USS *Constellation*
on the Dismal Coast

Studies in Maritime History
William N. Still, Jr., Series Editor

Iron Afloat: The Story of the Confederate Armorclads
William N. Still Jr.

To California by Sea: A Maritime History of the Gold Rush
James P. Delgado

Lifeline of the Confederacy: Blockade Running during the Civil War
Stephen R. Wise

The Lure of Neptune: German-Soviet Naval Collaboration and Ambitions
Tobias R. Philbin III

High Seas Confederate: The Life and Times of John Newland Maffitt
Royce Shingleton

The Defeat of the German U-Boats: The Battle of the Atlantic
David Syrett

John P. Holland, 1841–1914: Inventor of the Modern Submarine
Richard Knowles Morris

Cockburn and the British Navy in Transition: Admiral Sir George Cockburn, 1772–1853
Roger Morriss

The Royal Navy in European Waters during the American Revolutionary War
David Syrett

Sir John Fisher's Naval Revolution
Nicholas A. Lambert

Forty-Niners 'round the Horn
Charles R. Schultz

The Abandoned Ocean
Andrew Gibson and Arthur Donovan

Northern Naval Superiority and the Economics of the American Civil War
David G. Surdam

Ironclads and Big Guns of the Confederacy: The Journal and Letters of John M. Brooke
Edited by George M. Brooke, Jr.

*High Seas and Yankee Gunboats: A Blockade-Running Adventure
from the Diary of James Dickson*
Roger S. Durham

Dead Men Tell No Tales: The Lives and Legends of the Pirate Charles Gibbs
Joseph Gibbs

Playships of the World: The Naval Diaries of Admiral Dan Gallery, 1920–1924
Edited by Robert Shenk

Captains Contentious: The Dysfunctional Sons of the Brine
Louis Arthur Norton

Lewis Coolidge and the Voyage of the Amethyst, 1806–1811
Evabeth Miller Kienast and John Phillip Felt

Promotion—or the Bottom of the River
John M. Stickney

USS Constellation on the Dismal Coast: Willie Leonard's Journal, 1859–1861
Edited by C. Herbert Gilliland

USS

CONSTELLATION

ON THE DISMAL COAST

Willie Leonard's Journal, 1859–1861

Edited by C. Herbert Gilliland

The University of South Carolina Press

© 2013 C. Herbert Gilliland

Published by the University of South Carolina Press
Columbia, South Carolina 29208

www.sc.edu/uscpress

Manufactured in the United States of America

22 21 20 19 18 17 16 15 14 13   10 9 8 7 6 5 4 3 2 1

LIBRARY OF CONGRESS CATALOGING-IN-PUBLICATION DATA

Leonard, William Ambrose, 1837–1889.
USS Constellation on the Dismal Coast : Willie Leonard's journal, 1859–1861 /
edited by C. Herbert Gilliland.
pages cm—(Studies in maritime history)
Includes bibliographical references and index.
ISBN 978-1-61117-289-8 (hardback)—ISBN 978-1-61117-290-4 (e-book)
1. Leonard, William Ambrose, 1837–1889—Diaries. 2. Slave trade—Africa, West—
History—19th century. 3. Antislavery movements—United States—History—
19th century. 4. Constellation (Frigate)—History. 5. United States. Navy. African
Squadron. 6. United States. Navy—Sea life—History—19th century. I. Gilliland,
C. Herbert, editor. II. Title.
HT1332.L46 2013
306.3'620966'09034—DC23   2013019618

This book was printed on a recycled paper with 30 percent
postconsumer waste content.

Contents

List of Illustrations   vii

Acknowledgments   ix

Editorial Method   xi

Prologue   1

June 1859   6

July 1859   17

August 1859   25

September 1859   35

October 1859   43

November 1859   51

December 1859   62

January 1860   74

February 1860   82

March 1860   93

April 1860   98

May 1860   104

June 1860   116

July 1860   122

August 1860   128

September 1860   139

October 1860   153

November 1860   165

December 1860   178

January 1861   188

February 1861   205

March 1861   225

April 1861   248

May 1861   278

June 1861   297

July 1861   322

August 1861   344

September 1861   362

October 1861   378

Epilogue   386

Notes   389

Bibliography   399

Index   403

Illustrations

Maps

African Squadron cruising area   xiii

African Squadron Congo patrol area, 1860–61   xiv

Figures

USS *Constellation* gun deck   4

USS *Constellation* berth deck   5

USS *Constellation* spar deck   5

Charlestown Navy Yard   9

USS *Constellation* under way   28

Madame Ferreira's house on Prince's Island   53

St. Paul de Loanda   59

The U.S. Navy storehouse at St. Paul de Loanda   63

Lt. Donald McNeill Fairfax   79

USS *Portsmouth*   87

Typical page from Leonard's journal   111

USS *Niagara*   130

HMS *Arrogant*   136

The capture of the slave bark *Cora*   145

Boatswain John Hunter   166

Jamestown, St. Helena   186

USS *Saratoga*   206

Clipper ship *Nightingale*   223

USS *San Jacinto*   268

Flag Officer William Inman   298

William French   301

William French   301

Alexander Colden Rhind   305

Leonard's journal for the Fourth of July 1861   326–27

USS *Constellation* with studding sails set alow and aloft   357

The Portsmouth, New Hampshire, Navy Yard   380

Acknowledgments

This book would not have been published without the generous permission of William Leonard's descendant, Paul Sweeney, who still possesses the manuscript journal. Stan Berry and John Pentangelo meticulously prepared the working transcript. In addition John Pentangelo, former curator of the *Constellation*, read a preliminary draft and helped in many ways. Kate Dullnig, Michael P. Parker, and John Schroeder cheerfully read preliminary drafts and gave valuable advice. Chris Rowsom, director of Historic Ships of Baltimore, first suggested I look at the Leonard journal and has given steadfast support. Chris Robinson prepared the maps. The staff of the Naval Academy's Nimitz Library, including my daughter Alice Gilliland, was unfailingly helpful in many ways. Dale Cockrell lent his expertise on minstrel performances. Tony Hughes-Lewis and his cleaning lady, Vanda, helped clarify various questions about Madeira. The Huntington Library provided a copy of Captain Dornin's journal, with permission to quote.

At Historic Ships of Baltimore, Dayna Aldridge has been a tremendous help in verifying textual specifics.

Preparation of this edition was in part assisted by a sabbatical grant from the U.S. Naval Academy.

My wife, Carol, and my daughters, Anne-Marie, Alexandra, Elizabeth, and Alice, all expressed unfailing interest and support.

Editorial Method

William A. Leonard's journal of his cruise on the *Constellation* was written in an ordinary leather-spined blank book, 12.5 inches tall by 9 inches wide and 2 inches thick. He and others entered poetry, family information, and other material in it for decades afterward, but he bought it originally with the specific plan of recording his experiences aboard a ship of the U.S. Navy. The *Constellation* journal occupies the first four hundred pages of the book. The book has been kept in the family and is now (2012) in the possession of a direct descendant, Paul Sweeney.

Leonard's occasional remarks directly to the reader make it very clear that he intended his journal to be "published" at least to the extent of being read by friends and family. He saw himself as a reporter, and in that capacity at times made special efforts to seek out and obtain information, as when he lists all the officers of the ship or all of the possible mess bill items. I have edited his work in the firm belief that he would want it to be as accessible and attractive to readers as possible. What follows is Leonard's "title page" for his journal:

Items and Incidents

in the

cruise of the

United States Flag Ship Constellation

on the

West Coast of Africa

in the years

1859, 1860 and 1861

kept by

William Ambrose Leonard

of

Bunker Hill,

Charlestown,

Mass.

June 13th

1859

W.A. Leonard

My basic approach to editing William Leonard's journal has been to (1) keep all of his words; (2) modify the spelling, punctuation, and paragraphing in general (though not absolute) accordance with present publishing standards; (3) add comments and notes helpful to the ordinary twenty-first-century reader. My comments are interspersed within the original material to provide the reader as smooth and unified a reading experience as possible. I imagine the reader standing on the *Constellation*'s deck with Leonard, seeing and hearing what he sees and hears, while I whisper helpful information into the reader's ear.

The only words omitted in this edition of Leonard's journal are half a dozen words that he accidentally repeated, plus the running headlines at the top of every page, typically reading something like "Cruise of the U S Sloop of War Constellation Flagship of the Africa Squadron 1861." Because the pagination in this edition differs from that of the manuscript, keeping the headlines as they were would have been very cumbersome and intrusive. Additionally the summary comments for each day that now appear printed at the beginning of a day's entry have been moved from the margins in the original manuscript.

Leonard's usual punctuation was the comma, or at least marks that look like commas. The present editor has altered the punctuation to make it closer to standard practice, which has involved deciding (among other things) where sentences begin and end. At times a comma has been left where standard practice would not have permitted it, in order to maintain Leonard's rhythm of thought.

Leonard did not paragraph, but the present editor has made many paragraph breaks where appropriate.

Leonard was a fairly good speller, but corrections to his spelling have been silently made to bring it more into accord with standard spelling.

Like most writers of his day, Leonard was far more generous with capitals than presently would be considered correct. I have revised many capitals to lower case, though some have been retained.

Leonard's geographical names have been retained, as they are the common names of the time. If the modern name is different, it is given in parentheses at the first mention. Thus, for example, modern Luanda is referred to as St. Paul de Loando throughout the book.

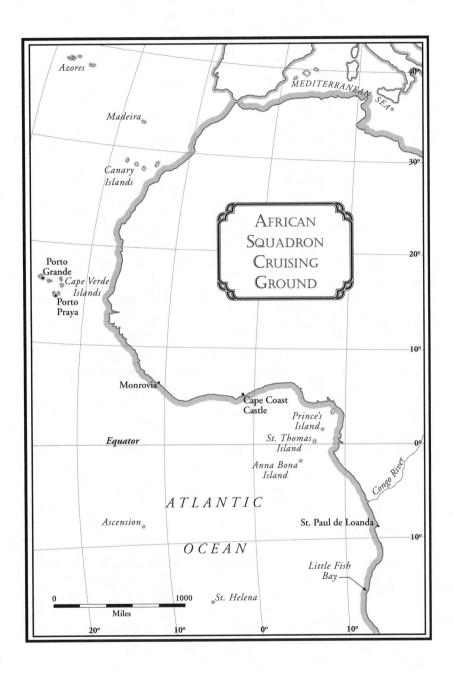

Azores

MEDITERRANEAN SEA

Madeira

40°

Canary
Islands

30°

AFRICAN
SQUADRON
CRUISING
GROUND

20°

Porto
Grande
Cape Verde
Islands
Porto
Praya

10°

Monrovia

Cape Coast
Castle

Prince's
Island

Equator

St. Thomas
Island

0°

Anna Bona
Island

ATLANTIC

Congo River

Ascension

St. Paul de Loanda

10°

OCEAN

Little Fish
Bay

0   1000

St. Helena

Miles

20°   10°   0°   10°

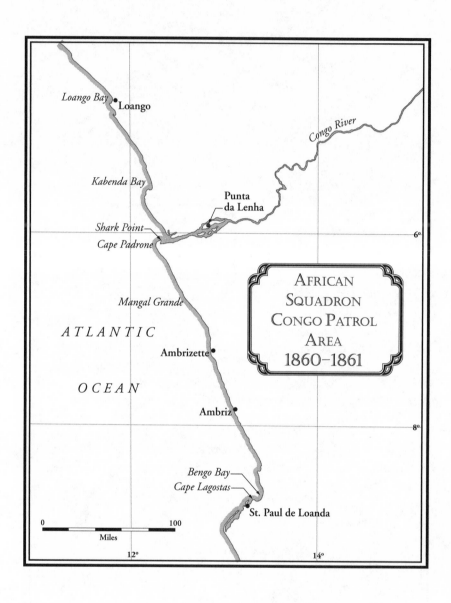

Loango Bay •Loango

Congo River

Kabenda Bay

Punta
da Lenha

Shark Point
Cape Padrone   6°

Mangal Grande

ATLANTIC

AFRICAN
SQUADRON
CONGO PATROL
AREA
1860–1861

Ambrizette •

OCEAN

Ambriz •

                                                                                8°

Bengo Bay
Cape Lagostas
                    • St. Paul de Loanda

0   100
       Miles
          12°   14°

Prologue

A three-masted wooden warship floats in Baltimore's Inner Harbor, embraced by modern office towers and market buildings. This veteran of distant seas and other centuries claims the center, while throngs of visitors eat ice cream cones and shop for jewelry or T-shirts in the shadow of its spars. For much of the twentieth century, this ship was believed to be the 1797 frigate *Constellation*. In fact, however, when the 1797 frigate was dismantled at the Gosport Navy Yard near Norfolk, Virginia, work was beginning on the 1854 sloop, likely reusing some timber from the old ship in building this very new one. The misidentification was maintained by deliberate deception, apparently to enhance the likelihood of the ship's being preserved as a historic relic. Naval records and the evidence of the extant ship's hull, though, make it clear that the vessel floating today dates from 1854. This second USS *Constellation* was the last all-sail ship constructed for the U.S. Navy, and as such it represents the ultimate in American design and craft of the Age of Fighting Sail. Also the only Civil War–era ship still afloat, Baltimore's *Constellation* is a twenty-gun sloop, 199 feet long and displacing 1,400 tons.

The confused identity had the happy result of causing the people and city of Baltimore, where the first *Constellation* had been built in 1797, to claim this ship as their own. Thus it has been preserved. Baltimore's claim is no less strong today, though the relationship has been revealed to be adoptive rather than one of birth.

Of the various assignments during a hundred-year career (1855–1955) with the U.S. Navy, the sloop *Constellation*'s most notable episode was the cruise from 1859 to 1861 as flagship of the African Squadron. The squadron's specific mission was to interdict slave ships leaving the West African coast. During the *Constellation*'s time as flagship, the squadron experienced by far its greatest operational success, even as at home, under the stress of slavery, the national fabric frayed and split at the seams.

Importing slaves into the United States was effectively ended when it became illegal after 1808, and U.S. law also forbade American citizens from engaging in the shipment of slaves anywhere, not just into the States. The U.S. Navy had been an occasional presence on the West African coast since 1820, when the USS *Cyane* escorted the *Elizabeth,* carrying the first group of freed American slaves to settle in what would become Liberia. However not until 1843 was the U.S. African Squadron formally established. Its creation was the result of the 1842 Webster-Ashburton Treaty (Treaty of Washington) between the United States and Great Britain.

Britain had made slave trading illegal throughout its empire in 1807, followed by the abolition of slavery itself beginning in 1833. Leading a global effort against the slave trade, Britain had since 1807 maintained a naval squadron along the African coast and developed a series of treaties and understandings with other countries to aid in suppression of the trade. Those agreements permitted the Royal Navy's African Squadron to stop and search ships flying the flags of various nations, with the most important exception being the United States. The British practice of stopping ships flying the U.S. flag had been a major issue in the War of 1812, something still very fresh in memory, and Americans were adamantly against signing away any bit of the sovereignty represented by the Stars and Stripes. Her Majesty's captains repeatedly watched ships full of slaves sail away unmolested under the American flag, to deliver their unhappy cargoes to the sugar plantations of Brazil and Cuba. The British government, noting that such a vacuum of authority could not be permitted to continue, urged action on the part of the United States. Hence in 1842 when Lord Ashburton came to America to negotiate with Secretary of State Daniel Webster the boundary between Maine and Canada, the issue of the slave trade was included. The two countries agreed that each would maintain a naval squadron mounting no less than eighty guns patrolling the West African coast. The British squadron already existed, but the Americans had to create theirs.

In 1843 Commodore Matthew C. Perry was sent with several ships to Africa to begin squadron operations. The mission was twofold: to intercept American vessels engaged in the slave trade and to protect growing American commercial interests in the region. The intent of the U.S. administration was that setting up the new squadron would not increase the Navy budget. With a huge global merchant fleet but a small navy of only a few dozen effective ships, the United States maintained squadrons around the world—the Home Squadron in home waters and the Caribbean, the Pacific Squadron, the Brazil Squadron, and the Mediterranean Squadron—and the U.S. Navy now stretched to add the stepchild African Squadron.

For most of its existence, the U.S. African Squadron was more a political token than a serious effort to interdict the slave trade. Between its establishment and the *Constellation*'s deployment in 1859, the strength and effectiveness of the squadron fluctuated. Occasionally it mounted slightly more than eighty guns, but more often fewer, and several factors caused those few to be even less effective than they might have been. Though clearly a dozen small ships with a half-dozen guns each would be more effective than three or four ships mounting twenty to forty guns each, the squadron for most of its existence followed the latter model, despite repeated recommendations by experienced naval officers. Steam vessels were recommended too, but none were sent. The squadron's base of operations (its "rendezvous") at Porto Praya in the Cape Verde Islands was a thousand miles from the main patrol area, so the transit ate up time that might have been spent on station.

In the early 1850s, British involvement in the Crimean War drew attention and resources from the Royal Navy's African Squadron, while the American squadron continued as more a token than an effort. Brazil outlawed the slave trade in 1850, and by the mid-1850s the trade into that country was effectively over. However, burgeoning demand in Cuba under the nonchalant Spanish rule, coupled with the sievelike naval interdiction, invited slave traders to make huge profits by shipping tens of thousands of slaves a year across the Atlantic to that island's plantations. The ships, crews, and capital involved were frequently American, with New York a major clandestine center. The American flag also remained a convenient device for keeping the British at bay, with very little risk of interference from the U.S. Navy. But in the late 1850s, the Crimean War ended, and Britain renewed attention to the Atlantic slave trade, now running almost entirely to Cuba. Increased British pressure stimulated the American government under President James Buchanan into meaningful action on the African coast. Secretary of the Navy Isaac Toucey began steps to increase the size of the squadron, add steamships, and move the base of operations. Conveniently a number of small coastal steamers acquired for an expedition to Paraguay became available when that force returned home. Sailing ships were still valuable, though, and the *Constellation* was chosen to be the new squadron flagship.

While domestic events moved swiftly from crisis to crisis toward the open civil war that would lead to the extinction of slavery in the United States, the *Constellation* raised anchor and sailed to patrol the West African waters as flagship of the African Squadron. It was tedious work in often miserable weather. Yet there was success—some of the most notorious slavers were stopped, and thousands of slaves were freed from unimaginably wretched conditions. What was it like to live and work aboard such a ship at such a time? William Leonard can tell us.

Boston born and bred, young Billy Leonard served aboard the *Constellation* from beginning to end of the African cruise and recorded all of it in his journal. The shipboard experience itself is what most interested him and what he expected to interest his reader. He paid very little attention to the inhabitants, flora, fauna, or physical geography of the African coast. Writing every day and often several times a day—sometimes by lantern light on the berth deck and sometimes sitting in the gig waiting for the captain—he illuminated the daily life of the enlisted sailor. Herein lies the great value of his book. Viewing his journal as a report to his reader, Leonard made special efforts to acquaint us with other members of the crew and to seek out and record details of how the crew was organized, where they worked, and what they ate. He also shared the exciting pursuit and capture of the slave ship *Cora*, the poignant farewell of the *Constellation*'s captain to his command, and his own thoughts on the life of a navy sailor. As we turn the pages, we step into his world.

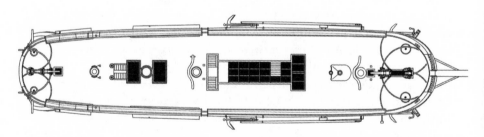

USS *Constellation* spar deck. Based on 1859 Yard Drawing in National Archives and Records Administration, College Park, Maryland.

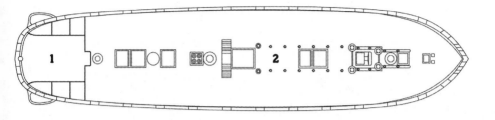

1- CAPTAIN'S CABIN
2- GUN DECK

USS *Constellation* gun deck. Based on 1859 Yard Drawing in National Archives and Records Administration, College Park, Maryland.

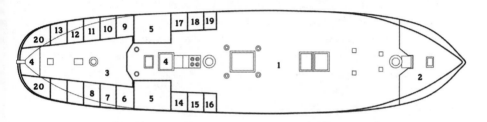

1- CREW BERTHING
2- SICK BAY
3- WARD ROOM
4- PANTRY
5- STEERAGE (MIDSHIPMEN)
6- 1ST LIEUTENANT
7- 2ND LIEUTENANT
8- 3RD LIEUTENANT
9- MASTER
10- PURSER

11- SURGEON
12- MARINE OFFICER
13- CHAPLAIN
14- BOATSWAIN
15- GUNNER
16- DISPENSARY
17- CARPENTER
18- SAILMAKER
19- PURSER'S ISSUING ROOM
20- STORE ROOM

USS *Constellation* berth deck. Based on 1859 Yard Drawing in National Archives and Records Administration, College Park, Maryland.

June 1859

William Leonard had gone to sea once as a thirteen-year old, on a China clipper. Now, at age twenty-one, he joined the Navy. An easy walk from Leonard's Bunker Hill neighborhood was Charlestown Navy Yard, one of the U.S. Navy's most important bases. From there ships got under way for duty in the Mediterranean, the Caribbean, the Orient, or the African coast. Since Leonard did not enlist for a particular ship, he could not know where he might be going. Clearly, though, he thought the experience would be interesting enough to record, and his friends had urged him to do so. By the time he had finished going about the Boston area making preparations on a cool rainy June day, he had acquired a large blank journal and written in it his first entry.

Though the twenty-first-century reader may be keenly aware that the America of mid-1859 was nearing civil war, at the time other topics claimed much public attention. Newspapers and illustrated weeklies headlined the sensational trial of Congressman Daniel Sickles, who had shot and killed his wife's lover in front of their house on Lafayette Square, across the street from the White House. The victim was the D.C. district attorney and a son of Francis Scott Key, while Sickles was a notorious womanizer, but a great deal of public sentiment favored Sickles as a defender of domestic virtue. Using the plea of temporary insanity for the first time ever in American jurisprudence, Sickles won acquittal. A few years later, the aggrieved husband, having become a Union general, lost a leg at Gettysburg.

For now, though, warfare in Europe absorbed American readers' attention. The battalions of French emperor Napoleon III, Austrian emperor Franz Joseph, and Italian hero Garibaldi maneuvered across the pages of city newspapers and Leslie's Illustrated. A Bostonian's finger might trace the troop movements through woodcut maps and panoramas accompanied by portraits of bemedaled leaders. Modern Italy was coalescing in the process of the

Austro-Sardinian War, also to be known as the Second War of Italian Independence.

Readers wishing to be entertsained by a historical cataclysm more remote in time might have turned to Harper's Weekly *for installments of Charles Dickens's new novel,* A Tale of Two Cities.

Of U.S. naval interest was the return of the successful Paraguay Expedition. The American government had sent nineteen ships with two hundred guns and 2,500 men to South America to demand indemnity for the death of an American seaman. The fleet sent to Paraguay included seven shallow-draft steamers leased for the purpose of projecting American power up the Rio Plata. Upon their return the navy exercised a purchase option, making these ships available for antislaving work, two for the coast of Cuba and four to join the African Squadron. That squadron had been created to meet U.S. obligations under the 1842 Webster-Ashburton Treaty with Great Britain. After years of neglect, the squadron's mission of interdicting the Middle Passage slave trade was now in 1859 getting serious interest from the Buchanan administration.

Slavery continued to vex the United States, as it had from the beginning. As the Boston Daily Advertiser *observed, "As usual of late years, the subject of slavery furnishes the chief question concerning our national politics at present."[1] Yet for all the dissension, the country was still a union in 1859, and most people expected matters to remain so. Even when Mr. Lincoln of Illinois had warned in his speech the previous year that "a house divided against itself cannot stand," he had explained, "I do not expect the Union to be dissolved—I do not expect the house to fall—but I do expect it will cease to be divided. It will become all one thing or all the other." In its column on newly published books, the* Daily Advertiser *mentioned a volume describing twenty-one men seen as possible U.S. presidential candidates in the coming year. The list included William Seward, Stephen Douglas, and Jefferson Davis—but not Abraham Lincoln.[2]*

On the day Leonard began his journal, he undoubtedly looked out at the ships in Charlestown Navy Yard and wondered which of those present might soon be taking him far from home. Each ship flew an American flag with thirty-two stars, representing the states in the Union. At noon over the stern of a twenty-two-gun sloop, a new flag rose to join the others. The USS Constellation *had been put back into commission, and preparations were beginning for its next voyage.*

June 13th

Shipped in the United States Naval Service in Boston and got a fit out from Moses Ingols.

Moses Ingolls owned a clothing store at 244 North Street, Boston.[3]

June 14th

At 10 A.M. went on board the U.S. Receiving Ship *Ohio*, laying at Charlestown Navy Yard. The U.S. Sloop of war *Constellation* and steam sloop *Hartford* are in the stream at anchor and are going to sea in a few days. The U.S. steam Frigates *Minnesota* and *Colorado* are here laid up in ordinary. The new steam gun boat *Narragansett*, built at this yard, is in the dry dock getting coppered. Besides there are three Line of Battle ships here: the *Ohio*, which is used as a receiving ship; the *Vermont*, which has never been out of the harbor; and the *Virginia*, which is on the stocks and has been there the last 34 years.

This being my first time on board a man of war, I of course was very green; however, by the kindness of an old salt who swung my hammock and showed me what to do I got along very well. At sundown all hands were called to muster, after which we got our hammocks, and were allowed till nine o'clock to do what we pleased. I being tired and very homesick, I went to my hammock to turn in. It was a more difficult job than I imagined, for on trying to get in I pitched head foremost on the deck at the other side of it. After trying several more times with the same results, I was shown how to get in by a fellow who seemed to have great sport at my mishaps.

June 15th

The flag officer of the U.S. Ship *Constellation* went on board of his ship; immediately on his arrival they hoisted his flag, and fired a salute of 13 guns. The U.S. Sloop of war *Hartford* also saluted him, and another from the Navy Yard, which salutes were returned by the *Constellation*. I was told today that I am going aboard the *Constellation*. She is going to the Coast of Africa, to relieve the U.S. Ship *Cumberland*, which vessel had been over two years in commission. The U.S. Ship *Hartford* is also going to be a Flag Ship; she is a splendid ship—she is destined for the China Station.

Flag Officer William Inman reported on June 16 that he had hoisted his flag aboard the Constellation *"this day."*[4]

Carrying the name of an illustrious eighteenth-century predecessor, this is the second Constellation. *Launched only five years earlier, this twenty-gun sailing sloop is the last all-sail ship built for the U.S. Navy, as the service continued its shift to steam. The* Boston Daily Advertiser *described it as follows: "This vessel is the finest corvette in the United States Navy, and carries a more formidable battery than any sailing ship of her size, in the world. She was inspected while cruising up the Mediterranean a few years ago, by all the British and French naval authorities on that station, who pronounced it the 'crack sloop.'"*[5]

The Constellation's *new mission would be to serve as flagship of the U.S. African Squadron. By the Webster-Ashburton Treaty of 1842, the United*

Charlestown Navy Yard. *Gleason's Pictorial*, February 1854. Gilliland Collection.

States and Great Britain had agreed that each would keep a naval force of eighty guns off the West African coast to interdict slave ships. The reality proved to be that neither side consistently maintained the full force, though the Americans were more desultory than the British. The Royal Navy was nearly ten times the size of the U.S. Navy, and the British had considerable commercial interests as well as actual colonies in West Africa. They also had for decades pursued a clear policy of eliminating slavery and the slave trade in their empire and throughout the world.

Though retaining slavery in its southern states, the United States too wished to suppress the transatlantic slave trade. A stronger motive for the United States to maintain an African Squadron was to prevent a regional vacuum into which the British would step, interfering with U.S.-flagged ships. The British had treaty arrangements permitting them to police the ships of various other nations as well as their own. However, the United States had no such agreement with Britain or any other country. Indeed quite the contrary—the Americans were vehement about permitting no interference with ships flying the American flag. The War of 1812 had been fought partly over that very issue. The net effect was that normally a U.S.-flagged ship could be stopped only by a U.S. Navy ship. At the same time, the U.S. Navy could not stop any ship legitimately flying the flag of another nation; they could arrest only American-flagged ships or ships claiming no flag at all, which were automatically considered illicit. Given a feeble U.S. Navy presence off the West African coast, plus the fact that American-built ships were of high quality and readily available, much—likely most—of the transatlantic slave traffic in this period moved on American ships and under the American flag. Their human cargoes were not shipped to the United States, however; the markets were Cuba and Brazil.

In the mid-1850s the Crimean War had drawn heavily on Britain's naval resources, distracting from its West African effort. Now, that conflict over, more Royal Navy ships are available for Africa. Now too, prodded by the British, President James Buchanan has determined to put some muscle into the U.S. African Squadron.

June 16th

Leonard provided here a table of the ship's officers. In the American navy at the time, the only ranks between midshipman and captain were lieutenant and commander, though when a lieutenant was in command of a ship he was titled "lieutenant commanding." The Constellation rated a captain as commanding officer. Below Captain Nicholas came the lieutenants in order of seniority, with the most senior—the first lieutenant—being the executive officer. Eastman, *the master, ranked just below the lieutenants. The four midshipmen were all recent graduates of the Naval Academy. Though Leonard listed Nicholas as the captain here in his entry for June 16, Nicholas did not take command until June 22, as will be seen in that day's entry.*

The captain normally occupied in solitary splendor a spacious cabin taking up the after end of the gun deck. It was divided for this voyage, giving half to the squadron commodore, Flag Officer Inman. Directly below, aft on the berth deck, cabins on either side of the central wardroom space went to the lieutenants and other more senior officers. Midshipmen and other junior ("steerage") officers occupied sleeping and dining spaces further forward.

Leonard joined the two hundred enlisted crew sleeping and eating on the large, open enlisted berth deck space.

Was drafted on board the U.S. Flag Ship *Constellation,* and went aboard of her in the afternoon.

Flag officer	Captain
Wm H. Inman[6]	John S. Nicholas.

Lieutenants

1st Charles McDonough ..	2nd A.C. Rhind
3d R. M. McArann ..	4th Trevett Abbott

Flag Lieutenant
James P. Foster

Thomas H. Eastman, Master	Purser John N. Hambleton
Fleet Surgeon Thomas L. Smith	Assistant Surgeon John M. Browne

Midshipmen
Wilburn B. Hall, Walter R. Butt, George Borchert,
and Theodore F. Kane[7]

Captain of Marines	Isaac T. Doughty
Lieutenant	Henry B. Tyler Jr.

Commodore's Secty	Apthorp Vanden Heuvel		
Purser's Clerk	James M. Worth	Captain's Clerk	S. Byard Wilson
Boatswain	Alfred Hingerty	Gunner	James Hutchinson
Carpenter	Henry M. Lowrey	Sail Maker	George D. Blackford

On my arriving aboard all hands were very busy taking in powder and ammunition. I was called aft by the 1st lieutenant and put into the After Guard, No. 238, and was also put into the steerage boat, the 3d cutter. On account of taking in powder there was no fire allowed in the ship, we therefore had a very late supper.

The least experienced crew members were generally assigned to the afterguard. "No. 238" was Leonard's billet and hammock number. The steerage boat, in this case the third cutter, was the one assigned for use of the junior officers; the senior officers' boat was the "wardroom boat," and the captain's boat was the gig.

June 17th

Being the anniversary of the Battle of Bunker Hill, we fired a national salute of thirty-three guns. The weather was very bad all day, raining all the time, thereby preventing a great many people from visiting the ship. It was very dull on board. Our captain's boat, the gig, went up the Mystic River to witness the regatta. In the afternoon all hands were called aft and spliced the main brace.[8] [*Oregon had become the 33rd state in February; however, the ship was likely still flying a 32-star flag, because the new flag would not be in effect until July 4.*]

The rain also prevented many planned activities ashore. Most public institutions in the city of Boston closed on that day so Bostonians could join the commemoration in Charlestown of the Battle of Bunker Hill. At sunrise, noon, and sunset, bells rang, and at noon an artillery salute was fired. Various parades, fireworks, and balloon ascensions were postponed, and the regatta Leonard mentioned (consisting of three rowing events for prize money) was one part of the celebration that rain did not prevent.[9]

June 18th

Being Saturday, all hands are very busy holystoning all the decks and cleaning the ship for tomorrow. Today one of the Marines was taken sick suddenly; his complaint proved to be the small pox. He was immediately taken to the hospital in Chelsea in our boat (3d cutter). Some of the boat's crew improving the opportunity by taking a run to the nearest rum shop and getting pretty well drunk, the consequence was a rough and tumble fight between the stroke oarsman and the bowman before we got into the boat, and a general row on our way to the ship, which was participated in by the coxswain and all hands. After closing up several of each other's eyes and knocking each other's noses out of joint, we concluded to go to the navy yard and have another drink all round, after which we returned on board.

June 19th

Being Sunday, the ship's company are preparing themselves for a general muster. At half past nine o'clock all hands were called to quarters for inspection, after which visitors were allowed to visit the ship in the afternoon. Some of the men went aboard the *Ohio* to visit.

The crew received their general quarters assignments. Each of the Constellation's *eight-inch shell guns required a crew of fourteen men plus a boy acting as "powder monkey." As side tackleman Leonard would stand to the left side of his gun, hauling on a rope (the side-tackle) used to point the gun left or right and to run it in or out. If the order were given to board or to repel boarders, the gun crew would take up small arms and Leonard would serve as a pikeman, which by 1859 could mean he would be armed with either a pike or a carbine.*[10]

June 20

Was stationed today at Quarters, at No. 4 gun of the First Division as first side tackle man and pikeman. At eleven o'clock the Governor of Rhode Island paid our ship a visit, and we fired a salute of 17 guns, all hands dressed in white frocks and blue pants.

June 21st

The gun deck divisions were called to quarters at nine o'clock, to drill at the large guns, and tell the guns' crews what to do. After drilling about an hour, we secured the guns. All the Top men are to work in the rigging. Went ashore in the boat in the afternoon and had a run.

June 22nd

The port watch are to work cleaning hawse, or taking the turns out of the chain cables. We have got both anchors down and at every turn of the tide, the ship swings, thereby taking a turn in them every time she swings. Every other day we clear them. Our Captain, S. Wilson, came on board today. We fired a salute of nine guns. He is very lame and has to be supported when he walks; Capt. John S. Nicholas is appointed to take his place.

Captain Wilson had fallen on ice in front of his house in January and severely injured his hip; he was still using crutches. Though he still had hoped to go to sea with the Constellation, *the doctors and secretary of the navy decided otherwise. However, his son, whom he had brought on as captain's clerk, remained aboard for the cruise to Africa.*

Capt. John S. Nicholas, fifty-nine, handsome, and of a distinguished Virginia family (his father had been governor), had been in the navy for forty-five years and commanded five ships prior to the Constellation. *His career had seemed to be finished in 1855 when the Navy Efficiency Board, established to remove excess officers, had "plucked" Nicholas, among others. Lobbying by some of the affected officers and their friends succeeded in reversing the decision of the board in some cases, including that of then-commander Nicholas, whose restoration to the active list brought promotion to captain. Perhaps suspecting he could not get a more desirable command, he had then specifically asked for assignment to the African Squadron.*

June 23

We are taking in wood and provisions, that come in launches from the navy yard. At 3 o'clock, roll. Our new captain, John S. Nicholas, came on board, and we honored him with a salute of nine guns. After looking at the ship, he gave orders for all hands to be called to exercise sail. He had the sails furled and loosed, reefed and mast headed several times, when he had the men piped down. He was very well satisfied with the exercise and made the remark that he would make a smart ship's company of them.

June 24th

Before the Civil War, the highest rank in the U.S. Navy was captain, with captains in command of squadrons being given the courtesy title "commodore." This still left such men at a disadvantage when meeting their counterparts from other nations, who could hold the rank of admiral, but sentiment in the United States associated that rank with undesirable class distinctions. In 1857 the navy came up with the odd compromise title of "flag officer," given a captain when commanding a squadron. (The rear admiral rank was established in 1862.)

Flag Officer William H. Inman was sixty-two, having begun his navy service as a midshipman on the Great Lakes in 1812. Like Captain Nicholas, he too had been "plucked" by the Navy Efficiency Board of 1855 but then restored by Congress in 1859. He had experience with steamships, useful now that the African Squadron was getting its first steamers. It can be noted, though, that not only was his flagship a sailing sloop but also throughout his time in command of the squadron, he never shifted his flag to one of the various steamers at his disposal.[11]

Our flag officer is living ashore and his boat goes ashore after him at 1 A.M. Today the boat's crew took French leave. At sundown, the boat not returning, the 3d cutter was sent in search of her. After pulling along the wharves for some time we found her at Long Wharf. Three of her men being in her, we took her and towed her alongside of the ship.[12]

June 25th

The U.S. Steam Sloop of war *Hartford* went past us on her way to China, where she is going to be flagship. Her officers gave a grand ball last evening on board of her, which was attended by several ladies and gentlemen from shore and all our officers. One of our gig's crew deserted after carrying our captain ashore. We manned the rigging and gave her three hearty cheers.

The USS Hartford *was a brand-new twenty-four-gun screw steam sloop. In 1864 in the Battle of Mobile Bay, while clinging to* Hartford's *rigging, Adm. David Farragut gave the command famously remembered as "Damn the torpedoes! Full speed ahead!"*

June 26th

Being Sunday, the boatswain's mate called the divisions to quarters to be inspected by the officers of the divisions. In the afternoon visitors were allowed to come on board and some of my friends came on board to see me. At sundown went ashore in the boat.

June 27th

The U.S. Sloop of war *Savannah* came to an anchor today astern of us; she saluted the navy yard and our flag officer. [She is] here to recruit ship [*that is, to improve the health of the crew*], as she has 100 men sick. We had several distinguished visitors on board. The ship *Rufus Choate* arrived here today from Liverpool.

A fifty-eight-gun frigate (not a sloop) with a 480-man crew, the USS Savannah *had just returned from two years off the coast of Mexico as flagship of the Home Squadron, monitoring the Mexican civil war known as the War of Reform. In addition to a great many cases of various other diseases, hundreds of the crew had been stricken with "intermittent fever," and Leonard's estimate of a hundred on the sick list when he visited is close to the number officially reported. Exposure to the debilitating climate with absolutely no liberty ashore for a year would surely have worsened not only the crew's health but its morale.*[13]

When the Constellation *joined the African Squadron, it was operating in what was commonly believed an especially unhealthy environment. "African fever" or "coast fever" (malaria or other fevers) took a steady toll on newcomers to the African coast. The navy had established strict sanitary regulations for operations on the African coast. The most important of these was that no sailor or officer could be ashore in Africa from late afternoon until late morning of the following day. Intended to avoid the "bad air" from which malaria takes its name, this regulation meant that navy personnel could not normally go much further up any African river than just past the mouth. However, the result was to keep everyone offshore during the morning and evening hours when mosquitoes, the real disease carriers, were active. What it also meant, of course, is that the crew of the* Constellation *could have overnight liberty only when their ship visited locations away from their patrol area. These dismal liberty conditions were another reason the African Squadron was not a navy favorite.*

June 28th 1859

Went aboard of the U.S. Sloop of war *Savannah*. Her men are going to have liberty. They give a very bad account of her officers. She has been twelve months in commission and have not had one hour's liberty. At one o'clock we returned on board of our own ship. All hands are to work clearing hawse.

June 29th

This day we done hardly anything in. The Boatswain piped to breakfast, after which we spread the awnings. All hands done what they liked. There are some of the workmen from the navy yard making several alterations.

June 30th

Sent down the main Topsail yard, to alter it in order to try a new patent reefing concern.[14] We are getting in more provisions and water. My boatkeeping day. At sundown we sent up the main Topsail yard.

The provisions, including barrels of bread and salted beef and pork were hoisted aboard from boats alongside and stowed below. The ship's water supply was pumped down into large iron tanks in the hold.

Each boat had a regularly assigned crew, Leonard having been assigned to the third cutter. When a boat was in the water awaiting use (they were stacked on the spar deck when the ship was underway), one man of the boat's crew, the "boatkeeper," was tasked with staying in the boat to keep an eye on it.

July 1859

July 1st

Today all hands were exercised at making sail in the afternoon. Small stores were served out to the messes by the purser's steward.

July 2nd

Being Saturday all hands are very busy cleaning the ship for tomorrow. Several recruits came aboard today from the receiving ship *Ohio*. Had a run ashore today in the boat. At sundown exercised the men at sending up and down topgallant and Royal yards.

July 3rd

Being Sunday were called to quarters for inspection, after which visitors were allowed to come on board. I had the pleasure of seeing my father and sisters; felt very lonesome after they went and tried very hard to get ashore in order to spend the 4th of July at home, had a very kind friend to stand my security, thanks to him, but it was no use—the 1st lieutenant gave orders for nobody to leave the ship that day.

Last to take his hand in farewell was Miss Bella Blood, who smiled as she descended the port side of the Constellation *and said, "Goodbye, Billy, keep a good heart, two years are not long."*[1]

July 4th

Being Independence Day, we dressed ship and fired a national salute of thirty-three guns. Our mess had a first rate dinner. I am boatkeeper today.

Fully dressed, the ship made a gay spectacle—American flags flew from the foremast, the mizzenmast, and the gaff, with the flag officer's broad pennant atop the mainmast and the jack at the bow; additionally multitudinous other flags flew on a line running in an arc from the bowsprit across the tops of the three masts and down to the spanker boom over the stern.

Gun salutes from other navy ships resounded as well, and the city of Boston fired salutes morning, noon, and dusk as part of a general celebration.

July 5th

Getting in provisions and water, our boat had a very narrow escape from being run over by the East Boston Ferry boat. One of our men was put in the brig for being drunk.

July 6th

The flag officer's official boat (his barge, *as an admiral's boat was called) having been seriously damaged, substitutions occurred that affected Leonard.*

About thirty more recruits came on board from the *Ohio.* Our barge got stove, so they are using the ward room boat for a barge until she gets fixed and we are used as the ward room boat and go ashore two or three times a day.

July 7th

A navy *ship carried enough crew to man half of its guns—either port or starboard—as normally only one side of the ship would be engaged. If, as sometimes did happen, opposing ships engaged both sides, the order would be "Man both sides!" and each gun crew would work a pair of guns on opposite sides, with most of the men running back and forth. The men of the* Constellation *practiced that evolution.*

At nine o'clock the drum beat to general quarters; we worked both batteries.

July 8th

Leonard and some of the other new recruits had to wear the ill-fitting uniform items they got from the "rendezvous," as a naval base or recruiting station was called.

All hands are dressed in white frocks and blue pants today. Some of us cut a very ridiculous figure, having nothing but rendezvous clothes; the frock I have got on is like a meal sack, it comes all over me.

July 9th

Saturday holystoned the spar and gun decks, very busy all cleaning up, for tomorrow we get fresh meat and vegetables; every day we are living first rate.

July 11th

Sunday, all hands were called to quarters for to be inspected, after which had a general muster round the capstan. The ship's company's names are called by the purser, each man answers to his name and rate, and passes round the capstan hat in hand. After muster we had a divine service, all hands attending. There were several ladies and gentlemen from the city; a clergyman from Charlestown officiated. During the service some noise was made in the port gangway and I was picked out by the officer of the deck as the one that made it. I was ordered to stand at the mast until the service was over. While standing there, a coasting schooner ran afoul of us, which broke up the service and got me clear of the mast. After getting her clear the visitors were allowed to come aboard. Had the pleasure of some of my friends. All hands dressed in white frocks and blue trousers and caps.

July 11th 1859

Leonard had an unpleasant encounter with Second Lieutenant Alexander Colden Rhind, who apparently had impressed officers on his previous ships as being arrogant, foul-mouthed, and generally difficult. By the time Leonard met him, Rhind had been court-martialed three times for such things as profane language, insubordination, and abuse of crewmen. Dismissed from the navy by the same board that had plucked Captain Nicholas and Flag Officer Inman, he too was reinstated in January 1859, after nearly four years out of the service. Though Rhind came from a distinguished New York family, he spent some of his formative years in the South. Now thirty-seven, he was engaged to Miss Fannie Page Hume, age twenty-three, who resided at "Selma," her grandfather's farm, near Orange, Virginia.

At 10 o'clock this day was called aft upon the quarter deck and reprimanded for what was done yesterday. On my denying the charge was told by him the least I said in a man of war the better it would be for me. After giving me a severe lecture, he told me that he would keep a sharp lookout for me, and if he did catch me foul, he would sweeten me, which I thought was not very encouraging in the beginning of a two years' cruise. This officer was our 2nd lieutenant, A.C. Rhind. I came to the conclusion that if he was going to watch me I could not do any better than to keep myself very strait or else I might be sorry for it. Nothing else occurred this day.

July 12th

At eight A.M. two launch loads of provisions came alongside from the navy yard, which took all hands all the forenoon to get them in, with the yard and stay. The fifer plays a tune and they walk away with the yard and stay; everything in a man of war is done with music.

The Constellation *had thirteen musicians.*

July 13th

Very busy all this day getting ready for sea, hove up one of our anchors took our barge and dinghy inboard, and at sundown sent up top gallant, and royal yards. At seven o'clock in the evening the pleasure yacht *Surprise* with a party of my friends from Charlestown just coming from a fishing excursion went by us singing three cheers for the red, white, and blue and Billy Leonard too, which made me very homesick all that night.

July 14th

At half past eight o'clock we were all ready for sea. We hove short and then our boat went up to the navy yard for the 1st lieutenant. Met my father and bid him good life, we returned on board at half past nine. The steaming boat *Walpole* is alongside of us. At ten o'clock we hove up the anchor, and was towed down the harbor to Nantasket Roads, where we came at an anchor. At four o'clock we went to the town of Hull with some of our officers, and then returned on board. We are going to sea tomorrow. Wrote two letters up home to M.L.M. [*Mary L. Moloney became Mrs. William Leonard.*]

July 15th   Going to sea/put back

At 10 o'clock we hove up our anchor and went to sea, having a pilot on board. We had a very light wind all day. Towards night it began to freshen and at 7 P.M. there was a good 9 knot breeze. The pilot now wished to leave us, but at the request of the flag officer he remained on board. The reason was the ship was very crank and it was necessary to put back to get in more ballast. At half past 12 we tacked ship and stood in for Nantasket Roads again.

A ship that was crank would roll quickly and not sail well; in the extreme case, it could easily capsize. Lowering the ship's center of gravity by adding ballast below or subtracting topside weight ameliorated the condition. Besides removing the two ten-inch pivot guns from the top (spar) deck, Inman ordered sixty tons of ballast added below.

July 16th   taking in more ballast

Early in the morning we came to an anchor in Nantasket Roads. In the afternoon we made preparations to take out our two large pivot guns, which being done we commenced taking in ballast which came down to us in a lighter from the navy yard.

July 17th

Sunday. We were taking in ballast all this day. In the afternoon all hands spliced the main brace, which is a glass of liquor. It is a beautiful day.

July 18th

The ballast is all in. We took out the shot and shell belonging to the pivot guns and put them in the lighter and then made preparations for sea.

Removing the pivot guns left the Constellation *with the twenty guns for which it was rated: sixteen eight-inch shell guns in broadside and four long guns firing thirty-two-pound solid shot—two aft and two in the bows.*[2]

July 19th   left the Pilot

At 10 o'clock we got underweigh [*sic*], with a good breeze, at 2 o'clock we hove aback the main topsail and left the pilot. Now our voyage commenced in earnest. Had about an eight knot breeze; the weather is very pleasant.

20th

The watch are to work in the rigging putting on chafing gear and the other watch putting the cables down the chain lockers. Had a good breeze all this [time] and going our course.

Chafing gear *was canvas covering on parts of the rigging that might rub together. The* cables *were the anchor chains.*

July 21st

At 10 o'clock the drum beat to general quarters and exercised the starboard battery. In the afternoon a bill was put up in the barber's shop telling the prices of articles required in the navy, which will be seen on next page.

dollars cts   *Prices of Articles required in the U.S. Navy*

dollars cts		dollars cts	Small Stores
$10.25	Pea Jackets		Small Stores
1.38	Jumpers	.26	Tobacca [*sic*] Plug
7.00	Cloth Jackets	.18	Soap a bar
4.00	Cloth Trowsers [*sic*]	.10	Beeswax a cake
1.60	Flannel Shirts	.25	1/4 pound White thread
1.15	Under Shirts	.25	do. do. Blue do.
1.15	Flannel drawers	.80	Ribbon a roll
1.38	Linen Frocks	.3	Tape do. Do.

dollars cts		Prices of Articles required in the U.S. Navy (continued)	
.74	. . . Trowsers	.5	Spool Cotton
6.00	Mattrasses [*sic*]	.3	Needles a paper
2.20	Blankets	.2	Thimbles
1.13	Silk Neckercheif [*sic*]	.33	Knives
.45 cts	yard Flannel	.20	Scissors
.15	. . . Nankin	.22	Scrub Brushes
1.86	. . . Shoes	.6	Blacking
1.86	. . . Pumps	.3	Dozen dead eye buttons
.70	. . . Caps	.15	Fine Combs
.40	pair yarn socks	.12	Coarse do.
.85	yard Satinet	.12	Tin Pot
2.56	Satinet Trowsers	.11	Tin Pan
.34	yard Duck	.14	Mustard a bottle
.40	Doz . eagle buttons	.11	Pepper do. do.
.25	do. marine do.	.11	Spoon
.18	small do./do.	.5	Skein Sewing Silk
1.20	Mess Kettle	.15	Pocket Handkercheif
.70	Mess Pan	.31	Razor
		.25	Razor Strop
	this is an exact	.35	Shaving Boxes
	Copy of the one	.6	Do. Brushes
	that was put up	.25	Blacking do.
	in the barbers	.15	Clothes do.
	Shop	.5 cts	Shaving Soap
	W.A.L.	.5	Grass a hand

The last item on the list, a hand of grass, may be mysterious to many readers. The official uniform hat for sailors in the tropics, like the hats worn there by civilian sailors as well, was a flat straw hat. Sailors wove their own from straw purchased from the ship's store.

July 22nd 1859   **at sea/Sail Ho.**

The first column is the division bill. They come out once a month and those who want any of the articles put down on their own division bill and has it charged to his account by the purser. The ship's company are divided into five divisions. The second column is the mess bill and comes out the first of every month, the cook of each mess takes charge of them and is handed in to the purser's steward by him. At eleven o'clock this day a sail was reported from the main Topsail yard, by the lookout, bearing two points on our lee bow, made her out to be a large ship, lost sight of her in the evening. Good wind and very pleasant weather all this day.

July 23d 1859

The wind died away and at 12 o'clock it was a dead calm, in the afternoon exercised sail at night had a good wind again. I had a lee wheel this day and a quarter lookout at night. The After Guard takes the lee wheel, the port gang-way and the Starboard quarter lookouts. Very pleasant weather.

The after guard consisted of the men—usually less experienced—who handled the sails on the after masts and also had the duties Leonard mentioned. Stand-ing the lee wheel watch, Leonard assisted a more senior man at the wheel, in whose lee he would normally stand.

July 24th

Sunday all hands were called to quarters for inspection, after which all hands were called to muster on the quarter deck, and the Articles of War were read by the 1st Lieutenant, after which we mustered round the capstan. Very fine weather.

The standard routine was to read the Articles of War (actually Rules for the Better Government of the Navy of the United States, *passed by Congress in 1800) on the first Sunday of each month. This is the first time Leonard men-tioned the practice, and the Articles were often be read on days other than the first Sunday of the month. However, they were read at least once a month, which was the real requirement. The complete Articles took nearly an hour to read aloud. A printed copy was posted where anyone could read it, but of course not all in the crew could be expected to be literate.*[3]

July 25th   sea Sickness

We are now in the Gulf Stream and are having some delightful weather, the wind is fair and we have got the fore topmast studding sail set. There is a very heavy sea running which makes the ship pitch heavily, causing some of our green hands to pay their compliments to old Neptune.

July 26th

This morning the port watch scrubbed hammocks. We have got a good breeze, and we are in hopes of making a quick passage to Madeira, where we are going to have 24 hours liberty.

July 27th 1859 **at sea**

The Starboard watch scrubbed hammocks. A sail in sight on our weather beam but cannot make her out. We made some very fine sailing this day, logging it fourteen knots an hour.

July 28th

This day the gun deck divisions were called aft on the quarter deck and were formed into companies for musket drill. I belong to the 1st company.

July 29th

At 10 o'clock the drum beat to general quarters. We exercised both batteries, also the howitzers on the spar deck. Fair wind and very pleasant weather.

The two twelve-pound Dahlgren boat howitzers were popguns compared to the ten-inch swivel guns they replaced, but if nothing else practice with them prepared the men for using them in boats or during a landing.

July 30th

Being Saturday the boatswain piped up all clothes bags in order to air our clothing. At 10 o'clock the port watch holystoned the gun deck.

July 31st **Spinning a tough yarn**

Sunday all hands were called to quarters for inspection. In the afternoon a sail was reported on our lee bow, good breeze all this day. At night I had a lookout from 8 to 10, which time was spent in listening to an incredulous yarn told by an old Quartermaster of the watch by the name of Daniel Malone.

August 1859

We have no wind and the ship is lying like a log on the water, the sea is as smooth as glass, not a ripple to be seen, the sun is very hot. In the afternoon all hands were called to exercise sail. After exercising about an hour the Boatswain piped down. The division bills are out, and that is all that was done this day.

August 2nd

All sail set, but it is a dead calm. At 10 o'clock the drum beat to general quarters; exercised the gun deck batteries and fired four rounds of shot and shell from each gun. In the afternoon the following order was put in the barber shop:

General Orders.

1st   The Watch only will be permitted to occupy the Spar deck unless all hands are sent up for any particular purpose.

2nd   The <u>watch</u> will be required to occupy their respective parts of the ship, when not called upon for work, at such times however the <u>entire</u> watch will assist in whatever may be going on, on that deck.

3rd   In bracing the forecastle men and fore top men, not required forward will be sent aft by the boatswain.

4th   It is all the time to be understood that the <u>watch</u> are not [to] sew or play games, and when any general work is going on requiring all the watch every man on the spar deck will immediately stand up and show by his movement a readiness to execute the orders from the Quarter deck.

5th   That part of the main deck designated for the use of the barber, is not to be occupied by any of the crew excepting when there for the purpose of their hair cut, or being shaved they are not to occupy the barbers chair at any other time.

6th   The watch below will be allowed to sew on the gun deck, and port side of the berth deck.

7th   At sea games will be confined to the gun deck. In port to the starboard side of the gun deck and port side of the spar deck, games will not be allowed on the gun deck, abaft the pumpwell, or on the quarter deck.

8th   The quarter deck at all times will be required as the parade of the ship where no irregularities will be permitted.

9th   The crew are not to spit on the decks at <u>meals</u> they are particularly to avoid this too common practice also to avoid loud talking.

10th   The men must have the mark of their respective watch on their arm, any man below in his watch, without leave, excepting to go to the Scuttle but will be punished.

[pointing hand] That part of the order which relates to the watched only being allowed the spar deck is not meant to apply from 6 P.M. until 8 P.M. and from 7 A.M. until 8 A.M.

     by orders 1st Lieut

August 3d 1859   at sea

We had a general fire quarters at half past 9 A.M. The men are discussing about the merits of the bill that was put yesterday. It is still a dead calm and every thing seems dull.

August 4th

During the morning watch we had several catspaws, or light gusts of wind. Towards 8 o'clock it settled into a pretty good breeze; the wind is fair and we have got studding sails set.

August 5th

There is a good breeze blowing now, and we are going through the water right merrily; holystoned the gun deck.

August 6th   Land Ho/we fire a signal gun/Feel very romantic

Early this morning Land was reported on our weather bow, which made quite an excitement, as it is the first land we got a glimpse of since leaving Boston. It proved to be the Island of Madeira. Towards evening the breeze fell away and we stood in calm. At 7 P.M. the wind rose again and we stood in. We were just getting ready to come to an anchor when we discovered we were in the wrong place. We immediately wore ship and stood out again, [but] the wind again died and left us becalmed. We now fired a gun which in a few minutes was answered from the other side of the Island; we now sent up a rocket and burned some blue lights which were also answered, we suppose by the U.S. Sloop of war *Cumberland,* which vessel we are to relieve. It is a beautiful night and the scene from where we lay becalmed is magnificent. It is a very high island and from the quantity [of] rockets, roman candles, blue lights, bonfires and other combustibles that are burning all over the Island, we came to the conclusion that it must have been some great holiday. All hands are up looking at the Island planning out what they are going to do when they get liberty. At 10 P.M. I turned in.

August 7th 1859   at Madeira

We had a good breeze this morning and stood in. We now found out that the place we run into last night was Fish Town. At 11 o'clock we came to an anchor in Funchal Roads, off the city of Funchal. The U.S. Sloop of war *Cumberland* is here; she has been laying here over four months waiting for us to relieve her. She is Flag Ship of the African Squadron. We gave her a salute of 13 guns, which she returned. We also saluted the Portuguese flag with 21 guns, which was also returned by the fort. Today being Sunday, we done hardly anything. Some of the *Cumberland*'s men came aboard in the afternoon, among whom I met with a schoolmate. He beset me with all sorts of questions about home. She is going home tomorrow; she has been in commission 27 months and bears the broad pennant of Commodore Conover. At night we swung clean hammocks, then all hands went in swimming.

"Fish Town" was actually the village of Camera de Lobos, five miles east of Funchal and in the twenty-first century still the center of Madeira's fishing industry.

That Commodore Conover had been sitting so long at Funchal with his flagship was symptomatic of the lackadaisical employment of the squadron under his command. Though the designated squadron rendezvous since the 1840s, Madeira was thousands of miles from the patrol area where slavers operated, so a ship kept there had no value to the squadron mission. However, Madeira was healthier and much more pleasant than any spot in the patrol area.

The African Squadron had never, since its inception under the terms of the Webster-Ashburton Treaty (Treaty of Washington) of 1842, been a top priority of the United States or the U.S. Navy but rather a stepchild of policy. Before the ink was even on the treaty, officers had recommended employing

USS *Constellation* under way. Courtesy of Historic Ships of Baltimore.

*steamships and placing the squadron base closer to the patrol area, to no avail.
Under Conover, however, the African Squadron had reached its nadir, with
only three ships—none of them steamers—and a commodore who showed
almost no interest in the mission. Complaints having accumulated from the
American press and especially from the British government, President James
Buchanan and Secretary of the Navy Isaac Toucey were making significant
changes.*

August 8th   ***Cumberland* sails for home**

This morning all hands scrubbed hammocks. At 9 o'clock went on board the
Cumberland; she is getting ready for sea. At half past 11 A.M. we returned
on board. At 2 P.M. the *Cumberland* hove up her anchor, and made sail. On
passing us we gave her a salute of 13 guns which she returned, after which she
manned her rigging and gave us three cheers, which we answered with a will,
while our band played home sweet home. We then run up the broad pennant

of Flag Officer Wm. H. Inman, commanding the African Squadron. We went ashore in the boat at sundown.

August 9th

Like everything else on the ship, the rigging required constant maintenance. The stays were lines supporting the masts; "rattling down" meant renewing the ratlines, the rope ladders the men used to climb up the masts.

All hands to work in the rigging setting up backstays and rattling down. We are going to have liberty as soon as the ship is cleaned up. This is a beautiful looking island. From where we lie, the harbor or roads is full of small vessels of all nations. An English mail steamer is at anchor here.

August 10th 1859   Tarring down/all hands Swimming

Today we commenced tarring down and by the looks of the rigging from a distance a stranger would suppose they were all monkeys hanging to the ropes. Once in a while a streak of tar comes on deck, let fall by some unlucky individual aloft, who if he is caught is punished for his carelessness, or has his eyes damned by the boatswain's mate. We finished tarring down at 4 P.M. At sundown all hands were piped overboard; two boats kept pulling round the ship in case some swimmers should get the cramp.

August 11th

Today we are taking in a supply of wood and water, in the afternoon we were rigging stages in order to paint ship tomorrow.

August 12th

All hands to work painting ship and doing other light work. There is plenty of fruit here now, such as peaches, pears, plums and cherries in abundance and very cheap indeed.

Vendors in small boats (called "bumboats") would come out to anchored ships to offer all sorts of local products; fresh fruit would be especially welcome after weeks on sea rations. Though Leonard did not often mention it, bumboats were usual almost everywhere in the cruising area.

August 13th

The American consul Mr [Robert] Bayman paid our ship a visit; we saluted him with seven guns.

August 14th

Sunday morning and a splendid day. We are dressed in white frocks, blue pants and caps, at 10 had a general muster and read the articles of war, in the afternoon the bay was covered with sailing boats filled with gaily dressed people.

August 15th

All hands washed clothes. The English mail steamer sailed today for South-ampton, England. Flag Officer Inman arranged to have the squadron's mail regularly sent home by way of England, on the scheduled mail steamer.

From this point on, most of the squadron's mail came and went via the regular English mail steamers to Madeira, Fernando Po, and Prince's Island. Inman took great pains to have the squadron's steamers meet the mail at those points. Even with the best efforts, though, the time lag of news from home was always a month or more.

August 16th

Today we were called to quarters and ordered to have white straw hats and also have our hair cut short.

August 17th

Our barber is very busy cutting the men's hair according to the order, and some of them are having a cut which they style dead rabbit.

Though the navy was requiring it, sailors and merchants operating on the African coast typically did have short haircuts or even shaved heads for comfort.

August 18th 1859

Today we scraped the masts and slushed them. The painter's gang were very busy touching up the paint work here and there. There is a large Portuguese Barque just come to an anchor. At sundown all hands went in swimming.

"Slushing" involved coating with lard the areas on the masts where the spars slide up and down; here Leonard's group was scraping off the old lard and then applying the new. When the standard salt pork or beef was cooked for the crew's dinners, the lard that boiled off was saved to be used for this purpose. Much more lard could be accumulated over time than was needed for the ship, and this could be sold ashore. The profits from such sales, used for ship enhancements, were the original "slush funds."

August 19th   Sloop of War *Marion*

Early this morning a sail was seen coming in, which proved to be the U.S. Sloop of War *Marion*, belonging to the African Squadron, and has been 18 months on the station. She saluted our flag officer with 13 guns and we returned it with 9 guns; her captain came on board of us.

The USS Marion *was a sixteen-gun sailing sloop about a third the size of the* Constellation.

August 20th

Being a great holiday ashore we hoisted the Portuguese flag and at noon we fired a salute of 21 guns; the *Marion* done the same. The forts on the island have been firing all day, all night, the whole island is like a massive bonfire.

Inman reported the USS Plymouth *was leaving this day for the United States.*

August 21st

Sunday. We had a general muster at 10.0.clock and the 1st lieutenant read the Articles of War. In the afternoon we had some visitors from shore, Dr. Maxwell's family who are residing here; he is attached to the U.S. Sloop of war *Portsmouth,* which vessel also belongs to the squadron.

Dr. Charles D. Maxwell had received permission to travel privately with his family to Madeira rather than make the transit aboard the Portsmouth. *Presumably he returned to the United States the same way.*[1]

August 22nd

Her Britannic Majesty's Steam Frigate *Termagant* arrived here and came to an anchor. She is nine days out from Plymouth, England. She is going to the Pacific station to join the squadron; she commenced taking in coal and water. We are not doing anything on board of us; we spread the awnings at 9 o'clock and do what we please till after supper.

August 23d   asking for liberty

The South American Mail steamer arrived here today on her way to England. Some of the petty officers went to the mast and asked for liberty, which we are going to have tomorrow.

August 24th 1859   in Madeira/first liberty

There has been a report circulated through that the Small Pox is prevailing here; our surgeon hearing this thought it prudent not to let the men go ashore until he investigated it. He went ashore and returned on board at half past 9 o' clock. He said there was a few cases of it in the eastern part of the city and cautioned the men not to go near that end of the city. On the strength of this the first lieutenant sent the first draft ashore, which was the first part of the

Starboard Watch, which consisted of 83 men dressed in white frocks, blue pants and caps; they are to be off at 10 A.M. tomorrow.

August 25th

During the night some of the draft came aboard dead drunk (or to use a man of war phrase Hog. O.). The men being all aboard at 11 o'clock, the 1st part of the Port Watch went ashore; the boats' crews are not going until the last.

The log of USS Marion *for this date reported: "At 11 furled sails in obedience to signal. At 12 fired a salute of 21 guns in company with the Forts onshore and the Flagship. Colors halfmast. At 1230 masted the colors and fired a salute of 21 guns after the landing of the Bishop of Madeira with Church pennant and Portuguese Flag at Fort—following the motions of Flag Ship." Don Patricio Xavier de Moura, formerly bishop of the Cape Verdes, had arrived to take up his post as the new bishop of Funchal. The celebration Leonard described on the twentieth was likely connected with the event. The bishop's formal installation did not take place until September 18.[2]*

August 26th

The second part of the Starboard Watch went ashore today, and at night we heard they were behaving very well.

August 27th   Hurrah for liberty/Jack ashore on Liberty/
                                    Visits the Mount Church

The 2nd part of the Port Watch and all the boat crews went ashore today at one o'clock. As this is the last draft going ashore, the boys determined to have a good time and as some of them say to make Rome howl. On getting ashore all hands made for the nearest rum shop and got a drink and a cigar, after which we paired in couples and started in search of pleasure. I in company with a young fellow belonging to Boston hired horses, which are very plentiful here and can be had very cheap, and started on a tour to the Mount Church, which is situated about three miles from the city of Funchal. We were accompanied by the guides, who everlastingly clung to our horse tails. After stopping on the road some half a dozen times to wet our throats and meeting with a host of beggars (the island is infested with beggars who won't take no for an answer) we arrived at the church.

We dismounted and with our guide we visited the church. After looking around the building, which is not much account, at least it is not half as grand as I [was] told it was, the view we got here was Truly Magnificent and the weather delightful. After listening to some traditionary tales told by our guide, we mounted our horses and commenced our downward descent. I being a poor rider, I came near being pitched head foremost over the horse's head. The road all the way down was splendid. All kinds of fruit and vegetables grow in abundance all over the island. We were now fast approaching the city, so we settled with our guides and dismounted and walked into the city. We now visited the Cathedral of San Miguel, which is a beautiful building, and several other buildings too numerous to mention. As it was now getting towards night we started to look out for some place to put up at a hotel in the Rua de Bispo.

The Church of Our Lady of the Mountain (Igreja de Nossa Senhora do Monte) remains a Funchal tourist spot, as does the cathedral.

August 28th [written in margin]

Early, it being Sunday morning, we got breakfast and brushed ourselves up, so as to go to church. It was a beautiful morning and the church bells were ringing merrily. We went arm in arm to the nearest Church of A Gracia de Sare, (church of the Messiah), where we stopped about half an hour and left it to visit some others, one in particular where the soldiers go to; here we were shown every attention and very much impressed by the ceremonies. The church inside is decorated in a splendid manner. The services were conducted in a manner different from what I have ever seen. We now left the church and started down towards the Grand Square, where we met some of our ship-mates, and we repaired to the French Hotel where my companion unfortunately got drunk and from that time until we got aboard (1 o'clock) I had to look after him.

The "church of the Messiah," the Portuguese of which Leonard garbled, is almost certainly the Igreja de Colégio, otherwise known as the Jesuit Church, built by the Jesuits in 1629 about a hundred meters from the Rua de Bispo.[3]

August 29th 1859   at Madeira

The liberty is all over, and all hands are talking about their adventures, some of which (if you can believe what they say) were almost Miraculous. At half past 10 A.M. the U.S. Sloop of War *Plymouth* arrived here from Cadiz with over 400 midshipmen on board. She is used as a school ship. She is on a roving commission and will stay a few days and then go home. Today all hands are very busy scraping the guns and gun carriages; in the evening all hands went in swimming.

The midshipmen aboard the Plymouth *were the entire student body of the U.S. Naval Academy, on the last leg of their summer cruise.*

August 30th 1859

My birthday—22 years old. The English Steam Frigate *Termagant* sailed today for the Pacific; the *Marion*'s crew are having 48 hours liberty.

August 31st

The U.S. School Ship *Plymouth* sailed today for home. We manned the rigging and gave her three cheers; the *Marion* also cheered her and she returned the cheers and dipped her ensign. The *Marion*'s crew are raising old harry ashore.

Actually, as Inman reported on August 20, USS Plymouth *sailed for home on that date. For whatever reason, Leonard's dating of events in the latter part of this month, as well as part of the following month, is surprisingly inaccurate.*

September 1859

September 1st   **our Flag officer on board the *Marion***

All hands scrubbed hammocks this morning. At half past 9 A.M. had a general quarters, after which the divisions bills came out for clothing and the mess bills for small stores. In the afternoon the flag officer went on board the *Marion* to inspect her; on his arrival on board of her they fired a salute of 13 guns and hoisted his pennant on the mizzen and we hauled ours down. At 5 P.M. he returned on board and we again hoisted his pennant. This afternoon the 2nd, 3d and 4th Lieutenants were very busy picking out fighting crews for the launch, 1st and 2nd cutters in case we should have a boat expedition. I do not belong to either of them. The launch carries two 12 pound howitzers and 30 men; she is commanded by our 2nd lieutenant.

September 2nd 1859   **at Madeira/First court martial**

The English Mail steamer sailed today for England. We are making preparations for sea. There is a court martial going on here today: one of our men (a seaman) ran away from one of the boats while she was ashore on duty. At 5 P.M. all hands were called to muster to hear the sentence of the Court, which was read by the 1st lieutenant. It was loss of 3 months' pay and 6 months' black list, which means the dirty work about the ship. (S.W.)

September 3d   **all hands up anchor**

Being Saturday we holystoned the gun deck, after which we sent up Top gallant and royal yards. At noon we hove short and waited the wind to spring up; at 5 P.M. we made sail and hove up the anchor and went to sea. In going out we came near running into a small brig that was at anchor outside of us. At night we lost sight of Madeira.

September 4   General muster

Sunday at 10 o'clock we had a general muster round the capstan. There is not much wind today, but it is very pleasant weather. We are going to Porto Grande, one of the Cape de Verde Islands. All hands dressed in white frocks, blue pants, and caps.

Porto Grande is actually the large natural harbor on the island of São Vicente (St. Vincent).

September 5th

We have got a good breeze this day, going about six knots. At 10 o'clock the drum beat to general quarters. We exercised the port battery; we went through all the maneuvers of boarding and repelling boarders.

September 6th

The port watch washed clothes. At 10 A.M. a sail was reported on our lee bow, which proved to be a large barque bound to the Northward and Westward.

September 7th

The Starboard watch washed clothes; in the afternoon the 1st, 2nd and 3rd divisions were called aft on the quarter deck for Musket Drill.

September 8th 1859   at sea/reading the stations/
first General Quarters at night/at sea

There being a very light wind this day, the 1st lieutenant called all hands on deck and read their stations to them. My stations are as follows: After Guard No. 238, loosing and furling on the Main Yard; in getting underway, Main deck capstan and afterwards on the Mizzen Topsail sheets; at reefing, Main Topsail Reef Tackles; in Tacking and wearing, lee main clew garnet and then the lee main braces; coming to an anchor, Main Topsail Clew Jigger and Bunt-lines. After supper we exercised sail.

At night about half past 11 o'clock, it being my watch below, was startled at the sound of the drum beating to general quarters. Turned out and dressed and was told by the Master at Arms to lash up my hammock with 3 turns and put it in the netting, and then go to my gun, which in doing I found it cast loose and ready for action. The battle lanterns were all lighted, the shot and shell were all up, and everything ready for an engagement. The drum now beat the retreat, and the watch went below. I cannot for the life of me describe the confusion there was on this occasion; in the hurry I lashed up shirt and jacket in my hammock and had to wait for them until the next watch.

September 9th

As we expect to get into port tomorrow we up [*sic*] the chain cables and bent them, and took all the chafing gear off of the rigging. We have got a good strong breeze.

September 10th   Land Ho.

The island of Santo Antão (discovered by the Portuguese on St. Anthony's Day) is one of the greenest of the Cape Verde Islands, especially on its northern and eastern sides, the direction from which the Constellation *probably approached.*

Early this morning the lookout at the masthead reported land in sight on our lee bow; made it out to be the Island of San Antoine, one of the Cape de Verdes, and very near Porto Grande. We have got a good wind and expect to get in this afternoon if the wind holds. The land is very high and looks very green. About 2 o'clock we came to

September 10th 1859   [St. Vincent]

anchor in the Harbor of Porto Grande opposite the town. It is one of the Cape de Verde Islands, and is one of the meanest looking places I ever saw. It belongs to the Portuguese, and is inhabited by Negroes. The English South American Mail Steamship Company have got a coal depot here, and that I believe is the only thing that keeps it alive. There is very good anchorage here, however, being completely landlocked. There is nothing grows here whatever, the people getting their supplies from the neighboring island of San Antoine. The U.S. Steamer *San Jacinto* is at anchor here, having arrived here during the week; she has been waiting for us. She has just come out here to join the Squadron. She saluted our flag officer with 13 guns; we returned her 9 guns for her captain. In the afternoon we got out all boats and at sundown sent down the Royal yards.

The first steam vessel ever ordered to the U.S. African Squadron, the USS San Jacinto *thus represented a major policy innovation by the U.S. government. The* San Jacinto *is a 1,500-ton steam screw frigate.*

September 11th 1859

Being Sunday, had inspection and a muster and the 1st lieutenant read the Articles of War. In the afternoon some of the *San Jacinto* men came aboard of us to visit. She left New York four days after we left Boston.

This afternoon the 1st lieutenant's clerk came to me and told I was shifted into the Mizzen Top and he gave me my stations, which are as follows: Mizzen

Royal yardman, reefing; on the mizzen topsail yard; tacking and wearing, weather crochic braces, afterwards in the Mizzen Top to haul taut the weather lift and shroud; making and taking in sail on the Mizzen royal yard. In the evening we swung clean hammocks.

After three months aboard, Leonard's shift to a new assignment brought new things to learn. What he heard as "crochic braces" was actually "crojack braces" or "crossjack braces." These lines held the crossjack, the lower yard on the mizzenmast.

September 12th

This morning all hands scrubbed hammocks. At 10 o clock we had general quarters. I forgot to mention that we had left one of our midshipmen; we left [him] on board the *Marion* as she was short of officers; his name is Hall. We went ashore in the 3d cutter this evening and the place is worse than I thought it was, being knee deep in sand. There is a kind of liquor here called Auguedent [*aguardiente, a type of brandy*] which is like fire.

September 13th 1859   at Porto Grande/all hands bury the dead

A very melancholy event occurred during the night: one of our men died. He was a young fellow from Cambridge, Mass. He was 25 years old; Thomas Phillips was his name. We went ashore in our boat and dug his grave and returned on board at 1 o'clock. At 2 P.M. all hands were called to bury the dead. His body was brought on deck by his messmates, where the burial service was read by the 1st lieutenant, after which the body was put into the 2nd cutter and brought ashore, our band playing the dead march. Our flag and the *San Jacinto*'s were at half mast.[1]

September 14th   at Porto Grande

All hands washed clothes. At 8 o'clock a large barque arrived here loaded with coal. At half past 4 o'clock the U.S. Steamer *San Jacinto* got underway and sailed round us two or three times and kept her port battery in operation. She wanted us to see what she could do. She is going to Porto Praya, where she is to wait for us.

September 15th

Today the 1st division exercised large guns and in the afternoon small arms. At 4 o'clock the US Steam gun boat *Mystic* arrived here and came to an anchor inside of us; she is to join the squadron. Went aboard of her and got some late newspapers. In the evening we swung clean hammocks. Some of the *Mystic*'s men are aboard of us.

On October 1, 1859, Flag Officer Inman wrote to the secretary of the navy, reporting among other things that "on the 24th ult. The U.S. Steamer 'Mystic,' Lieut. Comdg William E. Le Roy, arrived off this port and was signalized to this ship. She has had a successful voyage of 19 days from New York." Similarly the New York Times correspondent, in a report dated October 1, 1859, remarked that the Mystic arrived at Porto Grande on September 25, and the Boston Daily Advertiser's correspondent aboard the Constellation reported the Mystic arrived on September 24. The present editor does not know how to reconcile these reports with Leonard's.[2]

September 16th **remarkable phenomenon**

All hands scrubbed hammocks. At 10 o'clock a ship arrived here from New Bedford; she has been out ten months and has two hundred barrels of oil. There is a remarkable freak of nature to be seen here: one of the largest of the hill tops resembles a man's head perfect in every feature, and some say it looks like Washington's head, but as I have never seen Washington I can not trace the resemblance. In the afternoon the gun deck divisions exercised.

September 17th 1859 **to Porto Grande**

Today being Saturday we holystoned the gun deck, at 10 o'clock a young fellow was let out of the brig. He was court-martialed in Madeira for fighting and lost two month's pay and had thirty days in solitary confinement on bread and water. He looks very pale and felt glad to get out. (T.B.) In the afternoon the U.S. Steam gun boat *Sumpter* arrived here from New York to join the squadron; she has been out 38 days.

T.B. was Thomas Brady.[3] The New York Times correspondent reported the Sumpter as arriving on the twenty-second.[4] Inman also reported the arrival of the Sumpter on that date, seventeen days (not thirty-eight) from New York. The Sumpter was one of the steamers from the Paraguayan Expedition. Among the preparations for that expedition, the navy had leased seven shallow-draft commercial steamers suitable for river navigation and converted them for military use. After the business of the expedition was quickly concluded, it was more economical to purchase the ships outright than to fulfill the lease contract. This was done with an eye to using them on antislaving operations with the African Squadron or around Cuba.

September 18th

The English mail steamer arrived. It being Sunday we were called to quarters for inspection. Some of the *Sumpter* men came on board of us.

September 19th

This morning we had a boat expedition consisting of the launch, 1st and 2nd cutters, in order to learn the boats' crews their duties when called upon to man the boats. They returned at 5 P.M.

September 20th

All hands washed clothes. An American barque sailed from here today for the states; sent two cutters in her.

September 21st

We are awaiting here for the U.S. Sloop of war *Marion* to give her some orders; she was to sail from Madeira on the 18th of this month, after which we are going to Porto Praya.

September 22nd

The 2nd and 3d cutters went ashore early this morning and cast a seine for some fish. In trying to haul it in, it caught on a rock; we had to tear it to get it clear and had to return on board with no fish.

September 23

All hands scrubbed and washed clothes.

September 24th

The English mail Steamer sailed today. Holystoned the gun and spar decks.

In accordance with the arrangements he made a month ago, Inman advised the secretary of the navy that the best way to communicate with the squadron was by sending mail to Liverpool, to go from there by the English mail steamer to Fernando Po. Typically the communications lag between Washington and the flagship was about a month each way, but often it was longer. He also reported that the USS Mystic *arrived today from New York. Another steamer from the Paraguayan Expedition, the* Mystic *made the trip in nineteen days, despite strong gales along the way.*

September 25th 1859   at Porto Grande

Sunday. All hands dressed in white and at half past 9 o'clock the divisions were called to quarters for inspection. After dinner some of our ship's company went aboard the *Mystic* and *Sumpter* to visit; some of their men came aboard of us.

These two veteran ships of the Paraguayan Expedition were much altered after being leased for that operation. They had then been described by their commanders as scarcely seaworthy or suitable for naval purposes; one captain felt lucky to get home alive on his unreliable ship. The navy bought them anyway, then poured considerable resources into them. After reworking at the Brooklyn Navy Yard, the Memphis *was renamed the* Mystic, *and the* Atlanta *became the* Sumpter. *With improved engines, they also were given bowsprits and carved figureheads, "giving them a rakish clipper-like exterior," and other enhancements, so they could now be called "among the finest-looking vessels of their class in the United States navy."[5] By paying more for them secondhand than their owner had paid for them new and expending probably enough additional money to build even better new vessels, Secretary Toucey had made embarrassing naval sow's ears into silk purses.[6] Or at least they were better-looking sow's ears, for during their African deployment, the ships' officers will, like their predecessors, have had little good to say about them. However, despite problems with reliability and seaworthiness, they had exactly the characteristics American naval officers had been urging for the African Squadron for the past two decades—they were small steamers with shallow draft suitable for coastal and river patrol.*

September 26th   Quarters

At 10 o'clock this day we had general quarters for target practice. We fired six rounds from each gun and made some very good shots.

Regulations required each ship to fire six practice rounds from each gun every three months. Most gun drills were done without actually firing.

September 27th

The U.S. Steam gun boats *Mystic* and *Sumpter* sailed today for the coast. We were exercised all this day at cutlass drill.

September 28th   exercising

All hands washed clothes. In the afternoon we exercised sail: we furled and unfurled, reefed and unreefed, mastheaded the topsails several times, and gave general satisfaction.

September 29th   lose a kedge anchor

Today our launch got adrift from her moorings. She was almost on the beach before she was discovered, and we were all the forenoon in a hot sun dragging for it [the launch's anchor] in the 3d cutter. At 12 A.M. we had to give it up as a bad job.

September 30th   **Getting ready for sea**

We took in our launch, 1st and 2nd cutters, and are making preparations for sea. The division bills came out today; also the mess bills. An English coal ship came in and came to an anchor. At sundown we swung clean hammocks. We then went ashore in the boat.

October 1859

October 1st

Making active preparations for sea. At sundown sent up Topgallant and royal yards and took in all our boats, after which the Port Watch got the messenger up ready to heave up our anchor. At night the men had a fiddler in the gangway and had a good time.

W.A. Leonard

With this entry, as in various places later, Leonard inscribed his name. Readers will also sometimes encounter the names of family and friends at random locations. Additionally Leonard from time to time jotted down brief moral aphorisms that have no apparent connection to the events of the day. The messenger was a loop of chain or rope used on the capstan in the process of raising the anchor.

October 2nd 1859   **leaving Porto Grande**

At 9 o'clock we hove short to 15 fathoms and waited for a breeze, which generally comes in the afternoon at 4 o'clock. The breeze being very strong, all hands were called to loose sail and take one reef in the topsails, which being done we got up the anchor and stood out of the harbor. We are going to Porto Praya, which is about 150 miles from here and is another of the Cape de Verde Islands.

Porto Praya is the port and town (now called Praia) at the southern tip of the island of Santiago in the Cape Verdes.

October 3d   at sea/at Porto Praya/lose our Starboard Bow Anchor/
                              down Royal yards

We have got the N.E. trade winds, which are very strong at this season of the
year; we have got two reefs in our topsails. At 10 o'clock the log indicated we
were going 14 knots an hour. At 1 o'clock land was reported from the mast
head, which proved to be the island of Mayo about 30 miles from Porto Praya.
At 3 o'clock we sighted the island and at half past 4 P.M. we came to an anchor
off the town of Porto Praya, not before losing our starboard bow anchor and
about 45 fathoms of cable. They let go the anchor when the ship had too much
headway and in trying to check her the cable parted. The U.S. Steamer *San
Jacinto* is here waiting for orders from the flag officer. We got out all boats.

This is also a Portuguese possession and the appearance from where we lay
is very wild, but I understand that a little ways inboard there is a very fertile
soil, and I have no reason to doubt it, for alongside of the ship there are about
20 bum boats full of fruit and vegetables which they are offering at very cheap
prices. We are going to take in stores here; the store house for the squadron
is situated here, and there is an American consul here. We went ashore in the
boat and returned at sundown, when the Royal yards were sent down and by
some means our yard got foul and maybe we didn't get a blessing.

October 4th 1859 at Porto Praya/Breakers ahead

At 8 o'clock we saluted the Portuguese Flag, which salute was returned by
the fort. We then commenced to take in provisions and water by means of the
boats. In the afternoon we went ashore for the ward room officers and undertook to sail back. We had a good breeze but we had got but very little ways
when we discovered we were drifting on a shoal of rocks where the surf was
beating violently. We now were very close to them when one of the officers
(a marine officer) got so excited that he gave orders to down masts and out
boathooks. Although we were in a very dangerous position we could not help
laughing. After considerable work to keep her from striking the rocks, we got
her clear and pulled to the ship.

October 5th

At 10 A.M. the American Consul, Mr. [William H.] Morse, came aboard, when
we fired a salute of nine guns.

October 6th

The U.S. Steamer *San Jacinto* sailed today for Monrovia. At 4 o'clock we had
all our water and provisions on board; we got in all boats and sent up royal
yards.

October 7th

At 10 A.M. we got underway and made all sail for Monrovia, where we are going to take in about forty kroomen to man our boats. The U S government allows two to each gun, so as not to expose the white crew to the climate. At sundown we had a nine knot breeze.

The kroomen were members of an ethnic group dwelling in Liberia and adjacent portions of the West African coast who for generations had hired out to visiting ships, both naval and commercial. They brought their own canoes and organized themselves in groups under headmen but became members of the ship's crew during their time aboard. On U.S. Navy ships, headmen were signed on and paid as landsmen, their assistants as first class boys, and the rest as boys. The West African ports had no pier facilities; ships anchored out, and everything between ship and shore was transported in boats or canoes. Most such work was done by kroomen.

Inman reported sailing from Porto Praya on the fifth and arriving in Monrovia on the twenty-first.

October 8th

The port watch holystoned the gun deck, after which bags were piped up to air clothing. Had light winds all this day and had very pleasant weather. I had a wheel this afternoon. The port watch had 8 hours in, caught a large porpoise in the middle watch.

Willie Leonard Bunker Hill

October 9th 1859   at sea

Sunday at 10 o'clock had a general muster round the capstan, had a good breeze all this day; all sail set.

October 10th

The port watch scrubbed and washed clothes. In the afternoon the 1st division exercised large guns and the 2nd division had musket drill and the 3d division had single stick exercise.

The single stick was exactly that, though with a carved hilt, serving as a practice substitute for the cutlass.

October 11th

Very fine weather. Starboard watch washed clothes, the wind is from the N.N.E and we are going 9 knots.

October 12th   airing bedding

The wind died away and we are in the midst of a dead calm, the sun being very warm. The 1st lieutenant had all the hammocks out of the nettings and hung up in the rigging to air, which gives the ship the appearance of a Chatham Street Jew's shop.

October 13th

It is still a dead calm we have got the main Topsail aback and we are taking it easy; saw several large whales today.

October 14th   at sea

We had some very light cat's paws during the morning watch, which kept us pulling at the braces all the time; towards night however it settled into a steady breeze.

October 15th

The port watch holystoned the gun deck and in the afternoon all hands exercised sail. My wheel at 6 P.M.

October 16th

Sunday at half past nine called all hands to quarters for inspection, after which the 1st lieutenant read the Articles of War. The sun was very hot during the day.

Though the news did not reach the Constellation *for some time on this day, abolitionist John Brown led eighteen men on a raid on the federal arsenal at Harper's Ferry, Virginia.*

October 17th

The Starboard washed clothes. At 10 o'clock had general quarters, exercised both batteries and fished the masts.

October 18th 1859   at sea

Port washed clothes. We had several rain squalls during this day; we are fast approaching the rainy latitudes.

October 19th   rolling in the lee Scuppers/reefing

Very squally weather all this day with plenty of rain, which we took advantage of by rolling in the lee scuppers, and having a fresh water wash, which operation is a good treat to a sailor to get some of the salt out of their bones. At 12 o'clock in the midnight watch we had a very severe squall which took us all aback, all hands were called to shorten sail; put two reefs in the topsails and made everything snug for the night, after which the watch was piped down.

October 20th   Land Ho.

At 9 o'clock this morning the drum beat to general fire quarters. We are becalmed, not a breath of wind, and it is dreadful hot and sultry. At 2 P.M. the mast head lookout reported land in sight two points on our lee bow. At 5 P.M. it commenced raining, and which continued all night. The watch amused themselves by spinning yarns under the lee of the weather rail. Towards morning a very light breeze spring up.

October 21st   coming to an anchor/at Monrovia/
sling clean hammocks

Liberia was founded by the American Colonization Society in 1822 as a colony for freed American slaves and became an independent republic in 1847, with continuing public and private American support. By 1859 thousands of U.S. emigrants had settled there, mostly at Monrovia. By U.S. policy recaptured slaves from ships taken by the U.S. Navy were settled there as well. The Liberian government possessed a small (sixty feet in length) gunboat, the five-gun brig Quail, *given them by the British government.*

The wind freshening at 8 o'clock, we stood in for the land, and at 1 o'clock we came to an anchor in roads opposite the City of Monrovia, which is a beautiful looking place. It is the capital of Liberia and is chiefly inhabited by American Negroes and is in a very flourishing condition. It is a republic and its president is an American darkey by the name of Thomas Benson. There is two or three newspapers printed here, some of the people are very intellectual. There is plenty of fruit and vegetables which are to be had very cheap. There is a small brig of war at anchor inside of us, which belongs to the Republic. Their flag is similar to ours, with only one large star in it, which signifies the lone star republic. At sundown we sent down royal yards and slung clean hammocks. We are going to take in a supply of wood and water here.

Stephen Allen (not Thomas) Benson, Liberian president from 1856 to 1864, came to Liberia from Maryland at the age of six with his freeborn American parents.

22nd   trying the Cold water cure

All hands scrubbed hammocks, after which we washed the ship outside. After breakfast we commenced taking in wood and water. We are going to take in forty negroes here called kroomen, which belong to a tribe of that name they come from a place called Nefoo [Nifu], which is situated about 150 miles in the interior. They have already begun their applications and the ship is swarmed with them presenting their recommendations, (which they carry with them, slung around their necks in tin boxes) to our captain. They are a fine looking set of men. They now began to come a little faster than they were wanted and contrary to the orders of the 1st lieutenant they hung on to the ship's side, and resisted all attempts to drive them off. That official, getting a little riled, ordered the carpenter's mate to rig the force pump and have it manned, which being done he ordered the hose to be pointed at the (as he called them) Black Scorpions and such a scattering to get into their canoes which they made would have made a saint laugh. They were told to come again Monday.

October 23

Sunday. It being very rainy all this day, we dispensed with the usual inspection. In the afternoon an American brig arrived here from South America.

October 24th

Our Flag officer went ashore this day to dine with the president of the republic, and brought the ship's band with him. We had a run ashore in the boat in the afternoon.

At Monrovia, Inman received a letter from Rear Admiral Grey, commander-in-chief of the British African Squadron, saying that he had sound information that in the past two years seventy slavers had come and gone from the coast under the American flag, and of those eleven had been stopped by his ships and then sent on their way because their papers were valid. He specifically mentioned the Ellen, *stopped by HMS* Medusa *in September 1858, with locked-down hatches and the unmistakable smell of slaves aboard but good papers.[1] In his response Inman noted that the United States had instructed the ships of his squadron to cooperate with the British, also that four steamers had been added under his command and will, he promised, be "vigorously employed." As an example of cooperation between the two squadrons, he mentioned that Commander Brent had six months earlier sent correspondence about his ship (the USS* Marion*) and the HMS* Triton, *regarding the slaver* Orion, *to the secretary of the navy.[2]*

October 25th 1859   at Monrovia/Shipping the Kroomen

Taking in wood and water. The U.S Steamer *San Jacinto* arrived here today, twenty-three days passage from Porto Praya; she is going to take in about thirty kroomen. We shipped our kroomen today. They had to be examined by the doctors, some of them being rejected on account of their defects. We shipped forty in all. They had the queerest names I ever heard; after considerable trouble I learned the whole of them which are as follows:

Head Krooman		Second Head Krooman	
John Tobie		Jack Frying Pan	
	Tom Walker		
	Tom Pepper		
5	Tom Dennis	23	Jack Half Dollar
6	Bottle of Beer	24	Jack After Supper
7	Jack After Breakfast	25	Tom Out Hauler
8	Flying Jib	26	Fresh Water
9	Tar Bucket 1st	27	Tar Bucket 2nd
10	Black Bugger	28	Upside Down
11	Jack Smart	29	Ben Coffee
12	Ben Liverpool	30	Jack Poor Fellow
13	Beau Hickman	31	Bob Roberts
14	Two Forty	32	Jim Bobstay
15	Jim Crow	33	Jack Every Day
16	Jack Monrovia	34	Tom Freeman
17	Jack Savage	35	Prince of Wales
18	Josiah Anderson	36	Sea Breeze
19	Bill Harness Cask	37	Charley Mack
20	Jim Dough	38	Tom Rattlin
21	Bill Half Dollar	39	Jack Smoke Stack
22	Bill Boston	40	Sam Binnacle

These names were given to them by the crews of the vessels that trade on this coast, every one of which takes 10 or 12 of them to help them load their vessels. The U.S. government allows their vessels on this station two kroomen to every gun they carry. We are a 20 gun ship, therefore we are entitled to forty of them. The object in having them is to man the boats so as to keep the white men from being exposed to the sun, which is dreadful hot all along the Coast. They are a very hardy race of people and can stand a great deal of fatigue. They require no bedding; they sleep on deck.

October 26th   leaving Monrovia

This morning we got in all boats and sent up Royal yards. The *San Jacinto* sailed at 6 o'clock. She is to meet us down the coast. At 11 A.M. we hove up our anchor in the midst of a violent rain squall and left Monrovia. It rained all this day and night.

October 27th

It is still raining and the watch are washing their clothes. Towards evening it cleared away and we had a beautiful sunset.

October 28th   at sea/exercising the boys

Starboard watch washed clothes. It being a fine day and not much wind, the boys, and some of the landsmen, we exercised at reefing and furling sail; the Mizzen Topsail was used. After exercising about an hour, they were called down and got a great deal of praise for their smartness.

29th   at sea

The Port watch washed clothes. In the afternoon all hands were called to exercise sail, the watches working on their own sides. I, belonging to the port watch, would say that we beat them. We exercised the studding sails both sides. We are having some very fine weather.

October 30th

Sunday had division inspection as usual and read the Articles of War.

October 31st   at sea

The 1st division were exercised at the large guns, the 2nd division at small arms, 3d division at single sticks and the powder division at Carbine Drill.

November 1859

November 1st   Sail Ho

The divisions' bills are out and the men are busy putting down for clothing. The mess bills are also out. We have got a first rate breeze, giving about seven knots. We sighted and spoke a brig from Rio Janeiro bound to Liverpool 23 days out. We are bound to Prince's Island, where we are going to water ship.

November 2nd   at Sea

The Port watch washed clothes. At six o'clock we signalized a steamer from Cape Palmas, bound to London, England with the South American Mail. In the afternoon the 2nd division were exercised at large guns and the 1st division at small arm drill.

November 3d

The Starboard Watch washed clothes. At half past nine had general fire quarters, after which clothing was served out by the Purser.

November 4th

At 10 o'clock the drum beat to general quarters. We were at them for an hour, after which the drum beat the retreat.

November 5th

The Starboard Watch holystoned the gun deck, after which all bags were piped up to air clothing.

November 6th   at Sea

Sunday. All the divisions were called to quarters for inspection, after which we had a general muster round the capstan and read the Articles of War. At noon the wind died away to a dead calm at 4 o'clock a light breeze sprung up from the northward and westward, which towards night settled into a good breeze. We are going along at a first rate pace, about seven miles an hour.

November 7th

This morning the lookout at the masthead reported land on our lee bow, supposed to be Prince's Island. We hove to at night.
Willie Leonard

November 8th 1859   at Prince's Island/description of Island/
Madame Ferreira

Early this morning we filled away the main Topsail, and stood in for the land. At half past ten o'clock in the forenoon we came to an anchor at Prince's Island in fifteen fathoms water. The U.S. Steam Gun boat *Mystic* is at anchor here; she has been waiting for us.

It is a beautiful island, and from where we lay it makes a splendid appearance. It puts one in mind of reading some fairy tale of enchantment. It is covered all over with trees which are thick together as can be; there is abundance of all kinds of fruit and vegetables. The island abounds with all kinds of birds, among which the gray parrot is the most conspicuous; they keep up an incessant chattering from morn till eve. The ring tail monkey is very numerous here. The principal feature of the island is its mountain rivulet, which has its source somewhere in the mountain. It is almost always raining here, and such times there is a large waterfall to be seen on one of the highest peaks of the mountain. The water is very pure and cold. Our ships come here to get their supplies.

There is a large town at the other side of the island (it is a Portuguese possession); this side of the island is inhabited by negroes. There is an old Portuguese lady who (as near as I can make out) governs this side of the place. Madame Ferrara (as she is called by the people) is about 50 years old. She was born on the island, her parents being banished here for some political difficulties. She is highly esteemed by everybody who is acquainted with her. She has a large house here which overlooks the bay; the Portuguese flag may at all times be seen flying from its battlements. At sundown we got out all boats and sent down Royal yards. We are going to take in a supply of wood and water.

Madame Maria Ferreira had been for many years one of the wealthiest and most powerful figures on the island and held open house for officers of visiting ships.

November 9th 1859   at Prince's Island

This morning we commenced taking in a supply of wood and water. The U.S. Steam Gun Boat *Mystic* sailed today for the island of Fernando Po to get the

Madame Ferreira's house on Prince's Island. William Allen and T. R. H. Thomson, *A Narrative of the Expedition Sent by Her Majesty's Government to the River Niger in 1841*. London: Bentley, 1848. Special Collections and Archives Department, Nimitz Library, United States Naval Academy.

mail; she is to meet us at St Paul de Loando. At sundown we finished taking in wood and water, took in all boats and sent up Royal yards. We are going to cruise around the mouth of the Congo River after slavers; there is a great deal of talk among the ship's company about the prospect of getting prize money.

After a captured slave ship had been condemned by an American court, it was sold at auction and the proceeds divided. Half went to support a home for retired sailors; the other half was divided among the crew of the navy ship that had made the capture. The individual crew members received portions according to their rank. Additionally the U.S. government paid a bounty of twenty-five dollars for each recaptured slave landed alive in Liberia, and all of this money was similarly divided among the crew. The British paid similar prize money to their crews, including five pounds per recaptured slave.

November 10th   leaving Prince's Island

At 9 A.M. we hove up the anchor and made all sail for the Congo River. We have got a strong breeze from the Northward. In a very few hours Prince's Island was far astern of us. Wind N.E. by E giving about 6 knots an hour. The watch are very busy putting on chafing gear.

November 11th   at sea

At 10.0.clock the drum beat to general quarters; exercised the starboard battery. At noon the lookout at the masthead reported land on our starboard
beam. It proved to be the island of St. Thomas, about 25 miles distant. The
weather is very warm; it is cloudy and rainy. We are on the line [the equator].
Wind N.E. by E.

November 12th

The port watch holystoned the gun deck. It is very rainy here; being right on
the Equator it is very hot.

November 13th

Sunday. All hands were called to quarters for inspection; all hands dressed in
clean blue mustering clothes.

November 14th

There is a court martial going on today. Such business as this makes everything
look gloomy. In the afternoon the 1st division were exercised at large guns and
the 2nd division at small arms.

November 15th 1859   at sea/Sentence of a Court Martial

The starboard watch washed clothes. At 10 A.M. all hands were called to muster to hear the sentence of the court martial. The 1st lieutenant after reading
the charges and specifications he read the sentence of the court, which was as
follows: loss of two months' pay, thirty days solitary confinement in the brig
in double irons on bread and water. His charge was striking a man on the
quarter deck, they both being brought to the mast for fighting by the master
at arms (T.W. T.B.)

"Double irons" means manacles on hands and feet.

November 16th   Sail Ho.

The port watch washed clothes. At 11 o'clock land was reported by the lookout on the foretopsail yard. A sail was also reported bearing three points on
our lee bow; we squared away and bore down to her. She proved to be an
American trading brig after palm oil and ivory. Lost sight of land.

November 17th   at sea

This morning we took in the royals and topgallant sails and remained under
easy sail all day. The water here has a very dirty looking appearance; we are
in soundings. About every hour we cast the deep sea lead, get bottom at sixty
to ninety fathoms.

November 18th

This morning a sail was reported two points on our weather bow. We made all sail and gave chase, she also made sail and we did not gain much on her at night. She got away under cover of the darkness.

November 19th

The Starboard watch holystoned the gun deck, after which all bags were piped up to air clothing. Being Saturday, everybody is cleaning up for tomorrow for the usual inspection. I was very busy looking over my old letters and miniatures.

Leonard's miniatures would have been either small painted portraits or, more likely, daguerreotypes of loved ones.

November 20th   at sea

Sunday at half past 9 o'clock the divisions were called to quarters for inspection. There is land in sight. There is also a strong current running and the water has a very dark appearance; it is supposed to be the Congo River water.

November 21st   **at anchor at the mouth of the Congo River/ Barque *Orion* under arrest/her crew Sick with the coast Fever/Latitude 6.36 South**

This day we had a good breeze and fine weather, land in sight. At 1 o'clock we came to an anchor at the mouth of the Congo River in fifteen fathoms water. Shark's Point about seven miles distant. This is the principal mart for slaves on this coast. There is two large slave factories to be seen from where we are at anchor. The place presents a very wild appearance; it is said to be very sickly here.

Factor being the common word for a trader, a "slave factory" was the headquarters of a slave trader. The term was used interchangeably with barracoon, meaning a structure holding slaves awaiting shipment.

At 2 o'clock P.M. our flag officer went ashore in his barge. At 5 P.M. a vessel hove in sight off Shark's Point coming out of the river. Made her out to be the U.S. Steam Gun Boat *Sumpter* with our flag officer on board; she made signals to us to get underway; she also signalized that she had a barque under arrest supposed to be a slaver. We hove up the anchor and under the pilotage of the steamer we proceeded up the river and at half past six P.M. we came to an anchor inside of Shark's Point about two cables length ahead of the supposed slaver. She turned out to be the celebrated barque *Orion*, the same vessel that the U.S. Government had so much trouble about. All her crew are sick with the coast fever, or at least they pretend to be. She was taken by the U.S.

Steamer *San Jacinto* at sea and towed in here by her. She left her in charge of
the U.S. Steam Gun Boat *Sumpter* to wait for us. She is undoubtedly a slaver
and is to take a cargo of Negroes the first favorable opportunity. She is a very
pretty barque and belongs to New York.

*Shark's Point [Point Santo Antonio/Ponta Padrão] is the tip of land marking
the seaward end of the left (southern) bank of the Congo River. Its counterpart
on the right bank is French Point [Banana Point/Pointe Francaise]; between the
two points, the mouth of the river is five and a half miles wide.*

    Leonard's information was imperfect; the actual facts of the Orion's *story
merit attention for demonstrating the exasperation officers of the U.S. African
Squadron could experience.*

    Just before noon on November 22, the San Jacinto *anchored on the star-
board quarter of the* Constellation.[1] *Lt. J. F. Armstrong, commanding the* San
Jacinto, *reported simply meeting the* Orion *(a 449-ton barque), with a crew
from the* Mystic *on board, and letting it go on its way into the anchorage.[2]
Earlier, in October, the USS* Portsmouth *had boarded the* Orion, *let it go, then
stopped it again. In between the* Orion *had apparently gone up the Congo to
arrange for a later delivery of a cargo of slaves.[3] The* Mystic *had also boarded
the* Orion, *but although it had all the paraphernalia suitable for taking a cargo
of slaves, its papers were in order.*

    The Mystic's *captain did not feel he could arrest the* Orion, *given the recent
legal actions over the ship before it left New York. The* Orion *had sailed from
New York for Africa in January 1859 with the appropriate equipment and
cargo for a slaver, all legally declared because the New York court had recently
decided that nothing carried as cargo could incriminate. It was stopped at the
mouth of the Congo by a British cruiser, whose captain determined it to be
indeed a slaver and detained it. When the U.S. sloop of war* Marion *arrived a
few days later, the* Orion *was turned over to the* Marion's *captain, who sent it
to New York.[4] En route the* Orion's *captain confessed while dying that he had
been about to take a load of slaves. What happened next may seem incredible.*

    *The New York authorities released the crew for lack of evidence, but the
case against the ship itself remained open. Then the ship's owner (a New York
merchant) was able to get his property back by putting up a bond representing
the value of the ship, nearly eighteen thousand dollars. The bondsman actually
had no money but obtained the ship's release simply by swearing that he did.
The* Orion, *still fully equipped, was then transferred to its previous first mate,
Thomas Morgan, who actually wrote the U.S. secretary of state asking for
assurance that the British could not interfere with it. (The American government had already protested the British action.) Morgan then took the ship—
still under bond for potential forfeit pending settlement of its case—back to
Africa to try again to get a load of slaves.[5]*

Then in November 1859, off the African coast north of the Congo, the Orion *encountered the* Mystic. *Morgan, sick with "Congo fever" and saying that almost his entire crew was also incapacitated, brazenly asked for assistance in taking his ship to anchorage. The navy customarily assisted merchant ships in distress, and the* Orion *was still purportedly innocent, so the* Mystic *obliged, sending a dozen sailors aboard to work the ship until arriving at the Congo River—a navy crew sailing a slave ship to its destination while that ship's crew watched! The* Orion *could then wait until the navy ships left so it can load its slaves.*

November 22nd 1859   In the Congo River/
                                                visit to the *Orion*/not condemned/
                                                Black Fish/in the Congo River

This morning all hands scrubbed hammocks. As the water is fresh, all hands are having a good wash in the afternoon. The flag officer visited the barque on official business. He inspected her all over and had no doubts but that she was a slaver. She had a slave deck laid and the coppers were rigged all ready to take in her cargo. Our flag officer would not condemn her because she was taken before on the same grounds by the U.S. Sloop of war *Marion* belonging to this squadron, which vessel sent her home. She was acquitted, the government (as I understand) paying damages to the amount of $30,000. [*On this point Leonard seems to have been mistaken.*] She had good clearance papers from the New York custom house.

While the flag officer was on board of the *Orion* we had some very good sport; a large devil fish was seen swimming close to the ship. Our chief boatswain's mate, William Long, got permission from the Officer of the Deck to go after him. He had the 3d cutter manned by the Kroomen, and armed with a harpoon he gave chase and overtook the fish and stuck the iron into him. Now commenced the tug of war. This fish is a species of the whale and very dangerous, and they no sooner struck it than it turned and made for the boat. They sheered clear of it and it commenced to go to windward. They went at the rate of a mile a minute as near as I could judge and they looked pretty well frightened. Finally the iron broke and they returned to the ship. The ship's crew were all on deck and enjoyed the sport hugely, but what was fun to us, was not fun to the Kroomen, who were almost frightened out of their wits. At sundown we sent up the royal yards and took in all the boats. We are going to sea tomorrow—we are going to St Paul de Loando.

Slave ships were not built as slave ships but were merchant ships bought and converted for the trade. To avoid arrest the ship's character as a merchant was usually maintained until the very last minute, then just before loading the slaves the conversion was made. The "coppers" of a slave ship were large

*cooking pots—copper or iron—set up on deck to boil the rice or farina fed
to the slaves. They were a sure sign of a slaver; another very strong sign was
the presence of a slave deck, an extra deck of boards laid in the hold for the
slaves to lie on. While such preparations were among the reasons given to
justify arresting a ship as a slaver, they were almost never enough to satisfy the
American courts.*

November 23d 1859   leaving the Congo River

At ten o'clock we got underway and made all sail for St. Paul de Loando. We
saw several small sails to windward but did not give chase; we have got a
strong current against us. The weather is very chilly here.

November 24th   Homesick

Thanksgiving day felt very gloomy. I thought of the contrast between this one
and the last a year ago. Then I was with all my friends and had a good time;
today in a man of war with no friends on the Coast of Africa. Heigh ho, but
no matter it is no use to complain now, it is too late. At four o'clock in the
afternoon all hands spliced the Main Brace, which is nothing more or less than
a glass of whiskey. It has been very chilly all day.

*Aware of the increasingly dangerous stresses in the nation's fabric, Flag Officer
Inman indicated an especially timely meaning for the day in his letter to the
squadron of September 3, 1859: "A desire has been very generally throughout
our country to celebrate annually a Thanksgiving Union Festival. . . . The last
Thursday in November has been set apart for this object." Similarly in her ultimately successful campaign to make Thanksgiving the permanent nationwide
institution it became in 1863, Sarah J. Hale, editor of the popular magazine
Godey's Lady's Book, emphasized its value as "a renewed pledge of love and
loyalty to the Constitution of the United States."[6]*

November 25th   at sea

We have got a good breeze this day. At ten o'clock the drum beat to general
quarters and in the afternoon the sun came out very warm, when the hammocks were piped out of the nettings and hung in the rigging to air.

November 26th

At nine o'clock the bags were piped up to air our clothing, and at ten o'clock
the port watch holystoned the gun deck. In the first Dog Watch we scraped
and slushed the spars down. Our eight hours out.

St. Paul de Loanda. John S. Roberts, *The Life and Explorations of David Livingstone, LLD.* London: Adam, 1874. Gilliland Collection.

November 27th   **Land Ho.**

Today being Sunday and a very fine day, all hands were dressed in white. At half past nine A.M. all hands were called to muster. The 1st lieutenant read the Articles of War, and then we mustered round the capstan according to our rates. At twelve o'clock the Boatswain piped to dinner. Land in sight on our weather bow, supposed to be St Paul de Loando. At six o'clock we swung clean hammocks. Very fine evening,

November 27th 1859   **came to an anchor in St Paul de Loando/**
                                                        St Paul de Loando

At two o'clock P.M. we came to an anchor in the harbor of St Paul de Loando, right astern of the U.S. Steamer *San Jacinto*. She has been waiting here for us some time. There is a large French man of war steamer coming in; she is the Admiral's ship. The H.B.M. Steam Sloop of War *Archer* and gun boat *Spitfire* are here at anchor also. Several Spanish and Portuguese gun boats; the Portuguese Admiral's ship is also here. The U.S. Storeship *Supply* is here with naval stores for the squadron. The harbor is crowded with merchant ships of all nations. The Boston barque *John Gilpin* is here; she is going home in a few days.

The appearance of St. Paul de Loando from where we lie is very good. It looks to be a large city; it belongs to the Portuguese, and it is the principal place where their convicts are sent to. There are three large forts to be seen and they look to be well fortified. However, I can't say much about it now, as we are lying about three and a half miles from the shore. I will give a better description some other time.

Leonard did not get around to giving his promised description, but he found the city less impressive upon a closer look than it appeared from a distance. When David Livingstone visited there in 1854, he described it as showing signs of former magnificence but being in decay: "It contains about twelve thousand inhabitants, most of whom are people of color. There are various evidences of its former magnificence, especially two cathedrals, one of which, once a Jesuit college, is now converted into a workshop; and in passing the other, we saw with sorrow a number of oxen feeding within its stately walls. Three forts continue in a good state of repair. Many large stone houses are to be found. The palace of the governor and government offices are commodious structures, but nearly all the houses of the native inhabitants are of wattle and daub. Trees are planted all over the town for the sake of shade, and the city presents an imposing appearance from the sea."[7]

November 28th   great Saluting

We got out all boats this morning and at eight o'clock we sent down the Top Gallant and Royal yards and fired a salute of twenty-one guns for the Portuguese flag, which was answered by the fort; we then fired thirteen guns for the French admiral, which they returned; thirteen more were fired for the Portuguese admiral. We next saluted the English steam Sloop of war *Archer* with nine guns, which they returned. The *Spitfire* was also saluted with nine guns, which they returned. At ten A.M. the captain of the *Archer* visited our ship, and on his leaving he was saluted with nine guns, which salute was answered by the *Archer*.

France, with growing interests in Africa, maintained an African squadron comparable in size to the British one. Like the United States, they did not permit other navies to stop ships under their flag, but their squadron's presence discouraged its use by slavers.

November 29th 1859   at St Paul de Loando

Commenced cleaning ship inside and out. At twelve o'clock A.M. [*Leonard means noon*] the American Consul at this port, Mr. [John G.] Willis, paid the ship a visit. A salute of nine guns was fired for him. At five o'clock in the afternoon the American barque *John Gilpin* got underway and sailed for home; in passing us we gave them three cheers and our band played some national tunes. After hammocks were down some of the men enjoyed themselves by having a dance in the foretopmen's gangway until nine o'clock.

November 30th

Today all hands are to work in the rigging, setting it up and rattling it down. In the afternoon commenced to tar down and paint the ship outside. The English Steam Sloop of war *Archer* sailed today for the Congo River. The U.S. Steam Gun boat *Mystic* is here taking in coal. The U.S. Store Ship *Supply* commenced discharging her stores. We sent all our kroomen on board of her, besides five or six hands from each part of the ship to help them discharge her cargo.

The Supply's *cargo was being moved into the newly established naval store-house ashore.*

December 1859

December 1st   **discharging the Store Ship** *Supply*

As soon as the hammocks were up, we hove up the anchor and warped in about three quarters of a mile nearer the store ship. After breakfast thirty hands were sent on board the store ship to work, which causes a great deal of growling on their part. The weather is not very healthy here at present, it being very damp and chilly. At supper time our boys returned from the store ship. She is discharged. She is going to take in sand to bring home. We are going to send about thirty invalids home in her; so is the *San Jacinto* going to do the same.

W.A. Leonard

Thirty invalids was a large number for the ship's having been out only four months.

December 2nd 1859   **at St. Paul de Loando/building a Store House**

This morning our boat (3d cutter) went ashore to market and had a two hours' run we drank some native liquor called Auguedent and O Lord what stuff it is! Talk about Jersey Lightning warranted a dead shot &c. &c., it is nothing but water to this stuff. A smell of the bottle is a sure sign of a drunk, Fact, 'pon Honor. At seven o'clock we returned to the ship. There is a large store house building here for the American Squadron. They are going to break up the one at Porto Praya because it is too far out of the way. All our carpenter's gang go ashore every day to work upon it, also our armorer. [*The armorer was the ship's blacksmith.*] It will be a fine building when it is finished. The store ship *Supply* is taking in sand [*as ballast now that it had unloaded its stores*]. Some of our men went on board of her to work; in the afternoon they made a complaint to the officer of the deck, that the *Supply* crew are laying down on the booms laughing at our boys at work. He remedied the difficulty by putting his men in the hold to work.

The U.S. Navy storehouse at St. Paul de Loanda. National Archives, African Squadron Letters. Enclosed in Inman to Toucey, August 15, 1860.

The new storehouse, on leased ground fronting the harbor next to the custom-house, was a two-story stone structure, the upper floor being living quarters for the storekeeper and his assistant, and when completed would have a wharf and loading booms. The shift of supply base from Porto Praya to Loanda was part of a major strategic shift in the operation of the African Squadron, reflecting a significant change in the American government's policy regarding the Atlantic slave trade. Since the creation of the African Squadron in 1843, naval officers had been urging the establishment of a base nearer their patrol area rather than in the Cape Verdes a thousand miles from Liberia and three thousand miles from the Congo River. Building the Loanda storehouse represents a huge improvement in the squadron's efficiency, short-lived though it proved to be.

Meanwhile on this day in Harper's Ferry, Virginia, John Brown was hanged. Among those present were Col. Robert E. Lee, U.S.A.; Lt. Jeb Stuart, U.S.A.; Virginia Military Institute professor Maj. Thomas Jackson; and actor John Wilkes Booth.

December 3d   U S Sloop of war *Portsmouth*

Today the U.S. Sloop of war *Portsmouth* arrived here; she is one of the [*sic*] she went into commission on the 3d day of May 1859. As soon as she came to an anchor she saluted our flag officer with thirteen guns and we returned it with nine guns. At ten o'clock her captain came aboard in his gig. She has taken a slaver, a large ship called the *Emily* of New York. They put a prize crew on board of her and sent her home. She has been out here some time waiting for an opportunity to take in a cargo. The *Portsmouth* has been cruising off the Congo River.

The Emily *was taken September 20, after the commander of a British steamer flagged down the* Portsmouth *with information about it. It did not have slaves aboard but had all the other earmarks of a slaver, including a set of large boilers to cook food, lumber suitable for laying as a slave deck, suspicious papers, and its rigging modified from bark to ship. The prize crew brought it into New York on November 11.[1] With leniency typical of the New York court, the* Emily *was released on the grounds that, after all, it had been allowed to sail from that port with exactly the same cargo.[2]*

December 4th 1859   at St Paul de Loando

Sunday the divisions were called to quarters at half past nine o'clock, for inspection, after which the Articles of War were read by the 1st lieutenant. In the afternoon the men were allowed to visit the other ships. Today we got a lieutenant and a midshipman from the U.S. Steamer *San Jacinto* to replace the ones we let the Sloop of war *Marion* have. They are Lieutenant Loyal and Midshipman Farquer [*Lt. Benjamin P. Loyall and Midn. Norman H. Farquhar*].

December 5th   Boat Racing in St Paul de Loando

The men on board the *Portsmouth* are very anxious to have a trial with one of our boats. Yesterday they sent a challenge on board of us from their 1st cutters to our 1st cutters to pull them a race, the bet being each man putting five dollars on his own thwart. They pull fourteen oars, making the bet amount to ninety dollars. Our 1st cutters accepted it, and this morning was assigned as the time. The distance was two miles, the turning point being the Portuguese admiral's ship. As soon as the decks were washed down, the *Portsmouth*'s 1st cutter was alongside of us waiting for our boat. Unfortunately she was sent to market and had not returned, which made our boys feel bad; however, she returned at seven bells and they manned her. They got the word "Go" from our 1st lieutenant. They made a very good start of it and kept alongside of each other until coming back on the home stretch, when the *Portsmouth*'s boat gained and came in about two lengths ahead, winning the race and money. Considerable money changed hands among the officers. Our boat was the favorite.

December 6th 1859   at St Paul de Loando/Sinking the American Flag/
                                          sends the *Mystic* to St. Helena

The English Steam Gun boat *Viper* arrived here today and gave us the startling information that the celebrated barque *Orion* had been captured by Her Majesty's Steam gun boat *Pluto*. When the *Pluto*'s boat went alongside of her, she had the American ensign flying at her peak. The captain of the *Orion* had them [*the* Orion*'s U.S. colors*] hauled down and sunk. The *Orion* was full of negroes when she was taken. The *Pluto* put her in charge of a prize crew and sent her to the Island of St Helena. Our flag officer immediately sent the U.S. Steam Gun Boat *Mystic* to St Helena to get her captain, 1st and 2nd mates, and bring them here. We are very busy taking in the stores from the store house, which is nearly completed.

The Orion *had done what everyone expected. The* Orion*'s American flag would normally protect it from being searched by a British ship, especially given its legal and diplomatic celebrity. Typically a slaver of American origin would keep its U.S. identity and American captain, protecting it from British interference until ready to take on its cargo of slaves. Once the slaves were aboard, and especially if an American naval ship were approaching, the U.S. identity would be abandoned to avoid the death penalty American law* *provided for slavers, as opposed to transportation under English law. Intend-ing to free himself from U.S. law, the* Orion's *Captain Morgan threw his papers and flag overboard, though this created an identityless ship which was thus fair game for the British.*

Men from the Pluto *and from the* Mystic *(who had been aboard the* Orion *for days while helping the sick crew sail the slaver to the Congo) testified in court on St. Helena as to the American identity of the ship and officers. Indeed, too, close inspection could still discern "Orion, New York" beneath the new black paint on the stern.*

Trumping Morgan's negation of his ship's identity, Inman invoked the Tenth Article of the Webster-Ashburton Treaty of 1842, the first and only time that was done. The Tenth Article provides for extradition of each coun-try's citizens for various crimes. It does not mention slavery but does include piracy. As U.S. law made slaving the legal equivalent of piracy, Inman laid claim to the Orion's *officers as U.S. citizens engaging in piracy. In response the British authorities on St. Helena turned over Morgan and his two mates to Captain Le Roy of the* Mystic. *They were sent back to the United States for trial. There, however, after trial in Boston, they were found guilty only of a misdemeanor.*[3]

December 7th

Today we had general quarters and exercised the gun deck batteries at target shooting; made some very good shots and after the hammocks were piped down the ship's band were allowed to play on deck and all hands had a grand Breakdown in the port gangway.

By breakdown *Leonard meant some of the crew had an energetic dance (believed to be inspired by African American dancing).*

December 8th

Today we are taking in wood and water. It is very warm here now.

December 9th

All hands washed clothes. The carpenters are still to work on the store house. At 10 A.M. we had a boat expedition. After going through several important maneuvers they returned to the ship.

December 10th

Today being Saturday, all bags were piped up by orders of the 1st lieutenant to air clothing.

December 11th 1859   **at St Paul de Loando**

Being Sunday had the usual inspection by the officers of the divisions, after which the Articles of War were read by the 1st lieutenant. In the afternoon some of the men went on board the other ships to visit and some of their men came to visit us.

December 12th 1859   **General inspection by the Flag officer**

Today we had general inspection by the Flag officer. At ten o'clock the drum beat to General Quarters. We drilled at big guns for about an hour and then Small Arms, after which we had the Cut and Thrust exercise with broadswords. That being done we were called to quarters for a review. Everything proving satisfactory, the drum beat the retreat and we went to dinner at one o'clock.

December 13th

Several invalids from the U.S. Sloop of war *Portsmouth* came on board of us before going aboard the store ship, among which there is an old acquaintance from Charlestown (N. Story). She will take about 60 invalids in all. Our Boatswain is going home, also our Marine officer.

December 14th   **getting ready for sea**

We are making active preparations for sea, bending light sails, and securing everything for sea. There is a large Portuguese man of war brig coming in, and there are other sails in sight but cannot make them out. At sundown we got in all boats and sent up top gallant and royal yards. We are going to take a short cruise up to the Congo River. The *Portsmouth* is also going out with us—we are going to have a race.

December 15th 1859   **at St Paul de Loando**

The U.S. Steam Frigate *San Jacinto* sailed today for Kerbenda [Kabenda/ Cabenda] Bay to search for slavers. Her Britannic Majesty's Steam Gun boat *Trident* arrived here today. She has been cruising in the Bight of Benin. It is awful warm weather here now. We have fresh meat and vegetables every day for our dinner and the men are beginning to look very fat upon it. The store ship is still taking in sand. The French admiral's ship sailed today; she is going down the coast. Two small Portuguese brigs came to an anchor inside of us.

Writing the secretary today, Flag Officer Inman explained the tactic he would apply with the flagship and USS Portsmouth. *They would patrol along the tenth degree of east longitude, the* Portsmouth *running from the third degree*

south to the sixth degree south, while the flagship cruised between the ninth
and the sixth degrees. This would keep them roughly fifty miles offshore from
the main part of the coast from which slaves were embarked (the Congo River
and adjacent areas). Thus the navy cruisers would be far enough out that
they could not be seen from the shore, so the slavers would have to commit
themselves without knowing whether their coast was clear or not. Once they
emerged and sailed far enough out, they would be caught between the navy
cruiser and the shore. The African Squadron used this approach, though not
exclusively, throughout the rest of its existence.[4]

Aware, too, of the slavers' excellent intelligence network, Inman also began
the use of sealed orders, to be opened only after a squadron ship had gotten
under way. This eliminated any chance of crew chatter about a planned desti-
nation or patrol area being heard by a local and passed along the coast to warn
the slavers.

December 16th 1859

Today being general quarter day, the drum beat to general quarters. It being
very warm, we did not exercise a great deal after quarters. We were very busy
in making preparations for sea. There is a great deal of excitement on board of
us on account of the proposed race with the *Portsmouth*. There is considerable
money bet on the result, but the *Portsmouth* is the favorite at two to one being
bet on her. All the invalids were sent on board the store ship this afternoon. We
are going to leave our carpenter here with his gang until we come back, which
will be in a week or two; the *Portsmouth* and *San Jacinto* are going to do the
same. The store house is nearly completed and it looks very well indeed. They
are also building a wharf to the store house. We brought two storekeepers
out with us to take charge of it; they are two brothers by the name of Burney
[Birnie]. At nine o'clock I turned in.

December 17 1859   getting underway with the *Portsmouth*/
                                         Pride of the Navy/Racing with the *Portsmouth*/
                                                                    we beat her

Today being the day that we are going to have the race, all hands are very
much excited about it. Towards noon a good breeze springing up we both
hove up our anchors and made sail. We got the sail on both ships about the
same time. She had a good start ahead of us, being about half a mile. This trip
was got up solely to test the sailing qualities of both ships. There has been
considerable said about the *Portsmouth* beating everything she came across.
Her officers and men are confident of her beating us easily, and our boys feel
equally as sure of our ship, which was always the Pride of the Navy. The wind

being very light, we did not alter our positions a great deal. Towards four o'clock the wind became stronger and we gained on her very fast, and at five P.M. we were alongside of her; now commenced the race in earnest. We still gained on her very fast, and two hours after we left St Paul de Loando we were about two miles ahead of her. The wind being abeam, she now signalized to us to haul close on the wind, as that was her best sailing point, but it was no use, we tried her every way and beat her. We now hove to and waited for her. When she came close to us, we exercised Topsails with her and beat her again, thus proving ourselves the best ship.

Our captain feels mighty pleased, and well he may, for she is a noble ship; on her last cruise up the Mediterranean she was called the American Yacht, she sailed so well and always looked so neat. She beat some of the crack clipper ships. I understand there was considerable money changed hands among

December 17th 1859   at sea

the officers. Your humble servant won a dollar on the occasion. It being dark we soon lost sight of the *Portsmouth*. At twelve o'clock a sail was reported on our weather bow, the drum beat to general quarters, we lowered the 4th cutter and boarded her. She proved to be a large coal ship from Newcastle, England, bound to St Paul de Loando. Beat the retreat and made all sail for the Congo River.

December 18th   in the Congo River at anchor

Sunday and a delightful day. The *Portsmouth* is in company with us. At half past nine o'clock all hands were called to quarters for inspection. The *Portsmouth* is about five miles to leeward of us and there is a small sail ahead, which proved to be English Steam Gun boat *Spitfire*. At four o'clock land was reported, by the lookout at the masthead, bearing broad on our weather bow. At seven P.M. we came to an anchor at the mouth of the Congo River. It being very dark we could not see the *Portsmouth*. We fired a gun and burned some blue lights; they were answered by her. She is at anchor about five miles off.

December 19th   Sailing for Kabenda Bay

This morning came in very fine. The *Portsmouth* is at an anchor about three miles off. At half past our flag officer made signals for her to get underway, which she did. We also hove up our anchor and made sail. We are going to sail in company with her to Kabenda Bay. We have got a good wind, going about seven knots an hour. We still beat the *Portsmouth*, although they are altering her trim every hour. In the afternoon the wind died away and we are now in the midst of a dead calm.

December 20th 1859   **at sea in Kabenda Bay**

At daylight land was reported on our lee bow. The wind freshened towards the afternoon we are still in company with the Sloop of war *Portsmouth*. Late in the evening we came to an anchor, in Kabenda Bay. The *Portsmouth* also came to an anchor. A steamer was seen lying close inshore which proved to be the U.S. Steamer *San Jacinto*. We sent our 4th cutter on board of her.

December 21st   **Sail Ho a chase/Lost sight of her**

After breakfast our flag officer signalized to the other ships to get underway, and we also hove up our anchor. The *San Jacinto* now signalized that she had no provisions on board. We hove to and gave her all the bread and provisions we could spare. At two P.M. the Flag officer gave the *San Jacinto* orders to go to the northward and we in company with the *Portsmouth* sailed to the southward.

At four o'clock a sail was reported from the masthead, we made all sail and gave chase, we are overhauling her fast. At dark we wet our sail, the lookout reported that she had altered her course, we also altered our course and after her we went. At this state of affairs there began to be considerable excitement. Visions of prize money ran in the men's heads and to use a favorite expression, all hands were eager for the chase. It now being very dark, we lost sight of her at nine o'clock in the evening. Our captain thought it probable that she might have squared away and stood before the wind. He gave orders for us to square the yards, and set all our port studding sails, and in so doing as this Journal will show, he could not have done better, for at nine o'clock our boatswain, who was on the fore yard with a spyglass, reported a sail right ahead of us, about half a mile off laying to under bare poles. He now reported that she had made sail.

fire into her/She proves a Humbug/
again in Sight/Boarding her/she is a slaver

We fired a gun for her to heave to, but she paid no heed to it; we now fired a shot right into it, and at the same time the lookout on the cathead sang out that it was nothing but a floating island from the Congo River, which are very numerous in this vicinity. The event as it was created a hearty laugh among the officers and men, the last named gentlemen composing a song of 23 verses which they entitled hump, de, dooden, doo.

At twelve o'clock, just as the watch was getting relieved, the sail was again reported. This time she was too plain in sight to be mistaken, and at two o'clock she was right under our lee bow. We manned our 4th cutter with armed men, and in command of our sailing master, they boarded her. They were gone about an hour and we began to feel very anxious about them when the flag officer sent his boat to see what she was. On their returning they gave us the information that she was a slaver. The master remained on board of her with the 4th cutter's crew.

December 22nd   overhauling the Slaver

This morning all hands were eager to get a sight of the slaver. She is a full rigged brig and is manned by an entire Spanish crew; her name is the *Delicia*. She had no colors or clearance papers. The flag officer paid her a visit and he had no hesitation in pronouncing her a slaver: she had a slave deck laid and the coppers were all ready to be used. We took her officers and crew on board of our ship. They are a fine looking set of men, one of them in particular, having hard luck, it being the ninth time he has been taken in three years. The captain of her, however, was not taken. He went ashore the day before with the specie to purchase the cargo (that is their story and of course we cannot depend upon it). She was going to take in her cargo when she saw us coming.

The brig of itself is a miserable affair, being very old and leaky. She has got no stores on board, so we are very busy putting stores on board of her; she is hardly worth the trouble of sending home. She had a lower tier of liquor in her hold, and some of our men that were left to take charge of her during the night made too free use of it, the result being that six blue jackets and one marine are going to be court-martialed.

After considerable more humbugging with her, a prize crew of twelve men, and two officers, were sent on board of her. They were our 2nd lieutenant J.C. Mc Arrann [Robert M. McArann], and Midshipman Farquer [Norman H. Farquhar]. She got orders to proceed to Charleston, S.C. On her starting we manned our rigging, and gave her three hearty cheers, which was returned by our late shipmates, and in the midst of a violent rain storm we lost sight of the slave brig *Delicia*. We then filled away the main Topsail, and went in search of other adventures.

Captain Nicholas reported that the Delicia *was spotted at 3 P.M. on the previous day (December 20) twelve miles distant; after a chase of ten hours, they boarded it at 3 A.M. It had no flag, papers, or log (they had been thrown overboard), and the captain and supercargo, according to the first mate, were ashore shopping for six hundred slaves.[5] The prize crew brought the* Delicia *into Charleston on February 1. After the Spanish government put in a claim for the ship's having been under their flag, it was turned over to them, and the two Spanish mates held as prisoners were released.[6] The United States had no treaty permitting the arrest of Spanish ships.*

The prize crew, as was typical, was lost to the squadron once they took charge of their prize. Upon reaching the United States, the officers (after completing legal matters) awaited new orders, and the enlisted men were sent to a receiving ship for reassignment or discharge.

December 23d

Today another sad affair occurred; one of our ship's company died. His name was Henry Smith. He died with disease of the heart. He belonged to Roxbury, Mass. He was a general favorite with the ship's company. We buried him with Naval honors: we read the burial service and launched his body into the deep. The day was very fine. We have got a good breeze. The watch are to work in rigging.

December 24th 1859   at sea/Court Martial sentences

Fine breeze and pleasant weather. We are heading towards St Paul de Loando. They are court-martialing the men that were drunk on board the prize. At four o'clock all hands were called to muster to hear the sentence of the court, which was three months' pay stopped and six months' black list. There were six sailors and one Marine. The gun deck divisions exercised big guns in the midnight watch. I had a lookout, which time was spent in listening to a tough yarn told me by an old quarter master.

December 25th   Christmas present by the Captain

Sunday and Christmas day, what a splendid one I spent last year. I remember it as if it were but yesterday. I wonder if they think of me, but it is no use to give way to one's feelings when you can't be where you want to. At ten o'clock all hands were called to muster, after which I with a number of others was called aft upon the quarter deck, and rated to an Ordinary Seaman, which came entirely unexpected to me, it was a Christmas present by the captain. At five o'clock all hands were called aft to splice the main brace.

December 26th   Boys learning to steer

This day came in fine with a good breeze. At three bells in the forenoon watch the drum beat to general quarters. We went through the exercise of fishing the masts. In the afternoon we exercised sail and gave general satisfaction. This day the boys and Mizzen Top men were sent to the wheel in order to learn them to steer; this was done by orders of our 1st lieutenant, Mr. Mac-Donough. He is liked very much among the men.

December 27 1859 at sea

We have got a first rate breeze today giving about seven knots an hour. Steering to the southward and eastward. I am indebted to a fellow townsman by the name of John F. Powell for dates and other favors received at his hands.

December 28th

I will here state that I have become quite a tailor, and in every watch below when I am not writing I may be seen mending my unmentionables.

December 29th hove to

Today we have been under easy sail, it is very pleasant weather. At six o'clock in the evening the lookout at the masthead reported land supposed to be St Paul de Loando. At dark we hove aback the main Topsail and laid to for the night.

December 30th came to an anchor in St Paul de Loando

At day-break we filled away the main Topsail and stood in for the land. At one o'clock we came to an anchor in the Harbor of St Paul de Loando. The U.S. Store Ship *Supply* is still here, there is several trading vessels here also. At sundown we sent down the Royal yards, and got out all the boats. We are going to take in a supply of water and provisions here, there is plenty of fruit here now and can be had very cheap.

December 31st the Catamaran

This morning all hands are very busy cleaning ship inside and out. Got out the catamaran, which is a contrivance to scrub the copper. It consists of four large water breakers lashed together; it is manned by the black listers. After we had our breakfast we commenced to take wood, water and provisions.

January 1860

January 1st   **at St. Paul de Loando**

Sunday and New Year's day. At half past nine o'clock the divisions were called to quarters for inspection, after which we had a general muster round the capstan. In the evening all hands were called aft to splice the main brace, as is the custom on board of a man of war on holidays.

January 2nd

All hands to work taking in wood and provisions in the evening. All hands swung clean hammocks.

January 3d

All hands scrubbed hammocks. We finished taking in provisions this day.

January 4th   **Dancing**

Commenced setting up the rigging and staying the masts. At four P.M. we had her all a taunt ho. In the evening we got the fiddler up in the port gangway and danced until nine o'clock.

"All a-taunt oh" meant all the masts and spars were properly rigged and squared.

January 5th   **Target Shooting**

At ten o'clock this morning the drum beat to general quarters. The gun deck divisions were exercised at target shooting, the object being 1700 yards off. Some very fine shots were made by the 1st division, at 1 P.M. the drum beat the retreat. In the afternoon there was nothing done.

January 6th

All hands scrubbed and washed clothes. This being the usual General Quarter day, we had the regular exercise. We are having some first rate weather every day; we are wearing white frocks and hat and blue trousers.

January 7th

Holystoned the decks for tomorrow. A Spanish brig came in here today. It is a beautiful day.

Lieutenant McDonough was transferred from the Constellation *to take command of the* Sumpter.[1]

January 8th   **at St Paul de Loando**

Being Sunday, we had division inspection, after which we had divine service on the gun deck. All hands dressed in white frocks and hats and blue trousers.

January 9th   **the Store house is finished**

All the divisions went ashore today for target practice with small arms. They returned on board in time to get their dinners in the afternoon. All hands exercised sail. The Store House which has been building here for the last six months is finished. It is a fine building and reflects great credit on the workmen who were engaged upon it. The U.S. Store Ship *Supply* is getting ready for sea.

January 10th

A Portuguese trading brig arrived here today. She brings us news of the *Portsmouth*. She is cruising off the mouth of the Congo River, and the U.S. Sloop of War *Marion* is at Cape Coast Castle.

January 11th   **a Boat expedition**

We had a great boat expedition today. The launch, 1st and 2nd cutters were manned with their fighting crews, and we went through all the maneuvers of taking another vessel. We returned at five P.M. well pleased with the day's proceedings.

January 12th

The U.S. Sloop of war *Portsmouth* arrived here today.

January 13th

An English coal ship arrived here today from Newcastle, England. She made a very long passage of it, she being 112 days coming out here. It is very pleasant weather here now.

Inman reported that the Mystic *arrived at Loanda today, bringing the officers and crew of the* Orion *from St. Helena. Temporarily aboard the flagship, they would be sent to the United States; also on the* Constellation *as passengers were the gunner and fourteen crew from HMS* Pluto, *who brought the prize* Orion *to St. Helena.*[2]

January 14th

Holystoned the gun deck and also the spar deck, after which the bags were piped up to air clothing.

W.A. Leonard   Charlestown

January 15th 1860   at St Paul de Loando

All hands called to quarters for the usual inspection at half past nine o'clock in the forenoon. In the afternoon some of the men went on board the *Portsmouth* to visit, and some of her men came on board of us.

January 16th

Today five hands from each part of the ship were sent on board the store ship to help their men to bend her sails. She is going home very soon. Besides taking the invalids home she takes our boatswain, and a sergeant of Marines who is a townsman of mine.

January 17th

Today some more of the *Portsmouth*'s men came on board of us to be examined by our doctor. They are going home in the *Supply*.

Also going to the United States in the Supply *was a stone from Napoleon's tomb, which Lieutenant Commanding Le Roy of the* Mystic *brought back as a gift from St. Helena and Inman sent to Washington for inclusion in the Washington Monument, then under construction.*[3]

January 18th   amusements on board ship

The U.S. Sloop of War *Portsmouth* sailed today for the Congo River. Today the *San Jacinto* arrived here and came to an anchor. She gave our boys an invitation to come on board of their vessel and witness their Negro Minstrel band perform. Which they accepted; they came back highly pleased with the performance. The *San Jacinto* is to go to Cadiz for repairs. She will be gone about six months.

The San Jacinto *had been having constant problems with its machinery, especially with its shaft bearing, to the extent that it might soon break down completely and reduce the ship to sail power alone.*

January 19th   **getting up a Negro minstrel Band**

The U.S. Steamer *San Jacinto* sailed today for Cadiz. Our boys are going to get up a Negro Minstrel Band. We have got some very good singers on board of the ship. I have no doubt but what they will succeed in their undertaking. The U.S. Steam Gun Boat *Mystic* arrived here today from St Helena, having the captain, 1st and 2nd mates of the slave barque *Orion* in custody. [*But see the entry for January 13.*]

The term "Negro minstrel band" was commonly applied to a band of white performers wearing blackface.[4]

January 20th 1860   **at St Paul de Loando/**
                                                    the Slave Barque *Orion* again

The U.S. Sloop of war *Vincennes* arrived here today. She has been twenty-eight months in commission. The *San Jacinto* is her relief. We gave her the orders to go home; she is going to Boston, Mass. At ten o'clock the captain, 1st and 2nd mates of the *Orion,* was brought on board of us by the captain on the *Mystic* and given up to our flag officer. They are to be sent to the United States for trial; they are going in the *Vincennes.* The captain's name is Morgan. When the *Orion* was brought into St Helena, she had on board 871 negroes, 396 boys and 7 sex unknown. Before the vessel arrived 152 had died, which would make the total number, taken on board, when she left the coast of Africa 1023. Among those who died were 60 boys, 40 men, 8 women, 24 girls and 20 others sex unknown. The *Mystic* arrived at St Helena on the 21st of December from this port, when the barque was given up to them. The captain looks to be very sick. They are allowed to come on deck during the daytime, but at night they are put in double irons by the master at arms.

Replacement of the sailing sloop Vincennes *by the steamer* San Jacinto *was part of the new policy of furnishing the African Squadron with steamships, more effective in pursuing slavers, though unfortunately the* San Jacinto *presented its own problems. It had been having major shaft-bearing problems ever since leaving New York.*

However, the Vincennes *had long been rendered ineffective, not mechanically but by virtue of its commander. The* Vincennes, *under Commander Totten, had for some months been inspiring apoplexy among British commanders and statesmen, resulting in a detailed, "rather extraordinary" report landing on the desk of U.S. Secretary of State Lewis Cass just a month before. Though unlike Commodore Conover and his flagship, the* Cumberland, *the* Vincennes *had been present along the coast, Totten had shown a remarkable disinterest in pursuing slavers. Repeatedly Royal Navy officers had pointed out to him presumed slavers, and one even offered to use his steamer to tow* Vincennes *to the suspect vessel. Totten's consistent response was inertia, leaving the slavers to go about their business. Though he had been under Inman's command for the past five months, they met only now, as Totten and his ship left the African Squadron for home.*

January 21st

This morning we took in our launch, 1st and 2nd cutters and bent all our light sails; we are going to sea in a few days. Had general quarters at ten A.M., exercised the starboard battery.

January 22nd

Sunday had the usual inspection at half past nine A.M. There is a large steamer coming in supposed to be a Portuguese man of war. In the afternoon some of our boys went on board the *Vincennes* to visit.

January 23d 1860   at St Paul de Loando/
                                                  the Store Ship Sails for home

Today some of our men were sent on board the store ship [USS *Supply*] to help get her underway. At one o'clock they hove up her anchor and made sail. On passing us, we manned the rigging and gave her three cheers, which she returned. Our boys are glad she is gone; she has been an eyesore to us ever since she has been out here. The Portuguese man of war steamer came to an anchor and fired a salute of thirteen guns for our flag officer, which we returned.

January 24th   an appointment by the Flag officer

Today all hands were called aft upon the quarter deck. The 1st lieutenant read an appointment by the flag officer; Wm Long, our chief boatswain's mate, was appointed to the office of acting boatswain. He is a very good sailor and will make a first rate boatswain. Our own boatswain is going home in the *Supply*.

The boatswain, Alfred Hingerty, suffered some kind of stroke or paralysis and was being invalided home. He recovered sufficiently to return to the squadron in a few months.[5]

January 25th

All hands are to work taking in wood and water. Finished in the afternoon. At sundown we sent up the Top gallant and Royal yards.

January 26th   Change of officers/
                                                  leaving St Paul de Loando/
                                                  off Ambris/Send a boat ashore

The captain of the *San Jacinto*, having some difficulty with the flag officer, resigned and went home; the captain of the *Sumpter* was appointed to take

Lt. Donald McNeill Fairfax. Gilliland Collection.

his place. Our first lieutenant being the oldest one in the squadron was made captain on the *Sumpter.* We got the 1st lieutenant of the *Mystic* for our 1st lieutenant; his name is D.M. Fairfax. He has got a very good name in the *Mystic.* We also got a lieutenant from the *San Jacinto* before she went to Cadiz. His name is Johnson, a very good man.

Lt. Philip C. Johnson Jr., thirty-one, was a Maine native who graduated from the Naval Academy in 1855. Lt. Donald M. Fairfax, the new first lieutenant, came from the bluest Virginia blood, having been born in his family's namesake Fairfax County in 1821.

At six o'clock having a good breeze, we got underway and stood out of the harbor. As we were passing the U.S. Sloop of war *Vincennes* we manned the rigging and gave her three cheers, also a salute of nine guns; they also cheered and fired a salute of thirteen guns. She is going home in a few days; we left the captain and mates of the *Orion* on board of her.

We shaped our course to the northward, and for several days we cruised around Ambriz, a great slave depot. We now stood in for the land. On approaching it we discovered several small sails at anchor. We hove to and lowered the 4th cutter and sent her to see what they were. In about two hours she returned, reporting that they were three small trading schooners and we hoisted the boat, filled away the Main Topsail and stood out to sea again.

January 27   at sea/quite a [*sic*] excitement

At ten A.M. the drum beat to general quarters; exercised the starboard battery. We have got a light wind, it is very pleasant weather. At half past eight o'clock a sail was reported on our lee quarter. We gave chase and overhauled her; she proved to be a Portuguese barque loaded with salt, bound to St Paul de Loando.

At twelve o'clock, just as we were changing the watch, another sail was reported about 200 yards off. Just as we were passing her we could hear her drum beating to quarters, we immediately beat to general quarters, tacked ship and stood for her. We then fired a gun for her to heave to, which she did. We then lowered the 4th cutter and sent aboard of her to see what she was; she proved to be the U.S. Sloop of war *Marion,* bound to St Paul de Loando.

The "twelve o'clock" would be midnight, explaining why the Marion *was not reported until only two hundred yards off.*

In a letter of this date, apparently addressed to the captain of the Marion, *Inman said, "I perceive by the public Journals that complications exist in the relations between the U.S. and Great Britain. It is possible that these may result in war, of which we may not hear immediately." He gave directions on keeping the ship especially well prepared, with "provisions and water for three months," and ordered that if war does occur, the ship was to head home as rapidly as conditions permitted. Inman might have been reading about the "Pig War," or Northwestern Boundary Dispute, between England and the United States in late 1859.*

January 28th 1860   at sea

At daybreak land was reported on our weather bow, which proved to be Ambriz. Three small vessels were seen at anchor close under the land. We hove to and sent the 4th cutter to see what they were; in the evening the boat returned and reported them to be trading vessels. We then filled away and stood out again.

January 29th

Sunday all hands were called to quarters at half past nine for inspection as usual.

January 30th

After breakfast all hands were very busy in getting in all the chain cables, to overhaul the shackles and to clean out the chain lockers. It is a dead calm and it makes us feel blue, particularly as there is a sail in sight about seven miles off which looks rather suspicious. At five o'clock a light breeze sprung up, at dark we lost sight of the sail.

January 31st

This day came in with a good breeze and pleasant weather, nothing in sight. Saw a large school of porpoises in the afternoon.

February 1860

serving out the grog & ration money/
interesting particulars/at sea/negro singing

The 1st of January being the first month of the quarter we ought to have the grog and ration money served out, but being very busy all the month, we had no time, we therefore had it served out today. We also signed our accounts, which is done every three months, or quarter. A few remarks about this system here would not be amiss: those of the ship's company who do not wish to drink their grog can have it stopped and get the money for it, which is a dollar and twenty cents a month, or three dollars and sixty cents a quarter. The ship's company are divided into eighteen messes, three of which are marines, three petty officers, and twelve blue jackets.

Each man in the mess is allowed a ration, or in other words food enough to last him one month, which when turned into money, is equal to $6.50cts, which in three months amounts to $19.50cts. Now each mess has all the way from twelve to fifteen men in it; they therefore have the purser stop two or three of the rations and get the money for them, and they live on reduced rations, which is plenty enough. Each mess has got a caterer, whose business it is to look after all money matters and keep an account of what is expended, and when we get into any port where we can get any vegetables, he gets them. He is chosen by the mess, and is generally a trustworthy man. Each mess has also got a cook who sees to serving out the food and to keeping the mess things in order. Each mess has its own cook. Some of the messes have steady cooks who are allowed a ration, but when a mess has no steady cook, every man in the mess has to cook his week, or pay somebody to do it for him.

At mealtimes an oilcloth was spread on the deck for each mess of a dozen or so men, and they ate while sitting on the deck around it. (The officers, of course, had tables and chairs and were served by stewards.) The ship's cook and his assistant were permanently assigned with the actual cooking for the crew. The mess cooks carried the prepared food from the galley to the individual messes and, as Lawrence described later, cleaned the dishes and implements and the area of the deck assigned to their mess.

The master at arms regulates this part of the work. He is assisted by the ship's corporals. The berth deck is wholly under the master at arms's charge; he sees that it is kept perfectly clean and neat. It is inspected every day at half past nine o'clock, by the 1st lieutenant. The master at arms also has charge of all black-listers, and prisoners, and when anybody is sentenced by a court martial, he sees the sentence carried into effect with the assistance of the ship's corporals. He also has to see that everybody is in their hammocks, at nine o'clock when the ship is in port. Also sees all lights put out at ten o'clock except those that are required to light the ship, and those that have permission from the officer of the deck.

The ship's corporals are the police of the ship. They see that no boats come alongside of the ship without permission from the 1st lieutenant or the officer of the deck. They search all the ship's boats, and their crews, to see that they smuggle no liquor on board, but in spite of all their efforts it gets aboard some times. They stand watch and watch [*that is, they were in two duty sections, alternating watches*], they are at all times under the master at arms, who in fact is always considered the Chief of Police on board a man of war.

It is very pleasant weather, the Negro Minstrel band are progressing finely. They rehearse every evening. They are going to give their first performance when they get into St Paul de Loando, which will be in a few days.

February 2nd

Today we exercised large guns, small arms, and single sticks. We have got a fine wind, all sail set, steering a southeasterly course. There is a sail in sight to leeward, supposed to be an English gun boat.

February 3d

At five P.M. a sail hove in sight. We made all sail and gave chase, at nine P.M. we came up with her, fired a gun for her to heave to, which she did. We sent a boat on board of her, to see what she was, she turned out to be a New Bedford whaler. We hoisted the boat and went on our course.

February 4th   Land Ho/came to an anchor in St Paul de Loando

At daylight land was reported on our weather beam about 25 miles off, we stood in for it, and at 10 A.M. we came to an anchor in the Harbor of St. Paul de Loando. The U.S. Sloop of war *Marion* is here, and the *Vincennes* is also

here. We had supposed she had gone home; she is taking in wood and water.
We got out all the boats and at sundown sent down the Royal yards.

February 5th

Sunday, at ten o'clock all hands mustered round the capstan, after which the
1st lieutenant read the Articles of War.

February 6th   rigging a Stage

Commenced taking in water and provisions. The minstrel band are fixing up a
stage on the quarter deck for their performance, which is to come off tonight.
The bill will be seen on next page.

Grand
Minstrel Performance
given by the
Crew of the U. S. Flag Ship Constellation in return for one given them,
by the Crew of the U.S. steamer San Jacinto
Manager   Jarvis G. Farrar
On Monday Evening Feby 6th 1860.
The Performance will commence, with the company appearing
As Northern Darkies.

Overture, wood up . .	with variations. . .	Company
Opening Chorus .	Pirates Glee. . . .	ditto
Faded Flowers		J. G. Farrar
Lady Love		W. H. French
Angelina Baker		C. F. Gordon
Dear Lucinda		W. Jones
Hard Times		J. E. Elliot
Old Cabin Home		J. G. Farrar
Old Jaw Bone		C. D. Murphy

After which a

Guitar Solo . . . . by . . .		Peter Redovis
Fancy Dance		G. Francis
Accordean [sic] and Banjo Solo . . .		Gordon and French
Quartette [sic] Speed Away . . .		French, Elliot, Murphy and Gordon
Lucy Long, in character by G. Francis and general walk round . . . . by the .		Entire Company
Grand Lecture . . on Phronology [sic]. . .		W Jones

Following with the
Southern Darkies

Uncle Ned . . . with variations. . .		W Jones, Company

Going to the Shucking	Warren Harrington
Little more Cider	C. F. Gordon
Old Jim Brown	W. H. French
Fancy Jig	J. Elsie
Belle Brandon	J. E. Elliot
Ballad. . . when the swallows homeward fly	F. Keating
Railroad Collision . . . by the . .	Company

The performance to Conclude
with the
Celebrated Burlesque on the Lady of Lyons.

Claude Middletop	by	Frank Keating
Duke Aranza		J. E. Elliot
Pauline Dutch Apples		W. H. French

other characters by the company

The performance lasted until twelve o'clock and went off to the entire satisfaction of everybody that witnessed it. Besides our own ship's company, we had several of the *Marion*s and *Vincennes* boys on board who were highly pleased with the performance.

A romantic drama by Edward Bulwer Lytton, The Lady of Lyons *was a great hit when first staged in London and New York in 1838 and remained one of the most popular plays throughout the nineteenth century. It inspired a number of burlesques, of which the* Constellation *production was one.*

February 7th   *Vincennes* Sails for home

At eleven A.M. the U.S. Sloop of war *Vincennes* hove up her anchor, and made sail for home. We manned the rigging and gave her three cheers and fired a salute of nine guns; she returned the cheers and fired a salute of thirteen guns. The captain and mates of the barque *Orion* are on board of her; she is going to Boston, Mass.[1]

February 8th   forming a dramatic Association/at St Paul de Loando

At five P.M. A barque arrived here from Salem, Mass. She brought a mail for the squadron. I got two letters which I am very glad of, they being the first since leaving home, first rate news. Our boys, feeling highly elated with the success of the Minstrel Band, are going to organize a Dramatic Club. A meeting is to be held this evening in the main hold for the purpose. At four o'clock a Portuguese transport ship arrived here, from Lisbon, full of convicts; they are transported here. At sundown we got in all boats and crossed Royal yards. We have got in six months' provisions; we are going up the coast towards Madeira to recruit ship. We are to sail tomorrow; the U.S. Steam Gun boat

Mystic sailed today. After hammocks were piped down, all the boys assembled in the main hold. The meeting was called to order by the ship's barber, who was chosen manager, and a committee was chosen to select a couple of plays. After a little more unimportant business we adjourned until tomorrow evening.

February 9th   Selected the Plays

At half past nine o'clock had general quarters. In the evening we had a meeting according to appointment. The committee reported they had selected two plays, one being the two act drama called *Robert Maccaire*, and the *Farce of Box and Cox*, with several songs and dances between them. Your humble servant is cast to play in one of them.

Charles Selby's Robert Macaire, "A melodrama in two acts," was first produced in London in 1834. John Maddison Morton's Box and Cox was produced in London in 1847. Both plays were very popular in the nineteenth century.

In Robert Macaire, Leonard played the role of Clementine, a wealthy farmer's daughter betrothed to the innkeeper's son Charles.

February 10th

The U.S. Sloop of war *Marion* is going to sea with us. We are getting ready to start.

The USS Portsmouth arrived in the harbor today with its prize, the brigantine Virginian.

The Royal Navy steam gunboat Viper had found the Virginian up the Congo River at Punta da Lenha. It was anchored off one of the numerous slave factories in that area, flying an American flag but with papers and other evidence that the Viper's captain, Commander Hewitt, interpreted as suspicious. Leaving an officer and boat there, Hewitt steamed back downriver and notified Commander Colhoun of the Portsmouth. The American sanitary regulations would have made Colhoun reluctant to take either his sailing ship or a boat sixty miles in from the sea. At Hewitt's invitation, though, Colhoun sent a party upriver aboard the Viper to arrest the Virginian.[4] Inman made the required protest to the British commodore regarding Hewitt's having boarded an American ship but nevertheless sent the Virginian to the United States for adjudication. Throughout the existence of the African Squadron, its commanders and their British counterparts went through this pattern of protest combined with cooperation. The Virginian was sent to Norfolk, where the court found it innocent.[5]

The Viper was a six-gun bark-rigged screw steamer built for the Crimean War. The end of that conflict in 1856 made it convenient for Britain to shift a

USS *Portsmouth*. Naval History and Heritage Center, Washington, D.C.

number of such small, shallow-draft steam gunboats to service with the Royal Navy's African Squadron. Their counterparts on the U.S. squadron were the Paraguay-surplus steamers Mystic *and* Sumpter. *Indeed the ability to deploy ships such as the* Viper *to their African Squadron (which had been drawn down during the Crimean conflict) made it easier for the British to pressure the U.S. government into doing the same.*

February 11th   **at sea**

At ten o'clock we hove up our anchor and made sail, and in company with
the *Marion* we went to sea. We are steering a northerly course, all the watch
putting on chafing gear. At dark we lost sight of the *Marion*.

The Marion, *with a nominal crew of 150, had sent so many men home as
invalids or on prize crews that it was reported to have only 40 men left to work
the ship.*[6]

February 12th   **Divine Service**

Sunday at half past nine A.M. had division inspection, after which divine service was held on the gun deck. Our present 1st lieutenant, Mr. Fairfax, is a
religious man, and it is his intention to have divine service every Sunday while
he is in the ship. He is assisted by Lieutenant Loyal, who officiates as minister.
There is no compulsion used—those who wish to go can do so. There is a
religious society on board. They hold a prayer meeting every evening on the
berth deck.

Willie

*At the same time Leonard was sent to the ship in June, a group of twenty
religious "converts" was among the sailors sent to the* Constellation *from the
receiving ship. As appropriate for a squadron flagship, the* Constellation *did
have a chaplain assigned, but he never made it aboard. Granted a delay in
April 1859 to care for his ailing wife, Chaplain John Lenhart did not request
orders until July 1860, by which time the secretary did not "deem it expedient"
to send him.*[7]

February 13th 1860   **at sea**

Had a good breeze all this day and very fine weather. In the evening we had
another meeting in the main hold. We had a reading rehearsal of *Robert Maccaire;* we are to have two rehearsals a week, until further notice. The performance is to come off in Madeira.

February 14th   **Land ho,**

Today the gun deck divisions were exercised at small arms and single sticks.
Had a good breeze but the weather is very cloudy. At half past three in the
midwatch land was reported right ahead, supposed to be the Island of Anna
Bonde. Hove to for the night.

February 15th   **island of Anna Bonde**

Early this morning we made sail and steered in for the land. And at nine A.M.
we hove to within two miles of the land. This is a beautiful looking island.

It is inhabited by negroes. It is a Portuguese possession, who in fact own all the islands on this coast. Several canoes came alongside with some of the natives who speak very good English. We made sail again at eleven o'clock and shaped our course for the island of St. Thomas, which is about ten hours sail from here.

"Anna Bonde" is Annabon Island, also called Pagalu, about one hundred miles south of St. Thomas, in the twenty-first century politically part of Equatorial Guinea and still a beautiful, green island.

February 16th   at anchor off the island of St Thomas

At daylight land was reported which proved to be St. Thomas. At nine A.M. we came to an anchor about three miles off. The island is situated on the equator and it looks splendid from where we lie. We saluted the governor of the island with thirteen guns, which was returned from the fort. Sent a boat ashore, the messes got some very fine coffee here, very cheap, at sundown the boat returned. We are to remain here overnight. An anchor watch was set for the night. The dramatic club had a rehearsal after the hammocks were piped down.

February 17th 1860   at sea/lee Scuppers

At 11 A.M. we got underway and went on our course towards Prince's Island which is a little more than a degree north of the equator. At sundown, it commenced to rain, and rained incessantly all night. I took advantage of it by taking a roll in the lee scuppers and having a fresh water wash, which at all times is a rich treat to a sailor.

February 18th   wooding up at Prince's Island

At daylight we sighted Prince's Island and at noon we came to an anchor, in fifteen fathoms water. It is still raining. We got out all boats and commenced taking in wood and water. At sundown sent down the Royal yards. After hammocks were piped down, the dramatic company had a rehearsal in the main hold. We are getting along first rate. We also got up a subscription to get some money to help us along, which was responded to by the ship's company in a very handsome manner. We have no doubt of its success.

While the flagship's thespians rehearsed, the other squadron ships engaged in various actions having to do with American and European interests on the West African coast. In late February a man called the Prince of the Congo sought refuge with the factors (Dutch, American, and English traders) at Kinsembo (the main village of Ambrizette, on the coast near Ambriz) after fleeing Ambriz. Forced to surrender him after efforts to buy off the native king and leaders had failed, the factors saw him immediately shot in the head and cut to pieces and the pieces thrown in the river. They appealed to the USS

Portsmouth, *then at Loanda, for protection. Commander Colhoun sent his launch with a landing party, following with his ship as the wind permitted. After talking to the factors and some of the chiefs, with all agreeing things were by then stable, and a Netherlands navy ship having arrived, he departed.*[7]

February 19th   Sunday at Prince's Island

Sunday at half past nine o'clock all hands were called to quarters for inspection, after which divine service was held on the gun deck. It is a very pleasant day. The scene around us is beautiful beyond description; the island looks better than on our former visit. To me Sunday has a peculiar charm about it that I cannot fully explain. The very aspect of it, no matter under what circumstances, has a different appearance from any other day in the week. This one in particular being the most lovely one I have ever seen, whether it is from the beauty of the island or from my thought of former ones spent at home, I cannot say. Probably it is from the combined thoughts of both. Heigh, ho. Willie Leonard

February 20th 1860   at Prince's Island

Taking in wood and water. Our 1st lieutenant commenced giving the ship's company a run ashore in order (as he says) to stretch their limbs. About twenty go at a time for three hours; there is good bathing here and the men are improving it [taking advantage of it]. At sundown we had all the wood and water in. We are waiting here for the U.S. Gun boat *Mystic,* which is coming here with the mail from the island of Fernando Po. She is expected to be here on the 29th of this month.

February 21st

All hands washed clothes at 10 A.M. The gun deck divisions were called to quarters for target practice, the object being 1700 yards off. It was a rock about ten feet square; it being white washed, it made a very good object. The shots in general were very good as the captain was highly satisfied with them. At two P.M. I was called aft and with a number of others was told we might go ashore and stay until sundown. We went and had a bathe in the rivulet and a ramble in the bushes, until sundown when we returned on board.

February 22nd

Washington's Birthday. As soon as we turned out we cleaned the ship up for the day. At eight o'clock, the band playing the "Star Spangled Banner," we ran up an American ensign at each masthead and one at the peak. The purser provided the ship's company with a good dinner of fresh pork. At twelve o'clock we fired a national salute of twenty-one guns, and at supper time all hands were called aft to splice the main brace. The weather all day was splendid. The

Dramatic Club had a grand holiday rehearsal in the evening; we are getting on finely. The ship's band was allowed to play on deck until nine o'clock P.M.

"Clementine" does not have many lines, but they include "Do you know, Charles, I've such a beautiful new lace dress, and such a 'love' of a bonnet."[9]

February 23d 1860   at Prince's Island

Today we are scrubbing all the paint work inside and out. Finished it before supper. Some of the draft that went ashore today came aboard three sheets in the wind, and were very noisy and all for fighting, which caused them to be put in the brig in double irons, and the pleasing intelligence of having their liberty stopped in Madeira, which serves them right, as they were cautioned before going ashore.

February 24th   Squally

After the decks were washed down it began to rain and continued all day, with occasional very heavy squalls. We had some fears of dragging our anchor, stationed a hand in each chains with a lead. It looked rather gloomy all day; towards sundown it moderated, and at eight o'clock the moon showed in all its splendor.

As the new moon was on February 21, the splendor that night was delicate but especially appreciated after the preceding gloominess.

February 25   bending sail

This morning we took in the launch, 1st and 2nd cutters, and holystoned all the decks. After breakfast, we bent an entire new set of sails, the winds at this season of the year being very strong to the northward.

February 26th

Sunday. At half past nine A.M. the divisions were called to quarters for inspection, after which had divine service on the gun deck. We have got very bad bread on board of the ship at present; it is full of weevils, which getting into one's mouth is not very pleasant, I can assure you. We are going to get some when we get to Porto Praya.

Ship's bread was a form of hardtack, typically months—or even years—old by the time it reached the sailor.

February 27th

Had general quarters, exercised the starboard battery. At sundown we swung clean hammocks. The dramatics had a rehearsal.

Willie Leonard

February 28th 1860.   **at Prince's Island**

All hands scrubbed hammocks. After breakfast four hands from each part of the ship were sent ashore to scrub wind sails; I was one of the number. After we got through we had a ramble in the bushes; at seven bells we returned on board of the ship.

The wind sails were canvas scoops used to direct fresh air belowdecks.

February 29th   **leaving Prince's Island**

This morning we crossed Royal yards and got in all the remaining boats. We expect the *Mystic* here today. At eleven o'clock the *Mystic* came in here with the mail. At two P.M. we got underway, and before dark we were out of sight of Prince's Island. We have got a first rate sailing breeze.

March 1860

March 1st   **at sea/Sail Ho/Transferred to the Gig**

We had a light wind all this day and very pleasant weather. At seven A.M. a sail was reported from the masthead standing towards us; she proved to be a large coal ship bound for St Paul de Loando. At two P.M. the 1st lieutenant called me aft and took me out of the 3d cutter and put me in the captain's boat, which is called the gig, where I will have a first rate chance of seeing the elephant, head and tail. The men are putting down for clothing on their division bills. The mess bills are also out.

Being on the crew of the captain's gig was a plum job. It meant Leonard would get off the ship every time the captain did—much more than the average crewman—and would have some of his other duties reduced. He would also be better known to the captain, which proved advantageous at times.

March 2nd

Today we got the N.E. trade winds, but very light. In the afternoon they became stronger and at present we are going at the rate of six knots an hour with a prospect of going still faster.

March 3d   **at sea**

We have a good breeze this day. Saw a large whale, tacked ship several times during the day.

March 4th 1860   **at sea/Reefing**

Sunday at ten A.M. all hands were called to muster. The 1st lieutenant read the Articles of War, after which we mustered round the capstan. In the afternoon the wind began to freshen, and at four P.M. all hands were called to shorten sail. We double reefed the topsails and made everything snug for the night.

March 5th

At daybreak the wind abated a little; shook a reef out of the topsails and set the top gallant sails over them.

March 6th

The port watch washed clothes this morning but on account of the wind being so very strong, there was not much washing done. The men don't like to have their clothes blown away.

March 7th

Starboard watch washed clothes, and the clothes lines look as if a gang of thieves had plundered them.

March 8th   close reefing

The wind now became still stronger, we were obliged to close reef the fore and mizzen Topsails and put three reefs in the main. The weather is good but Lord Harry how it does howl.

March 9th   heavy weather

Today the wind is still the same with no signs of its moderating. There is very heavy head sea and the ship pitches awfully, causing some of the boys to get wet jackets. These are the regular N.E. trade winds. After the hammocks were piped down we had a rehearsal of *Robert Maccaire*. It is getting on finely.

March 10th   at sea

The weather this morning is still the same. The port watch holystoned the gun deck. This day the men are generally very busy getting ready for tomorrow's muster.

March 11th   at sea/Close reefing

Sunday. At half past nine A.M. the divisions were called to quarters for inspection, after which we had divine service on the gun deck. At eleven A.M., the wind moderating, we shook out the reefs and set the top gallant sails. Towards evening it began to blow again and we were obliged to furl the top gallant sails, and close reefed the topsails. It blowed big guns all night.

March 12th   sprung a yard

The wind moderating, shook out one reef and set top gallant sails over them, in the afternoon we sprung our fore top gallant yard, sent it down and got up a new one, which operation kept the fore top men busy all the watch.

March 13th [Real speed]

The wind went down considerable, we therefore shook out all the reefs and set the Royals and top gallant sails. In the afternoon, the wind being a couple of points free, we gave her the fore topmast studding sail. We are almost flying through the water, the log line indicating thirteen and fourteen knots an hour.

March 14th Death of a Krooman

Last night one of our Kroomen died. At ten o'clock all hands were called to bury the dead. The ship was then hove to with the main Topsail aback. The ensign was at half mast. The 4th lieutenant read the burial service, and his body was launched into the sea. Filled the main Topsail and stood on our course. The weather is getting rather chilly.

March 15th

Today the wind began to blow again. Had to close reef the topsails and hauled up the main sail. Towards night it blowed a living gale, and kept at it all night.

March 16th 1860. at sea

This day the wind again moderated; we shook out the reefs and set everything. At nine o'clock the clothes bags were piped up to air clothing. Had a rehearsal in the evening.

March 17th

Very pleasant weather with all sail set. There is a Temperance Society forming on board of the ship, having the Gunner as president.

March 18th

Sunday, at half past 9 A.M. had division inspection, after which had divine service as usual on the gun deck. The wind began to blow towards noon; we single reefed the Topsails, and set the top gallant sails over them.

March 19th

Saw a sail to windward, supposed to be a whaler as there is a large school of whales to be seen to windward.

March 20th

The weather here at present is very chilly, or at least it feels so to us, just coming out of the warm latitudes. We are not allowed to lay on decks on account of it, by orders of the Fleet Surgeon.

March 21st

The weather being very pleasant, we shook out the reefs and set all sail, had a lee wheel in the afternoon watch.

March 22nd   exercising the boys

Today the boys and landsmen are exercised at reefing, making and taking in sail, the Mizzen Topsail being used for the occasion. Had a rehearsal in the evening.

23d   mending

Today I am very busy mending an old pair of trowsers, and by the looks of them (if a body can judge of appearances) they wanted mending. It is a very pleasant day and is very warm.
W.A.L.

March 24th 1860.   at sea

Holystoned the gun deck. Fine weather and a strong breeze; piped up bags to air clothing and holystoned the berth deck.

March 25th   Close reefed

Sunday at half past nine all hands were called to quarters for inspection. We are still in the N.E. trade winds, and they are getting stronger. At five P.M. took in the Royals and top gallant sails and double reefed the topsails; in the midnight watch had to furl the mizzen and close reef the fore and main Topsails.

March 26th   Land ho.

Blowing heavy, under close reefed fore and main topsails, fore topmast staysail and spanker, going at the rate of seven knots an hour. At sundown, the lookout at the mast head reported land, broad on our lee bow. At eight P.M. we hove to until morning.

March 27th   foul of a dutch Brig

At daylight we filled away and stood in for the land; at ten A.M. we came to an anchor in Porto Praya under close reefed topsails. In coming to an anchor, we got foul of a Dutch brig; we carried her fore top gallant mast, flying Jib boom and injured her rigging considerable. We sustained but very little injury but we have got to make the damages good. At sundown we sent down Royal yards and got out all our boats.

March 28th

Today the Boatswain and a number of our men went aboard the brig to repair damages. At ten o'clock the American consul, Mr. Morse, came on board; fired a salute when he went away. We brought him ashore in the gig, this being the first time I pulled in her. There is a very heavy swell here, which makes it very difficult to pull. Had a short run up into the town and returned on board at sundown.

March 29th 1860   Porto Praya/a run ashore

Today we commenced taking in wood and water; we are also taking in a supply of bread, what we have got being full of maggots, and weevils. Some of the men to work on board of the brig; they are almost done. In the afternoon we went ashore in the gig with the captain's wash clothes. We had a good run of over two hours all over the town.

March 30th   visit of the Governor

The governor of the island visited the ship today and dined with our flag officer. On leaving he was saluted with seventeen guns. All hands to work getting in wood and water. Today some of the men that were to work upon the brig made too free with the schnapps that were on board of her; consequently they were put into the brig, when they came aboard of us.

March 31st   watering ship

All hands to work getting in small stores, wood and water. As I now belong to the gig I am excused from all work. At one o'clock the captain went ashore to dine with the consul. On landing the captain told the coxswain he might give the boat's crew a run until sundown—didn't we have a time! I bet we did! Today we finished taking in wood and water and the men are done on the brig. She looks much better than she did before.

April 1860

April 1st

Sunday all hands were called to quarters for the usual inspection, after which we had a general muster and the 1st lieutenant read the Articles of War. An English barque sailed today. The U.S. Steam Gun Boat *Mohican* has been here. She has got a large mail for us. The captain gave us [the crew of the gig] the privilege of going ashore in the afternoon, which we availed ourselves of and had a good time.

The Mohican *was a newly built thousand-ton, six-gun steamer, sent under the new policy of the Buchanan administration to strengthen the African Squadron. Unfortunately nobody got to read their mail for a while. The* Mohican *left Porto Praya two weeks earlier, heading for Monrovia. As it expected to meet the* Constellation *there, it took the squadron mail with it.*[1]

April 2nd 1860   Porto Praya/getting ready for sea

Today the grog and ration money were served out. We also signed accounts with the purser. The mess bills are out and so are the division bills. We were ashore most all day getting stores for the captain. In the afternoon a Portuguese brig came in here from Porto Grande with a mail for us. At sundown we sent up Royal yards and got in all boats. We are going to sea tomorrow. Had a rehearsal in the evening.

Unfortunately for Leonard, the Portuguese brig had no mail for him. He received mail seven times during the twenty-six-month deployment.

April 3d   left Porto Praya

At ten A.M. we got underway with a double reef topsail breeze. We are going to the northward, to Madeira to recruit ship and give the men liberty. I had a lookout in the first watch.

April 4th

We have got a good strong breeze, and very pleasant weather. All sail set. We have got the N.E. trades yet. We are in good spirits with a prospect of liberty ahead, having had none for over eight months.

April 5th

At 10 A.M. the drum beat to general quarters. Exercised both batteries. At eleven A.M. the drum beat the retreat. We have got a good breeze and very pleasant weather. Had a rehearsal of *Robert Macaire* in the evening.

April 6th

We are having delightful weather here now. All sail set, we tacked ship several times during the day.

April 7th

This morning the starboard watch holystoned the gun deck. All sail set, tacked ship several times during the day.

April 8th

Sunday all hands were called to quarters for inspection, after which had divine service on the gundeck. Several sails in sight. We are in a calm at present but there is a good sign of wind.

April 9th 1860.   **at sea/Laughable/Funny/worth reading**

A sail in sight; she appears to be a large square rigged vessel. We have got a head wind now and we tack ship twice in a watch. In the evening we had a rehearsal. Bye the bye—I had almost forgotten to mention what a variety of doings there are on board of this ship of an evening after hammocks are piped down, nor do I believe I can describe it and do it justice. However, I will do the best I can.

I will commence with the berth deck. 1st comes the religious society who hold a prayer meeting on the starboard side, forward next to the sick bay. Next in order is the Temperance Society, who are discussing the advantages derived from taking the pledge; they occupy the port side of the deck. Next comes the Dramatic Club, who are spouting Shakespeare in the main hold. Then comes the negro minstrel singers with their instruments, making night hideous with their yelling. Now comes the gun deck. First there is a crowd of about twenty who have got a fiddler perched upon the breach of a gun dancing breakdowns. Another crowd singing sailor songs and still another crowd skylarking, while on the spar deck, the quiet part of the ship's company are promenading, talking over last cruise, or listening to some old weather beaten tar, telling his miraculous adventures when he was a young man. While your humble servant is sitting on the combings of the fore hatch smoking a pipe, thinking of home.

April 10th

Very light wind this morning. A sail was reported which proved to be an American merchantman. Sent a boat on board of her, she is from Liverpool bound to New Orleans. The boat returned and we again proceeded on our course.

April 11th 1860.   at sea

Moderate breeze and fine weather, a sail in sight on our weather beam.

April 12th

Passed several sail today; we are right in the track of vessels now, and the horizon is covered with them. We still have got a first rate breeze.

April 13th

At ten A.M. had general quarters exercised the starboard battery. In the afternoon we exercised sail.

April 14th

Very fine weather. The port watch holystoned the gun deck. Signalized an English mail steamer. In the afternoon we scraped the spars and slushed them. I had a lee wheel in the dog watch.

April 15th

Sunday. All hands called to quarters for inspection, after which had divine service on the gun deck as usual, two sails in sight to windward. Very pleasant weather, with all sail set.

April 16th

The gun deck divisions were exercised at big gun drill and the master's and powder divisions were drilled with carbines. Had a rehearsal of *Box and Cox* in the evening.

April 17th   Spirit room

The starboard watch washed clothes. Two hands from each part of the ship were sent into the spirit room to break it out. They got at the whiskey and made themselves roaring drunk. They got in double irons and some of them got gagged; some of them are to be court-martialed. Fine weather.

April 18th   **Sentenced**

Today three of the men that were in the spirit room yesterday were court-martialed for being riotous. At five P.M. all hands were called to muster. They had three months' pay stopped and deprived of all liberty while in the ship.

April 19th 1860   **at sea/land ho/dead calm**

This morning the wind died away to a dead calm. Very foggy at noon, towards evening the fog cleared up and land was reported from the masthead, supposed to be the Island of Madeira. We are lying like a log upon the water, not a breath of wind in the last dog watch. The boys are planning out what they are going to do when they get ashore on liberty.

April 20th   **out all boats/towing Ship/at Madeira**

In sight of land but not a breath of wind, very pleasant indeed at noon, having no wind or any prospect of any. The captain gave orders to get out all boats and tow her in; we are within ten miles of the town of Funchal. At two P.M. the Flag officer went ashore in his barge. The boats now commenced towing the ship, with our boat (the gig) taking the lead, at three o'clock, a light breeze springing up, the boats were recalled on board, and at 5 P.M. we came to an anchor in the Bay of Funchal. There are several small vessels here. Everything looks green. It presents a beautiful appearance from where we lie at anchor. We are going to refit all our rigging, and paint the ship inside and out. At sundown we got the launch out, and sent down the topgallant and royal yards and unbent sails. We are going to have fresh provisions while we lie here. All hands are in excellent spirits and are all talking about the good times we are going to have [on] liberty. We went ashore in the gig with a large bird and some oranges, as a present from our captain to the American consul, Mr. Bayman. The name of the bird was a flamingo; we got him at Porto Praya.

Ashore Inman was greeted by Capt. Thomas A. Dornin, who had been sent over to take command of the San Jacinto. *Dornin arrived at Madeira aboard an English ship from Liverpool on April 1, when he learned that his ship had gone to Spain for repairs. He had been enjoying the hospitality of the consul's home while awaiting the flag officer's arrival.*[2]

April 21st 1860.   **Madeira**

Holystoned all decks and cleaned the ship outside, she is going to be caulked all over. As tomorrow is Sunday, we did not do much except cleaning up. In the afternoon we went ashore in the gig and had a good run. In the evening a serenading party came close to the ship; it being a lovely moonlight night, the singing was very well.

April 22nd

Sunday. All hands dressed in white. At half past nine A.M. all hands were called to quarters for inspection, after which divine service was held on the gun deck. We could hear the church bells ringing ashore, and how pleasant it sounded. Had several distinguished visitors aboard in the afternoon.

April 23d

Commenced setting up the rigging and rattling down; a gang of caulkers are also to work upon the ship. In the afternoon we commenced tarring down, which was finished at supper time. A small brig came in here today.

The captain hired eighteen local workmen to caulk the ship, a task that took them more than a week. Additionally the ship required replenishment of its bread stores. The bread taken aboard from the Supply *in Loando proved to be so weevilly that 9,100 pounds were thrown overboard. Captain Nicholas contracted for locally baked bread, but baking five tons of bread taxed the local bakeries so much that it was not ready until the middle of May.[3] Likely no one aboard the* Constellation *was unhappy at such a delay at Madeira.*

April 24th   a run ashore/noted rendezvous for sailors

Today we commenced painting the ship inside. An order was passed that the barges, gigs and 4th cutter's crews be excused from all work while we lie here. At one o'clock the captain went ashore to dine with the consul. He gave us permission to have a run until sundown. We had a good chance to visit some of the most popular places where a blue jacket frequents when he gets ashore here. Among the most prominent are Bubull Alley, Red Sea, Pistereen Alley and a host of others too numerous to mention. The city is in a much better condition than when we were here before. At sundown we returned to the boat and went aboard.

April 25th 1860.   at Madeira

Our captain goes ashore every day and we have very good times. We had a rehearsal of *Robert Macaire* in the evening. The company are making active preparations for the performance.

April 26th   distinguished arrivals

The English mail steamer arrived here today, having on board our flag officer's wife and daughter. They are going to live here while we lie here. She also brought out Captain Dornin, U.S.N. He is to take charge of the U.S. Steamer *San Jacinto,* which vessel is now repairing at Cadiz. We finished painting the ship today; the dramatic club are painting their scenery.

Actually as has been seen, Dornin arrived weeks ago. As arranged in their con-
versation when Inman arrived, Inman sent Dornin to Portugal and thence to
Cadiz to catch the San Jacinto.[4]

Inman's having brought his family out to Madeira suggests that he antici-
pated emulating his predecessor in spending a good deal of his deployment
there. Indeed an opinion aboard the ship was that it would remain in Madeira
until August.[5] However, the secretary of the navy had other ideas.

April 27th

Our captain and the captain of the *San Jacinto* went ashore in our boat and
stayed till twelve o'clock at night. The ship is finished throughout and we are
expecting liberty pretty soon.[6]

April 28th   commence giving liberty
This morning the 1st lieutenant began to give liberty. The 1st part of the port
watch and the 3d cutter's crew were ordered to dress themselves in clean blue
mustering clothes, with jackets, and go and get their money from the purser.
They got one month's pay and forty-eight hours' liberty. They went ashore at
nine o'clock in high spirits. We went ashore in the afternoon in our boat and
they were enjoying themselves first rate. At sundown one or two of the draft
were sent on board by the 1st lieutenant for being drunk and noisy.

The practice was to pay liberty men only a certain amount of their accumu-
lated pay, for their own protection.

April 29th

Sunday, had a general muster today around the capstan, after which had divine
service.

April 30th

The liberty men are all coming off and they behaved themselves finely with
only one or two exceptions.

Writing on this date, Inman acknowledged Secretary Toucey's orders to rear-
range the assignments of the lieutenants; he also reported scurvy on the Portsmouth *due to its long time at sea.*

May 1860

May 1st   **at Madeira**

The 1st part of the starboard watch are ashore on liberty. The English Steam Frigate *La Forte* arrived here today from England. An English gunboat also arrived here; she is named the *Trident* and she has been on the coast over four years.

The Constellation *exchanged salutes with HMS* Forte, *a brand-new fifty-gun steam screw frigate, flagship of Rear Admiral Hon. Sir Henry Keppel KCB, Commander in Chief of Her Britannic Majesty's Naval Forces on the Cape of Good Hope and West Coast of Africa Station—successor to Rear Admiral Grey, mentioned earlier, and Inman's British counterpart. The* Trident *was a six-gun paddle sloop.*

Inman received an order from Toucey sending the Constellation *back to the African coast. Inman ordered Captain Nicholas to be ready to leave by the eighth. Nicholas responded that it would take longer than that to get the ten thousand pounds of bread needed to replace the bad bread obtained in Loanda from the* Supply. *He expected to be ready by the twentieth.*

May 2nd   **on Liberty/a visit to Fish Town/Serenading**

The liberty men belonging to the 1st part of the Starboard watch being all off, the 1st lieutenant gave orders for both 2nd parts of the watches and all the boats' crews to get ready to go ashore after dinner. We got ashore at one P.M. We set our feet upon the beach, the gig's crew resolved upon sticking together. We procured a guide and he got us an entire suit of shore clothes. We visited several places of note, and in the afternoon we got horses and went to Fish Town, which is about five miles from the city of Funchal. We arrived there about half past three o'clock in the afternoon. After remaining there about an hour, we turned back to the city, where we arrived about half past five P.M. We then visited a billiard saloon and played about a dozen games, after which we began to think of getting something to eat. We went to the French Hotel and we had a good supper. We then repaired to the Grand Plaza where the governor's band were playing. All the beauty and fashion of Madeira were there. The band played until eight o'clock. At nine o'clock we went to our lodgings and after a social game of high, low, jack, we turned in for the night. I being very tired, I soon fell asleep, but I had hardly slept an hour before I was awakened by the sound of singing accompanied with some instrument that (for the life of me) I could not make out. (I afterwards learned it was called a guitar.) They had me almost crazy for an hour, after which they went away and left me to my slumbers.

Inman wrote to acknowledge the secretary of the navy's letter of February 4, 1860, taking Inman to task. Inman stressed the need of the men of the squadron for liberty; the secretary replied on June 16 that liberty may be given on St. Helena.

Also on this date, Inman acknowledged the secretary's letter of March 27, which said (Inman quoted), "To render the African Squadron more efficient for the purposes for which it is maintained on the Coast of Africa, the limits of its cruising ground towards the North will hereafter be restricted to the 20th parallel of North latitude. You will regard your instructions of the 6th of July last as modified to conform with the order. No vessel will leave the cruising ground without special permission from the Department." The twentieth parallel being well south of Madeira, the Constellation *did not again visit that pleasant island.*

Clearly the flag officer and the secretary had different desires regarding employment of the squadron, a situation not improved by the communications lag. Generally it took no less than a month each way for mail between Washington and the flagship and sometimes considerably more. Thus—as happened a number of times—Inman might take a certain action and then learn months later it was disapproved. One issue repeatedly causing friction was the assignment of officers, for which Inman was chastised more than once after shifting officers from one ship to another to make up deficiencies.

May 3d 1860.   **at Madeira/on Liberty**

At five P.M. [A.M.] we were all up and ready for a tramp. After getting breakfast, we started up town to see what our boys were about; they were enjoying themselves first rate. We now took a ramble down some of the most noted rendezvous for the blue jackets, and here Jack reigned king. Some of our boys were pretty well corned and of course we had to drink or fight. We preferred the former. We, however, got clear of this crowd and paid a visit to the Mount Church. As I had been there on a former visit I cannot give it a better description. We returned to the city at six P.M. and then to our lodgings, where we had a good time for the evening. One of us was here taking very sick and one of us had to watch him, all night.

May 4th   Return on board

This morning we donned our sailor clothes ready to go on board at eight o'clock. We ate a good breakfast and started to go on board, leaving our sick boatmate at the hotel; we did not wish to remove him on account of his being very sick. On our way to the boat we met the Fleet Surgeon and told him the case. He in company with us went to the hotel to see him. After consulting with him about ten minutes, he gave us orders to bring him on board on a litter, which we did. We got aboard at half past ten A.M. We left our boatmate in the sick bay, and immediately went ashore with the captain and staid till eleven o'clock at night.

May 5th

Liberty being over, the dramatics are making preparations for the performance which is to come off next week. The governor's band have volunteered their services for the occasion. They number twenty-three pieces, and with thirteen of our own, we will have music enough at all events.

Bandsmen were a regular part of every naval ship's company and were specially recruited for that role. As has already been seen, they played for normal shipboard evolutions as well as for special occasions.

May 6th 1860.   at Madeira/another Liberty

The liberty men are all off, with one or two exceptions. Two men had a row and are ashore yet. They will be court-martialed; the 1st lieutenant is after them. As a general thing the men behaved themselves finely. The flag officer and captain says it has been the quietest liberty they have seen for a number of years, and in consideration thereof he is going to give us another liberty of twenty-four hours before we leave here. As for my part I do not care about any more liberty, as our boat is ashore every day and night. [*That is, by virtue of being on the crew of the gig, Leonard got all the time ashore he wanted.*]

May 7th   Governor gives a ball

The governor gives a grand ball this evening, and all of our officers are going there. At four o'clock we brought the captain ashore so as to attend the governor's ball. We remained ashore all night. We have fixed on the evening of the 10th to give our performance; we have got everything ready and we are confident of giving it in good style. There is going to be quite a number of ladies and gentlemen from shore on board that evening.

May 8th

Our 1st lieutenant commenced giving us the other twenty-four hours liberty. He sent the 1st part of the starboard watch ashore. The purser is living ashore, so they have to get their money from him. The petty officers and seaman are allowed five dollars, ordinary seamen and landsmen and boys three dollars,

Inman reported Lieutenant Commanding McDonough, captain of the USS Sumpter *(and previously first lieutenant of the* Constellation*) to the secretary for insubordination. The secretary responded on June 6 directing preparation of charges for a court-martial. Because of the mail delay plus the requirement to have officers of certain rank on the court, the court-martial did not take place until August 20.*

May 9th

Today the 1st part of the port watch went ashore at ten o'clock. We went ashore in the forenoon to get some fixings for the theatre. In the afternoon we had a full dress rehearsal on the berth deck which went off to the entire satisfaction of the company. We are all in excellent spirits.

May 10th 1860

Today being the day of our performance, the dramatic troupe are very busy, all day fixing up the stage. We have got the ship decorated in fine style, with flags and streamers. We had several baskets of flowers and bouquets presented to us by the American ladies residing on the island, and take it altogether we made a grand gala day appearance. At four P.M. it began to rain and it made us feel very gloomy. Towards six P.M. it cleared up, and the audience began to assemble, and long before the time for commencing arrived every seat and standing place was occupied. At this time the greatest excitement prevailed. The governor's band gave us some elegant music.

The plays selected for the occasion were the two-act drama of *Robert Macaire,* and the laughable farce of *Box and Cox.* The cast of characters were very good, as you will see by the bill, which I copied word for word. The bills were printed ashore. The only objection in it is the way the names were given in; however, that was not the company's fault, that part of the business was entrusted to the purser's steward, who thinking to have a good joke had them printed as they are on the bill, which is as follows:

Grand Dramatic Entertainment
by the
Constellation . . .Amateur. . . Association
*_____*_____*

the above named association will give their first entertainment on board the U.S. Ship *Constellation* on Thursday Evening, May 10th 1860. The performance, will commence with the popular drama,—entitled *Robert Macaire,*—after which songs, and dances—to conclude with the laughable trifle entitled *Box and Cox.*

The performance will commence at 7 o' clock, precisely. The gentlemen of the *Constellation* with their friends are respectfully invited to attend.

D. Benjamin,

Manager.

The following is a cast of Characters
Robert= = =Macaire
or the two murderers
adapted from the French by Charles Selby

Robert Macaire—disguised as Redmond	by Mr. John Hunter
Jacques Strop— = = Bertrand . . .	P. Steward.
Pierre headwaiter.	John Powell.
Sargeant Loupy.	Isaac Nodine
Germuel	Thomas McCrachend
Dumont	C.D. Murphy.
Charles	Albert Comstock.
Francois	H.W. Higgins.
Marie	Mrs. Liddous French.
Clementine	Miss Rachel Leonard

After Which

A grand pas de deux, la Vasoviana-by-Signora Francisca & Monsr Elsezniski

Comic Song—Billy O Rourke . . .	Don Pedro O Dailie,
Aria, from the Bohemian girl-the heart bowed down .	Signor Stewardino
Grape vine Twist	Uncle Ned
Grand pas seul, la Polka, ...	Signorina lignum Vitae Francisca

---

To conclude with the laughable trifle, by J. Madison Morton Esq.—entitled
Box and Cox.

Box—a printer	.	.	.	.	.	by Mr. P. Steward.
Cox—a hatter	.	.	.	.	.	P. Doran.
Mrs. Bouncer	.	.	.	.	.	Miss Angelina Cloney.

The performance went off to the entire satisfaction of everybody who were there, among whom there were about thirty English and American ladies, and gentlemen, who are residing in Madeira. The flag officer's wife and daughter, the officers of our own ship and crew, some of the English Steam Frigate *La Forte*'s officers and men and several Portuguese ladies and gentlemen. The performance ended at half past ten o'clock precisely. The boats were all called away to take the invited guests ashore; we went ashore in the gig with a party of six gentlemen, one of whom (an English officer) gave our coxswain two dollars to drink his health with, which we did I can assure you.

In coming off of the beach, the boat got capsized, whether it was from the effects of drinking the gentleman's health, or the heavy surf on the beach, I cannot say—most likely the former. After righting the boat we returned on board, where the boys belonging to the club were having a first rate time, a collation being given them by the midshipmen. At a very late hour we turned into our hammocks well pleased with the evening's sport.

The dramatis personae here mingled sailors' real names with fictitious stage names. "Miss Rachel" Leonard sent copies of the playbill home to his family and friends. The song and dance interlude included the popular "Varsouviana Polka"; the anonymous Irish jig "Billy O'Rourke Is the Boy"; a nostalgic baritone aria from the 1843 opera The Bohemian Girl, *by Michael W. Balfe and Alfred Bunn; the minstrel "Grapevine Twist"; and another polka.*

May 11th

Commenced clearing away the wreck of the theatre. At nine o'clock the liberty men came off; another draft went ashore at eleven A.M. Our boat's crew are going on liberty on Sunday. The English admiral's ship (the *La Forte*) sailed today for the Cape of Good Hope.

May 12th

Holystoned the spar and gun decks. The boys are having a great deal of talk about the performance; they all say it was beyond their expectations. I am going ashore tomorrow, and am in hopes of having a good time in the evening. All of the liberty men were off. The second liberty the men behaved a great deal better than the first. The barge's, gig's, 4th cutter's and the dinghy's crews are going ashore tomorrow.

May 13th   **at Madeira on Liberty/Visit to the Church of St. Roque**

Sunday again on liberty in Madeira. The 1st lieutenant, being a very religious man, gives some of the men privilege to go ashore and attend church, and it is astonishing, what a crowd of the men that became religious, but that soon got played out, some of them returning on board three sheets in the wind and the others shivering. At half past nine o'clock divine service was held on the gun deck as usual. We were ordered to get ready to go ashore. Our boat's crew were told to come back at sundown, on account of the captain wanting to use the boat. He is going to let us go again some other time.

We got ashore at half past ten o'clock; it was a splendid day. We went to the French Hotel, and staid there till dinner time, which was at one P.M. We then took a stroll around the plaza. At two o'clock we hired horses, and started for the Church of St. Rougue, which is situate about five miles from the City of Funchal. We understood from our guides that there was an interesting ceremony to come off. The roads were lined with people, all dressed in their holiday costume. We were all mounted, and of course, were the centre of attraction. We were dressed in blue jackets and pants, white frocks and hats.

We arrived at the church about four o'clock P.M. We left our horses in charge of the guides and entered the church, which is a magnificent one. We were shown to some seats by one of the Padres, who in fact showed us every attention. At half past four o'clock the services commenced; they were very impressive. It consisted of offering six boys, and six girls, by their friends, to the services of the church. It is customary to do so once a year.

After the ceremony they formed a grand procession and marched to the Convent of St. Augustine, where we left them, and returned to our horses and started back to the city well satisfied with our day's visit. We next proceeded to the French Hotel where we had an excellent supper, and returned on board.

In the twenty-first century, greater Funchal has grown to include the Church of San Roque, but in Leonard's day the neighborhood was a separate village. The huge church on an elevated spot continues to dominate the area.

May 14th

At nine o'clock the captain went ashore. I, being boat keeper, I had to stay in the boat. At twelve o'clock we returned on board. The English gun boat sailed today for England. Some of our boys are very sick from the effects of the hard usage they gave themselves while ashore on liberty.

The following prescription applied more specifically to when a boat was waiting next to its ship, but the principles would apply elsewhere as well: "Duties

Cruise of the U.S. Ship Constellation

January 15th 1861.

at
St. Helena

This morning all hands scrubbed hammocks, an American Barque, the Aurelia of Boston arrived here, we went ashore in the gig and had a very good run, in the evening we had the last rehearsal of Ambrose Gwinett we are going to give our performance to morrow night.

January 16th

fixing the
Stage

Early this morning the dramatic troupe began to fix up our stage and scenery for the performance at 9. O. Clock we went ashore and got some things for it. there is considerable talk about it here ashore, at 1 P.M. we returned on board, at 2 o. clock the preperations for the theatre being over, the boys began to make arrangements for the performance at 3. O. clock a steamer was signalized from the Fort on ladder hill. which proved to be the U. S. Steam Frigate San Jacinto. and at ½ past 4 P.M. she came to an anchor. we have been expecting her this last three days. at 6.0. clock our audience began to assemble we had all the officers belonging to the St. Helena, Regiments and their Ladies besides several of the citizens all the officers from the U.S. Steam Frigate San Jacinto, and 60 of her crew, the crews of an American Barque and Whale ship, and our own officers and men the performance commenced at ½ past 7 o. clock. with the 3 act drama of Ambrose Gwinett after which a song and dance then the popular farce of the Widows Victim. a song. and concluded with the laughable farce of Boots at the Swan. the performance ended at ½ part 11 O. clock and gave entire satisfaction. but I must say that the way we were treated after the performance, was in my opinion rather shabby it is a customary thing on board of an american man of war to give the performers a little to drink while

arrival
of the
San
Jacinto.

our
audience.

in Regard to Boat Keepers. See that they sit up properly in their boats; that they rise and salute all officers in passing boats; that they keep their boats from fouling each other and the ship's side; and that they are in uniform. Do not allow them to wash clothes in their boats, nor to converse with men on board ship."[1]

May 15th

Commenced taking in a supply of wood and water, which we finished before night. We went ashore in the evening with the captain's steward to get some stores for the captain. We had several good games of billiards; went aboard at seven P.M.

May 16th 1860   at Madeira/the Gig's crew Serenading/A Gentleman

This day came in very fine. In the evening the gig's crew went ashore to serenade several American families who are stopping here for the summer, among which were the consul's, and Dr. Maxwell's families. They were very much surprised at the serenade as it was entirely unexpected by them, in a foreign land to be serenaded by a party of man of war's men.

At half past eleven o'clock we started towards the grand square, singing all the way. In passing a billiard saloon which is frequented by our officers, we struck up a popular negro song, which brought out one of our lieutenants by the name of Foster (a perfect gentleman), who made us sing several songs, and as he said were sung tip top style. We then in company with Mr. Foster proceeded to a hotel, where we drank his health, at his expense, till we were pretty well in for it. We then went to the billiard saloon and finished the night in a very jovial manner. It was daylight before we separated.

May 17th   unexpected orders/at Madeira

At seven A.M. we returned on board, and at half past eight we went ashore with the captain. We have just got the unwelcome news that we are going to sea in a few days; it makes all hands feel blue. It was the intention of the flag officer to spend the 4th of July here, but he has got orders from the Secretary of the Navy by the English Mail Steamer that arrived here last night to go to sea, and not to come any higher than 20 degrees north. As Madeira is in 35 degrees north, this is our last visit here. Vessels on the station will hereafter go to St. Helena to recruit ship. The orders are very obnoxious to the officers, and I understand they are going to remonstrate against it. The flag officer's wife and daughter have just arrived here, and several of the other officers' families are also here. They feel bad about it, as they intended to spend the summer here. The officers are going to give a grand ball on board this ship tomorrow afternoon. We had a breakdown in the gangway in the evening.

Leonard was mistaken about the orders having arrived the previous night, because as has been noted, Inman acknowledged the order to stay below twenty degrees north in his letter to Toucey of May 2.

May 18th   Grand Ball in Madeira/Gander Sets

The first thing we did this morning, we holystoned the spar deck. After breakfast the quarter master commenced to decorate the quarter deck. At twelve A.M. they had it finished. The quarter deck presents the appearance of an immense flower garden: the flags and streamers of all nations were festooned overhead in a beautiful manner, and I must say it makes a very beautiful ballroom. At two P.M. the invited guests began to assemble, and in less than an hour the assemblage, were all on board. Among the guests were several English and American ladies and gentlemen, two Portuguese dukes, all the naval officers of our ship in full dress uniform. The dancing commenced at half past three o'clock. The ship's company were allowed the privilege of looking on.

At half past four o'clock the dancing ceased and the party retired to the gun deck for dinner, the after part of the ship from the main mast to the taffrail being reserved for that purpose. [*As the taffrail is on the spar deck, Leonard seems to have meant to say that the area on the spar deck from the mainmast aft to the taffrail was reserved for the purpose of dancing.*][2] At five o'clock dance was again resumed, the boys now got up sets of their own in the port gangway which they styled gander sets, and I have no hesitation in saying that they had the best time of it. At half past six o'clock the party broke up, and at seven o'clock all hands were called aft to splice the main brace.

The crew, having no females to dance with, jokingly referred to their dance sets as "gander sets."

May 19th   Leaving Madeira

Early this morning we sent up top Gallant and Royal yards, took in all boats, and got the messenger up, and made extensive preparations for sea. At half past three o'clock all hands were called to get up anchor. The anchor came up very slowly; in fact all hands felt like leaving home, and well they might, for this is indeed a Dismal Coast. At sundown we lost sight of the beautiful island of Madeira.

May 20th 1860   at sea/General muster

Sunday and a beautiful day. At ten A.M. had a general muster, the Articles of War were read by the 1st lieutenant, after which we mustered round the capstan. We are going to Porto Grande.

May 21st   exercising

A good breeze and pleasant weather, in the afternoon the 1st division exercised large guns, the 2nd division small arms, and the 3d division single sticks. I had a quarter lookout in the midwatch.

May 22nd

Fair wind, going about seven knots an hour, the 2nd division exercised large guns, the 1st division small arms, the 3d division single sticks and the powder division carbines.

May 23d

The wind is still fair, and the weather good. In the afternoon the 3d division exercised large guns, the 2nd division small arms and the 1st division single sticks.

May 24th   Single Stick Practice

The port watch washed clothes. At half past nine o'clock we were called to quarters and an order was read to each division. As near as I can recollect it was as follows: the captain will give the sum of ten dollars to the best single stick player in three months. All hands are practicing in the gangways; the passers by are in danger of getting their eyes knocked out by the ones who are practicing.

May 25th

The starboard watch washed clothes in the afternoon. All hands were exercised at making and furling sail. There is no wind at all; the ocean looks like one sheet of glass.

May 26th   at sea/at sea looking after a Sunken Rock/Land ho

This morning we have got a light breeze, going about three knots, the [*sic*] gave orders to keep a bright lookout ahead; he expects to see a hidden rock, that was reported by the same vessel that went over it. At noon being in Latitude 17.55 north, Longitude 23.24 West, the very spot where it was reported to have been seen, we hove aback the Main Topsail and tried to get soundings with the deep sea lead, but it was no use. It being a very calm day, the officers had their glasses pointed in every direction and if there had been any rock here we could have seen it. After looking some time longer with the same success, we filled away the Main Top Sail and stood on our course. At sundown land was reported by the lookout on the fore topsail yard, bearing two points on our lee bow. We have got a good breeze now. The land is supposed to be the island of San Antonio, one of the Cape de Verdes. At nine o'clock P.M. we hove to for the night.

Inman directed Nicholas to verify the "Louisa's Rock," reported in a Boston paper of July 1859, a Captain Jones reporting it at Lat 17.55 N and Long 23.34 W. Nicholas, with an eye to the most precise navigation possible, arranged to be within twenty minutes' sail at meridian (when taking the noon fix), then sailed directly over the spot. No rock.[3]

May 27th   **came to an anchor in Porto Grande**

Sunday. Early in the morning, we made sail, and stood in for the land and at ten o'clock A.M. we came to an anchor in the harbor of Porto Grande. We are not going to stop here long; we are going to Porto Praya. We are going to sail tomorrow.

May 28th   **Perilous adventure/sailed for Porto Praya**

This morning the gig's crew took the 3d cutter and went fishing, but could not catch anything. On returning to the ship, we were very much annoyed by the gambols of a very large whale, and her two young ones. They came nigh demolishing the boat and those that were in it several times. It might have been good sport for them, O, but I must say it was poor fun for us.

At five o'clock we got underway and made all sail for Porto Praya. We had hardly cleared the land when the wind died away to a dead calm. We had several light catspaws during the night.

May 29th 1860.   **at sea**

We had very light winds during the forenoon. Late in the afternoon a good breeze sprang up and kept it all night.

May 30th   **Land ho**

This morning, land was reported which proved to be the Island of St. Jago. At eleven A.M. we came to an anchor in Porto Praya. We got out all boats and at sundown we sent down Top Gallant and Royal yards.

May 31st   **at Porto Praya**

Today all hands are very busy taking in provisions, and water. At eleven A.M. the American Consul came on board, and we learnt from him that the U.S. Sloop of war *Portsmouth* sailed from here a week ago. She took a slaver in this port and sent her home, she also brought a mail for us that was brought out here by the U.S. Steamer *Mohican;* she expects to find us at Madeira.[4]

June 1860

June 1st

Today we went ashore in the gig to get some stores for the captain. We are going to sea tomorrow. At sundown, the provisions being all in, sent up Top Gallant and Royal yards. The port watch to work getting up the messenger. At seven o'clock the boatswain piped down hammocks.

June 2nd leaving

At ten we got underway for Prince's Island with a good strong breeze, the watch on deck to work putting on chafing gear.

June 3d at sea

Sunday. At nine A.M. the divisions were called to quarters for inspection, after which we had a general muster ref the Articles of War, after which had divine service on the gun deck. We have a good breeze and all sail set. Saw a school of porpoises in the dog watch.

June 4th 1860 at Sea

The port watch are to work on the gun deck getting the chain cables, to overhaul them and clean out the chain lockers. We have got a good breeze and pleasant weather.

June 5th

Today we have the regular monthly stores served out. We have got a good breeze and pleasant weather.

June 6th

Today being a very fine day, the 1st lieutenant had all the hammocks piped into the rigging to air bedding.

June 7th

This morning the lookout at the masthead reported a sail on our weather bow. It is a dead calm. At night the breeze springing up, we lost sight of the sail.

June 8th

At 10 A.M. we had general quarters, exercised the starboard battery. I had a lookout in the mid watch.

June 9th

Today being Saturday, we holystoned the gun deck and cleaned up for tomorrow.

June 10th   **There she blows**

Sunday. At the usual hour the divisions were called to quarters for inspection, after which we had divine service on the gun deck. A very large whale came close alongside of the ship, which created quite an excitement among some of our men who have been whaling.

June 11th

In the afternoon the 1st division exercised large guns, the 2nd division small arms and the 3d division single sticks. We have got a good breeze and pleasant weather.

June 12

Today the second division exercised big guns, the 1st at small arms and the 3d division at the single sticks. We are jogging along at the rate of six and seven knots an hour.

June 13th 1860   **at sea**

One year in commission. One year ago we were in Boston harbor, now we are on the coast of Africa. We are having very pleasant weather and all sail set.

June 14th   **an old Salt**

This morning the weather calm and remained so all day. In the afternoon all hands exercised sail. I being in the ship one year, I can give a good description of some of the most noticeable characters, and I will do so in the course of the

Journal. I will commence with the captain of the forecastle starboard watch. Alexander McIntosh, or Old Mac, as he is familiarly called, is an out and out man of war's man. He belongs to the western part of New York, and has been in the service thirteen years. He is a good sailor and a good natured man. He is about six feet high and can tell as tough a yarn as the next man living. By his looks a person would say he had seen hard times. He is now one of the most prominent members of the Temperance Movement on board of this ship. He is also captain of No 4 gun. He always makes a good shot. I had a lookout in the midwatch.

June 15th

At ten o'clock this forenoon the drum beat to general quarters. After dinner the gun deck divisions were exercised at single sticks and small arms. At five o'clock P.M. a good breeze sprang up and at eight P.M. we logged twelve knots.

June 16th

This morning the starboard watch washed clothes and holystoned the gun deck. At nine P.M. piped up all bags to air clothing, which as the men say is a sailor's pleasure, to over haul his bag and see what they have got. We have had some very pleasant weather the past week and all hands are in excellent spirits.

Willie Leonard

June 17th 1860   at sea

Sunday, and the Anniversary of the battle of Bunker Hill. A day that is celebrated in a very good style where I belong, or in fact in the very town where the battle was fought 17th of June 1776. At half past [9] A.M. the divisions were called to quarters for inspection, after which had divine service. Very pleasant weather with all sail set.

June 18th   at sea

The Anniversary of another great battle, that of Waterloo. The reason I put this down was this: we have got a very old marine on board of this ship that was in the English army all through the Peninsula War, and he was spinning us a yarn last night in the mid watch about some of his campaigns, that is the reason I thought of the Battle of Waterloo.

June 19th

We are now in the vicinity of the equator and we are getting plenty of rain. The ship's company are improving the opportunity by having a fresh water wash. It continued raining all day. We are becalmed. We had no wind all night.

June 20th

It continued raining all this day, and the boys begin to think it is too much of the good thing. Especially as it is a dead calm.

June 21st

No wind yet. We are lying like a log upon the water, but it looks like a good breeze from the eastward. At two P.M. we got it, a fine seven knot breeze,

June 22nd

We have got a first rate breeze. It rained during the forenoon, but it cleared up in the afternoon. We are pretty close to the land according to reckoning. At twelve o'clock midnight we braced the main yard aback and remained so during the night. It is very warm here now, it is about one degree to the northward of the Line.

June 23d 1860   **at sea/land ho/at anchor in Prince's Island**

Early this morning we made sail, and at ten A.M. the lookout on the fore topsail yard reported land two points on our lee bow. At two o'clock in the afternoon we came to an anchor at Prince's Island in seventeen fathoms water. The U.S. Steamer *Mohican* is here; she saluted our flag officer with thirteen guns, and we returned one of nine guns. She is a perfect beauty and carries thirteen guns. She is to join the African Squadron at sundown. We got out all boats and sent down royal yards. All hands are going to have a run ashore here.

The Mohican *was a brand-new thousand-ton six-gun steam sloop, just commissioned in late November. Prior to the* San Jacinto's *arrival in September, the African Squadron had never included a steamship. Now with the* Mohican, *the squadron included four. Leonard's attribution of thirteen guns to the* Mohican *was a slip of the pen, repeating the number of guns in the salute.*

June 24th

Sunday and a very pleasant day. At half past nine A.M. the divisions were called to quarters for inspection. In the afternoon some of the *Mohican*'s men were aboard of us on a visit. After supper some of our men went ashore for a run until sundown. At eight P.M. set the anchor watch.

June 25th

This morning our flag officer went on board the *Mohican* to inspect her. On arriving on board they saluted him with thirteen guns. Today we commenced taking in a supply of wood and water. It is very fine weather here now.

June 26th

We finished taking in wood and water. In the afternoon the gig's crew went ashore to clean the boat and scrub the awning; had a very good bathe in the creek. We returned on board at four o'clock. The U.S. Steamer *Mohican* sailed today for the island of Fernando Po to get the mail for us.

June 27th

The 1st lieutenant sent two hands from each part of the ship [ashore] to scrub windsails. All hands are very busy cleaning the ship outside and holystoning inside. At five o'clock the men came off pretty well drunk and were put in the brig.

June 28th   at Prince's Island/Bum Boating

At ten A.M. the gun deck divisions were exercised at large guns. There is an eccentric darkie here, who comes off in the Bum Boat every meal time. He calls himself the General. When the U.S. Sloop of war *Portsmouth* was here, they fitted him out with an entire suit of officer's full dress uniform and he feels mighty proud about them. I don't think they could have selected a more comical looking one, it would make a horse laugh to see how consequential he is. A Bum Boat is a curious institution. It is nothing more nor less than a traveling variety store.

Although Leonard did not mention it, bumboats would have come out to the ship at nearly every place visited, offering the sailors local fruits and vegetables, souvenir birds and animals, etc.

Inman now ordered Lieutenant McDonough from the Sumpter *back to the* Constellation. *Since being suspended from command, McDonough had continued inconveniently to occupy the entire captain's quarters on the* Sumpter *while awaiting his court-martial, for which the secretary's order had yet to catch up with the squadron. McDonough remained aboard the* Constellation *without assignment until his trial.*

Inman received a report from Commander Brent of USS Marion *describing his actions in early March at Kinsembo, where Commander Colhoun had led a party ashore in February. Brent and the captain of HMS* Falcon *led parties ashore (Brent brought fifty men from the* Marion) *for two nights to protect the local factories (Dutch, English, and American) during a scrap between the natives and Portuguese troops led by the governor of Angola. Brent halted the governor's advance by threatening to open fire if his men moved a step further. A likely side effect of Brent's naval excursion (made despite the sanitary regulations forbidding overnight stays ashore) was to prevent the Portuguese from annexing the region north of the river, which might well have put these legitimate factors out of business and left the area more vulnerable to slave trading.*[1]

June 29th   visit of the English Admiral

In the afternoon the U.S. Gun Boat *Mohican* arrived here from Fernando Po. She did not bring the mail but left it with the U.S. Steamer *Sumpter*, which vessel left before she did. She brought the English Admiral from Fernando Po. He is going to join his vessel at St Thomas's. At eleven A.M. he came on board of us, when a salute of fifteen guns was fired for him. Our flag officer placed the U.S. Steamer *Mohican* at his disposal. Late in the evening the *Sumpter* arrived with our mail.

Admiral Keppel was a tiny man with flaming red hair. While loaning him the use of the Mohican, *Inman also handed him copies of correspondence from several American merchant captains, voicing complaints about treatment by ships of the British squadron.*[2] *The curiously balancing relationship between the two countries, enacted by their naval representatives on the African coast, was no better dramatized than here. Both naval squadrons were tasked with interdicting the slave trade, and they often cooperated very cordially. At the same time, the U.S. government strongly opposed any British interference with American ships, so although those ships were commonly used by slavers, protesting such interference with them was part of the U.S. African Squadron commander's job.*

June 30th

This morning we sent up top gallant and royal yards and made preparations for sea. The U.S. Steamer *Mohican* sailed today for St. Thomas's with the English admiral on board.

July 1860

July 1st   going to sea

Sunday. Early this morning we got underway and made all sail for St Paul de Loando. At ten A.M. all hands were called to muster, read the Articles of War and passed round the capstan, after which we had divine service. In the afternoon all hands were to work putting on chafing gear and doing other jobs round the ship. We have a good breeze.

July 2nd 1860.   at sea

We are now on the Equator, not a breath of wind. It is very wonderful. It commenced to rain at sundown and rained all night.

July 3d

Today we are crossing the Line for the third time. There is a very light breeze, with plenty of rain. At seven P.M. we got a good steady breeze, and kept it all night.

July 4th   4th at Sea

Independence Day. We are now just sixty miles south of the Equator. It is a very dull day and awful foggy. We have got a light breeze. At five P.M. all hands were called to splice the main brace. Felt miserable all this day.

July 5th

This morning the fog cleared up and the sun came out in all its splendor. There is a good prospect of having some fine weather—we have got a good breeze.

July 6th

Very pleasant day. I am busy making a set of hammock clews. My old ones gave out last night and let me down head foremost. The fall stunned me; it was almost an hour before I could collect my senses. When I did come to, my topmates were having a good laugh over the accident. It is man of war fashion to laugh when anything of that kind occurs.

July 7th   Boxing/at sea

The men are enjoying themselves in the foretopmen's gangway with an exhibition of the manly art of self defence. They have got the Heeman and Sayers Fever; each party has its particular friends. Such an excitement there is on board of an evening one would suppose the renowned champions themselves were on board in connection with this. It would not be out of place to mention a particular individual on board of this ship by the name of Daniel Benjeman, or as he is familiarly called, Ben the Barber. He is the ship's barber. He is known throughout the entire navy, and as he styles himself a regular navy man. There is not any thing going on board of the ship but what he is at the head of it. He is a good hearted soul and very accommodating and talk, O lord he can blow like a steam engine.

Leonard's mail that arrived June 29 at Prince's Island seems to have brought newspapers with stories about the two prizefighters, or possibly the Harper's Weekly *for May 5, which featured a double-page illustration of the bareknuckled, first-ever "World Championship" boxing match between the formidable Englishman Tom Sayers and American John C. Heenan, "the Benicia Boy," at Farnborough, England, on April 17.*

July 8th

Sunday we did not have the usual inspection today on account of its raining. It rained down in torrents all the forenoon, toward evening it cleared up. We have got a very good breeze, all sail set.

July 9th

This day came in calm in the afternoon. All the gun deck divisions were exercised at small arms and the powder divisions were drilled with carbines.

July 10th

The 2nd and 3d divisions were at large gun drill all the afternoon. The 1st division were at single stick exercise.

July 11th

This morning the 3d division exercised big guns. After supper, there being no wind, all hands were called to exercise sail. After an hour's drilling the boatswain piped down.

One of the complaints Inman passed to Admiral Keppel involved Capt. J. S. Clark of the American barque Edwin. *As the* Constellation *sailed south to Loanda, Captain Godon of the* Mohican *dropped off the admiral and was now visiting Cape Coast Castle on the British Gold Coast, investigating the case. Clark had had a grudge against a krooman who lived near Cape Palmas in Liberia and planned to cut out his tongue and throw him overboard. The krooman got away, but Clark and his mates fired on his canoe and two others, killing two kroomen and wounding several. Proceeding to Cape Coast Castle, he discharged his four American seamen at their agreement but did not give them the customary passage money home. Clark then complained of his treatment by the local authorities. Godon, who really had no jurisdiction over most of the issues, took no action, and apparently Clark got away with his crimes.*

July 12th

At nine A.M. the drum beat to general fire quarters. This is a separate thing altogether from the regular fighting quarters: in case the ship catches fire each man has got his station where he is got to [go] when the drum beats. At half past nine the drum beat the retreat.

July 13th

At ten o'clock this day we had general quarters. In the afternoon, it being a fine day, the hammocks were piped out of the nettings to air bedding. We have got all the starboard studding sails set.

Leonard did not mention an encounter on the way from Prince's Island to Loando that was described by the Boston Daily Advertiser's *correspondent: "On the passage from Prince's Island, we chased a barque for 17 hours, firing five blank cartridges before she hove-to. We sent a boat to her, in charge of Sailing-master T. H. Eastman, and on his getting alongside was informed that she was the French barque* Vendique, *40 days from Marseilles, bound to Kabenda, with a cargo of bread and aguardiente; also, that he would not be allowed to come on board—when the boat returned without even asking for her papers. It being dark at the time, her colors, if any were set, could not be seen. It is the opinion of many on board that she was a slaver, and that one of her crew, understanding French, was placed in the gangway and represented himself as her captain."[1] As the American government had no treaties providing reciprocal arrest of suspected slavers with any other nation, the* Constellation *could not stop a genuine French ship, or any ship except one under the U.S. flag (or one with no flag), even if it had been full of slaves.*

July 14th

We have got a good breeze and very pleasant weather, all the starboard studding sails set.

July 15th 1860   at sea

Sunday, at half past nine A.M. called the divisions to quarters for inspection, after which divine service was held on the gun deck. The afternoon we were becalmed all sail set.

July 16th   Sail ho

We are still becalmed. At ten A.M. a sail was reported on our weather beam. Could not make her out; at dark we lost sight of her.

July 17th

We are still becalmed and the air is very sultry. Towards evening a light breeze sprung up and it freshened during the night.

July 18th   exercising

This morning we have got a good breeze, all the port studding sails set; very warm weather.

July 19th   exercising

This day came in calm. At four o'clock P.M. all hands were called to exercise sail, each watch working on their own side, one trying to beat the other. We ran the studding sails up and down on both sides a dozen times, made and took in all sail about half a dozen times, and then the boatswain was ordered to pipe down.

July 20th

We are still becalmed. There are several large looking sharks swimming around the ship. There is a curious superstition among seafaring men, about sharks; they say that when a shark follows a ship it is a sure sign that somebody is going to die on board. Their belief in it is so great that they will cite cases that come within their own personal knowledge and even go as far as to take an oath on it.

July 21st   **Sail ho.**

This morning the port watch holystoned the gun deck. We have got a good breeze and expect to get in tomorrow. At five P.M. a sail hove in sight; she proved to be a store ship just leaving St Paul de Loando.

The store ship was the chartered Cochituate, *from Boston, which among other things had put ashore in Loando two of the* Constellation's *former officers, Boatswain Hingerty and Midshipman Farquhar. Hingerty took up his former duties, while his replacement (acting boatswain William Long) resigned and was sent back to the United States.*

July 22nd 1860   at Sea/land ho/came to an anchor
                                                   in St Paul de Loando

Sunday all hands were called to quarters for inspection at half past nine A.M. at ten o'clock the lookout at the masthead reported land, which proved to be St. Paul de Loando, and at two P.M. we came to an anchor in the harbor. The U. States Sloop of war *Marion* is here; so is the U.S. Steam Gun boat *Sumpter.* At sundown we got out all boats, and sent down Top Gallant and Royal yards. We got a large mail here and I received some letters, and several packages of papers from home. In the letters I received some very melancholy news, it being the death of two of my dearest friends.

A letter from Anna Moloney contained a poem lamenting the death of a friend named Lizzy.

July 23d

Today we went ashore in the gig and returned on board at eleven A.M. At noon we saluted the Portuguese flag with twenty-one guns, which they returned with twenty-one guns. The U.S. Sloop of war *Marion* saluted our flag officer with thirteen guns, we returned a salute of nine guns. At sundown all hands swung clean hammocks. Very fine weather here now.

July 24th

All hands scrubbed hammocks and after breakfast we commenced taking in water and provisions. We are also cleaning the ship inside and out. We are going to paint ship tomorrow.

July 25th

Commenced painting ship the first thing this morning. We had a run ashore this forenoon and had quite a ramble among the Negro huts.

July 26th

There is a general court-martial going on here now on board of the U.S. Sloop of War *Marion*. One of the boatswain's mates struck the 1st Lieutenant; it will go very hard with him.

July 27th

This afternoon our captain and the captain of the *Marion* went ashore in our boat to the Navy yard and returned at sundown.

July 28th 1860.   **in St Paul de Loando**

The English ship *Grampion* arrived here today from Liverpool after a very long passage of 116 days. She is loaded with coal.

July 29th

Sunday at half past nine A.M. all hands were called to quarters for inspections as usual. In the afternoon several of our boys went on board the *Marion* to visit.

July 30th

All hands scrubbed hammocks. The gig's crew went on a fishing excursion in the forenoon.

July 31st

Today we had general quarters and division exercise, very fine weather.

August 1860

August 1st   **at St Paul de Loando**

All the respective divisions are drawing clothing and the messes are drawing small stores. In the afternoon the 1st division went ashore to shoot at target, after which we had good run on the beach.

August 2nd

Today we finished taking in provisions; we now commenced to take in wood and water.

August 3d

This day we had a grand boat expedition. In the afternoon the gig's crew went ashore, and had a good run; after returning on board we had a grand Breakdown in the gangway.

August 4th

Two Portuguese brigs arrived here today, fine weather.

August 5th

Sunday, all hands were called to quarters at half past nine A.M. for division inspection, after which we had a general muster round the capstan. In the afternoon several of the ship's company went on board the U.S. Sloop of War *Marion* to visit.

August 6th 1860   **St Paul de Loando**

This morning all hands scrubbed and washed clothes. Went ashore in the gig at three P.M. and returned at sundown.

August 7th

At ten o'clock we took the captain ashore; he is going to dine with the American consul. At sundown he returned on board the ship.

August 8th **a surprise the U.S. Steamer *Niagara***

This morning we are making preparations for sea. We went ashore to get some little stores for the captain. In the afternoon a very large sail hove in sight, supposed to be a steamer. As it was getting dark we could not make her out. At seven P.M. she came to an anchor; sent our gig alongside of her to ascertain what she was, to our great surprise, she proved to be the U.S. Steamer *Niagara* with the Japanese Embassy on board. She put in here being short of coal. It is the first time I ever saw her, she is a monster, and withal a perfect beauty. She is on her way to Japan. Our captain let her have the use of our Kroomen to help them coal ship, also to take in wood and water.

Inman reported the Niagara *arriving on the sixth.*[1] *Inman assigned all the kroomen from the* Constellation, *the* Marion, *and the* Mystic—*seventy-three in all—to the* Niagara *temporarily to assist in coaling and watering.*

The Niagara's *previous visit to the African coast just two years before was very different. Then it had carried to Liberia two hundred Africans from the slave ship* Echo, *taken near Cuba.*

Just prior to that mission, the Niagara's *large size had made it the choice to lay the American end of the first transatlantic cable. After a failed attempt in 1857, the second attempt the following year was successful, though the cable was operational for only three weeks.*

Now the Niagara *was taking home the first diplomatic mission sent from Japan to the United States. The Japanese—four emissaries and their suite— were entertained in Washington, New York, and elsewhere with grand balls and receptions. Having come by way of the Pacific, on July 7 they boarded the* Niagara *to be taken home to Japan by crossing the Atlantic and rounding the Cape of Good Hope. At 5,500 tons displacement, the* Niagara *was the largest ship the U.S. Navy possessed, making it the choice for this latest of several unique assignments. To house the Japanese delegation, a special 4,000-square-foot cabin had been built upon the spar deck, with splendid staterooms and quarters for staff and servants, at great expense to the American government.*

August 9th **saluting**

This morning the U.S. Steamer *Niagara* saluted the Portuguese flag with twenty-one guns, which salute was returned from the fort. She also saluted our flag officer with thirteen guns and we returned her nine. Today the Japanese went ashore to visit the place, and the natives crowded around them so they

USS *Niagara*—Dickinson College. From *Gleason's Pictorial*, November 6, 1858. Image courtesy of the House Divided Project of Dickinson College.

could hardly get along the streets. They called them "American women." In the afternoon we made preparations for sea: at sundown we sent up top gallant and Royal yards. We are going tomorrow only for a day or two, merely to air ship.

August 10th

At eleven A.M. we hove up the anchor, and made sail. We went outside the harbor. We are to return in a day or two. Land in sight, very plain. There are several small vessels beating in, mostly trading vessels. At sundown we took in the Royals and top gallant sails and cruised at the mouth of the harbor all night.

August 11th 1860   outside of Loando/exercising/came to a anchor

At daylight this morning we are still in sight of the harbor. We are about ten miles off; it is a dead calm. The shipping in the harbor can be seen plainly, particularly the *Niagara*. At five P.M. all hands were called to exercise sail. As we had left our kroomen in Loando, thought we could not furl or loose sail as quickly as if we had them. We proved it otherwise: every man done his best and the sails were furled, loosed, and made quicker than any other time since the ship went into commission, so our captain said. A light wind now springing up, we shaped our course for the harbor and at nine P.M., (it being very dark, we dared not run in) we came to an anchor off Point Agustus and set quarter watches for the night. At twelve P.M., the watch being renewed, some of us missed our muster. The result was we had to toe a mark for four hours.

The Constellation *was in Bengo Bay, eight miles north of Loanda; what Leonard heard as "Point Augustus" is actually "Point Langosta," or Cape Langosta, the southwest terminus of the bay.*[2]

August 12th   at anchor in St Paul Loando

Sunday. At daylight we hove up the anchor and made sail for the harbor, and at ten A.M. we came to an anchor in our old place in seventeen fathoms water. The U.S. Steam Gun boat *Mystic* arrived here yesterday, having captured two vessels (they had no cargos). She sent them home with prize crews. The U.S. Steam Frigate *Niagara* is still coaling ship. At sundown we sent down Royal and Top Gallant Yards.

The Mystic *captured the brig* Thomas Achorn *off Kabenda in late June and the brig* Triton *off Loango in mid-July. When the skipper of the* Thomas Achorn *spotted the* Mystic, *he mistook it for a British steamer and flew the American flag (a reasonable error, as the* Mystic *was one of the first U.S. Navy steamers ever to appear on the African coast). Flying the American flag, he would be safe, as the United States did not sanction interference with American-flag ships by anyone. As it happened, though, the flag made him fair game for Lieutenant Commanding Le Roy's* Mystic. *No slaves were aboard, but the cargo and equipment made it clear what the brig's purpose was, and nobody in the crew denied it.*

The Triton, *of New Orleans, had no colors or papers, as they had been thrown overboard, and its name on the stern was painted over. It was learned that it had been sent to pick up the slaves originally purchased for the* Delicia, *which the* Constellation *had taken the previous December. Midn. Norman H. Farquhar, who earlier had taken the* Delicia *into Charleston, had returned to the squadron and had been put in charge of the* Triton's *prize crew. He arrived in Norfolk, Virginia, on August 24. The* Triton *was condemned and sold. The case in New York against the* Thomas Achorn *was dismissed.*

Midshipman Butt and Lt. James P. Foster were detached from the Constellation *to the* San Jacinto.

August 13th   a fat prize

The U.S. Steamer *Mohican* arrived here and came to an anchor. She has captured a large slaver having 997 negroes on board and a very valuable cargo of palm oil and ivory in her hold. She was taken off the Congo River, her name is the *Ariel,* and she belongs to New York. At two P.M. we went ashore in the gig and had a run till sundown, some of the boat's crew being very merry when they got on board the ship.

W. A. Leonard

The captured slaver was actually the Erie, *of New York, which had cleared from Havana on about January 20. None of the men aboard admitted to being either captain or mate, and many said they were just passengers. However, the Havana clearance paper named Nathaniel Gordon as captain. The* Mohican's *Captain Gordon did not believe Gordon's claim that he had sold the ship up the Congo and was now merely a passenger.*

Under the command of Lieutenant Dunnington and Midshipman Todd, the Erie's *prize crew first sailed to Monrovia to disembark the recaptured slaves. In the interval 130 recaptives died. After legal proceedings in New York, the ship was condemned and sold. More remarkably Captain Gordon was also found guilty of owning and commanding a slave ship and condemned to death. Despite appeals for clemency, President Lincoln approved the sentence, and on February 21, 1862, Nathaniel Gordon was hanged. He is the only person ever executed by the United States for being a slaver.*

August 14th 1860   St Paul de Loando
                                                running on a sand bar

This morning the captain visited the *Marion* and returned on board at noon. In the afternoon a large American vessel hove in sight. At four P.M. she got aground in crossing the bar. She immediately hoisted the American Ensign union down as a signal of distress. We sent all our boats to her assistance. So did the *Niagara, Marion, Mohican* and *Mystic* but before the boats reached her, she was afloat and at eight o'clock P.M. she came to an anchor astern of the *Niagara.* She proved to be a chartered coal ship sent here from Philadelphia. She has been 106 days coming out here. Her name is the *Sebastian Cabot.*

Midn. Wilburn Hall returned to the squadron aboard the Niagara.[3] *Spotting him when visiting the* Niagara, *Inman plucked him for his flagship to avoid the possibility of the* Constellation *being unable to send a captured slaver home for lack of an officer. Each prize sent home usually reduced the squadron by two officers as well as a dozen men. Because replacements were few and irregular and some officers were invalided home for various medical problems, lack of officers was chronic and at times acute. At this time the* Constellation's *sailmaker, G. D. Blackford, was being sent home for ill health, and Midshipman Kane was transferred to the* Mystic.[4] *The secretary of the navy repeatedly voiced strong disapproval of Inman's juggling of officers from ship to ship, though it seems to have been justified given the constant attrition.*

August 15th

Some of the Japanese ambassadors paid our ship a visit in company with the captain of the *Niagara.* On leaving they were honored with a salute of seventeen guns.

August 16th

The English Steam Sloop of War *Archer* arrived here in the afternoon. We took our captain on board of the *Archer.* Then they both went ashore to dine with Sir Henry Humphries, the English Minister at this port. We returned on board at sundown.

The Archer *was a twelve-gun screw sloop.*

August 17th   *Marion* ordered home/Theatre on board the *Archer.*

Early this morning the gig's crew went fishing. At nine A.M. the U.S. Steam Gun boat *Sumpter* arrived here, with the *Marion's* orders for home; the *Sumpter* got them from the *Portsmouth,* which vessel has had them four months. She will sail in a few days for Portsmouth, N.H. She has been in commission thirty-three months. In the evening our flag officer and captain went on board Her B. M. Steam Sloop of war *Archer* to witness a theatrical performance given by her crew. We had to wait for the captain and therefore had a chance to see it. The acting was very good indeed and everybody went away very well pleased.

August 18th 1860.   St Paul de Loando

Holystoned all decks. After breakfast all bags were piped up by an order from the 1st lieutenant to air clothing.

August 19th   another prize taken by the *San Jacinto*

Sunday at half past nine A.M. had division inspection, after which had a general muster and divine service in the gun deck. At twelve o'clock A.M. the U.S. Steam Frigate *San Jacinto* arrived here, and came to an anchor astern of us. She has taken a slaver with six hundred and seventy eight (678) negroes in her. She also brings us the news that the U.S. Sloop of War *Portsmouth* is at Prince's Island watering ship. In the afternoon the best part of the ship's company went visiting the other ships, and some of their men visited us. It is a beautiful Sunday afternoon.

Writing Secretary Toucey on August 14, Inman reported the San Jacinto *entering harbor as he wrote.[5] He then reported the* San Jacinto's *capture of the* Storm King, *taken a week earlier without papers and with 619 slaves on board. When that ship was leaving its home port of New York on May 1, 1860, it was under legal restraint as a suspected slaver, but the marshals sent to board it let it go on promise of a bribe of $1,500.[6] It was brought back to New York by a prize crew and condemned by the court, but first the recaptured slaves were taken to Liberia to become settlers there.*

August 20th   General court Martials on board the
Marion and *San Jacinto/Marion* sails for home

Today we brought our captain on board the U.S. Sloop of war *Marion*, as there is going to be a general court-martial on board of her, and our captain is a member of the court. They are going to try one of her men for striking the 1st lieutenant. As they fired the gun from the *Marion* another was fired from the U.S. Steam Frigate *San Jacinto* and the Jack run up to the masthead. They are [also] trying Lieutenant Charles McDonough for disobedience of orders; he has been under arrest for the last two months in our ship. At two P.M. the court-martial being over on board the *Marion*, she immediately hove up her anchor, and stood out of the harbor for home. We gave them three cheers, so did the *Niagara, Mohican,* and *San Jacinto*. After passing the last named vessel she made sail, and fired a salute of thirteen guns for our flag officer, which we returned with nine. She has been in commission about thirty-one months. We went on board the *San Jacinto* with our captain after supper and staid until ten P.M.

The Marion *went to Monrovia to drop off its kroomen and home from there. It had about forty sick men aboard, from its own crew and transferred from other ships, plus a half dozen officers being sent home for various reasons.*[7]

August 21st 1860.   St Paul de Loando/Negro Minstrels

This morning we went ashore in the gig and had a first rate run. In the evening most all of our boys went on board the *San Jacinto* to witness a negro minstrel performance, given by some of her crew. It was a very good exhibition and they deserve credit for it. Some of the *Niagara's, Mohican's, Mystic's* and *Sumpter's* crews were there and all of their officers.

August 22nd   sailing of the *Niagara*

This day the U.S. Steam Frigate *Niagara* sailed for Japan. She is going to stop at Cape Town, and several other places. In the evening we sent up our Top Gallant and Royal yards. We are going to sea tomorrow.

August 23d   going to sea/up anchor

This morning we took in all boats and got up the messenger. And at two P.M. we got underway in company with H.B.M. Steam Sloop of War *Archer*. We have got very light winds. We are not to remain out very long.

After a long and acrimonious exchange of letters, Inman suspended Commander Godon from command of the Mohican, *intending a court-martial for insubordination.*[8] *The* Mohican's *first lieutenant, Lieutenant Patterson, relieved him.*

August 24th   at sea

A dead calm, exercised the gun deck batteries. St Paul still in sight. We are now heading for it. The *Archer* is to leeward, firing at target. At three o'clock P.M. we came to an anchor in St. Paul de Loando and at sundown Royal yards. [*That is, they brought down the royal yards, as was customary every day in port or at anchor.*]

August 25th   again in St. Paul de Loando

This morning we got out all boats, and commenced taking in wood, and water. As the U.S. Steam Gun boat *Mystic* is short of men, we sent about fifteen men

HMS *Arrogant*. Photograph © National Maritime Museum, Greenwich, London, Image A8115.

to her and a midshipman to make out her complement. Finished taking in wood and water at sundown.

August 26th

Sunday at 10 A.M. all hands, were called to muster, after which had divine service on the gun deck as usual. At one P.M. the U.S. Sloop of war *Portsmouth* arrived here; in the afternoon I went on board of her to visit.

August 27th 1860.   St Paul de Loando/Death on board the *Arrogant*

In the afternoon H.B.M. Steam Frigate *Arrogant* (being the admiral's ship) arrived here and came to an anchor, the shock of which caused the death of one of her lieutenants. He has been sick some time; out of respect for his memory she did not salute us. We went alongside of her in the gig. The lieutenant will be buried tomorrow.

The Arrogant *was a forty-six-gun steam screw frigate with a crew of five hundred.*

August 28th   Burying a lieutenant in port/the Funeral Cortege,/ arrival at the Landing the procession on shore/ arrival at the cemetery/Burial

Funeral of one of the Lieutenants of H.B.M. Steam Frigate *Arrogant* at St Paul de Loando August 28th 1860

At two P.M. preparations were made on board the English admiral's ship to bury the lieutenant. At half past two the flags of all the shipping in the harbor were hoisted at half mast and the cortege began to move. All the boats of the *Arrogant, Archer, Falcon, Spitfire* and *Buffalo* (English) [and] *Constellation, Portsmouth, Mohican, Mystic,* and *Sumpter* (American) formed in two lines. The band came first, playing a dead march, after which came the launch towing the pinnace, which had the coffin in it. All the Marines were in the launch, then came all the English and American boats with all the officers in them formed in two lines, the English on the right of the body and the Americans on the left. The English admiral in the rear of his boats, and our flag officer in his barge brought up the rear of our boats. They pulled with muffled oars to the landing place, which is about three and a half miles from where we are lying at anchor, the band playing a dead march all the way. On arriving at the landing, the body was placed upon a howitzer carriage (brought ashore from the admiral's ship expressly for the occasion). The procession was then formed, the band came first playing a dead march, then came the body drawn by twenty of the *Arrogant*'s crew with eight of his brother officers as pall bearers. After the body came all the English and American officers on foot. Next came the civic and military officers of the city followed by the English admiral and our flag officer in a barouche, drawn by six horses. Next in order was the Marines belonging to the different English vessels; they numbered about 200. The next in order was the blue jackets to the number of 700 hundred; they marched 4 deep. They brought up the rear of the procession.

After marching an hour and a half we arrived at the cemetery, which is three miles from the landing, followed by thousands of the natives. The impressive service of the Church of England was then read, and his body lowered into the grave, in the midst of three volleys of musketry fired by the Marine Corps. Minute guns were fired from the admiral's ship during the entire route of the procession. The funeral throughout was a very solemn affair. At six P.M. we returned on board of our own ship, very much impressed with the events of the day's proceedings.[9]

August 29th

At eight o'clock the English admiral's ship *Arrogant* saluted our flag officer with thirteen guns and we returned him fifteen; she also saluted the Portuguese flag with twenty-one guns. We are taking in a supply of wood and water.

McDonough's court-martial was now in progress.[10]

August 30th 1860

My Birthday. The U.S. Steamer *San Jacinto* sailed today for the Congo River. Very warm here at present.

August 31st

The division and mess bills came out for next month. In the afternoon the English steam Sloop of war *Archer* sailed for St. Helena in order to give her men liberty.

September 1860

Today all hands are drawing clothing and small stores. In the afternoon we went ashore in the gig and had a good run. We returned on board at sundown.

September 2nd   **Sunday**

Sunday at half past nine A.M. had a division inspection, all hands dressed in blue frocks, white trousers, and hats. At ten A.M. had a general muster, read the Articles of War and passed round the capstan, after which divine service on the gun deck. In the afternoon the men were allowed to visit the other men of war lying in the harbor.

September 3d   **arrival**

All hands washed clothes at eleven o'clock A.M. a large steam frigate [the *Bartholomew Diaz*] arrived here, which proved to be the Portuguese admiral's ship. The Prince of Portugal, (the present King's brother) is acting as admiral. We gave him a salute of twenty-one guns, as also did the *Arrogant,* which salutes were returned from the frigate. The forts on shore also saluted him. There is great excitement about him ashore; in the evening the City of St Paul de Loando was illuminated for him. He is on a visit to all of the Portuguese possessions on this coast.

Lieutenant McDonough's court-martial was over, sentence approved. He tendered his resignation, apparently on grounds of ill health, and went home on the merchant bark Ann & Mary.[1]

September 4th   **prince ashore**

Today our flag officer paid an official visit to the Prince of Portugal on board of his own ship, and on his leaving they fired a salute of thirteen guns, which was returned from our ship. The Prince went ashore in the afternoon and was received at the landing by all the nobility. The city was illuminated in the evening.

September 5th 1860   St Paul de Loando

Today we are watering ship. In the afternoon our flag officer and captain went on board the *Arrogant* to dine; after supper the captain went ashore and returned at sundown.

September 6th

Today a Spanish barque arrived here. She is a very suspicious looking craft and we are watching her movements very closely.

September 7th

Today we are very busy getting ready for sea. Took in all boats and at sundown we sent up Top Gallant and Royal yards. The English Steam Gun boat *Spitfire* sailed at seven P.M. for the Congo River. Two Spanish Man of war Gunboats arrived here from Havana. They are bound to Manila; they put in here for coal.

Meanwhile, Inman decided not to court-martial Commander Godon, but to restore him to command of the Mohican, *which was ready for sea after caulking and loading supplies.*

Also, Sailmaker Blackford of the Constellation *had been sent home on the* Marion *for health reasons.*

September 8th   visit of a Prince/arrival of his highness/
manning yards/saluting

Visit of Don Louis, Prince of Portugal, to the U.S. Sloop of War, *Constellation*, Flag officer W.H. Inman September 8th 1860

At two P.M. preparations were made to receive Don Louis of Portugal, politically known as the Duke of Oporto, now acting as Admiral and having command of all the naval forces belonging to the crown of Portugal. His brother Don Pedro is now king. At half past two o'clock his Royal Highness arrived on board, on which occasion the yards were manned, all hands being dressed in white frocks, blue trousers, and caps. It gave the ship quite a beautiful appearance. All hands were then called to quarters to be received by the Prince. He remained on board about an hour, and on his leaving, the yards were manned as before, and a salute of thirteen guns was fired for him as Commodore, which salute was returned by the Portuguese frigate. He is quite young, being 21 years of age. He is said to be a very good sailor. He is of a very fair complexion and in height about five and a half [feet].

When King Pedro V died in a cholera epidemic in November 1861, the Duke of Oporto became King Luis I. With a strong interest in science and especially oceanography, he financed research voyages and founded a major aquarium in Lisbon.

Going to sea/exciting time/no damage done/At sea

At four o'clock P.M. all hands were very busy making preparations to get underway. At half past four we hove short, and made sail and was just heaving up the anchor, when it was discovered we were drifting rather too close to the English admiral's ship, the *Arrogant*. We braced the yards up sharp and tried to cross her bow; we had barely cleared her when it was discovered that our anchor that had been dragging all this time had caught the chain of the frigate, which accident brought us up all standing. The wind, now catching our sails aback, was fast drifting us down upon the frigate. It now appeared to both ships' companies that there would be a fearful collision; however both ships paid out cable, and as if by a miracle the wind caught our sails on the other tack, and just brought us clear of the *Arrogant's* bow; not, however, before she had rigged in her flying jib boom (all hands in both ships being long before called to their stations for saving ship). We still kept paying out chain, and we again swung close under her stern, thereby taking a round turn in her cable. It was a miracle that we did not come together. If we had, it is the opinion of all, that there would be several lives lost. As we were now out of danger and at anchor astern of the *Arrogant,* she lowered a boat and sent a lieutenant on board of us to know if we were in want of any assistance. We thanked him very kindly and told him no. We again made sail, slipped our cable 115 fathoms, and stood out of the harbor with a very good breeze. We are going to the Congo River for two weeks.

Slipping the cable meant the anchor chain was run out to its full length into the water so the ship could leave it and the anchor behind, departing without taking the time to sort things out to weigh anchor. A buoy attached to the end of the cable (in addition to the customary buoy on the anchor itself) permitted retrieving the chain and anchor when the ship returned to Loando.

September 9th 1860.   St Paul de Loando/at Sea/
sail ho./Shifted into the main Top

Sunday. All hands were called to quarters for inspection at half past nine A.M., after which had divine service on the gun deck. During the services a sail was reported by the masthead lookout bearing broad on our weather beam, she is supposed to be the U.S. Steamer *Mohican*. At eleven A.M. another sail was reported on our weather bow. At twelve o'clock we spoke her; she proved to be an English barque loaded with coal bound for St. Paul de Loando. Land still in sight at two P.M. I was called aft to the 1st lieutenant's desk, and by him shifted into the Main Top as topsail yard man No 116: At tacking and reefing, at the lee Main Topsail brace; in getting underway, paying down cable on the gun deck; coming to an anchor, in the Main Top; at loosing and furling sail, on the Main Topsail yard.

With his reassignment Leonard received a whole new set of stations and associated duties. However, he remained in the crew of the captain's gig.

September 10th   sail ho/company/court martial

At daylight a sail was reported which proved to be the U.S. Steam Gun boat *Sumpter.* Signalized to her to come within hail, which she did. Our flag officer then gave her orders to keep company with the flagship until further orders. His object in doing this was in case a sail hove in sight he could send her to see what it was. It being very calm, at ten A.M. a sail was reported on our lee bow. Sent the *Sumpter* to ascertain what she was. At two P.M. she returned, and reported the sail to be the U.S. Sloop of war *Portsmouth.* In the afternoon two of our men were tried by a court-martial, one for theft and the other for cutting a krooman with a knife. After supper the 1st division exercised big guns, the 2nd division small arms, and the 3d division single sticks. The powder divisions were exercised with carbines. It is very calm weather here at present. The *Sumpter* is in company with us yet; her light was to be seen all night.

September 11th 1860   at Sea/sail ho/a Whaler

Foggy weather with a light rain. At six A.M. a sail was reported on our weather beam, which proved to be the U.S. Steamer *Mohican.* At ten A.M. another sail was reported a point on our weather bow, which turned out to be the U.S.S. *Portsmouth.* At eleven A.M. the lookout on the Main Topsail yard reported another sail on our lee bow, which proved to be an American whaling barque. At seven P.M. a boat from the whaler came alongside. Her captain stated he was short of provisions. Our flag officer told him to keep in sight until morning and he would furnish him with what he wanted. Very pleasant weather, with a light wind, two lights in sight all night, one the whaler's, and the other the *Sumpter*'s. At twelve o'clock midnight we hove to until morning.

September 12th   U.S.S *Portsmouth*

At seven o'clock this morning a sail was seen two points on our weather bow, sent the *Sumpter* in chase. At nine A.M. got out two boats and filled them with provisions for the whaler; she in return gave us 550 gallons of sperm oil. At two P.M. the *Sumpter* returned, and reported the sail to be the *Portsmouth.* She is coming towards us. All the divisions are exercising large guns. At five P.M. we spoke the *Portsmouth.* Our flag officer ordered her to keep in sight until morning. In the midnight watch a light was reported on our weather bow, supposed to be on the land.

September 13th

Early in the morning we made signals to the *Portsmouth,* to send a boat on board the flag ship. The flag officer gave her his orders, we then made all sail and stood before the wind, very light wind and foggy weather. At two P.M. lost sight of the *Portsmouth;* the *Sumpter* is still in company with us.

W.A. Leonard

September 14th 1860.   at Sea/sail ho

At seven A.M. a sail was reported on our weather bow. At ten A.M. the drum beat to general quarters; exercised the port battery. The sail reported proved to be the *Portsmouth.* At five o'clock P.M. all hands exercised sail. The *Sumpter* still in company with us.

September 15th   sail ho/*San Jacinto*

At daylight a sail was reported which proved to be the U.S. Steamer *San Jacinto.* We signalized to her to come within hail, which she did, and her captain came on board of us. We then gave her some oil, and then stood on our cruise. At one P.M. a sail was reported on our weather bow; she proved to be an English cruiser.

September 16th   Whales

Sunday morning all hands were called to quarters at half past nine A.M. for inspection, after which church was held on the gun deck. A school of whales are playing close to the ship. At seven P.M. the flag officer hailed the *Sumpter,* and ordered her to keep in sight till when he then would part with her. I had a lookout from eight until ten first watch.

September 17th

A very beautiful morning. The *Sumpter* quite close to us. At three P.M. we parted with the U.S. Steam Gun boat *Sumpter.* We then stood in for the land. At seven P.M. we passed a floating island and at nine o'clock we hove to for the night.

September 18th   land ho

At daylight we wore ship and stood in for the land. At six A.M. land was reported. On nearing it we discovered the U.S. Steamer *Mystic,* at anchor, signalized to her to get underway. Our flag officer gave her his orders. We then made sail and stood on our course. This is called Loango Bay. The divisions exercised after supper. At half past five o'clock P.M. we sighted a large sperm whale. Fine weather and a good breeze.

September 19th 1860.   at sea

At three P.M. the 3d division exercised large guns, the 2nd division small arms and the 1st division single sticks. Very dark and foggy all night. The port watch eight hours in. All sail set.

September 20th   another race with the *Portsmouth*/beat her again

At half past two P.M. a sail was reported on our lee bow; we bore down to her and made her out to be the U.S. Sloop of war *Portsmouth*. She hove to in order to let us come up with her. On passing her she made sail and stood right in our wake. Her object was soon discovered, she wanted to try her sailing qualities again, they were not satisfied with the beating they got. They said that their bottom was foul then, and it now being very clean they thought they would beat us this time, but it was of no use, we beat her worse than before. I guess this will take the conceit out of them. At eight P.M. she was out of sight astern. It is a splendid moonlight night. Tacked ship several times during the night.

September 21st

Early this morning a sail was reported, which proved to be an English man of war steamer. At seven A.M. another sail was reported bearing broad on our lee bow. At eight A.M. we lost sight of it. In the afternoon the gun deck divisions were exercised at big guns, small arms and single sticks. At eight o'clock P.M. we shortened sail and then hove to for the night. Had a pleasant weather all day and a good wind.

September 22nd   sail ho

Early this morning a sail hove in three points on our weather bow, standing right down for us. She proved to be the U.S. Steamer *San Jacinto*. On making us out she stood in the opposite direction and we soon lost sight of her. Another sail was reported which proved to be a Portuguese brig of war. We then hove to for the night.

September 23d 1860   at sea/General Muster

Sunday all hands were called to quarters at half past nine o'clock in the forenoon, for inspection, after which had a general muster. The Articles of War was read by the 1st lieutenant, after which all hands went round the capstan answering to their name and rate. At ten o'clock saw a large school of whales. Had a wheel from two till four. At seven P.M. we took in sail. Had a good wind all day. In the midwatch [from midnight to 4:00 A.M.] it died away to a dead calm.

The capture of the slave bark *Cora*. *New York Illustrated News*, December 22, 1860. Historic Ships of Baltimore.

September 24th 1860   Fishing

At nine A.M. a sail was reported on our weather bow, which proved to be the U.S. Steamer *San Jacinto;* she is coming down to us. This forenoon the forecastle men caught enough fish (bonitas) to furnish all the messes. They also caught two large sharks, one being seven feet five inches in length. It is a dead calm. The gun deck divisions were exercised at their usual drill. At one P.M. the *San Jacinto* was quite close to us. She sent a boat alongside of us, her captain coming in it. There is a summary court martial going on now—one of the men struck a krooman. Several of our officers visited the *San Jacinto* in the evening and returned at 9 P.M. Very warm during the night; it is a dead calm.

September 25th 1860.   Sail ho.

The *San Jacinto* is in company with us at 9 [A].M. we gave her some provisions and at three P.M. we parted with her. Very warm; there is a five knot breeze blowing. At four P.M. a sail was reported on our lee beam. We squared away and stood down to her, set all our studding sails and at six P.M. we made her out to be the U.S. Steamer *San Jacinto*. We then took in the studding sails and hauled close on the wind starboard tack aboard. We now had a good stiff breeze going about nine knot.

1860.   at sea/sail ho

At seven bells in the last dog watch, the lookout on the starboard cat head reported a sail on our weather bow, about two miles off. She perceived us about the same time; she immediately braced her yards up sharp and stood close on a wind. It was a splendid moonlight night, the moon being then at its full. We gave her chase, but I will try and give an account of the chase, in good shape, beginning on the other page.

U.S. Flag Ship Constellation

William J. Martin		Boston Mass
	at Ira B. Shaws	No 5½ Bromfield
		Street,

Mary E. Leonard		Charlestown Mass
	at Home	

This Journal is kept by William A. Leonard of Bunker Hill Charlestown Mass U.S.A.

Wm Sennott. {5½} Boston Mass

Mary E. Leonard   Brothers
Jane A. Leonard   and
James Leonard   Sisters
Catherine Leonard
Charles Leonard
Ellen M. Leonard

Mary E. Carroll address 13 Everett St Charlestown, Mass.

Mary L. and Anna M. Moloney
                 address 13 Everett st Charlestown Mass.

Chase, and Capture of the American Slave Barque *Cora* of New York, with 705 negroes in her. By the United States Flag Ship *Constellation*. September 25th 1860

It was a beautiful moonlight evening. Just as the messenger boy of the watch had struck six bells, the lookout stationed on the starboard cathead reported a sail on our weather bow standing right down to us with studding sails set on both sides. On seeing us she hauled down her studding sails, and hauled up sharp on the wind. We no sooner saw this than we did the same, she being about two points on our weather bow, about 2 miles ahead of us. We could see that she had on every stitch of canvas that would draw, determined to outsail us if she could. At half past eight o'clock we saw that we had gained considerable on her.

By this time there was not a man or boy on board of us, but what was up on deck witnessing the chase, and full of excitement as to whether she was a slaver or not, some betting she was and others she was not. We were fast gaining on her. At half past nine o'clock No 1 gun's crew were called to quarters, and loaded their gun with shot. Soon after we hove a shot across her forefoot, in order to make her heave to. But she still continued on her course. Now the boys were all excitement, not one of the watch below could sleep a wink, they were all on the spar deck, watching the barque. She now began to fall to leeward, and we were fast gaining on her. At ten o'clock we fired another shot at her, but it was of no use, she kept right on. She now was only a half a mile ahead of us. She now cut away one of her quarter boats, she done this as a decoy: she thought that we would heave to for the boat and give them a chance to get away. We could see that there was nobody in the boat, so that was no go. As we were now to windward of her, we set the fore topmast studding sail. They now saw plainly we were gaining on them fast. They set all their port studding sails, and kept off a point or two, and then commenced throwing overboard water casks, spars, booby hatches, kedge anchors, and in fact everything that was moveable in order to lighten her.

We were now within hailing distance of her; our captain gave an order to fire one more shot at her, and then if she did not heave to, to fire a shell into her. The shot was fired, which cut away her fore topmast studding sail halliards, but still she would not heave to. But on hearing our captain give the order to load the gun with shell, and prime, they backed their main topsail and hove to. We also hove to. Our captain then hailed her and ordered her to clew down her royals, and haul up her courses, which she did very slowly.

We then lowered the 4th cutter and sent her to board the barque, each man being armed with a pistol and cutlass, our 1st lieutenant and sailing master having command of the boat. We were now about fifty yards from her; we could see our party boarding her very plainly, the moon shining very brightly about this time. Pretty soon our 1st lieutenant hailed our ship in the following style: "*Constellation* Ahoy!" "Halloa," was answered from our ship. "We have got a fine fat prize, chock full of darkies," was the rejoinder. On hearing this, our ship's company gave three hearty cheers, which made the welkin ring. Our captain now gave orders to lower away the gig and bring her captain, mates and crew on board of our ship. Your Humble Servant, being one of the gig's crew, had an opportunity of seeing the Elephant.

When we got alongside of her, the officers and crew of the slaver were ordered into our boat by the 1st lieutenant. They numbered twenty-nine in all. [*The list sent the secretary of the navy numbered twenty-five.*] The captain, 1st and 2nd mates, and a passenger supposed to be the super cargo we left on board. We then took the crew to our own ship and then returned to the prize. This being the first slaver I ever saw with slaves in, my curiosity led me upon the slave deck. The scene which here presented itself to my eyes baffles description. It was a dreadful sight. They were all packed together like so many sheep—men, woman, and children entirely naked, and suffering from hunger and thirst. They had nothing to eat or drink for over 30 hours. As soon as the poor negroes were aware that we were friends to them, they commenced a shouting and yelling like so many wild Indians. They were so overjoyed at being taken by us that I thought they would tear us to pieces. We then took the supercargo (not however before leaving men enough on board the barque to take care of her until the morning) and then returned to our own ship.

On getting aboard, our boys crowded around us, to get the news. It being now eight bells or twelve o'clock midnight and my watch below, I went down and turned into my hammock to dream over the events of the night. Being very tired I soon fell asleep.

Adieu, W.A.L.

September 26th

At four o'clock this morning, it being our watch on deck, the men stood gazing at the barque, which is but a very little ways astern of us, talking about what a splendid prize she is. They are not far out of the way, for she is indeed a beauty, everything about her being perfect. She sailed from New York and has been out here three months, laying the best part of that time in the Congo River. On the night of the 24th of this month, she took in her niggers. The night being very cloudy, they made sail and stood out to sea, and in so doing they ran right into our sight. It was bad for them, but first rate for us. At six o'clock A.M. a sail was reported from the mast head on our weather beam. At seven A.M. we lost sight of it.

In the afternoon a prize crew of nine men and three marines was picked out, and at five P.M. they were sent aboard of her. I now had another chance of visiting her and I must say she is a perfect model of beauty, everything in tip top condition. Our boatswain and a gang of men are to work setting up her rigging, the barque's crew having slacked up all her shrouds, and backstays in order to make her sail faster. We have been lying to all day, with the main topsail aback. Our boats have been very busy all day running to and from the barque. There is considerable to find out who is captain of her; it appears that she had two separate crews with two captains, one crew being Spanish and the other American. They are going to send the Americans home, and let the others go when we get back to St. Paul de Loando. The passenger is to go with them. He is a New Yorker.

Slavers to the West African coast typically carried two captains and often two crews. An American captain and crew were part of the American identity the ship retained until the slaves were aboard. The American flag, papers, and captain protected the ship from interference by the British, whose treaty arrangements enabled them to interdict ships of most other nations trading on the African coast but who were denied such privilege by the U.S. government.

Once the slaves were aboard, however, the risks changed. An American slave captain or sailor arrested by the U.S. Navy could be convicted of piracy under U.S. law, with a possible death sentence. Such extreme measures did not apply to non-Americans (indeed they were not prosecuted by U.S. authorities) so just before the presence of slaves aboard made a ship undeniably a slaver, the American captain would turn it over to the non-American captain, with a "sale" of the ship. The new captain and crew then took the ship and slave cargo westward across the Atlantic. For the same reasons, any American found aboard a slave ship would claim either to be of some other nationality or else that he was merely a passenger.

September 27th 1860.   at sea/Slaver gets her orders/
                                           she sails for home cheering

This day, we sent ten of the barque's crew (Americans) also the captain and two mates, also Americans, on board of her; they are to be brought home to be tried. Our flag officer then put her in charge of our sailing master, Thomas Eastman, and Midshipman Hall. She will go to Monrovia to land her slaves and then to Norfolk, Virginia. At three o'clock in the afternoon, all business being settled, we hoisted in all our boats, the barque squared away and stood on her course, we also stood on our course. We then manned the rigging and gave her three hearty cheers, which they returned with interest. She now set all her port studding sails and hoisted the American ensign at her peak and a pennant at the main. It was thus we parted with the slave barque *Cora* of New York.

Master Thomas H. Eastman and Midn. Wilburn Hall, with four seamen, three ordinary seamen, four landsmen, and three marines, were the prize crew. They went first to Monrovia to land the recaptives, of whom 694 out of 705 were landed alive—a very high percentage. From Liberia they sailed for Norfolk for legal proceedings. Three slave ship officers and Charles the cabin boy went with them as prisoners; Capt. John Latham and eight others were sent to New York aboard the supply ship Relief; *two crewmen joined the crew of the* Constellation; *the remaining crewmen were landed on the African coast.*

Inman's letter of September 26 to the civil authority stated that the Cora *was taken at eleven o'clock after a chase of three and a half hours and that "several guns loaded with shot were fired toward her, but not to touch her. She made every effort to escape, by throwing overboard a boat, a wooden hatch, casks, spars, etc."*

According to Morgan Frederick, who claimed to be the first officer, the ship had left New York under John Latham on June 27 and had arrived at Punta da Lenha, Congo River, on August 27. It had anchored off Mangal Grande on September 24 and taken the slaves aboard at eleven that night. Twenty-four hours later the ship was taken by the Constellation.

Leonard did not mention that one lucky sailor received from Captain Nicholas a $50 reward for being first to sight a slaver. For the future Nicholas raised the prize to $120 after the wardroom officers kicked in $50 and the steerage officers offered $20.[2]

September 28th   sail ho/Court martial/Death/gloomy

At six A.M. land was reported on our lee beam. At half past ten A.M. a sail was reported from the masthead; it proved to be the English man of war steamer *Spitfire.* At eleven A.M. three small sails were discovered lying at anchor close under the land. At three P.M. another sail was reported two points on our lee bow, which proved to be a sailboat. Today one of our men was tried and sentenced to lose three months' pay by a summary court-martial for disobeying orders. At six P.M. Corporal James Edwards died with disease of the heart; he belonged to the Marine Corps, and has been twenty-one years in the Naval service. He was respected by the whole ship's company. He is to be buried tomorrow. It makes all hands feel gloomy. The land has been in sight all day on our lee beam. We are now heading for St Paul de Loando. We expect to be there in a few days.

W.A. Leonard

September 29th 1860.   **at sea/Burial of Corporal Edwards/ hove to/general quarters at night/a yarn**

At nine o'clock in the forenoon the hands were called to Bury the Dead. The body of Corporal Edwards was brought on deck by his messmates, the ensign was hoisted at half mast and the band playing the dead march, the Marines were drawn up in the Starboard Gangway. On placing his body down, the drum was rolled, it being muffled, after which the funeral service was read by our 4th lieutenant, and his body consigned to the deep by his brothers in arms, who fired three volleys of musketry over him, after which the boatswain piped.

The port watch holystoned the gun deck in the afternoon. All hands signed accounts with the purser. He then served out grog and ration money. It now being dark and being close to land, we hove to for the night. At eleven o'clock the ship's bell rung for fire, and the drum beat to general fire quarters. After going through several important maneuvers, it being twelve o'clock, the drum beat to retreat.

It is laughable to see the confusion there is when the drum beats to general quarters at night. All the hammocks are down and the watch below asleep. All hands must lash up their hammocks, with only three turns, and put them in the nettings and then go to their gun or station and cast loose their gun ready for action. (The guns which are first reported are the bullies of the ship, and there is no end to their blowing.) Then the watch below is piped down by the boatswain and the usual routine again commences. I had a lookout on the port quarter in the middle watch, which time was spent in listening to a long yarn about the *Columbia* Frigate, spun by an old quarter master by the name of Daniel Malone.

September 30th 1860.   **at sea/land ho./came to an anchor**

Sunday morning land in sight at six to port. We tacked ship, and stood in to the land. At half past six a sail was reported which proved to be a Portuguese man of war brig. At half past nine o'clock, all hands were called to quarters for inspection, after which had divine service on the gun deck. At half past two P.M. we came to an anchor in St. Paul de Loando. The U.S. Gun boat *Mystic* is here. At nine o'clock in the evening a vessel was burning blue lights off the mouth of the harbor. It is supposed to be the store ship *Relief,* which is expected here.

October 1860

at St Paul de Loando/
arrival of the Store ship *Relief*

At daybreak, the U.S. Store Ship *Relief* was discovered lying at anchor, off the point. At six o'clock she got underway and stood in, and at half past seven A.M. she came to an anchor, inside of it. She is loaded with stores, and is from the Charlestown Navy Yard. We got a large mail bag from her; I got some letters and papers, which I am very thankful for. After breakfast all hands were very busy in getting up our anchor and chain which we left here the last time we were here. At twelve o'clock the anchor was cat headed and the decks was washed down. At two bells all hands were piped to dinner. My boatkeeping day. At three P.M. the gig went ashore with the captain and returned at sundown, after which all hands swung clean hammocks. We are going to take in wood, water and provisions while we lie here.

W.A.L.

To "cat head" or "cat" an anchor was to haul the anchor's crown snug against a large timber (the cathead) projecting from that side of the bow. Then the upper part of the anchor was swung up against the side of the ship and lashed there, "fished." This secured the anchor, preventing it from swinging into the side of the ship when the ship was under way.

The newspapers (from July and earlier) devoted much coverage to the Italian war, including Garibaldi's triumphant entry into Naples. Considerable ink was also devoted to the balls, receptions, and other activities involving the Japanese delegation, whom the men of the Constellation *had already encountered when the* Niagara *stopped at St. Paul de Loando back in early August.*

October 2nd 1860   St Paul de Loando/Pete Campbell the Slaver/
                          we have got the Captain of the Yacht *Wanderer*

This morning we commenced to take in wood, water, and provisions. We have
still got the Spanish captain and crew, also the American passenger of the
barque, on board of us. They are going to be sent ashore here, [except] two
of them have shipped with us. The passenger, who (by the way) is named Pete
Campbell, is a very comical fellow, he is about 5 feet 8 inches in height, of
a stout frame, and a very good looking man. He has an eye, like an eagle's,
which pierces through you when he looks at you. I say he is a comical man on
account of his propensities for making fun. He has sailed out of New York as
mate, and he says he was a passenger in the barque, but there is not a shadow
of a doubt but what he is either her captain or in some way connected with
the vessel. But the crew stick together like bricks and they all tell one story.

At eleven A.M. the captain of the *Mystic* came on board of us, when the
slaver's crew were brought before him. The *Mystic* boarded the *Cora* the day
before she was taken. He identified the Spaniard as being her captain; he also
gave us the startling news that he is the—or was the—captain of the celebrated
Yacht *Wanderer*, of which there has been so much talk about. His name is
Latham. He was immediately put in irons. He will be sent home in the store
ship. He is a very gentlemanly looking man of a light complexion; he is master
of several languages. The rest of the barque's crew will be set at liberty tomorrow. They feel very bad about their captain. He says himself he is not what
they represent him to be, and he is confident of being released when he gets to
the United States.

The yacht Wanderer *was indeed a celebrated case. The Atlantic slave trade
had for decades involved importing slaves to Brazil or Cuba, with few if any
being brought into the United States, which American law made too difficult
and dangerous. Wealthy Charlestonians financed the* Wanderer's *slaving voyage partly out of the usual desire for profit but also as a challenge to the laws
against importing slaves into the United States. The elegantly outfitted yacht
sailed from New York in June 1858 on what was purportedly a gentlemanly
tour to Africa. At an appropriate time, the gentlemen crammed aboard nearly
five hundred slaves, brought out in canoes from Kabenda, north of the mouth
of the Congo River. As the yacht departed, the USS* Vincennes *spotted it and
tried to intercept, but with the* Wanderer *going twenty knots to the* Vincennes's
*eight and a half, the pursuit was hopeless. The four hundred plus slaves who
survived the passage across the Atlantic were landed six weeks later on Jekyll
Island, Georgia.[1] Legal actions against various men involved were ultimately
fruitless, though the vessel itself was condemned and sold at auction—to be*

bought by Charles Lamar, one of the original backers. In the course of the legal defense efforts, unsuccessful attempts were made to challenge the constitutionality of laws against importing slaves to the United States and elsewhere.

The claim that the captain of the Cora, who when first arrested called himself "Loretto Ruiz" but later said he was John Latham, had been the captain of the Wanderer is apparently recorded in no contemporary document other than Leonard's journal.[2] The identity of slave ship captains, as was the case here, was often very obscure, as being an American and a slaver captain made one vulnerable to hanging for piracy. False names and false nationalities were common, as with "Latham," who claimed initially to be Ruiz from Spain and simply a passenger rather than a member of the crew, much less captain.[3] Latham was later described as "a fine-looking man, about five feet ten inches in height, light complexion, with light hair and whiskers, large, prominent, light eyes, and having the look of a German or Dane."[4] Though the identities of the men on the Wanderer were clear, the question of which should be called the captain was not, and it is not clear which Lieutenant Le Roy of the Mystic might have been looking at. All the subsequent official correspondence and legal paperwork, however, identifies the man taken on the Cora by the name "John Latham." At least in his taste in ships and standard of shipboard living, Latham closely resembled the gentlemen of the Wanderer. The Cora was a fine, fast ship beautifully maintained, and the New York Times noted that "in [Cora's] cabin was found every luxury suitable for a tropical climate, consisting of the choicest wines, preserved meats, fruits. &c., &c." Indeed the customhouse clerk remarked that "probably no vessel ever cleared from New York with so complete a cargo for a 'pleasure excursion' except the Wanderer."[5] The Boston Daily Advertiser's correspondent reported that a boatload of luxurious food and wines was transferred to the Constellation for the benefit of the wardroom officers.[6]

Whatever his real identity or other false identities, while jailed in New York awaiting trial, Latham was taken shopping for new clothes. At Brooks Brothers' store, he slipped away from his escort, not to be seen again. The mate, Morgan Frederick, by his own account later, escaped from the ship's cabin while anchored out in New York Harbor by bribing his guard, then picked up his baggage from the local marshal and disappeared. A year and a half later, he was identified and arrested while serving as a U.S. Navy master's mate aboard the New York receiving ship North Carolina.[7]

As for the Cora itself, after completion of the legal process, it was sold at auction at Elizabethport, New Jersey. The buyer, according to the New York Times, immediately fitted it out to return to Africa for another load of slaves.[8]

October 3d 1860   at St. Paul de Loando/Dancing

We are still taking in provisions. At ten o'clock, the slaver's crew were sent ashore. At two P.M. the gig's crew went ashore, where we fell in with Pete Campbell. We had several drinks together. At sundown we returned on board, when the boys had a grand dance in the foretopmen's gangway. The ship's band furnished the music. At nine P.M. all hands were piped into their hammocks.

Leonard's description of Pete Campbell accords with that given by Wilburn Hall in his narration decades later of his experience with the Cora. *Hall says Campbell got away from Loanda with the help of Masonic brothers, then took passage to Cuba aboard another slave ship. The two met a bit later on the street in New York, and again four years after the Civil War, at which time, Hall reported, Campbell was performing as a circus clown.*[9]

October 4th

This day the U.S. Sloop of War *Portsmouth* arrived here from the Congo River. We are still taking in provisions.

October 5th

Today we finished taking provisions. The Store Ship *Relief* finished taking out her cargo. We went ashore in the gig on an errand for the captain; we returned at sundown.

The Relief *returned to the United States, taking the captain and eight of the crew of the* Cora *for legal proceedings.*[10]

October 6th

In the afternoon the U.S. Steam Gun boat *Sumpter* arrived here with our mail from the island of Fernando Po. We were very busy all day taking in small stores. We are going to sea next Monday for a short cruise around the mouth of the Congo River.

October 7th   getting ready for sea

Sunday. This morning all hands were called to quarters for inspection, after which divine service was held on the gun deck. In the afternoon some of the men visited the different ships in port as is the custom on every Sunday. At five o'clock we took in all boats, and sent up Top Gallant and Royal Yards. The *Portsmouth, Mystic* and *Sumpter* are the vessels lying here now belonging to the squadron.

October 8th 1860. **St Paul de Loando/leaving St Paul**

This day we are getting ready for sea. At three P.M. we got underway, made sail and went to sea. At six P.M. we had a strong wind from the N.E. Very squally during the night. My lookout from ten till twelve.

At Inman's order (as was his general practice), the Portsmouth *left late at night, to avoid its departure being seen and reported through the slavers' excellent intelligence network all along the coast.*

October 9th **at sea/land ho/she turns out to be a whaler**

At two P.M. land was reported on our lee bow, which proved to be Ambriz, which is a little to the southward of Congo River. At three P.M. a sail was reported on our lee bow. We made sail and bore away for her, and at half past seven P.M. we overhauled her. The drum beat to general quarters, we lowered the 4th cutter and boarded her. She proved to be an American whale ship by the name of *Montague*. Our boat returned and we filled away and allowed the whaler to go on her cruise.

October 10th **sail ho**

At six o'clock this morning a sail was reported from the fore top-sail yard. She proved to be the English man of war steamer *Spitfire*. At ten A.M. another sail was reported on our weather bow, which turned out to be a Portuguese topsail schooner (a trader). In the middle watch we caught a large porpoise.

October 11th **Dramatics again**

The starboard watch scrubbed hammocks. The steamer *Spitfire* is in sight. In the evening the *Constellation* Dramatic Association had a meeting in the main hold. They are making preparations for another performance. On account of some misunderstanding some of the late company have resigned; they have chosen a new manager. On that account I left. I hope they will prosper.

October 12th 1860 **At sea/sail ho/**
San Jacinto captures another Slaver/sail ho

At five A.M. the port watch scrubbed hammocks. At eleven A.M. a sail was reported from the mast head, which proved to be the U.S. Steamer *San Jacinto*. She lowered a boat, and her captain and several of her officers came on board of us. They have captured another slaver, on the tenth of this month, with seven hundred and fifty (750) negroes in her. She was a brig belonging to New York; her name was the *Bonita,* and was entirely new. She also had on board three of the barque's [the *Cora*'s] crew that we left ashore in St. Paul de

Loando, one of whom died on board the *San Jacinto*. Yesterday, at three P.M. we parted company with the *San Jacinto*, and at five P.M. we sighted a sail right ahead of us about ten miles off. We gave her chase and at eleven P.M. we spoke her; she proved to be the English Gun boat *Spitfire*.

The Bonita's *slaves (715, not 750) had been loaded the day before, and such was the skill of the slavers that it took only fifteen minutes to get them all aboard.*[11]

Lt. James Foster and 1st Lt. (Marines) John L. Broome command the Bonita's *prize crew. Commander Dornin, the* San Jacinto's *captain, sent the* Bonita's *captain back with them for trial in the United States but kept the rest of the crew to be transferred to the supply ship* Relief *to go back on that ship as prisoners. This is because disease and prize crews had made the* San Jacinto *very short of officers and men, and he would have had to put a larger prize crew on the* Bonita *to guard the twenty additional prisoners. Normally, too, a marine would not be a prize crew officer, but Broome had merchant marine experience and so was pressed into service.*[12] *Personnel shortages were a constant problem for the squadron. Lieutenant Foster confronted problems of his own when he arrived with the* Bonita *in Charleston.*

October 13th   land ho

At nine o'clock the drum beat to general quarters. Exercised the port battery. At one P.M. a sail was reported. We gave chase. At four P.M. land was reported on our lee bow, at seven P.M. we lost sight of the sail. We then hauled up close on a wind so as to keep off of the land. Lights were seen all night all along the land.

October 14th   sail ho/the *Relief* again

Sunday. All hands were called to quarters at half past nine o'clock for inspection, after which had divine service, during which a sail was reported standing in for the land, which proved to be the U.S. Store ship *Relief*. At two P.M. we came to an anchor in Kabenda Bay. The *Relief* is at anchor here; she is the vessel we were chasing the day before. There is a very heavy swell here. At eight P.M. the anchor watch was set for the night.

October 15th 1860   at Kabenda Bay

The starboard watch washed clothes. We are waiting here for the *San Jacinto*; she is expected here. The *Relief* is also waiting for her. The reason why only one watch [washed] clothes, is because this is the cruising ground. If a sail should heave in sight we would get underway and give chase. We are about four miles from the land and it is very foggy. A bumboat comes alongside every meal time; they are full of monkeys and parrots; we are not allowed to have any kind of an animal on board.

The Constellation *was stricter about pets than some navy ships; the gray parrots were especially popular with officers and enlisted, and monkeys were not uncommon, with assorted other species also sometimes acquired.*

October 16th   **sail ho/we get underway/a cruiser/*San Jacinto*/ under easy sail an account of the lookouts**

The port watch washed clothes. At four bells, it being my masthead, I reported a sail off our starboard quarter; could not make her out. At nine A.M. the Quarter Master of the watch made her out to be at anchor, which looked very suspicious. At eleven A.M. we got underway to see what she was, [and] at two P.M. we came up to her; she proved to be an English cruiser at anchor. We took in all studding sails and hauled close on the wind. At three P.M. a sail was reported on our lee bow. Squared yards, set studding sails and stood down for her, made her out to be the U.S. Steamer *San Jacinto*. Spoke her, she told us that the vessel that was ahead of us was the H.B.M. Ship *Wrangler,* which vessel has just come on the coast. We then took in Royals and Top Gallant sails, and kept to the northward under easy sail. At two in the middle watch had a gangway lookout. There are six lookouts kept at night: two on the catheads, two in the gangways and two on the quarters. They are relieved every two hours. When the bell strikes the half hour, each man has to halloa out his post. If he should fall asleep he is punished by a court martial. In war time the punishment is death; in peace three months' pay is stopped with thirty days solitary confinement on bread and water in the brig.

The Wrangler *was a small, barque-rigged screw steam vessel, built during the Crimean War for coastal and inshore operations.*

October 17th 1860.   **at sea/court martial/Sentence of two men by a court martial/a hard sentence**

The starboard watch holystoned the gun deck. There are two Summary Court-Martials going on here now. At 4 P.M. the court-martials are over. At 5 P.M. all hands were called to muster to hear the sentence of the court, which was as follows: the first was a marine, who refused to do duty with his knapsack; his sentence was loss of two months' pay (twenty-two dollars), thirty days in solitary confinement on bread and water, and two months' black list. The other was a blue jacket. He called the captain of the main top a white livered hound. He reported him to the 1st lieutenant, who preferred charges and specifications against him. His sentence was very hard and caused considerable murmuring among the men. It was the loss [of two] months' pay (twenty-eight dollars, he being an ordinary seaman) reduced to the next inferior rank (a landsman) and two months' black list. After which the boatswain piped down. At 6 P.M. took in Royals and Top Gallant sails, tacked ship several times during the night. My halliards from 10 till 12.

October 18th   general fire quarters/sail ho

Port watch washed clothes. At four bells the lookout at the mast head reported land on our lee beam. At five bells a sail was reported on our weather beam; made her out to be a steamer, at half past 9 A.M. the bell rung and the drum beat to general fire quarters. After several maneuvers, beat the retreat. First part of the Main Top men to work on the Main top gallant backstays. At 3 P.M. tacked ship in hauling round the head yards. The Kroomen made a great deal of noise stamping with their feet, which is against the 1st lieutenant's orders. He ordered the head one to punish them for it. He took a rope end and went at them with a will. A sail was reported, which proved to be the U.S. Gun boat *Mystic*.

October 19th 1860.   At Sea/chase of a Suspicious looking Sloop/
                                 spoke her/heave her to/a slaver/let her go

The starboard watch washed clothes. At 9 A.M. a sail was reported which is about two points on our weather bow. Tacked ship several times during the forenoon and at 1 P.M. we had gained considerable on her. We made her out to be a large sloop; we have got strong suspicions of her. We tacked several times in the afternoon, and at 7 P.M. we spoke her. She did not give us a very satisfactory answer, we hove her to, and sent our 4th cutter alongside of her. She proved to be a slaver, as her captain told the officer in command of the boat. We could not take her as she had no niggers in her, she had good papers and Spanish Colors. The captain of her told our lieutenant that he calculated to take 280 niggers. Take him altogether he was as independent as a down east yankee. At half past seven the boat returned, we hoisted her and made sail and allowed the sloop to go on her way, after which we took in Royals and Top gallant sails, and remained all night under easy sail.

According to another Constellation *crew member, the sloop's crew was all packed up and ready to be taken off as prisoners when their ship was boarded. If the* Constellation *had been British, that would have been the case.*[13]

October 20th

Port watch holy stoned the spar deck. At half past 7 A.M. a sail was reported which turned out to be the *Flying Dutchman*. At 9 A.M. the starboard watch holystoned the gun deck. At 2 P.M. land was reported which turned out to be the celebrated Cape Fly Away. My mast head is the last dog watch under easy sail all night.

"Cape Fly Away" was the slang term given to low-lying clouds mistaken for land.

October 21st

Sunday. Came in rainy, with no wind, had divine service, my mast head, from 10 till 12. We are hove to with Royals and topgallant sails furled and the courses hauled up. In the afternoon it cleared off splendid. We remained under easy sail all night. My halliards from 10 till 12 in the first watch.

The courses are the lowest (and largest) sails—the mainsail on the mainmast and the foresail on the foremast.

October 22nd 1860. At sea

At four o'clock this morning we had a heavy rain squall, port watch washed clothes. At half past 9 A.M. the 1st division was called to quarters and cleaned their gun truck and pins.

October 23d Cruising off the Congo River

This day came in fine with a good breeze. I am gun deck sweeper this week, was elected last Sunday. Am very busy repairing my clothes; we are cruising under easy sail, the 2nd and 3d division are exercising small arms and single sticks. At night we hove to. It is very cloudy.

October 24th

At four o'clock this morning a very strong breeze was blowing. We are hove to, the mizzen topsail is on the cap, the reef tackles are hauled out. At 8 o'clock it was very pleasant weather again. All sail set. In the afternoon the divisions exercised.

October 25th

Fine breeze and pleasant weather. The Dramatic Club have a rehearsal tonight; we are getting on first rate. We are going to play when we get to St Paul de Loando, where we are now going to.

October 26th land ho/boarded by the quarantine boat/
Yellow Fever/came to an anchor in St Paul de Loando

At daylight land was reported from the mast head; wore ship and stood for it. At 12 A.M. was becalmed. At 3 P.M. it began to breeze up we set studding sails, and in about half an hour we took them in. The master having missed his reckoning, we made the land about 70 miles to leeward of St Paul. We hauled close on the wind and commenced beating up to the harbor; at half past 7 P.M. we were almost at our anchorage, when a Portuguese boat came alongside with a quarantine flag flying. She informed our captain that the Yellow Fever was raging ashore, which news caused considerable excitement on board. We came to an anchor; however, the flag officer gave orders not to let anybody out of the ship and not allow any boats alongside until further orders.

October 27th   we go ashore/Shifted again

At 4 A.M. we lowered our boat and went fishing. At 5 P.M. sent down Royal yards. At three o'clock in the afternoon H.B.M. sloop of war *Archer* came in, and our captain went on board of her. She has just come from St. Helena. The captain after remaining on board of her some time concluded to go ashore; both captains came into the boat. After a hard pull against wind and tide, we landed them. The captain gave the boat's crew strict orders not to leave the wharf. At 7 P.M. we returned on board. During the forenoon my station was again shifted, my number now being 114. Main top Gallant Yard man. We then slung clean hammocks.

October 28th   the Gig's crew quarantined by orders
of the Flag officer at St Paul de Loando/
at St Paul de Loando/watering ships

Sunday. The Doctor went ashore yesterday to investigate into the sickness. He returned and gave orders for nobody to leave the ship. It being Sunday and our captain going to give a dinner, he sent his steward and the boat ashore, to market. On coming alongside of the ship at seven o'clock the 1st lieutenant hailed the steward and asked him if he had left the boat. On his answering that he did, he ordered us to pull out to the launch, (which was moored about two cables' length astern of the ship.) and make fast to her and stay there until further orders. We waited about an hour and a half. When our recall was hoisted, we came on board, when our boys began to laugh at us, asking us if we had just come out of quarantine. We are taking in water, at 9 A.M. got out all boats. We are not going to stop here long. At half past ten A.M. had church, the men dressed in white frocks, hats, and blue trousers. At twelve o'clock H.B.M. Steam Gunboat *Sharpshooter* arrived here. At four o'clock the *Archer* got underway and steamed down to Freshwater Bay, where we are going as soon as we take in our provisions. A Portuguese steamer sailed at 5 P.M. We are taking in water all day.

The Sharpshooter *was an iron-hulled, six-gun, first-class screw gun vessel.*

October 29th   taking in 6 months provisions/King's Birthday

Got breakfast at six o'clock this morning. Two hands from each part of the ship to work in the water tanks. At 9 A.M. the gig went ashore, to get stores for the captain. There is nobody allowed off the wharf, on account of the yellow fever. I have learnt that there have been eleven persons died daily with it, and singular enough, it has not touched the negroes here, but every white person that catches it dies. At twelve o'clock we returned on board. All hands are to work cleaning launches. We are taking in six months' provisions. It is my boatkeeping day, had a very late supper and spliced the main brace. The gun deck is lumbered up with provisions, we are going to sea tomorrow. A French steamer is signalized from the fort. Today is a holiday here, the king's birthday. We fired a salute of twenty-one guns and hoisted the Portuguese flag at the fore.

October 30th   the gig a fishing/ship gets underway/
came to an anchor/Dramatic

Had breakfast this morning at six o'clock. At seven o'clock the gig's crew went fishing and had a first rate time. While we were out fishing the ship was discovered to be underway and going to sea at the rate of three knots an hour. We immediately got up our anchor and pulled after her; she however came to an anchor off Point Augustus, which is about 14 miles from the City of St. Paul de Loando. We got alongside of her at half past two P.M. The English Man of War Steamers *Archer, Sharpshooter,* and *Buffalo* are at anchor here. We had a rehearsal in the main hold at seven o'clock in the evening. We are going to give a performance next Thursday evening. It is very fine weather here.

October 31st   Target Shooting/at anchor off Point Augustus

This morning all hands scrubbed and washed clothes, had breakfast at 8 A.M. All hands dressed in white frocks, hats, and blue trousers. The *Archer* is target shooting. The Gun boat *Sharpshooter* left here last night. We are waiting here for the U.S. Steamer *Mystic.* She is expected here from the Island of Fernando Po with a mail for the squadron. In the afternoon the gun deck divisions were exercised at target shooting, the shots made were very good. We then had a boat sail; our boat sails like a witch. We had a rehearsal in the evening; it bids fair to be a good performance. We then turned into our hammocks.

U.S. Sloop of war *Constellation*	22 guns
U.S. Steam Frigate *San Jacinto*	16 guns
U.S. Sloop of war *Portsmouth*	16 guns
U.S. Sloop of war *Saratoga*	18 guns

U.S. Steam Gun Boat *Mohican*   6 guns
U.S. Steam Gun Boat *Sumpter*   4 guns
U.S. Steam Gun Boat *Mystic*   4 guns
Total 86 guns
These vessels comprise the African Squadron
Feb, 10th 1861

November 1860

1st This morning all hands scrubbed hammocks. This being the day that we are going to give the performance, the company are very busy making preparations for the occasion. In the forenoon we went on board the English Steam Sloop of war *Archer,* and gave her officers, and men, an invitation to come on board and witness the performance, which they accepted.

At 1 P.M., the hammocks being piped down, we commenced to set up our stage and scenery; at 4 o'clock we had everything arranged, and it made a very neat appearance. As ill luck would have it, it commenced to rain about 6 P.M. However, we did not stop for that. I had almost forgot to mention that on account of the yellow fever being in the city of St. Paul de Loando, we could not send any invitations ashore, or get our scenery and some of our dresses, that we had engaged when we were here before, so we had to do with what we had left at the Madeira performance.

At half past seven o'clock we were all ready to commence, the call boy's bell rang and up went the curtain. The plays selected for the occasion were three farces, viz *Vermont Wool Dealer, Widow's Victim,* and the roaring farce of the *Omnibus,* with several songs and dances.[1] The entertainment went off to the satisfaction of everybody present, among whom I noticed the captains of H.B.M vessels *Archer* and *Buffalo,* besides their lieutenants, and some of their crews, our own officers and crew, particularly our flag officer, who seemed to be highly pleased with the performance. I sustained the character of Mrs. Rattleton in *The Widow's Victim* and had great praise for the way in which I rendered it.

At half past ten o'clock, the performance being over, the officers gave the dramatic troupe a collation. We had plenty to eat and drink (some of the boys had to be helped into their hammocks). We have got a splendid wardrobe, especially the ladies' dresses, some of which are very costly. We are going to give another performance when we get to the Island of St. Helena.

Boatswain's Mate John Hunter. Historic Ships of Baltimore.

In the Green Room during the performance, there were some very laughable scenes. It was raining and everything was wet, caused by the rain dripping through the awnings. There were ladies, gentlemen, waiting maids, boot blacks, servants, soldiers, robbers, Scene shifters, niggers, bar tenders, and a host of others too numerous to mention all huddled together in the only dry spot that could be found. As the actors got through their parts they would change their clothes; some of them forgetting where they had left their own clothes, or being misplaced by others they commenced to grumble. One instance in particular [amused] us very much. A young fellow (a boat mate) C.F.G. [O. S. Charles F. Gordon] by name, (who by the way made a splendid appearance as Julia Ledger, in the farce of the *Omnibus*) after getting through his part, he took off his ladies' apparel, all but a chemise; he then commenced to look after his clothes. Just imagine his horror on discovering that his pants were not where he had left them. He made use of an expression on the occasion, that was very unladylike; it was, "Who in Hell has got my pants? Never mind, here is a pair," and he seized onto a pair belonging to our chief boatswain's mate (who was at that time on the stage, doing the character of Jerry Clip in the farce of *The Widow's Victim*) and put them on. When Jack H——r [Boatswain's Mate John Hunter] got through his part, of course he was minus his unmentionables. After searching some time, he gave it up in despair and had to do with a pair of knee breeches that he had been acting in. After having several hearty laughs at Jack and Charley's expense, we turned into our hammocks highly satisfied with our evening's sport. On the next page there is an exact copy of one of the bills.

W.A. Leonard

See next page
[doodle of hand pointing]
Dramatic Soiree
on board
U. S. Flag Ship Constellation
given by the
Constellation Dramatic Association

Isaac L. Nodine. . . . . Manager
John L. Nicholson. . . . . Prompter

* * *

On Thursday Evening Nov 1st 1860.
the performance will commence with the
laughable Farce entitled the
Vermont = Wool = Dealer

Deuteronomy Dutiful the wool dealer . . by Mr. Strowe
Mr. Waddle . . . . T. McCrachen
Captain Oakley . . . . J.G. Farrar
Con Golumby [?]. . . . . by . Mr. T.W. Igo
Bob . . . . W. Harrington
Slap a barkeeper. . . . . . . Gus Henry

* * * * * * * * * *

Miss Amanda . . . . by . . Mr. C.F. Gordon
Belly S. Higginbottom
after which a
Comic Song . . . . by . . Mr. P. Daley
following with the

Widows = Victim
a farce in one act

Jerry Clip a stage struck barber . . . . J. Hunter
Byron Tremain Pelham Podge . . . . P. Doran
Mr. Twitter . . . . J. Cameron
Tinsel John . . . . J. Hunter
Moustache Strappard . . . . . . " "

<<<* * *>>>

Mrs. Rattleton a charming young widow . . . W.A. Leonard
Jane Chatterly her maid in love with Jerry . . W.H. French
Mrs. Twitter . . . . Alvah Olds
cook, housemaid, waiters &c &c by the company
the whole to conclude, with the
laughable farce of the

Omnibus.

Pat Rooney . . . . J. F. Powell
Mr. Ledger . . . . Thomas
McCrachen
Mr. Dobbs . . . . T.W. Igo
Master Tom Dobbs . . . . . . W.H. Strowe
Farrier Boy . . . . P. Downey

Julia Ledger . . . . by . . C.F. Gordon
Mrs. Dobbs . . . . J. Cloner [?]

Miss Damper　　.　　.　　.　　.　　.　　.　　.　　S. Higginbottom
Miss Jemima Damper　.　　.　　.　　.　　.　　.　　W. Phillips

<<<***>>>　　　　　<<<***>>>

N.B. The ship's company are respectfully invited N.B. to attend the performance to commence at half past seven o'clock precisely. The ship's band will be in attendance and will play some of their most popular airs.

As Mrs. Rattleton, Leonard played the widow of the title, described in the play text as "a young widow, extremely handsome, extremely accomplished, and extremely irresistible."

W.A. Leonard
Point Augustus
November 1st 1860

November 2nd 1860

All hands washed clothes. The dramatic company are busy setting things to rights. At 8 A.M. loosed sail. The U.S. Gunboat *Mystic* arrived here with no mail; she has gone up to the town for coal. The steamers *Archer* and *Buffalo* warped up close to us today. In the evening the Dramatic Club had a meeting and elected a new set of officers; we are getting up a subscription to get some more money.

November 3d 1860　　at Point Augustus/Sentence of a court Martial/ sail ho/*San Jacinto*/she goes to Congo

Holystoned all decks. At 9 A.M. all hands were called to muster to hear sentence of a court martial; the prisoner was a marine, his offence was sleeping on his post. His sentence was loss of two month's pay (22 dollars), and two hours extra post duty each day for fifteen days with his knapsack and accoutrements. At 1 P.M. a sail hove in sight which proved to be the U.S. Steam Frigate *San Jacinto*. Made signals to her, she came close under our quarter. Our flag officer hailed her and gave orders to send a boat on board the flagship, and her captain came on board. She has been to Elephant Bay. She got orders to cruise to the Congo River. She then made sail, and was soon out of sight. We are at anchor here in twenty-two fathoms of water. At sundown we got in all boats.

Elephant Bay is south of Benguela in modern Angola. Thwarted by the yellow fever in Loanda, the Constellation *headed to "Fish Bay" (Little Fish Bay), south of Elephant Bay. Little Fish Bay, though ineligible for overnight liberty by virtue of being on the African coast, was a relatively attractive location for crew recreation ashore and the purchase of fresh vegetables.*

November 4th   waiting for the mail

Sunday morning all hands are very busy, in cleaning their brightwork, and brushing their clothes, ready for muster. At half past 9 A.M. the respective divisions were called to quarters for inspection, after which had divine service on the gun deck. We have got everything ready for sea; we are waiting here for the U.S. Steamer *Mohican,* which vessel is expected here with the mail from Fernando Po, on receiving which we are to weigh anchor and start for Fish Bay, which is about ten days' sail from here. All hands are criticizing on the performance; they give us a good deal of praise. In the afternoon the gig went sailing.

November 5th 1860   Point Augustus/got underway/
                                         sail ho/chase her/give up the chase

At eight o'clock this morning we crossed the royal yards. We got news that the yellow fever is increasing up to the city. The U.S. naval storekeeper is not expected to live. At 11 A.M. we got underway for Fish Bay. A sail was reported from the masthead supposed to be the *Mohican.* We fired two guns for her to heave to, which she paid no attention to, she kept right on her course. At 1 P.M. we gave up the chase; the flag officer left orders for the *Mohican* to follow us with the mail. We have got a good breeze, going about six knots an hour.

November 6th 1860   Land ho/at sea

Very cloudy weather, with rain, the wind is dead ahead. The dramatic company had a very interesting meeting in the main hold last evening. I am main top sweeper on the gun deck, this again. At five o'clock land was reported, on our lee beam; it proved to be Loando a little to the southward of St. Paul.

Willie Leonard

Though the day was uneventful aboard the Constellation, *back home the political earth was shifting. It was election day, resulting in victory for Abraham Lincoln. President Buchanan, reflecting the apprehensions of many, referred to it as "that event . . . which now threatens to plunge our country into total ruin."*[2]

November 7th   Caught a Flying Fox/White rat

Port watch washed clothes. We have got a good breeze, and very pleasant weather. There is a very strong current running here against us, and we are making but very little headway. One of our men caught a flying fox, and they are having great sport with him.[3] We are running quite close to the land. almost within a stone's throw of it. It looks very barren, not a green spot to be seen. At 5 P.M. the 3d division exercised big guns. The captain of the fore hold caught a large rat which was perfectly white. The ship is infested with rats and cockroaches. We tacked ship several times during the night. In the midnight watch I had a gorgeous lookout.

November 8th 1860. at sea/Mending clothes

Starboard watch washed clothes. There is a man stationed in each chains, heaving the lead, as there is very shallow water here. The watch below are very busy mending their clothes; the gun deck looks like a mammoth tailoring establishment. The divisions are putting down for clothing on their division bills.

November 9th court martials/am elected main top Sweeper

Port watch holystones the gun deck. Fine breeze and pleasant weather. There have been thirty court-martials since the ship has been in commission. We have to be very careful what we say or do, or else we will be court-martialed; the men are beginning to feel dissatisfied. There is going to be a court-martial in a few days; a man called a boatswain's mate a damn liar.

I am anxiously waiting for my sweeping week to be over. The part of the ship that I have to sweep for is where all hands smoke at meal hours; after they get through I have to clean up after them, which is not a very agreeable job. However, my week will be up next Monday. Tacked ship several times during the night. Very light wind. We are in latitude 13 - 14 south, course S.E. by E.

November 10th Sentence

Saturday. The port watch holystoned the gun deck. We have got the port studding sails set. At 6 P.M. all hands were called to muster to hear sentence of a court-martial. The charge was calling a boatswain's mate a Damn Liar. His sentence was reduction to the next inferior rank, an ordinary seaman (he being a seaman); six months' black list, to consist of two hours each day in his watch below cleaning bright work. A ten o'clock this night we had a severe rain squall.

November 11th land ho

Sunday and a splendid day; it is very warm. All hands dressed in white frocks hats and blue trousers; at half past 9 A.M. all hands were called to quarters for inspection, at 10 A.M. had divine service on the gun deck. Land in sight all day, on our lee beam, called it Elephant Bay.

November 12th out of commission/at sea

Starboard watch washed clothes. After breakfast the purser began to serve out clothing to the ship's company. At twelve o'clock I gave up my commission as main top sweeper, and I am not sorry for it, I can assure you. At noon we were in latitude 12.52 S., we are going about eight knots an hour. We are 170 miles from Fish Bay. Land in sight all the afternoon. At night the heavens began to blacken up, and assume a very threatening aspect. In the first watch the wind began to freshen, and it now commenced to thunder, very loud, and the lightning began to assume all sorts of fantastic shapes. It was *really* a terrific sight to behold, in the midst of which we took in royals and top gallant sails. It did not amount to much, however. At eleven o'clock we again made sail and tacked ship. We are making but very little headway as there is a strong head current of four knots an hour running against us. The ship's company are very anxious to get to Fish Bay as there is plenty of vegetables to be had there very cheap.

November 13th 1860.   at sea

Port watch washed clothes, at half past nine o'clock had division inspection the 1st division exercised small arms, the 3d division big guns. In the evening the dramatic club had a meeting in the main hold. We have got a good breeze, but it is dead ahead, and we are making but very little headway on our course; we are now about ninety-eight miles from Fish Bay.

November 14th   Trimming ship

This day came in cloudy, my masthead from 10 till 12. We were in latitude 14.24 south at noon. The wind being fair, we set top gallant studding sails, in the forenoon we ran the two forward guns aft in order to alter the ship's trim, to see if she would sail any better. We are about fifty miles from Fish Bay. At 8 P.M. the wind died away to a dead calm; we took in the royals and flying jib, and hauled up the mainsail and let her stand that way until the middle watch when a light breeze sprang up.

November 15th   lose a yard/came to an anchor in Fish Bay

This morning, the wind freshening, set all sail, the land in sight on our lee beam at 6 A.M. In tacking ship, the main top gallant yard got foul of something aloft when the yards were swinging, and parted right in the slings. We immediately sent down the remains of it. There is a very heavy sea and the ship is pitching very violently. Fish Bay is about ten miles off. At two o'clock we discovered we were some ways to windward of Fish Bay; we therefore squared yards, and set the starboard studding sails, and at half past three o'clock we came to an anchor, in Fish Bay. The U.S. Steam Gunboat *Mystic* is here, she arrived here last Tuesday with our mail, there is also an American whaling barque called the *Rascius* at anchor here, also a Portuguese trading brig. The U.S. Sloop of war *Portsmouth*. left here on the 11th of this month. At sundown we got out all boats, sent down royal and top gallant yards, and swung clean hammocks.

November 16th   **description of the Place/*Mystic* sails**

All hands washed clothes, after which all hands were very busy cleaning the ship inside and out. Having had a run ashore in the gig, I will attempt to describe the place. It is a Portuguese settlement and it presents almost the same appearance as Porto Grande, although there are twice as many houses, and white people (that is if one can call a Portugee white). It is called Fish Bay on account of the numerous quantities of fish of a very good quality that is caught here, and it is a rendezvous for all trading vessels on this coast to get a superior kind of vegetables that are to be had here. There is very good anchorage here: we are within a half a mile of the beach and have twenty-one fathoms of water. The U.S. Gun boat *Mystic* sailed at one o'clock for the Island of St. Helena to give her men liberty. I sent three letters in her. At three o'clock we fired a salute of thirteen guns for the governor of this place, which was returned from the fortress. There is a regiment of infantry here. At 5 P.M. the caterers of the messes went ashore to get vegetables for the messes.

Fish Bay (Little Fish Bay/Mossamedes/Namibe) was the southernmost settlement of the Portuguese territory. It offered a good harbor, supplies of fresh water, and abundant fish. Local farms provided plenty of Irish potatoes, other vegetables and fruits, beef, mutton, pork, and poultry.[4]

November 17th 1860.   **at Fish Bay/a good Dinner**

Holystoned all decks. It is beautiful weather here in the daytime, but rather chilly in the mornings, and evenings. We are taking in a supply of sand today. We made a first rate dinner today on fresh meat and vegetables; we are going to have fresh meat every day while we lay here. The flag officer has gone ashore, to pay a visit to the governor. At 4 P.M. a steamer was signalized off the point and at 5 P.M. she came to an anchor, ahead of us. She is a Portuguese mail steamer from St. Paul de Loando.

November 18th   **Sunday in Fish Bay**

This being Sunday, all hands are busy getting ready for inspection. The 1st lieutenant is going to give all hands a run ashore here, and has commenced this day with the petty officers. At half past eight o'clock two English steamers arrived here. They belong to the African Exploring Expedition; one is named the *Livingston* and the other is the *Spitfire*.

While I am writing this, the ship's bell is tolling for divine service that with the chime of the bells that are ringing in the Portuguese church ashore, makes one's thoughts refer back to some very quiet Sabbath morning at home. There is a Dutch settlement, about eight miles from this town, where all the vegetables are raised. At 1 P.M. the gig's crew went on board the whaler. She is from New Bedford. She has been out twenty-six months, and has got eighteen

hundred barrels of oil. She is going home in the spring. After having a good
look at her, we returned on board of our own ship. We are going to make
extensive alterations while we lie here, so as to have her look well before we
get to St. Helena.

The Spitfire, *a four-hundred-ton, three-gun paddlewheel steamer, was towing
the other vessel, which was actually the exploring steamer* Pioneer. *They were
on their way to the Cape of Good Hope, whence the* Pioneer *would be taken
on to Dr. David Livingstone for use on his expedition up the Zambezi River in
Mozambique on the southeastern coast of Africa. Livingstone hoped to open
the Zambezi to navigation and encourage commerce, including the cultivation
of cotton, which could supplant that grown with slave labor in the American
South. The* Pioneer, *with its five-foot draft, proved incapable of its intended
purpose, constantly grounding in shallows or on sandbars as well as encoun-
tering rapids. Slavery was no less prevalent in eastern Africa than on the West
African coast patrolled by the* Constellation, *and Livingstone's expedition
freed several groups of slaves during its travels.*

November 19th 1860.   Fish Bay/setting up rigging and Tarring down

At daybreak, all hands were set to work in the rigging, setting it up, and tarring it down. We housed topgallant masts, and overhauled the topgallant rigging. At half past nine o'clock the gig's crew went fishing. Mr. Johnson, our 3d
lieutenant, and Dr. Brown [John M. Browne] went with us, we had very good
success, and at half past two o'clock in the afternoon we returned on board.
At 3 P.M. we went on board the whaler, to get some fish lines, and from there
we went ashore. After rambling about the town for more than two hours, and
being pretty tired we returned on board the ship. At sundown the work on
the rigging was all finished, but for the life of me I cannot say which is got the
most tar, the rigging or the deck. Anyhow it will give the starboard watch a
good holystoning job. The two English steamers sailed today. The Dramatic
Troupe had a very interesting meeting in the evening and transacted some very
important business, and had some very exciting debates. At eight o'clock we
adjourned. We are to have a rehearsal on Wednesday evening.

November 20th   Hard Luck/at Fish Bay/a row/painting

Holystoned the spar and gun decks. After breakfast the gig went fishing. We
dropped anchor in fifty-five fathoms water; after fishing here about an hour,
with no success, we tried to haul up our anchor, and go out farther, but we
could not haul it up. It was caught under a rock. After several fruitless attempts
to get it up, we gave it up. We tried to buoy it with one of our awning stan-
chions, but we had no sooner let it go when it sank, thereby losing stanchion,

over sixty fathoms of deep sea lead line, a 42 pound lead, and a small grapnel. We returned on board at one o'clock. In the afternoon we took in eight barrels of oil, from the whaling barque *Rascius*. At 2 P.M. a draft went ashore on liberty. The gig's crew went ashore, to get some fishing lines for the captain. On our way back to the boat, we dropped into a rum shop, and before we left it we had a row among ourselves, during which I got myself pretty well cut up, one eye blackened and my face all scratched up. I am ashamed to be seen, I look so bad. At sundown we returned on board. All hands are very busy painting the ship outside, and the quarter gunners are touching up the guns.

November 21st

The paint work not being dry, all hands slept in very late, had breakfast at seven o'clock, after which a draft of twenty men went ashore on liberty until six o'clock. The gig's crew took the launch and went fishing. At 9 A.M. the Portuguese mail boat sailed for Lisbon. During the afternoon some of the liberty men came off pretty well corned; it is awful liquor here, regular chain lightning, or minie rifle stuff.

November 22nd   the gig's crew get a run

All hands are scraping the gun deck, also the spar deck, the latter being full of tar. Had breakfast at 7 A.M. Another draft went ashore this forenoon. In the afternoon the gig's crew went ashore for a run, and till sundown we had a sociable time, with a small party that came ashore in the draft at 3 P.M. The 1st lieutenant and master at arms came ashore to hunt up the drunken men, some of which are raising the old harry here. One young fellow got his head cut open by the master at arms. We returned at sundown. There are five or six of the boys drunk and making a great noise. They were put in the brig by orders of the 1st luff.

November 23d 1860.   Fish Bay

This morning all hands washed clothes. We are painting the ship today, she looks splendid. There are two or three of the men that went ashore yesterday going to be court-martialed; the 1st lieutenant has already put some of the drunken ones into the After Guard. It is very dull on board. Nobody went ashore today.

November 24th

Holystoned the gun deck. We are still painting the ship inside. The gig's crew went fishing. The whaling barque *Rascius* sailed today. We are the only vessel that is laying here now. We went ashore in the gig in the afternoon, and had a first rate time; returned at sundown.

November 25th   **Sunday**

Went fishing this morning, it being Sunday. We had inspection at half past nine o'clock, after which had divine service on the gun deck. There is a large barque just coming to an anchor, astern of us. Some of our men went ashore in the afternoon on liberty until sundown.

November 26th   **heavy surf/get wet through/a proposition/**
                                           at Fish Bay/minie Rifle Rum

At four o'clock this morning, the gig's crew went fishing; we had very good luck, and returned on board at eight o'clock. At 4 P.M. we went down to the Dutch settlement with the captain and purser and landed them. There was a very heavy surf running at the time, and for half an hour, we had as much as we could do to keep the boat from going broadside on to the beach. After getting ourselves wet through we got her off, and anchored her. We now proposed that one of us should go up, and see if he could get something to drink, as we were wet through and very cold. It was no sooner proposed, than it was acted upon—one of the boys went up and returned in about fifteen minutes, with a Bottle of the Article, which we hailed with delight, but in so doing we proved that the old adage is correct which says "Never count your chickens before they are hatched," for on putting the bottle to our lips, the smell that came from it made us sneeze. That was enough, in fact it was enough to make a horse sick to look at it. At sundown the captain and purser came into the boat and we arrived on board at 7 P.M. after a very hard pull against both wind and tide.

The "Dutch" settlement was a German community fostered the previous decade by the Portuguese authorities.

November 27th   **exercising the Launch**

This morning all hands washed clothes. At nine o'clock the second company of small arms men went ashore on a target excursion; at twelve o'clock they returned, having completely riddled the target. At one o'clock the launch was called away, with the fighting boat's crew; she is sailing round the bay firing her twelve pound howitzer every ten minutes. At three o'clock she returned on board. Another whaling barque arrived here today, she is eighteen months out, and has five hundred barrels of oil.

November 28th   **visit to the Dutch settlement/at Fish Bay/**
                                                    Launch practicing

Today all hands scrubbed hammocks. As soon as we scrubbed our hammocks, the gig was sent down to the Dutch settlement, on an errand for the captain.

We sailed down and arrived there about half past six in the morning, we beached the boat, and left the boat keeper to take care of her. We then started up to the settlement. We had a very pleasant walk over hedges and ditches, across a large brook, and arrived on a large farm, where the field hands were to work, the birds were singing merrily, everything around us seemed to be contented. On walking a little farther, we were all taken aback on seeing the old farm house, which was situated on the edge of a large brook and looked for all the world like a New England farm house. After giving the farmer our errand, which was to get some wood for the ship, we with longing looks retraced our way back to the boat and returned on board. At 9 A.M. the first company of small arms men went ashore to shoot a target. We made some very good shots and returned on board in time for dinner. In the afternoon the launch's crew went ashore to practice howitzers. We sent down an old main topsail and bent a new one. We went ashore after supper to get the captain's wash clothes. It being my boatkeeping day, I went in bathing. We returned on board at sundown. The dramatic company had a rehearsal in the evening.

November 29th

The gig went fishing this morning. After breakfast had a grand boat expedition, in which all the boats in the ship were engaged. Am very sick today. In the afternoon we painted all the boats. In consequence of being sick I turned in as soon as hammocks were piped down.

November 30th   getting ready for sea

I feel first rate this morning. We went fishing and only caught two fish. All hands washed clothes, at eight o'clock we sent up topgallant yards. After breakfast we went ashore and scrubbed our boat inside and out. Went ashore in the evening and had a run. At sundown, we got in all boats and the Port watch were sent on the gun deck to get the messenger up. We are going to sea tomorrow and I believe we are going to St. Paul de Loando. The Dramatic company had a rehearsal in the evening.

(Patience is a great Virtue)

December 1860

December 1st

At six o'clock this morning, sent up the royal yards and got swinging booms alongside. At nine o'clock all hands were called to make sail, after which we hove up the anchor, but there being no wind, we drifted close in to the land and had to let go the anchor again. At 10 A.M., the sea breeze coming in, we again hove it up and went to sea. In the afternoon we had a good breeze, we set all the port studding sails; we are going to St. Paul de Loando.

December 2nd

Sunday, and a beautiful day. We have got the S.E. trade winds and we are rolling down to St. Paul's at the rate of six and seven miles an hour. At half past nine o'clock all hands were called to quarters for inspection, after which had a general muster on the quarter deck. The 1st lieutenant read the Articles of War, after which had divine service, on the gun deck as usual in the first dog watch. The after guard and mizzen top men are getting up the sea clothes lines.

December 3d

This day came in rainy, with several severe squalls; at eight o'clock it cleared up and the rest of the day we had very fine weather. At 4 P.M. the 1st division was called to quarters, and exercised big guns. The 3d division exercised small arms. At sundown we were only eighty miles from St. Paul de Loando. We are however in the midst of a dead calm and it is very warm.

December 4th 1860

It was calm all night. At daylight land was reported on our weather bow, which proved to be St. Paul de Loando. In the afternoon we got a light wind, and at five o'clock we came to an anchor in the harbor of St. Paul de Loando, about ten miles from the city. It being very dark, we were all in a bustle and confusion until half past nine o'clock, when the hammocks were piped down and all hands turned in. I had the first anchor watch from eight till ten; was very sleepy.

December 5th   get underway/no sickness/rain squall/came to an anchor/
at St. Paul de Loando/waiting for the mail

At half past four this morning, the hands were turned to. The 4th cutter was manned with the Kroomen, and they were sent up to the city to make enquiries about the yellow fever. The gunner went with them. We washed the decks down with sand, and at eight o'clock we sent down royal yards and got the swinging booms out. At 10 A.M. the 4th cutter returned, and reported that there was no sickness up to the city. She also reported that the U.S. Steam Gunboat *Mohican* was at anchor. Made sail and stood up the harbor. When we got at the mouth of it, a violent squall struck us; as we were close to a lee shore, and having plenty of time to get in, the captain [thought] it best to stand off until it was over. We tacked ship, thereby avoiding the squall, and saving all hands from getting wet through. After it passed over, again tacked ship, and stood in towards the harbor, and at half past five o'clock we came to an anchor in the harbor to windward of the U.S. Steam Gun boat *Mohican*. At sundown all hands swung clean hammocks. The dramatic club had a rehearsal of *The Widow's Victim* in the main hold, in the evening. We have come to the conclusion to have that as part of the performance, by request. An American barque sailed from here today for the U.S. We are going to take in wood and water here, and then wait for the U.S. Steam Frigate *San Jacinto,* which is expected here with the mail from Fernando Po. Then we are going to the island of St. Helena to give the men liberty.

The Mohican *had curtailed a planned patrol because of a boiler leak.*[1]

December 6th   **go ashore**

All hands washed clothes today. We are dressed in white frocks, hats and blue trousers. We are taking in wood and water. In the afternoon the captain went ashore in the gig, but the boat's crew were not allowed to go off of the wharf. We returned at sundown.

December 7th

All hands scrubbed hammocks. We are still taking in wood and water. In the afternoon a Portuguese brig came to an anchor astern of us. The gig went ashore in the afternoon and we had a run.

December 8th   *Portsmouth*

Went fishing this morning; it is dreadful warm weather here now. In the afternoon the U.S. Sloop of war *Portsmouth* was signalized from the fort as coming in. At half past eight o'clock she came to an anchor right astern of us. She has just come from the Congo River.

December 9th 1860.   **St. Paul de Loando/general court martial**

Being Sunday, the divisions were called to quarters at half past nine o'clock for inspection, after which divine service was held on the gun deck. In the afternoon the men went visiting the other ships in the harbor. The U.S. Steam Frigate *San Jacinto* came in here in the evening with the mail from Fernando Po. There is going to be a general court martial on board the U.S. Sloop of war *Portsmouth* tomorrow; our captain, 1st and 4th lieutenants are members of the court. Very warm weather.[2]

December 10th   **court martial on board the *Portsmouth***

All hands washed clothes. After breakfast the captain went on board the *Portsmouth*. At 10 A.M. the signal gun was fired, to commence the court martial. We staid on board of her until dinner time, the boats having some trouble to get their grog, but by the kind endeavors of Burns the Chief Boatswain's Mate, we got it, and went on board of our own ship, and got our dinners. We then returned on board the *Portsmouth*. The court martial is ended, [so] we then took the captain on board, and then went ashore in the gig with the steward. It is a boy who they are trying on board the *Portsmouth;* he struck the Officer of the Deck with a sight cover while on duty. We have got to go to Fish Bay for a clean bill of health, and then we are going to St. Helena. We are getting ready for sea. In the evening we had a rehearsal of *Boots at the Swan* and it went off first rate.[3]

December 11th 1860.   **St Paul de Loando/get underway**

This morning, we sent up the royal yards, and rigged the fish gear, and got the messenger up. At four o'clock we hove up the anchor, made sail and went to sea. We have got a good breeze, we tacked ship several times during the night.

December 12th   **at sea**

This morning we are drawing our regular monthly clothing, it is very fine weather, and we have got a good breeze. The 3d division exercised large guns. Tacked ship several times during the night.

December 13th   **a dead body**

The port watch washed clothes. Very fine weather. We are steering a S.W. and by S. course, but there is but very little wind. This morning the body of a man was seen floating by the ship. He had nothing on but a shirt; he probably fell overboard from some vessel in the night time.

December 14th

The starboard watch washed clothes. At ten o'clock the drum beat to general quarters and at 11 A.M. beat the retreat. We have got a head wind, are making but very little on our course. The dramatic company had a rehearsal of *Ambrose Gwinnett* in the evening; it is a three act drama, and a very nice one.[4]

December 15th   sewing

The port watch holystone[d] the spar deck this morning. After breakfast the starboard watch holystoned the gun deck, at nine o'clock the bags were piped up to air clothing. I am doing a little in the mending line, I must say that I make very poor work with a needle.

December 16th 1860.   at sea/Southern Cross and Magellan Clouds

Sunday, and a very warm day, all hands dressed in white frocks, hats, and blue trousers. At half past 9 A.M. all hands were called to quarters for inspection, after which had divine service. At twelve noon, we were in latitude 11. 47. south. In the evening the Southern Cross and Magellan clouds were to be seen. The Cross is composed of four very brilliant stars, in the shape of a cross. The Magellan clouds are three small white clouds. They are stationary; they are to be seen on any fine evening in these latitudes. Towards evening the wind became stronger.

December 17th   drilling

The port watch washed clothes. It has been raining all the watch. In the afternoon the 1st division exercised big guns, the 2nd division small arms and the 3d division single sticks. We are 170 miles from Fish Bay. At three o'clock we have still got a head wind. In the evening we had a very good rehearsal of *The Widow's Victim.*

December 18th   sail ho the *Mohican*/court martial/extra drilling

The starboard watch washed clothes. At ten o'clock a sail was reported on our lee beam, which proved to be the U.S. Steamer *Mohican*. She left St Paul de Loando yesterday in the afternoon. Preparations were made for another court martial, the offender being a Marine. After supper the 1st division were exercised at small arms drill, and through the stupidity of a few numbskulls, we were kept at it for two hours, also a prospect of being twice as long the next time. The court martial is ended. We had a very heavy squall in the first watch, took in royals and topgallant sails.

December 19th 1860.

We have got an eight knot breeze. This morning at half past nine o'clock, all hands were called to muster to hear the sentence of a court martial, which was one month's police duty and deprivation of all liberty on foreign stations. His offence was not obeying orders quick enough to satisfy the wishes of a newly made corporal. We had several squalls during the night, with a little rain.

December 20th

The port watch holystoned the gun deck. At noon we were in latitude 14 south, and 60 miles from Fish Bay, in the afternoon the winds began to freshen, and at sundown we single reefed the topsails, and set top gallant sails over them, in the midnight watch we shook out the reefs, and made all sail, land in sight. A sail was reported standing across our bows, but she was soon out of sight.

December 21st

Land in sight all along our lee beam, supposed to be in the vicinity of Fish Bay. At night we took in all our light sails, and waited for daylight. We had several heavy squalls during the night. It is very warm.

December 22nd

In the morning we made all sail and stood in for the land. On coming close to it we discovered that we were fifteen miles to the leeward of the port, we hauled close on a wind, and at three o'clock we came to anchor in Fish Bay. We did not furl sail, as we do not intend to stop here but an hour or two. The flag officer went ashore in his barge; we also went ashore in the gig and had a run. At 5 P.M. the flag officer returned and all hands were called to get up anchor, which we did with a will. All hands are in good spirits, at the prospect of being in St. Helena. Soon we have got a roaring breeze—in the midwatch we were going ten and eleven knots an hour. It is very pleasant weather.

December 23d

Sunday, all hands were called to quarters for inspection at half past 9 A.M., after which had divine service on the gun deck. In the afternoon I had a mast head look out from two until four o'clock; it was very chilly. All hands are talking about what they are going to do when they get liberty in St. Helena. We went ten knots an hour all this day.

December 24th

Starboard watch washed clothes. We have got all the port studding sails set, we went eleven knots all this day, and we are rolling heavily. We had a rehearsal of *Ambrose Gwinnett* in the evening; it went off first rate. At 5 P.M. all hands exercised guns. It is a very dull Christmas eve to me.

December 25th   Christmas day very dull

Tuesday and a Christmas Day. It rained in the morning but cleared up towards eight o'clock. The port watch washed clothes. I must say it is very dull to me, in fact more so than any other day in the week. Whether it is from thinking of former ones, or from having the blues, (which I am subject to) I cannot say. At noon, we were 600 miles from St. Helena. We now have got regular S.E. trade winds, all sail set. At four o'clock all hands were called aft to splice the main brace. We are going at the rate of eight and nine knots an hour, it is very pleasant weather here now.

December 26th 1860.   at sea

This morning is rather chilly. We are going ten knots an hour; at noon we were 390 miles from port. We are scraping iron work and getting things ready for port; the ship looks first rate. In the afternoon we set the port lower studding sail, and in the evening the Dramatic Club had a very good rehearsal of *The Widow's Victim*.

December 27th   at sea

This morning the port watch washed clothes. We are going eight knots an hour; we expect to get in tomorrow. I am longing to see the island, I have heard so much talk about it and read about it too that I have pictured to myself a rare sight. I wonder if it is anything like what my imagination pictures it to be; if it is it will be worth seeing.

December 28th 1860.   land ho/St. Helena/first impressions/thoughts/
swinging clean hammocks/come to an anchor
at the Island of St Helena/fortifications/
Napoleon Bonaparte

The starboard watch washed clothes. It is very foggy. At seven o'clock land was reported, which caused quite an excitement throughout the ship. It proved to be the island of St. Helena. It is very high land: we are fifty miles from it and it can be seen very plain; on a clear day it can be seen eighty or ninety miles. All hands are looking at it and criticizing on its appearance. On coming nearer to it, I was struck with its deserted and barren looking appearance. I thought then, what must the feelings [have been], of the great Napoleon Bonaparte when he first sighted the island, situated in mid ocean. They must have been heart rending to him. I am going to make it my business to visit his tomb and will give a description of it in my own way.

At 2 P.M. we are about seven miles off. We expect to be in about half past five o'clock. The closer we get to it, the drearier it looks. At 4 P.M. we swung clean hammocks and unbent all the studding sails. Our flag officer is going to live ashore while we lie here, which will be about three weeks. The dramatic club are going to give a performance. When the ship gets cleaned up, we are going to have liberty here.

At five o'clock we came to an anchor off the island. The U.S. Steam Gunboat *Mohican* is here, having arrived at twelve o'clock. The American clipper ship *Live Yankee* is here with a cargo of coolies, also three English ships with the same cargoes. There are about forty old hulks here, principally East India men, and Slavers that have been condemned. The island from where we lie looks like a barren rock. It is provided with natural fortifications, and the only landing place there is, is so well fortified with cannon and mortars that all the force that could be brought against it would be useless, every fissure and gully in the rocks a cannon can be seen. Again my thoughts wandered back to the time when the great Napoleon first landed here. What must that great man [have] thought, when the vessel that brought him here dropped anchor? I can almost fancy the look of despair he cast at this barren rock, and well he might, for it is indeed a desolate looking island. It is a great stopping place for vessels to and from the East Indies and China, who stop here to water ship. Two or three arrive here daily at sundown.

Sent down royal yards and fired a salute of twenty-one guns for the English flag, which was returned from the fort. We also fired a salute of nine guns for the American consul who came on board at 8 P.M. An English East India man came to an anchor astern of us at 9 P.M. The *Live Yankee* sailed. The dramatic club had a rehearsal of *Boots at the Swan* in the evening.

In a single glance, Leonard's eye encompassed major policies and practices of the global labor market of his day. The hulks of condemned slavers he observed at St. Helena represented a difference between American and British slavery suppression policy. A ship condemned as a slaver by an American court was sold at auction, which at times resulted in the ship going right back to Africa for another shipment of slaves. Noticing similar results from their similar process, the British had changed their law so that a condemned slave ship had to be broken up, not sold intact.

The coolie ships Leonard noticed were among those participating in the legal coolie trade. As the slave trade came under pressure in the early to mid-nineteenth century, the demand for labor in New World colonial possessions caused enormous growth in another practice. Many thousands of men per year were taken from India and China under indenture contracts to work on plantations in the Caribbean and South America, in mines in Peru, and on the guano islands off the Peruvian coast. Their living and working conditions and their life expectancy were little different from those of the African slaves they replaced, though they were technically free men.

December 29th 1860. at St. Helena/a run ashore in the gig/ drinking houses

This morning, all hands were very busy cleaning out the 1st, 2nd and 3d cutters. At seven o'clock the English East Indiaman sailed. At half past 8 A.M. Boston barque *Storm King* arrived here from the Mozambique Channel; she is bound to Salem, Mass. At 9 A.M. we went ashore in the gig, and had a two hours' run up to the town. The town looked quite natural to me; everything looks home like, and everybody talks English, not like the coast where they ask you if you say this or that. The town is called James Town; it is situated in a valley between two large hills. There are two streets in the town: one called Napoleon St., which is the best road to Longwood, and the other is Jamestown St., which is the provincial thoroughfare. This street is about half a mile long—that is as far as the houses go. It terminates at the hospitals, of which there are two, one used for the soldiers and people of the island and the other as a sailors' hospital. This street also leads out to Longwood, which is where the tomb of Napoleon Bonaparte is situated. The street is full of drinking houses, kept on the European system. Among the most prominent are the Jolly Tar, Jolly Sailor, Spotted Dog, Heart of Oak, the Ship Anchor and Crown, and a host of others too numerous to mention. After rambling about two hours, we returned on board. It is very hard to land here, there being a very heavy surf at the landing place. In the afternoon we went ashore, and had another run until sundown. At 6 P.M. the English ship *Netherby* arrived here from the East Indies.

December 30th 1860 at St. Helena

At half past nine o'clock all hands were called to quarters for inspection, after which had divine service on the gun deck. Two English ships arrived this morning; in fact there is not a day passes but one or two vessels arrive here. We are going to commence giving liberty tomorrow morning; the 1st part of the starboard watch, and all the boats' crews are going in the first draft. We are going to have a month's pay and forty-eight hours' liberty. The *Mohican*'s crew are also to have liberty tomorrow.

The crew undoubtedly were owed much more than a month's pay, but the policy when sending the men on liberty was to give them only what was deemed a reasonable amount, to protect them from their own imprudence.

Jamestown, St. Helena. From Matthew C. Perry, *Narrative of the Expedition of the American Squadron to the China Seas and Japan*. Washington, D.C.: Nicholas, 1856. Gilliland Collection.

December 31st 1860   at St. Helena

All hands washed clothes. In the forenoon the purser served out grog, and ration money. Some of our men were sent on board the barque *Storm King*, to take out some of her cargo. She is going to make some repairs, as she leaks badly. At 2 P.M. the 1st part of the starboard watch and the boats' crews were ordered to dress themselves in clean blue mustering clothes and go ashore on liberty. At half past 2 P.M. the Boston Ship *Warren Hallett* and two English ships arrived from China and two more sailed at 4 P.M. Our flag officer went ashore in uniform. He was received by a detachment of the St. Helena Regiment and a full band. As soon as he landed the fort on Ladder Hill gave him a salute of thirteen guns, which was returned by our ship.

There is a remarkable flight of steps on this island: they begin at the base of Ladder Hill, and extend to the fort on top of it. I do not know how many steps there are, but as soon as I get liberty I am going to make it my business to count them. They are wooden steps, not cut into the rock as some people say they are. There is a banister on both sides of them all the way. A person looking up at them from the bottom, would feel rather timid in ascending or descending them, as they look almost perpendicular. The English soldiers and natives of the island run up and down them with a very reckless speed.

Some of our liberty men have come off already, three sheets in the wind. The dramatic club have a rehearsal of *The Widow's Victim* this evening. We had several ladies and gentlemen on board the ship today visiting. It is delightful weather here.

January 1861

at the Island of St. Helena

New year's Day. Some of our liberty men came off this morning, badly cut up. An English mail boat from Cape Town arrived and sailed from here this forenoon. At 11 A.M. a large four-masted French ship came to an anchor, also two English ships; there is a large English clipper ship hove to about ten miles from the island. At twelve o'clock she squared her yards, and was soon out of sight. Two ships sailed from here. In the afternoon we went ashore in the gig, and had a good run. We are taking in water today, and it is very good. Some more of the liberty men came off this evening, badly cut up. Our boys and the *Mohicans* are having a civil war ashore. I had an anchor watch from ten till twelve.

The Civil War at home was about to break out as well. Under the command of Lt. James P. Foster, the slave brig Bonita, *the capture of which Leonard mentions on October 12, 1860, had made its way to Monrovia and landed 616 slaves surviving from the 622 aboard when the ship was captured. Since then it had been making its way back to the United States through extremely rough weather. Adverse gale winds made it impossible to get into Norfolk as ordered or New York, and finally Foster took refuge at Charleston. His mainsail was split, his rigging and spars rotten and battered, and most of his crew sick. The timing was bad, too. He arrived in Charleston on December 20, the very day the South Carolina convention, meeting in Charleston, voted to secede from the Union.*

While his country disintegrated around him, Foster frantically telegraphed Secretary Toucey, asking, "What shall I do?" The district court insisted he bring in his single prisoner, the slaver captain, which he reluctantly did on

December 28. After the court declared it had no jurisdiction, Foster attempted to take the prisoner back to the ship. A mob gathered outside the courthouse forcibly took his prisoner from him while Foster appealed to the sheriff, who looked on and did nothing. Thus another slaver captain escaped justice. Foster's ship was taken from him, too, by armed men, and his requests for a tow to leave the harbor were rejected. Getting his ship back, and with cooperative weather, a week later he was able to sail to Savannah (Georgia being still in the Union) and take his crew by train to New York.[1]

January 2nd   the *Rascius* again/at St. Helena/
                              costumes/badly cut/get brought up
                                          with a round turn

This morning three English ships arrived, and two sailed. The four-masted French ship sailed in the forenoon. At nine o'clock, we brought our captain, purser and flag officer's secretary [ashore]; they are going to visit Napoleon's Tomb. We had a two hours' run. The American whaling barque *Rascius* arrived here today; she is lying off and on. In the afternoon two French barques came in, also an English barque; at 5 P.M. the English barque *Eveline* sailed from here for Hull, England.

At half past 5 P.M. we went ashore for the captain. He was to come off at sundown, [so] we had a couple of hours' run. We went up to the town and met some of our boys, who were pretty merry. They were dressed in all sorts of costumes, their own clothes being stolen from them during the night while they were drunk. The draft is almost all off, [and] we are not going to have any more liberty until the *Mohicans* get through theirs. One of the *Mohican*'s men has had his throat cut and is not expected to recover. It was done by one of his own shipmates.

At 6 P.M. we started to go down to the boat. We met the 1st Lieutenant of the *Mohican* and saluted him. If we met him once we met him a dozen times before we got to the boat. The last time we met him we again saluted him as before. His attention being attracted at something at the time, he did not observe us. On turning round he hailed us somewhat in the following manner: "I say men, when you pass me, I want you to salute me, I am not so damn small but what you can see me." This sally completely took me by surprise, I never felt so mortified in my life. I had some words on the end of my tongue to reply to him, when some good spirit held it back. I should like to salute him on American soil, but this is mutiny, and I had better say no more about it at present.

At half past six o'clock the captain came down and we returned on board. There is great talk and blowing tonight by the liberty men that came off, all telling their adventures while they were ashore. We have got about ten of the

wild in double irons, under the sentry's charge. I am getting very anxious to have my liberty. The 2nd part of the port watch are the next ones to go ashore.
W.A. Leonard
Charlestown, mass.

January 3d 1861

This morning two English ships arrived here. The gig went ashore at five o'clock this morning and we had a run of two hours. At 9 A.M. the 2nd part of the port watch went ashore; there is also a draft from the *Mohican* ashore. In the afternoon the captain went ashore to dine; he gave the boat's crew a run till sundown. The draft that went ashore today are behaving themselves first rate. At seven o'clock we returned on board.

January 4th 1861

This morning some of the liberty men came off. An American barque sailed in the afternoon. We had an hour's run ashore, and returned at five o'clock. In the evening some more of the liberty men came off dead drunk. In the evening the dramatic club had a rehearsal of *Boots at the Swan*.

January 5th 1861

Several vessels passed in sight of the island this morning, showing their numbers as they passed. At one o'clock the 2nd part of the starboard watch were ordered to get ready and go ashore. The gig's crew were also ordered to get ready and go. As we had belonged to the 1st part of the port watch, the order took us by the surprise. Our 1st lieutenant being ashore, we were determined to ask him. As this is the commencement of our liberty it deserves a separate heading.

Preface

I hope the reader of my account of the liberty in St. Helena and visit to the Tomb, and Residence, of Napoleon Bonaparte, will not judge it too harshly. I do not make any pretension to be a writer; if I did I would make the reading of it as interesting to you as the reality was to me; however, I think by reading it the reader will have some idea of what there is written. I write this journal simply to gratify my own curiosity, to see my own adventures in writing and fulfill the wishes of my friends who requested me to write them.
W.A.L.

1861
FORTY EIGHT HOURS LIBERTY IN
THE ISLAND OF ST. HELENA

WITH A DESCRIPTION OF A VISIT TO THE TOMB OF
NAPOLEON BONAPARTE ALSO HIS RESIDENCE AT LONGWOOD

At two o'clock, we went ashore, and met our 1st lieutenant on the landing. We asked him about our friend; he told us he would see about it when he got on board the ship. We then went up town and waited in a public house, by the name of the Heart of Oak and in about half an hour, the object of our anxiety appeared, which circumstance put the party in excellent spirits, we then smiled all around, had some cigars, and then visited some of the most popular resorts, among which, the Spotted Dog, Jolly Tar, and Victoria were the most prominent. As we three (by the way, three constituted our party—their names were John F. Powell, Adner Legg and myself) intended to have a quiet time, we went to a private boarding house and made arrangements for our meals and lodgings while we stayed ashore.

After eating supper we visited the town by gaslight (or rather by candle light). We called into several of the dancing houses, where some of our boys were having (to use their own term) a gay old time. During our visits from place to place, we met several of our men in company with soldiers belonging to the St. Helena Regiments (by the way these same soldiers have a queer way of introducing themselves; they draw you into a conversation about your family affairs, they find out what you are, and who you are, and then by tracing their own generation a little ways back they find that you are a relation, or an old friendship of the family. Of course you must then drink with them, and if you are so unfortunate as to get drunk, you are completely stripped of money and clothing.)

Leaving the dance houses and soldiers to their prey, we visited several other places, and as it was our intention to visit the tomb and residence of Napoleon Bonaparte on the following day, we repaired at an early hour to our lodgings, and retired for the night with pleasant visions of a good night's rest. But in this we were sadly disappointed, for before we had been in bed half an hour, we were swarmed and attacked by fleas, which infest every house on the island and as this is that part of the year, which is called the flea season, they came down on us with a vengeance, and it was that part of the night or morning, when the small hours began to look large, that we closed our eyes to sleep, and when we did get asleep, being very tired, we slept soundly until long after the sun had risen.

After nearly ten years in power, Napoleon had been forced to abdicate in 1814 and was exiled as ruler of the island of Elba, off the Italian coast. The following year he returned to France, where his hundred days in power ended at Waterloo. He sought asylum with the British, who sent him to St. Helena. He

spent the rest of his life there, dying in 1821. In 1840 Great Britain granted
Louis-Philippe, king of France, permission to remove the emperor's body
to Paris, where it has remained entombed in splendor under the dome of the
Invalides. In 1858 Longwood and the tomb were given to France.

Visit the Tomb of Napoleon Bonaparte
Also His Residence at Longwood

Second day. Sunday January 6th 1861.

After brushing ourselves up, and getting breakfast, we left our lodgings, and
started up town, and met twelve or thirteen of our fellows, who were perfectly
sober, and after several of their adventures during the night were related to
us, they proposed that we should join them, and visit Napoleon's Tomb and
Longwood, his residence. As this was our original intention we accepted the
proposal with pleasure. On our way by the barracks, we met two regiments
of English soldiers on their way to church, headed by a brass band of twenty
pieces playing a quick march. They looked very clean and neat. On our way
out we stopped at the upper end of the town, on account of one of our boys
making a proposition that we should take something to drink along with us,
as the road was a very long one, and a hard one to travel. The proposition was
no sooner made than agreed upon; we then mustered together, and got several
bottles of ale and porter, two bottles of wine, and 1 bottle of brandy. We then
made a start in earnest. After turning the first corner of our route (which was
the James Town Street road) we broached two of our bottles, and drank them.
At this point two of the party, getting frightened at the looks and height of
the mountainous road that was before us, resolved to turn back. They bid us
good bye and a pleasant journey, and then started back to the town. We then
resumed our march up the mountain.

The road all the way up was very steep and rocky, and arriving at the
first peak, or bluff (which was about one mile from where we left the two
who went back) we sat down to rest, and broached two more bottles. At this
place, some more of the party, being anxious to get out to the Tomb, started
on and left us sitting down. After resting here about fifteen minutes, our party,
consisting of five, again started on our journey. After tramping about another
mile we stopped and drank the last (as we supposed) of our stock of liquor.
Two more of the party, getting very restless at our stoppages (which were
quite often) started on themselves. They were no sooner out of sight than our
shipmate (who by the way was a very comical fellow) hauled out a pint bottle
of brandy. This we did not care much about, but as we had a hard road to
travel yet before us, we partook of a little, which revived our spirits, and we
again started on our journey, and we learnt from a party, who were going in

the same direction, we were about one mile from the Tomb and one mile and a half from Longwood. This time we started on with the full determination of not stopping until we reached the Tomb. I will here mention that the views we got, while traveling up the mountain, were indeed beautiful. The farms, houses, and country residences of the citizens, which were situated in the valleys below us, presented a very picturesque appearance, and the deep ravines, that met our view at different turns of the road, were terrific to behold.

Arrival at the Tomb

We had almost reached the gate, which is the entrance to the valley wherein the Tomb is situated, when a comical incident occurred to one of our number. A sudden gust of wind lifted the cap off of his head. He immediately started in pursuit of it down the mountain. After running about half a mile, and just being on the point of picking it up, it took another start, and went in another direction. We sat on the grass, and laughed at his attempts to regain his cap until we had pains in our sides. He, however, after several more attempts at last regained it. We then started and reached the gate. The gate, and framework attached to it, is built of wood. It has a large brass bell attached to it, which rings when the gate is opened, and gives notice to the man who has charge of the tomb that there are visitors approaching. We passed through the gate, and after a few minutes' walk we arrived at the Tomb, which is situated inside of a wooden fence, with a small house or sentry box at its entrance, for the keepers, who are French soldiers, one of whom (a corporal) on perceiving us, joined us, and explained everything to us. We gave him a few shillings for his trouble, he gave us a leaf apiece, off of a geranium plant that grew at the side of the tomb, which is situated inside of a neat iron railing, (the space that the tomb occupies to the best of my judgment is about 13 feet long by 10 in width).

The tomb is built of stone, with a large marble slab, cemented on top of it. The remains of the old willow tree that he used to sit under, can be seen yet. It is nothing but an old stump, with no signs of life in it. Before leaving the enclosure, we picked up a stone apiece, as a relic of the tomb, which I intend to bring home with me. We then started out registering our names on the book at the sentry box (which book is kept there expressly for that purpose) passed to the right of the tomb, and drank a glass of water from the same spring that Napoleon used to drink from, in his morning ride, from Longwood. Here (as the French guide told us) Bonaparte would sit for hours, meditating. This was the only spot on the island that he loved. He expressed a wish that if he died and was buried on the island, here he would like to lie. A little further on we came across two small houses which as our guide informed us was where he and the other keeper lived. As we had gained about all the information that was of any interest about the tomb, we asked him the direction to Longwood. He gave us the directions, telling us that there was a tavern on the road, where if we wanted we could get refreshments.

Start for Longwood

We then bid him goodbye, and after 5 minutes' walk, we arrived at the tavern, where we learnt from the landlord that the rest of our party started for Longwood twenty minutes before. Not, however, before we [had] our dinners ordered for us by them. When we got back we then had a lunch, and started on after the rest of the party. On the road we met with a jackass, which one of our boys mounted, and he made the road all the way along by his endeavors to keep on his back.

After walking about half an hour, and meeting with nothing very interesting, we caught sight of the house at Longwood. The mist here was very thick, it was heavy enough to wet us through. I will here mention that the trees, as we came along the roads, presented to us a very peculiar appearance, all leaning in one and the same direction,. which is caused by the wind always blowing in one direction, which is from the S.E., causing the trees to lean to the N.W.

Arrival at Longwood and Description of the House

On approaching the house we met five of the party returning to the inn. They congratulated us on our appearance, and told us they had ordered dinner for themselves and us, and would wait for us at the inn (which by the way went by the name of the Rose and Crown). We then left them and went towards the house, which is enclosed within a wooden fence. The house and grounds covers, (as near as I could judge) about two acres. The gate is similar to the first gate at the tomb. A bell is also attached to this which rang when we entered. We walked up the path, or avenue, which was handsomely laid out, and on approaching the principal entrance to the house, we were met by a French sergeant who takes care of the house and grounds. We entered the house, first registering our names upon his book. We then in company with the sergeant visited every room in the house, [he] explaining everything as we went along.

Napoleon's House at Longwood

The first room we entered was his reception or drawing room. This is where the book is kept where visitors register their names. Every six months this book is sent to Paris. The second room was his parlor, and the very room wherein he died. In this room is a marble bust of himself placed on the very spot where he breathed his last. On the other side of the room is a large mirror, resting on a mantle of black marble, exactly opposite the bust. The next room was his dining room. There was nothing in this room whatever. The sergeant then invited us into his own private apartment and offered us a glass of wine, which we accepted with many thanks.

We then went outside of the house, through a back gate, where we saw an artificial fish pond, where Napoleon used to spend part of his time meditating, and looking at the fishes as they were swimming in the water. The pond is shaped in the form of his Cocked Hat, the dimensions of it being about 16 to 18 feet long and about four to six feet wide. There is a granite margin all round it.

We again entered the house by another door, passing through a servant's room, into the chamber wherein he was first taken sick. Our guide here told us, that this room being very close, the doctor ordered him to be removed into the room wherein he died. There is in this room hanging over the mantle a small mirror. I will here say that as we were passing through the different apartments, and listening to the account of Napoleon's habits, which our guide told us, a feeling of deep melancholy crept over me, which in this room turned into awe. I could not help thinking what must have been the sufferings of so great a man. We next passed into his billiard room, and from there to his bathing room, after which we visited his library; these last three had nothing in them whatever. The upper floor was then visited but as they had no connection with him but belonged to members of his household, a description of them is unnecessary.

We then passed out of the house, which is built of wood. It is an old fashioned cottage built house with two wings. It is painted cream color. Sometime after the death of Napoleon, the house was used as a farm house, the wings being used as stables, but since the French Government has taken possession of it they have recently had it repaired throughout and it now presents the same appearance as it used to when he was living.

Napoleon's Tomb looks today exactly as Leonard described it.

Longwood today also looks much as it did in Leonard's day and remains the property of the government of France.

Returning from Longwood

Having now seen everything of interest that was to be seen, we took a farewell leave of our guide (who was a perfect gentleman) and proceeded on our way back to the inn (Rose and Crown) where our companions were waiting for us to join them. We trudged on, not meeting with any incidents on the road. We arrived there in half an hour and found our companions seated at table, waiting for us. We sat down with them, and after partaking of a hearty dinner, we settled accounts with the landlord, and started on our way back to the town.

As I have given a description of the country on our way out it would be useless to say anything more about it. On our way back some of the party (I being one of the number), feeling very tired and our feet being very sore (mine in particular) took off our shoes, and walked barefoot, and on reaching the environs of the town, we bathed our feet in a stream of water that ran from the mountain, put on our shoes, and walked into town, where we arrived at five o'clock pretty well tired with our day's journey. Meeting with several of our boys, we went to a public house and had some very good ale to drink, after which we went to our lodgings, ate a good supper, and retired at an early hour. And being fatigued with our day's walk, we soon fell asleep, and slept so soundly that our tormentors, of the previous night (I mean the fleas) made no impression on us whatever.

**Monday. January 7th Last day ashore, and the
Visit up Ladder Hill.**

Long after sunrise this morning, we awoke, and after finishing our toilet, and eating a good breakfast, we left the house to pay a visit to Ladder Hill, also to pay particular attention to count the steps, as there had been several disputes as to how many there are. We arrived at the foot of the hill at ten o'clock and commenced the ascent. We counted every step separately until we reached the one hundredth step, where we sat down, and compared our accounts, which we found correct. We then proceeded up, resting at each hundredth step until we reached the top, counting very carefully as we went up, making the amount 651 steps—no more, no less. We then visited the fort, and barracks, and then started on our way down the ladder, which we found much easier than the ascent, as there is two wooden banisters all the way. As that was about all we wanted to see about the famous ladder, we took a stroll till dinner time. There are two hotels in the town, one is Storees, [?] or the St. Helena Hotel, which is situated in the square, (which is called St. James Park) and the other is Smith's or the Commercial Hotel. There are also eight Public houses, or Tap rooms, whose names I have mentioned before. There are at present three churches in the town: one in St James Park (Church of England), one half ways up James-town St. which is called Bertrams Church (Baptist) and the other in process of building, and is intended for the Roman Catholics. This is near the hospital. The principal features of St. James Park are the custom house, court house, post office, St Helena Hotel, the church, barracks, jail and a large garden. There is also a large barrack for the soldiers in Jamestown St.

As it was getting near dinner time, we went to our lodgings, and after eating a first rate dinner, and having two hours yet before our time was up, we laid down for a nap, and did not wake until half past 3 P.M. Our liberty being up [in] one hour and a half, we immediately started for the landing, meeting the other draft coming ashore. We hired a shore boat and arrived on board at four o'clock. We reported ourselves to the officer of the deck. Thus ended our first and probably last liberty in the island of St. Helena. The names of the party were as follows:

J.W. Thomson	C.F. Gordon	W.A. Leonard
J.F. Powell	Adner Legg	Thomas Brady
George Brooks	M. McQuade	M.Marshall
M. Whitehouse	Hugh de Vaney	James Lavin

We are very tired. We enjoyed our liberty first rate. I never would have forgiven myself if I had not visited the Tomb of Napoleon and Longwood. At six o'clock an English barque arrived here. The dramatic troupe are now turning their attention to theatrical matters. We have not fixed upon a particular time, [but] it will be next week; we are waiting to hear from our manager, who is living ashore with the flag officer.

Ladder Hill, with its (now 699) steps more vertical than those of many a ladder in ordinary use, remains a tourist attraction in the twenty-first century.

January 8th 1861.   at St. Helena

This morning we again commenced our usual duties. At eight o'clock an American ship sailed from here. At 10 A.M. we went ashore in the gig and had a run; returned at dinner. In the afternoon two English ships arrived. Turned in very early tonight.

January 9th

This day several vessels passed in sight of the island in the afternoon. All the liberty men came off; all hands now have had liberty. We had several visitors today, principally English officers and their ladies.

Though Leonard's liberty was very successful, some of his shipmates had less happy results. The Boston Daily Advertiser's *anonymous correspondent complained: "Our 'blue jackets' have had an unsatisfactory liberty of forty-eight hours, being while ashore, harassed and driven about by a squad of police. Those who were guilty of the sailor-like offence of getting drunk, were sent off to the ship in charge of an officer, who received a fee of five dollars for his trouble. In this way the sum of $145 was paid to the police, and charged to the accounts of the men, and all further liberty stopped."*[2]

January 10th

This morning an American ship arrived here, and dropped anchor. The 1st lieutenant is going to commence giving the Kroomen liberty tomorrow morning

At home at her family farm near Orange, Virginia, Fannie Page Hume received the letter her fiancé, Lieutenant Rhind, had begun November 4 in Loando and finished at Little Fish Bay November 15. She noted in her diary that Florida and Alabama had seceded today and Mississippi the day before. She wondered "what changes might not be produced" before Rhind returned home.[3]

January 11th   *Mohican* sails

It is very squally here this morning, with a little rain. Two ships and a barque arrived here today; the U.S. Steam Gunboat *Mohican*, sailed in the afternoon for St. Paul de Loando. We had a rehearsal of *Ambrose Gwinnett* in the evening.

January 12th

This morning we holystoned all decks. An English barque arrived here and sailed the forenoon. We are going to have a grand ball on board, also a theatre next week. It is very fine weather here now.

January 13th

Sunday. All hands dressed in white frocks, blue caps, and trousers. At half past nine A.M. the divisions were called to quarters for inspection, after which we had divine service on the gun deck. At 2 P.M. we went ashore and had permission from the captain to remain until sundown.

January 14th

All hands washed clothes. Two English ships arrived here and a barque sailed. At 4 P.M. we went ashore in the gig and had a two hours' run, in the evening we had a rehearsal of *Boots at the Swan,* and *The Widow's Victim.*

January 15th 1861.   at St. Helena.

This morning all hands scrubbed hammocks. An American barque, the *Aurelia,* of Boston, arrived here. We went ashore in the gig and had a very good run. In the evening we had the last rehearsal of *Ambrose Gwinnett;* we are going to give our performance tomorrow night.

January 16th   fixing the Stage/arrival of the *San Jacinto*/
our audience/our last Theatrical Performance

Early this morning the dramatic troupe began to fix up our stage and scenery for the performance. At nine o'clock we went ashore and got some things for it. There is considerable talk about it here ashore. At 1 P.M. we returned on board, at 2 o'clock the preparations for the theatre being over, the boys began to make arrangements for the performance. At three o'clock a steamer was signalized from the fort on Ladder Hill, which proved to be the U.S. Steam Frigate *San Jacinto,* and at half past 4 P.M. she came to an anchor. We have been expecting her this last three days.

With the arrival of the San Jacinto, *the men of the* Constellation *learned that Lincoln had been elected president by a large majority. That news had reached the* San Jacinto *when the* Mystic *delivered its mail at Loanda on January 1. Leonard was apparently so caught up in his thespian activities that he neglected to mention it.*[4]

At six o'clock our audience began to assemble: we had all the officers belonging to the St. Helena regiments and their ladies, besides several of the citizens, all the officers from the U.S. Steam Frigate *San Jacinto,* and sixty of her crew, the crews of an American barque, and whale ship, and our own officers and men. The performance commenced at half past seven o'clock with the three act drama of *Ambrose Gwinnett,* after which a song and dance, then the popular farce of *The Widow's Victim,* a song, and concluded with the laughable farce *Boots at the Swan.* The performance ended at half past 11 o'clock and gave entire satisfaction, but I must say that the way we were treated after the performance, was in my opinion rather shabby. It is a customary thing on board of an American man of war to give the performers a little to drink while the performance is going on, also after it is over. We did not get any (but one before it started) during the plays, and were actually drove into our hammocks after it was over by the 1st lieutenant and Master at Arms. He even prevented two of the officers from giving us any. The boys turned into their hammocks in no very good humor, I can tell you. Below is an exact copy of one of the bills which we had printed ashore:

The Constellation Dramatic Association
<<<((((((((I))))))))>>>

the above association will give a
Dramatic Entertainment
on board the U.S. Flag Ship Constellation at St. Helena
on Wednesday Evening January 16th 1861
<<<*>>>   <<<*>>>   <<<*>>>

the performance will commence with the popular 3 act drama entitled Ambrose Gwinnet after which the Farce of the Widows Victim. the whole to conclude with the laughable farce in one act entitled the Boots at the Swan.

the performace will commence at ½ past 7 precisly [*sic*]
a lapse of 18 years between Second and third acts
Ambrose Gwinett

Ambrose Gwinett . . . W.H. French
Ned Grayling . . . J. Hunter
Gibbert . . . Mr. T.W. Igo
Collins . . . J. Cameron
Lable . . . G. Henry
Reef. . . F. Fader
Lucy Fairlove . . . Mr. W.A. Leonard
Jenny . . . . Mr. J. Cloney
George . . . Mr. J. Stenson
Blackthorn . . . A. Legg
Will Ash . . . W. Harrington
Bolt. a jailor . I. L. Nodine
Officer . . . J. McNamara
1st sailor . . . H. Rudolph
2nd do . . . E.B. Nichols
Mary . . . Master Alvah Olds
villagers by the entire company

after which the popular farce of the

Widows Victim
Jerry Clip . . a stage struck barber . . . (Mr. John Hunter
Tinsel John. . . . .) . . . . (
Moustache Strappado . . . . (
Mr. Twitter . . . . Mr. John Cameron
Byron Tremaine Pelham Podge . . . . P.B. Doran
        *   *   *

Mrs. Rattleton a charming young widow . . W.A. Leonard
Jane Chatterly . her maid . . . . W.H. French
Mrs. Twitter . . . . B. P. Guilford

The performance to conclude with the laughable farce Entitled
the
Boots at the Swan
Higgins . . . . Mr. J. Cloney
Frank Frisky . . . . A. Legg
Jacob Earwig the boots at the swan . . . . J.F. Powell
Pippen . . . . E.B. Nichols
Mrs. Moonshine . . . . Mr. C.F. Gordon
Emily . . . . B.P. Guilford
Sally Smith . . . . W.H. Strowe
Betty Jenkins . . . . Master A. Olds

<<<<<<<~~~>>>>>>>

everything about this performance carried on in good manner: the acting was very good, as we were told by the English and our own officers; our dresses was splendid, we had scenery and costumes from ashore furnished us by the manager of the theatrical club ashore. This will be the last performance we will give on board of the U.S. Ship *Constellation*.

Know thyself is an ancient and Wise Motto
Have, no Chum, in a Man of War

January 17th 1861.   **at St. Helena/Breaking up the Theatre/**
getting ready for the Ball

This morning the boys are clearing up the wreck of the theatre, and the way they demolished the scenery and other fixings was a caution. After breaking it up they threw it overboard and at eight o'clock all traces of our recent theatre were invisible. It is the talk of the whole ship's company the way we were served. As there is considerable trouble on board of an American barque that is at anchor here, two of her men refusing to work, they were brought on board of us, and two of our men were sent in their places. At two o'clock the quartermasters commenced rigging up the quarter deck for the ball, which is to commence at four o'clock. As we went ashore, I did not see much of it. Anyhow it lasted until nine o'clock in the evening. The *San Jacinto* is giving her men forty-eight hours' liberty and one month's pay. In the evening the American barque sailed for Hull, England.

January 18th   **Misfortune/the Boat's crew leave me ashore/**
at St. Helena/laying myself liable to a court martial/
the Boat sent for me by the captain

Today our captain went on board the *San Jacinto* and returned. At 10 A.M. an English ship arrived here from Melbourne, bound for Liverpool. In the afternoon the gig went ashore, and we had a run up town and returned in time for supper, after eating which we again went ashore to get the steward, who was to come off at sundown. We therefore had a good chance for a run. We separated and agreed to meet each other at the landing at sundown. I in company with a Spaniard (the one we took from the slaver) started up town to visit some folks we were acquainted with. While we were ashore on liberty, after staying here about half an hour, the Spaniard went out, saying he would wait for me at the corner. I staid about five minutes longer. I started to go down to the boat, the Spaniard (Pedro)[5] having gone down before me. On arriving at the landing, the boat was gone. On looking I saw she was half ways to the ship. I halload after them but it was no use, they did not hear me. I was now in a quandary whether to go aboard in a shore boat or not. After deliberating about five minutes or more, I came to the foolish conclusion to remain ashore, thereby laying myself liable to a summary court martial. With this intention I went up town and met some of the *San Jacinto*'s men, who were on liberty. I stated the case to them, and they generously furnished me with some money, and in company with them I spent the night and part of the next day. At eight o'clock the boat again came ashore, with an order from the captain to bring me on board. I met the coxswain of the boat at half past 8 P.M. and he in a very insulting manner ordered me to go on board, which I did not take any notice of it. I have no doubt if he had asked me in any kind of a gentlemanly manner I would have gone aboard without any further trouble; as it was I told my official coxswain to go to a very unreasonable locality.

January 19th   a reward is offered for me/am caught/
                                          brought aboard put in irons

At eleven o'clock this forenoon, as I was taking a nap in one of the public houses, my slumbers were awakened by the two of the St. Helena Police, who informed me that there was a reward offered for me, and a description of my person being sent with the reward, they had no hesitation in saying that I was the person. They marched me to the landing, and brought me on board the ship, where I was immediately put in double irons, and put in the brig where there was another prisoner besides myself. He is serving out a sentence of thirty days on bread and water for not paying proper respect for an officer while ashore on liberty.

January 20th   in the Brig

Sunday. On account of being in the brig I do not know what transpired on deck. The only [thing] that relieves the time is the change of sentries every half hour. In the afternoon we had the company of a krooboy, who was triced up to a beam for some misdemeanor. I felt very uncomfortable in double irons and am in great suspense to know what they are going to do to me. At night all hands swung clean hammock; mine was slung by a friend, J.F.P. [John F. Powell, a member of the gig's crew.]

January 21st   Liberated/put back in the boat/
                                          got off through the captain's influence

This morning all hands scrubbed and washed clothes. At half past nine o'clock I was taken out of the brig by the Master at Arms, who told me that I was free, and was also told by him that I would have to go in the boat as usual. This to me sounded rather strange. I thought I would be taken out of the boat [at] all events. I think myself very fortunate in getting off so easily. It was through the captain's influence I got off; it is according to the Articles of War a court martial offence. My character up to the present time has been very good; this I know must have had great influence with him. At 3 P.M. an American whaling schooner, the *Fanny* of Sacketts Harbor, arrived here. At 5 o'clock an English barque sailed from here. After supper the gig went ashore, but nobody got out but the coxswain. Returned at sundown. Very fine weather.

January 22nd

All hands scrubbed hammocks. We had several visitors on board the ship today. An English barque sailed today. An English ship laying off and on. The *San Jacinto* is still giving her men liberty.

January 23d   asking for more liberty

We are taking in wood and water. The ship's company are very anxious to have twenty-four hours more liberty. The petty officers went to the mast about it, and the 1st lieutenant told them point blank no, as the ship is to be reported ready for sea Saturday. In the afternoon the captain dined on board the *San Jacinto*. We staid on board of her until nine o'clock.

January 24th 1860   at St. Helena

This morning we holystoned all decks. In the afternoon we went ashore, but all the crew had to stay in the boat. At six o'clock we returned on board. In the evening the boys had a dance in the gangway until nine o'clock.

January 25th

All hands washed clothes. It is my boatkeeping day. At 4 P.M. the gig went ashore for the captain's steward. The captain told them they might have a run until sundown. I was ordered to stay in here for punishment. At sundown we returned on board.

January 26th   preparing for sea/Leaving the island of St. Helena/
news of the *Saratoga*

This morning we holystoned all decks, after which we sent up royal yards, and got up all the fish gear. After breakfast we took in all boats, and got up the messenger, and at eleven o'clock we were all ready to heave up our anchor. We are waiting for the flag officer. At one o'clock he arrived on board, and at half past 1 P.M. we hove up the anchor and made sail, first putting a single reef in the topsails, the breeze being rather fresh at the time. We then set topgallant sails over them, and in two hours' time we were a good distance from the island of St. Helena, although it was very plain in sight. We now shook out the reefs, and set royals, and flying jib. We left our Marine officer on board the *San Jacinto* at his own request to drill the marines on board of her; he is to join us again in about two weeks. At sundown the island of St. Helena was out of sight. We have got a first rate breeze; we are going the rate of seven and eight knots an hour. Where we are going I do not know for certain; it is rumored that we are going to the Congo River. We have got news that the U.S. Sloop of war *Saratoga* is at St. Paul de Loando.

January 27th 1861.   cutting a Krooman

Sunday at half past nine o'clock the divisions were called to quarters for inspection after which all hands were called to muster. The Articles of War were read by the 1st lieutenant, after which we had divine service on the gun deck. Today one of our men struck a krooman on the forehead with a stick and cut him badly. He was put in the brig with double irons. He will be court martialed.

January 28th   court martial/Sentence

The port watch washed clothes. We have got a good breeze, and are going about eight knots an hour. In the afternoon the officers are having a summary court martial upon the man that cut the krooman. After supper the 1st division exercised large guns, the 2nd Small Arms and the 3d single sticks. We have got all the starboard studding sails set. At half past five o'clock all hands were called to muster to hear the sentence of a court martial, which was as follows: reduction to the next inferior rank (an ordinary seaman, he being an able seaman); two months' black list, to consist of cleaning bright work. The charges brought again him were taking the law into his own hands and saying at the mast that a white man could get no justice on board this ship, it is very hard to get punished for a nigger.

January 29th

Starboard watch washed clothes this morning. In the afternoon the divisions are at the usual exercise. Very fine weather, going about ten knots an hour.

January 30th 1861

This day came in very fine, the divisions exercised in the afternoon. In the dog watches the men were amusing themselves with boxing gloves.

January 31st   at sea

The starboard watch washed clothes; the hammocks were all piped out of the nettings to air bedding, as it was a very fine day.

February 1861

1st   at sea/on the cruising ground

At half past nine this morning, the drum beat to general quarters. Exercised the port battery. At half past ten beat the retreat. We are now in our cruising ground. We had several rain squalls during the night.

February 2nd

The port watch holystoned the gun deck. The division and mess bills are out today. The weather looks very dark and squally.

February 3d   off Congo River

Sunday. It is raining, we had to dispense with the usual inspection. We are now in the vicinity of the Congo River. We expect to meet the mail, which is coming from Fernando Po in one of our gun boats. It was a dead calm all night.

February 4th

The starboard watch washed clothes. It is still a calm, and very warm. My mast head from ten till twelve. We are going to St. Paul de Loando.

February 5th   land ho/we are Saluted by the *Saratoga*/
shipping in St Paul de Loando

Early this morning, land was reported, all along our lee beam. We tacked ship and stood in for it. It proved to be St. Paul de Loando. On nearing the mouth of the harbor we were saluted by a vessel with thirteen guns. Made her out to be the U.S. Sloop of war *Saratoga*, which has just come out here to join the squadron. We returned her a salute of seven guns. At five o'clock we came to an anchor. The *Mohican, Mystic,* and *Sumpter* are here; the barque *John*

USS *Saratoga*. Special Collections and Archives Department, Nimitz Library, United States Naval Academy.

Gilpin of Boston and three other American barques are here; the English gun boat *Wrangler* is here; there is a large American ship coming in. After supper we got out all boats and sent down royal yards. The *Saratoga* brought us a mail. I got two letters from home (W. L.).

February 6th 1861   **St. Paul de Loando/inspecting the *Saratoga***

This morning all hands are very busy cleaning the ship, inside and out. At 9 A.M. the flag officer went on board the *Saratoga*, to inspect them. On his arrival they saluted him with thirteen guns. In the afternoon the American coal ship *Mazeppa* arrived here from Philadelphia after a passage of sixty-five days. At four o'clock a Portuguese gunboat arrived here with some important personage on board, as they are manning yards and saluting him all over the harbor. We had a run ashore today in the boat.

The Saratoga *brought out seventeen marines as replacements; they were transferred to the flagship.[1] Inman dispatched the* Saratoga *to cruise between Kabenda and Snake's Head, alerting its captain to keep a special eye out for several ships known to be up the Congo at Punta da Lenha; among the suspect vessels was the thousand-ton clipper ship* Nightingale.

February 7th **witness a governor's reception**

At eleven o'clock last night the *Saratoga* sailed for the Congo River. The English sloop of war *Archer* and gunboat *Sharpshooter* arrived here today. In the afternoon we went ashore in the gig and had a good run until sundown. There is a new governor appointed for this place. He arrived here yesterday; it was he that all the saluting was for yesterday. We happened to be on the wharf when he was received by all the officials of the place, and soldiers, and several thousands of the people. They welcomed him in a very good manner. We then returned on board.

Inman, receiving instructions from the secretary, orders Commander Godon, the Mohican's *commanding officer, to take on duties as purser aboard the* Mohican, *despite Godon's previous strong protests. The ship's purser had been sent home sick, and the squadron had no replacement, but funds had to be handled somehow to cover local expenses and pay the crew. Godon asked to be relieved of command but was denied.*

February 8th

This morning all hands washed clothes. At nine o'clock A.M. the U.S. Steam Frigate *San Jacinto* arrived here from St. Helena. She reports the U.S. Sloop of war *Portsmouth* there giving her men liberty.

February 9th **ship *Nightingale* of Boston**

At 1 P.M. the captain went aboard the *Mystic* to dine. We then went ashore with the steward, and returned on board at sundown. It is schreeching hot here now. That is the only way that I can express the state of the weather at present. The report here now is that the Congo River is full of slavers. The American ship *Nightingale* of Boston is out here after a cargo of Black Ebony.

The clipper Nightingale, *to be mentioned again later, was one of the most famous ships of the day. Built in Maine in 1851, it was designed to carry fifty passengers in luxury between New York and London for Prince Albert's Great Exhibition of that year, after which it was intended for the China tea trade. Displacing 1,066 tons and 178 feet long, it proved to be not only exceptionally beautiful but remarkably fast. Indeed it repeatedly proved itself the fastest ship in the world. It was named after singer Jenny Lind, the "Swedish Nightingale," whose U.S. concert tours in 1850–52 had made her and promoter P. T. Barnum very wealthy. Financial problems caused the ship to be sold into ordinary trade instead of going to the Great Exhibition and eventually to be bought by slavers, as Leonard here reports.*

February 10th 1861   at St. Paul de Loando

Sunday. The English Gunboat *Sharpshooter* sailed today. At 10 A.M. a Portuguese brig came in. In the afternoon the *Mystic* sailed for Congo. It being Sunday, we were called to quarters for inspection at half past 9 A.M. Divine Service as usual in the afternoon. Went visiting the other ships in port.[2]

February 11th   taking in 6 months provisions

All hands washed clothes. The gig went ashore after breakfast and returned at 1 P.M. We are now taking in six months' provisions. We expect to sail in a few days. The English Steam Sloop of war *Archer* sailed from here today. She has got orders to go home. We were taking in provisions until a very late hour.

February 12th   orders the fleet to meet on the 4th of March

This morning the gig went fishing. At 8 A.M. a Portuguese man of war brig arrived here, a Portuguese barque sailed. It is rumored about the ship that the flag officer has given orders to the whole squadron to meet him in Kabenda Bay on the 4th of March, when he will give them his final orders. It is also rumored that we are not going to St Paul de Loando again. In the afternoon the gig went ashore, and returned at sundown.

Writing to a friend at home, Captain LeRoy of the Mystic *commented that, given the latest mail from home, "many out here seem to think disunion certain." Still, continued LeRoy, "a steamer from the Cape de Verdes a few days since brought our Flag Officer a note from the English Consul there stating they had news from England to the 1st Jany & that the news there received from the U.S. represented matters as quieting down." He also noted that Inman had deposited the squadron archives ashore.* [3] *As this was so his relief could retrieve them, clearly Inman expected to go home very soon.*

Fannie Hume, receiving the letter Lieutenant Rhind had mailed December 27 from St. Helena, remarked that "no tidings of our political turmoil had reached him."[4]

February 13th   leaving St. Paul de Loando for the last time

Twenty months in commission. All hands scrubbed hammocks. At eight o'clock crossed royal yards. The main top men got fits, on account of their yard. Their royal yard men had to send it down again and try it over. The *San Jacinto* sailed this morning for the Congo. We are going to sea at 3 P.M. At 10 A.M.

the gig went ashore and returned at dinner time. At 3 P.M. we got underway and went to sea. We have got a splendid breeze; we soon passed the English Gunboat *Wrangler,* which vessel was a good ways ahead of us. We are going to the Congo River.

Raising and crossing the royal yards was done every morning at eight o'clock when a U.S. Navy vessel was in port and also of course done prior to getting under way. The smartness of this action was one measure of the general excellence of a ship's crew, readily observed by officers and men on other ships in the vicinity, as well as by flag officers or commodores. Having to "try over" would have been embarrassing, especially for the flagship. When other squadron ships were in port or at anchorage with the flagship, they were supposed to follow the lead of the senior ship in crossing yards each morning.

As has been noted earlier, the Constellation *was very fast for its type of ship, and as seems to be recorded here in Leonard's account of its passing the* Wrangler, *under the right wind conditions a good sailing ship could outrun the steam vessels of the day.*

February 14th 1861   at sea/cruising after the *Nightingale* of Boston

The starboard watch washed clothes. We are on the lookout for the ship *Nightingale,* of Boston. She is reported to be out here, for a cargo of slaves. The Kroomen were sent to the mast head to look out (Rather a late move after being in commission 20 months). At twelve o'clock noon a sail was reported which proved to be the gunboat *Mystic.* After supper we bent a new mainsail. The *Mystic* is still in sight. At 6 P.M. the royals and topgallant sails were furled, the courses hauled up and the main topsail braced aback, and remained so all night. A fine moonlit night.

February 15th   toothache/a Dutch Jew

Port watch washed clothes. At six o'clock we made all sail and set all the port studding sails. I am suffering severely from a very bad toothache, the last three days. It drives me almost crazy. At night we again took in all the light sails, hauled up the courses and remained so until morning.

Another of our celebrities is Peter Anderson, the foremast man. He is a Dutchman, and one of the shrewdest ones I ever saw. He is called by three or four different titles by the ship's company, such as Dutch Peter, Jew, Down Easter and Nettles, the latter sobriquet being given him on account of his always making them and selling them to those who are too lazy to lay them up for themselves. His usual charge is a plug of tobacco (which is equal to 26 cts). He not only deals in nettles, but in fact everything that he can make— anything—knives, bag lanyards, clothes stops, shoes &c &c. Take it into consideration that tobacco is worth sixty and seventy cents a plug on this coast, he makes an immense profit. He is a very accommodating man and is a very lively one; he keeps the whole ship's company in a continual laugh when he has a mind to. This I believe is his third cruise in the U.S. Navy. There are several more whom I touch up in the course of the journal.

W.A. Leonard

A nettle (or knittle) was a short piece of cord used to sling a hammock.

February 16th 1861.   at sea/court martial/sail ho

The port watch holystoned the gun deck. It is a dead calm. At 9 A.M. a sail was reported on our lee beam. There is a summary court martial going on today. The sail proved to be the U.S. Sloop of war *Saratoga*. She hove to and her captain came on board. At night we lost sight of her. Tacked ship several times during the night.

February 17th   sail ho/the *Mystic*/sail ho/land ho/a rain squall

Sunday at 8 A.M. a sail was reported on our lee bow; we squared in and stood down to her, we also saw a steamer in chase of her, which proved to be the U.S. Gunboat *Mystic*. At half past 9 A.M. the divisions were called to quarters for inspection. At 10 A.M. spoke the *Mystic,* who reported the other sail to be an English barque after palm oil and ivory. We then hauled close on a wind and left the *Mystic* to pursue her course. At 2 P.M. another sail was reported on our weather beam, there is land all along our lee beam. The sail proved to be a large Portuguese man of war steamer.

At night it began to thicken up and looked very squally. At twelve o'clock it burst upon us. We took in all the light sail and furled them, single reefed the Top-sails and lowered them on the caps and left them so all the middle watch. It did not blow, however, but the rain poured down in torrents. I never saw it rain so in my life—it came down in such quantities that it almost blinded me—it thundered and lightened awfully. In the morning watch it cleared up and we made all sail.

February 18th   sail ho/board her/at sea/sentence of a court martial

This morning the starboard watch washed clothes. It still looks very rainy. At 9 A.M. a sail was reported on our lee bow standing for us. On her coming near us, we hove to and sent a boat on board of her. She had English colors at her peak. She proved to be the English barque *Guilford*, of Liverpool. She is trading on the coast for palm oil and ivory. She is the same one we were in chase of yesterday and the one that *Mystic* boarded. In the afternoon the 1st division exercised large guns, the 2nd division small arms and the 3d division single sticks. We have everything ready to go to quarters at night in a moment's notice.

At five o'clock all hands were called to muster to hear sentence of a court-martial. The charges were treating a superior officer with contempt. The sentence was twenty days in solitary confinement in single irons on bread and water and one month's black list to consist of cleaning brightwork two hours each day in his watch below. (Joe Fitzsimmons)

It was very cloudy all night. At 11 P.M. took in royals and topgallant sails; it remained calm all night. In the morning watch set all sail. A light breeze is springing up; set all the port studding sails.

February 19th   sail ho/exercising the main Royal yard men

At 6 A.M. sighted three sails. One was the barque that we boarded yesterday, and the other proved to be the U.S. Steam Gunboat *Mohican.* We made signals to her, but she did not answer them. In the afternoon we got a six knot breeze, at four o'clock the royals were taken in; the main royal being furled rather slow, the captain being on deck took notice of it. He made them loose and furl it six times in succession. At 5 P.M. the divisions went through the customary exercise. It was a dead calm all night and very warm.

February 20th   again elected main Top Sweeper

This day came in cloudy, with no wind. At twelve o'clock this day I was again elected Main Top Sweeper, on the gun deck. Which job I detest; however, it will give me the opportunity of writing a great deal more than if I was on deck. The divisions exercised as usual. We had very light winds all night and it was very warm. I had a gangway lookout from ten until twelve o'clock in the first watch.

February 21st 1861.   at sea/Shark/Captain of the Mizzen Top/
                                      a narrow escape from Death

Port watch washed clothes. It is still a dead calm, and very warm. At 10 A.M. a light breeze sprung up. We are making to the southward, starboard tacks aboard [sic]. At eleven o'clock we caught a large shark, eight foot long. At 5 P.M. we had a very heavy rain squall; it cleared up towards eight o'clock and we had a very clear night.

Another of our Noticeable Characters is Alexander Wilson, captain of the mizzen top. He is a man that stands about 5 feet 6 inches and of a very dark complexion, which the men keep a twitting him all the time about, calling him such names as Moke (a vulgar phrase in a man of war for a negro), Krooboy, and in fact every name they can think of that applies to the dark specimens of humanity. Which he listens to with a very good grace, he has got one of the very best tempers for a man that I ever heard of. He is all the time spinning yarns that are as incredulous as the stories in the Arabian Knights, and to make the story more laughable, he is always the hero of his own yarn. He came very near being killed, the first time we left Porto Grande. In getting underway, he was on the fore topsail yard (he being captain of the fore top at the time). When the topsails were hoisted, the fore went foul, the boom tricing line being fast in the top. It parted and the boom came down, striking Wilson on the head and knocking him aloft the yard. He struck the topmast rigging, which fortunately threw him into the belly of the foretop sail, thus saving his life. He was then caught by his topmates and brought upon deck, and into the sick bay where his life was despaired of for four days after the fall. He is now, however, in first rate health and as funny as ever. He has been quartermaster, captain of the fore and mizzen top, which he is now acting. He is a native of Baltimore, Maryland U.S.A.

February 22nd   At sea

Washington's Birth Day. It is very cloudy this morning. At nine o'clock it cleared up, and it now has the appearance of a very fine day. It turned out to be a beautiful day. We had no wind. However, at five P.M. all hands spliced the Main Brace in honor of the day. It remained a dead calm all night.

February 23d   sail ho/beat the *Saratoga*/sail ho/
the *Portsmouth*/a heavy rain squall

It is still a calm. At daylight three sails were reported, one supposed to be the *Saratoga* and another the *San Jacinto*. At 9 A.M. the starboard watch holystoned the gun deck, at 11 A.M. we got a good breeze, set all the port studding sails. The Sloop of war *Saratoga* is astern of us coming up very fast. At four o'clock the breeze freshened up, and we are leaving the *Saratoga* fast, having at 5 P.M. gained one mile and a half. She now gave up the chase and stood in another direction. We now have got a good breeze. At four bells in the first watch (ten o'clock) a sail was reported on our starboard bow. She showed signal lights which no other vessel but the *Portsmouth* has got. At five bells we spoke her, both vessels hove to, and her captain came on board. She left Kabenda at nine o'clock this morning, in search of us. She is just from St. Helena. She expected that we had her orders to go home; they thought the *Saratoga* was their relief, in which they got disappointed. Our flag officer gave her orders to cruise off the Congo River.

All the middle watch a rain squall was brewing around us, which at half past three o'clock burst upon us. We took in all the light sails and furled them, lowered the topsails on the caps, and hauled out the reef tackles. The thunder was very loud, and the lightning was very vivid. During the flashes we could see the *Portsmouth* to leeward under the same sail as we were. It did not blow much, however, but rained unmercifully, which gave the boys wet jackets.

February 24th 1861

at sea/Sunday in a man of war during
a rain storm/Bad Bread/sail ho

Sunday, at daylight made all sail. It is still raining, and continued raining all the forenoon, which caused us to dispense with the usual Sunday morning's inspection and church. A man of war is one of the dullest places in the world, during a rain storm; they are so open that they are always wet, the watch below moping about the gun and berth Decks like so many old maids. The individuals that catch fits on such occasions are the gun deck sweepers, who are all the time with a swab in their hands, drying up the deck. At noon it stopped raining, and the afternoon was fine. Our bread is getting very bad, being as full as it can be with maggots and weevils, which to a sensitive person gives quite a shock, when he feels one in his mouth. At 5 P.M. a sail was reported, right ahead, made her out to be a brig, we gave her chase, at dark we lost sight of her.

February 25th

sail ho/chase a suspicious looking sail/
she proves to be the *Portsmouth*/at sea

This morning the port watch washed clothes. It is a beautiful morning. At 10 A.M. two sails were reported; one is the *San Jacinto* and the other we are in chase of. She proved to be the Sloop of war *Portsmouth*. At 5 P.M. the divisions exercised. At night we furled the light sails, hauled up the courses and hove to. At half past eleven in the first watch a sail was reported right ahead, we immediately made all sail and gave her chase. Supposing her to be a slaver, we got everything ready for boarding her: we ran the two forward guns into the bridle ports ready for action. At four bells in the middle watch we came up to her, when our supposed slaver turned out to be the U.S. Sloop of war *Portsmouth*. She hove to and sent a boat alongside of us. We also hove to. At seven bells we again took in all the light sails, hauled up the courses, and hove to. The *Portsmouth* under easy sail is going to the southward. In the morning watch we again made all sail; set all our starboard studding sails. It is very fine weather.

February 26th

sail ho/*San Jacinto* and *Sumpter*/
cruising off the Congo River

At 6 P.M. two sails were reported on our lee bow; one is supposed to be the *San Jacinto;* the other we have not made out yet. We are standing for the *San Jacinto*. At nine o'clock we fired a gun for her to heave to. It is very warm this forenoon. At half past ten this forenoon the sails were close alongside; one is the *San Jacinto,* and the other is the Gunboat *Sumpter.* We hove to, and both captains came on board. The captain of the *Sumpter* gave us the information that a brig has cleared the coast with a cargo of slaves (probably the one we were in chase of and lost sight of). He also says that the clipper ship *Nightingale* is in the Congo River waiting for an opportunity to come out with a cargo. At 11 A.M. we parted company with the steamers, and stood on our course. It is a very fine day; we have got an eight knot breeze. We are in the vicinity of the Congo River. At 5 P.M. the divisions exercised. We had a good breeze all night. In the first watch we sighted one of our gun boats, but she was too far off to make out which one it was.

February 27th   rumor

This day came in very fine, with a good breeze. At three bells in the morning watch a sail was reported on our lee beam. We are close to the mouth of the Congo River. We are going five knots an hour. At three o'clock we bent new topsails. We had a very good night of it. It is rumored around the ship that our Kroomen are going to leave us on the fifth of March in Kabenda, which puts the men in very good spirits, as they have been the cause of a great deal of trouble since they have been in the ship.

God, and our Native Land.

An Interesting chapter on Miscellaneous Matters

The ship's company are divided into 5 separate divisions. Viz:

1st Division

is commanded by the 2nd Lieutenant, and the oldest midshipman. It comprises the eight forward guns. Also the launch, the largest boat in the ship, belongs to this division: she carries two howitzers (12 pounders) and 30 men. There are 60 men in this division, 14 men and a powder boy to each gun.

2nd Division

is commanded by the 3rd Lieutenant and the next oldest middy. It comprises the 6 next guns abaft the 1st division. The 1st and 2nd cutters belong to this division. Each man is furnished with a cutlass, pistol, and ammunition. There are 45 men in this division.

3d Division

is commanded by the 4th Lieutenant and the youngest middy. It comprises the 6 after guns. The 3d and 4th Cutters belong to this division. The boats' crews are armed the same as in the 3d division. There are 45 men in this division.

4th Division

is the spar deck, a master's division and is under his charge. They look out for the sailing of the ship when the other divisions are at quarters, and if anything is shot or carried away they repair it. The Boatswain and his mates, of which there are 4, belong to this division. There are 25 men in this division, besides two men from each gun on the gun deck called sail trimmers, who when the Boatswain pipes a peculiar whistle, have to go on the spar deck and assist the master to make, and take in, sail.

5th Division

is the powder and magazine division. Their station is the berth deck, shot lockers and shell rooms. They pass the cartridges, shot and shell from the berth deck to the powder boys of the gun deck division, by means of small tackles, made expressly for the purpose. This is the largest division in the ship. It is in charge of the Gunner and his mate.

Quarters

A gun's crew are divided into 2 parts, 1st and 2nd. The only time they work separate, however, is when both batteries are worked, which is very seldom. They are numbered, the 1st being captain. Every odd number is his part: 3 is the 1st loader and 2nd boarder, 5 is the 1st sponger, 2nd boarder, 7 is the 1st shot and wad and pikeman, 9 is the 1st handspikeman, and 2 boarder, 11 is the 1st train tackleman, fireman and port guard, 13 is the 1st side tackle man and pikeman. This is all the 1st part of the gun's crew. Then comes the second part, which begins with No. 2, who is 2nd captain and 1st boarder; 4 [is] 2nd loader [and] 1st boarder; 6 [is] 2nd sponger, 1st boarder; 8 is 2nd shot and wad and pumpman; 10 [is] 2nd handspike, 1st boarder; 12 [is] 2nd train tackleman, sail trimmer and port guard; 14 second side tackleman and pike man. Those with a powder boy make a gun crew complete.

As the normal expectation was that in combat only one side of the ship would be engaged, the ship carried enough crew to man half the guns fully—either the starboard or port battery. Should the ship find itself between two opponents, half of each gun crew would man the opposite gun. In the case of either boarding an enemy ship or needing to repel boarders, the gun crews then became pikemen and boarders.

At quarters there are certain signals, or orders, which apply to the different stations of the gun's crew, in case we should board a ship, or repel them from boarding us. [When] the fighting captain gives an order to call away the 1st boarder, a rattle is sprung. When the 1st boarders go where they are ordered to, at the 2nd spring of the rattle ("all boarders"), a double roll of the drum calls away all pikemen.

In case of a general fire on board the ship, the bell rings and the drum beats to quarters. The ship's bell calls away the firemen, who are furnished with fire buckets with three fathoms of line attached to them. The pumps and hose are rigged by the carpenter and his gang, 1st boarders get all the ship's water buckets and bring them in the lee gangway, the scupper plugs and ports are put in and lowered. The pumpmen man the pumps. The Marines are drawn up on the quarter deck with loaded muskets, ready for any emergency, while the spirit room is guarded by the corporals. The magazine is the gunner's charge, who at an order can flood it in a moment's notice by means of a cock or cassett in the magazine room. All combustible matter is under the officers of divisions' charge, that is if it is in his part of the ship, who if he thinks it will endanger the ship can order it to be thrown overboard.

When the drum beats to general fighting quarters all hands go to their stations, cast loose one, or both batteries (that is in case the order should be one or both), the 1st captain of the gun reports his gun ready to the officer of his division, who when the division is ready, reports to the 1st lieutenant (who is the fighting captain), who in turn reports to the captain. All orders come from the captain, through the 1st lieutenant, and by the captain's clerk to the officers of the divisions.

Every Friday in each week we have general quarters. After going through some of the most important maneuvers the drum beats the retreat. There is also a detachment of Marines on board the ship, commanded by a Marine lieutenant, who take an active part in general quarters, to cover the men when they are boarding. They number 40 men, 2 orderly sergeants, 4 corporals, and 24 privates.[5] The master's division are provided with carbines, so they can fire from the tops and rigging.

Small Arms

The gun deck divisions are formed into companies of small arms men, called battalions: the 1st commanded by the 2nd lieutenant, and a midshipman; the 2nd by the 3d lieutenant and a middy. They are exercised at musket drill one day each week. Sometimes in port they go ashore for target practice. They are also drilled one day each week at broadsword exercise, and still another day for large gun drill. During wet or stormy weather, it is dispensed with. Thursday is General Fire Quarters; Friday is General Fighting Quarters; Saturday, general holystoning; and Sunday is general inspection.

Boats

There are 8 boats in the ship: the launch; 1st. 2nd. 3d and 4th cutters; the barge, or flag officer's boat; the gig, or captain's boat; and dinghy, which is the smallest boat in the ship. Each boat has got a coxswain, whose duty it is to look after their boats, and all the gear belonging to her. They also act as 2nd captains of tops, with exception of the dinghy's coxswain, whose rate generally goes to the ship's painter, or extra boatswain's mate. Each boat is furnished with masts and sails. The launch, 1st and 2nd cutters, are used in port to provision and water ship; the 3d cutter is steerage boat; and 4th cutter is the ward room boat. The barge is the flag officer's, and gig the captain's; the dinghy is used by everybody.

Watches

The ship's company are divided into two watches, Starboard, and Port. Each watch is divided into 5 separate parts, viz. Forecastle, Fore Top, Main Top, Mizzen Top and After Guard. Each part [has] about 16 men, who are also divided into parts called Quarter watches, with 1st and 2nd captains. Each part of the ship has its particular duties to perform, and nothing else. Each watch is commanded by a lieutenant and midshipman, who are called Officers of the Deck. Each watch has got a boatswain's mate, whose duty it is to repeat the orders from the quarterdeck, and see them executed. There is also a part of the Marine Corps, who stand watch at sea; they are in the charge of a corporal of Marines. There is also a ship's corporal attached to each watch, whose duty it is to see the ship's regulations kept and in port to keep off all boats, and [keep] strangers from coming aboard, unless by permission from the officer of the deck. They also assist the Master at Arms, to take charge of all prisoners, and at night to see all lights put out except those which are required to light the ship.

Petty Officers &c. &c.

Master at Arms

has charge of the berth deck, and prisoners that are sentenced by court martial, and with the assistance of the ship's corporals, to see that their sentences are carried into effect. He also sees that the berth deck is kept in good order, and [is] to see that the messes are properly regulated and see that the ship's company swing their hammocks in their proper numbers, and in port to see everybody in their hammocks at nine o'clock, excepting those that are required on watch. He is a first class petty officer, his pay being 25 dollars a month. He is known to the ship's company by the curious sobriquet of "Jimmy Legs." (For further information about the master at arms, and messes, see page 83.)

Yeoman

has charge of the storeroom. His duty is to take charge of all articles required for the ship's use, such as Hardware, Rigging, Blocks, &c. &c. He keeps an account of everything that is expended by him. His pay is 30 dollars a month. The storeroom is situated in the forward part of the ship, on the orlop deck. Its entrance is by way of the fore passage.

Painter

has charge of all oils, and paints, has a locker to himself which is forward of the yeoman's room, or what is called the eyes of the ship. He does all the painting that there is to be done, with the assistance of such of the ship's company that know how to paint. He has got a coxswain's rate or 24 dollars a month.

Armorer

or ship's blacksmith, sees to fixing all iron work. He has a forge, and all the tools required at his work. He is assisted by a mate. He is a second class petty officer, 20 dollars a month.

Cooper

has all the coopering work to do, and opens all the provisions, and sometimes he assists the carpenter. He is also a second class petty officer, 20 dollars a month.

Carpenter's Mate

is a first class petty officer with 24 dollars a month. He does all the carpenter work with the assistance of the carpenter's gang. His work is overseen by the ship's carpenter, who is a warrant officer.

Sail Maker's Mate

is a second class petty officer (20 dollars a month). He mends all the sails, hammocks, awnings, and such other work that may be required of him. His work is overseen by the Sail Maker, who is also a warrant officer. He has also charge of the sail rooms, of which there are two, one in the forward passage, and the other in the cockpit.

Gunner's Mate

is a first class petty officer. His duty is to look after all the guns and their gear, and everything that is appertaining to them. He is assisted by the quarter gunners. His work is superintended by the gunner, a warrant officer. He looks after the powder magazine, shot, and shell rooms.

Quarter Gunners

are second class petty officers (20 dollars a month). They are stationed in the division, to keep the batteries, small arms &c in order. There are six of them, three in each watch, who at sea, they are stationed on the main yard, and look after the mainsail. They also have the foretopmast studding sail tack and boom brace to look after; also the after guy belonging to the lower boom, and with the assistance of the quartermasters and after guard, the main rigging comes in their line of duty.

Quarter Masters

are 1st class petty officers, five of which get 24 dollars, and the other gets 25 dollars a month. He is the signal quartermaster. Their business is to see to the steering of the ship, and to see all provisions properly weighted when they are served out to the ship's company. They also look out for all flags and signals, lead lines and compasses. Coming into harbor they are stationed at the wheel, and in the chains heaving the lead. They assist the other parts, in the main rigging.

Boatswain's Mates

are 1st class petty officers. The range of their duty is very extensive. There are four of them in the ship, three of which stand watch and the other officiates as master's mate on the gun deck. They are each provided with a silver pipe, or whistle. When an order is given by the officer of the deck they pipe, and repeat the order, and also see that it is done. A boatswain's mate is supposed to be the best sailor man, and of course they superintend all the sailor men, when they are to work. When the ship's company has any complaints to make, they generally get the Chief Boatswain's Mate to speak for them, as he is counted one of the leading petty officers. They are superintended by the boatswain, who is a warrant officer.

Captains of the Fore and Main hold

the captain of the main hold is a second class petty officer. His duty is to see that the provisions are properly stowed, and to take care of everything that is put under his charge. Water and wood comes in their line of business. The captain of our fore hold has got no rate, he is a seaman; his duty is the same as the other captain.

Ship's Corporals

are second class petty officers; 20 dollars a month (for duties see page 83; on messes and page 217 on master at arms).

Purser's Steward

is a first class petty officer. His duty is to serve out all provisions and keep an account of them; he also assists in serving out small stores and clothing. He is assisted by Jack of the Dust. In some ships he is allowed a ration with his pay.

Jack of the Dust

is not a petty officer. He is allowed a ration with his pay. He assists the purser's steward in all his duties. The bread rooms, whiskey tub &c &c are under his charge.

Ship and Wardroom Cooks

the ship's cook is a first class petty officer, Ward room cook a 2nd class. Their duties are to cook for the ship's company and officers and keep their galley and cooking utensils in order. They are each allowed a mate to assist them.

Commodore's and Captain's Cooks

are second class petty officers. They cook exclusively for the commodore and captain.

Commodore's, Captain's and Wardroom Stewards

are second class petty officers. The steerage steward has got no rate; the steerage officers are allowed a landsman, and make up the deficiency out of their own pockets.

The wardroom officers (the more senior officers below the captain) had their own mess, cook, and steward, as indicated. The junior ("steerage") officers berthed and dined separately from them.

Warrant Officers' Cooks and Steward

are also landsmen, they do the same [as for] the steerage officers. They are also allowed a boy to wait upon them at table.

Doctor's Steward

has got no rate. He is generally a seaman, and looks after the dispensary, and serves out the medicines.

Coxswains

for coxswains (see boats on pages 216–17 and 2nd captains of tops).

Captains of the Fore Castle

are 1st class petty officers. Their duty is to look after the forward part of the ship. The sails they have to look after are the fore sail, fore topmast staysail, jib, flying jib, and fore topmast studding sails. They also look after the fore rigging and all the gear from the foremast to the flying jib boom end. The anchors come in their line of duty. The forecastle men have to steer the ship and heave the lead. There are two second captains, who are coxswains (24 dollar men); they have charge of the second parts of the watch.

Captains of the Fore Top

are second class petty officers. All the gear from the fore top upwards belong to them. The fore topsail, topgallant sail, royal topgallant studding sails and main topmast staysail belong to them. The 2nd captains are coxswains.

Captains of the Main Top

are the same as the captains of the fore top. Their sails are the main topsail, topgallant sails, royal and topgallant studding sails. The 2nd captains of this are also coxswains.

Captains of the Mizzen Top

are the same as the other captains. Their sails are the mizzen topsail, topgallant sail and royal. The second captains of this top have got no rates; they are seamen. The men that fill this station are generally promoted the first opportunity. The boys are put in this top to learn. The captains of the tops also have a certain part of the deck to look after; they are also captains of guns.
W.A.L.

Captains of the After guard

are 2nd class petty officers. Their duty is to look after the spanker and main trysail, and with the assistance of the gunner's mate, quartermasters, and quarter gunners, to look after the mainsail and main rigging. The afterguard also has the mizzen rigging to look after. The 2nd captains are the same as the 2nd captains of the mizzen top.

Seaman

get 18 dollars a month. They are supposed to know how to steer, heave a lead, send down a mast or yard, bend a sail and a host of other jobs too numerous to mention.

Ordinary Seaman

gets 14 dollars a month. He is supposed to know how to handle sail, reef, and steer, send down a royal or topgallant yard, and topgallant mast.

Landsman

is supposed to know nothing about sailor work whatever. He is, however, supposed to learn, and they are generally put into the tops and if they are any way smart, they are promoted, as also do other grades.

1st and 2nd Class Boys

1st class get 10 dollars, 2nd class 8. They are equally divided in each watch. They are employed to run with messages from the quarterdeck and look after the side ladders, and are sometimes during the cruise put into the mizzen top to learn.

Idlers

there are a great many in a ship's company who come under this head, such as bandsmen, 1st lieutenant's clerk, cooks, stewards, ward room servants, and everybody who does not stand a night watch, such as carpenter's mate, gunners and sailmaker's mates, ship's servants. In working ship through the day, they are sent on deck. These with the exception of Officers, and the Marine Corps, make up the ship's company. I do not wish the reader to infer from my description of the different grades and their duties, that is all that is required of them, it is not. What I have described is only a part of their duties, but is the principal part, however. I will now in a manner describe the Marine corps.

Orderly and duty Sergeants

The first named takes charge of all the Marine clothing, and does all the writing, and sees to all money matters. He also drills the Marines. The duty sergeant is the one that sees the Marine duty executed. He stands a watch the same as a corporal. An orderly sergeant's pay is 20 dollars a month. Duty sergeants get 17 dollars. This is for the 1st enlistment; 2 dollars a month more for the 2nd and 1 dollar a month more, for each subsequent enlistment.

"Orderly sergeant" was a nineteenth-century rank established to recognize senior sergeants (who might command marine detachments too small to be commanded by an officer). "Duty sergeant" was not a rank but denoted, as Leonard indicated, a sergeant who was not an orderly sergeant.

Corporals of Marines

of which there are 4. They get 13 dollars a month, and an advance upon their pay in cases of reenlistments, the same as sergeants. They stand watch, and see all posts relieved in proper time. They are also considered as police in the ship.

Privates

of which there are 40 commanded by a lieutenant. They have their own peculiar duties to perform, such as sentries upon the cabin doors, spirit room, scuttlebutt, brig, and in port on the spar deck. At sea they stand watch. Their pay is 11 dollars a month, and raises according to their enlistments in the same ratio as sergeants' and corporals'. (For more information see quarters on pages 215 and 216.)

The clipper ship *Nightingale*. From the *Monthly Nautical Magazine and Quarterly Review*, February 1855. Special Collections and Archives Department, Nimitz Library, United States Naval Academy.

Ship's Barber

is another prominent fixture in a man of war. He generally ships as an ordinary seaman (14 dollars a month). On arriving on board of his own ship, he selects a part of the ship which he thinks will suit his purposes (provided it is forward of the main hatch on the starboard side of the deck) and commences operations. The men are shaved as often as they are ashore, which they pay him yearly for (about 3 dollars a head is the usual charge). The one we have got is the most accommodating one in the U.S. Navy.

February 28th 1861.   cruising off the Congo River/
                                          watching the *Nightingale*/
                              her sailing powers/blowing/Reefing

This day came in dark and foggy. At seven o'clock it commenced to blow; took in all the light sails, and at half past seven we double reefed the topsails. For the last three days we have been cruising off the mouth of the Congo River in consequence of information that we got from the Gunboat *Sumpter,* which was that the ship *Nightingale* is in Congo waiting to run out, with a cargo of slaves. There are two English steam gunboats at anchor in Congo waiting for her, and I believe the whole American squadron about the mouth of the river watching to see when she comes out. It is reported that her captain is an old hand in this trade, having made six successful trips. Our men are having great arguments about her sailing qualities. Those that have seen her, say that if she once gets out of the river and has a good breeze, there is not a vessel afloat can catch her. They also allow that we are some on sailing, but would be nowhere alongside of her. She is a full clipper and was built expressly for the World's Fair at London. There was a light rain falling all this forenoon. At noon, the wind moderating, we shook out one reef and set topgallant sails. At 6 P.M. it again commenced to blow. We took in topgallant sails and double reefed the topsails. We are in the Congo River yet. It was a very pleasant night.

March 1861

March 1st 1861.   land ho/sail ho/at sea/sail ho/At Sea/Sail ho/
                                  Mystic/good news the *Jamestown* sails as our relief/
                                  the *Saratoga* takes a Prize/no niggers/know nothings

This morning came in very fine, the port watch washed clothes, land in sight
all along our lee beam. We are now sailing in five fathoms of water. Three
sails in sight, supposed to belong to the squadron. We are steering towards
the land, which is Kabenda. It is very warm today. Hands are dressed in white
frocks, hats and blue trousers. Two more sails were reported at 11 A.M. We are
signalizing to one of them, which is one of the gun boats.

At twelve o'clock the *Mystic* came close to us and sent a boat alongside.
She gave us the gratifying intelligence that the U.S. Sloop of war *Jamestown*
sailed for the coast to relieve us as flagship, which news all hands hail with
delight. We have been talking of home for the last three months. On nearing
the land a sail was reported lying to an anchor, which proved to be the U.S.
Sloop of war *Saratoga*. Our flag officer made signals for her to get underway,
which she did, and at 3 P.M. she came close to us, when both vessels hove
to. She sent a boat alongside with her captain. She has taken a prize, a small
schooner, about 60 tons burthen. She has got no slaves in [her], however she
has got the name on her stern blacked over. Enough of it can be made out to
tell she belongs to Newburyport. Her crew are the genuine know nothings.
They do not understand any language whatever. She has got no flag or papers.
She is not worth taking anyhow; she will probably be burnt. After giving the
Saratoga her orders, both vessels made sail and stood on our courses. In the
middle watch we had a very heavy rain squall. Under topsails and courses all
night.

The Saratoga *seized the ninety-ton* Express *on February 25. The prize was neither sent to the United States nor burned. It was decided it was in such poor shape that it would endanger a prize crew, and apparently it was not even worth the trouble of burning, so it was released.*[1]

March 2nd   blowing/all hands reef topsails/sail ho/
                                                      At sea/Patching and mending

This day came in wet. In the forenoon the port watch holystoned gun deck. At 10 P.M. it commenced to blow rather heavy, all hands were called to reef topsails, after which the watch was piped down, left the yards on the caps all the forenoon. It rained until 1 P.M., when it ceased. At 2 P.M. a sail was reported on our weather beam, and at half past 3 P.M. we made her out to be the U.S. Sloop of war *Portsmouth.* She is standing in the same direction as we are. We are now under single reef topsails and topgallant sails. It has every appearance of being a bad night. I am very busy tailoring this last three days, mending and patching up my old clothes. Contrary to our expectations the weather turned out to be very good all night.

March 3d   land ho/4 sails in sight/another interesting character/
                                 At the Battle of Buena Vista/at sea/Mess Bills/
                                                      First step towards Home/Sport

Sunday. In the morning watch, we shook out the reefs, and made all sail. Land in sight all along our lee beam. Four sails in sight belonging to the squadron. At half past nine o'clock the divisions were called to quarters for inspection, after which divine service was held on gun deck as usual. We are now expecting to see the U.S. Steam Gun boat *Mohican,* which is coming here with the mail from Fernando Po. It is a beautiful day. All hands dressed in white frocks, blue trousers and caps.

Another of our characters is a Marine, by the name of Michael Keenan. He is a native of some part of the north of Ireland, as his tongue will tell. He now hails from Philadelphia, where he has a wife and family. He is a very industrious man, always doing something. He has been berth deck cook for the orderly sergeants' mess ever since we have been in commission, for which he gets ten dollars a month besides his regular pay, which is fifteen dollars, it being his third enlistment. He also makes a few dollars by washing clothes and scrubbing hammocks. He has been all through the Mexican War under General Scott. He received a slight wound at the Battle of Buena Vista. He is always very lively, and is also a strict Temperance man. He can make some of the queerest noises with his mouth that I ever heard. He is in very good humor since he heard the news of the *Jamestown* coming out to relieve us.

We had small stores served out to us yesterday for this month. I with considerable trouble borrowed one of my own mess bills, which I give an exact copy of on the next two pages. These bills are printed and the blank places filled out by the purser's clerk. This bill is for this month, and it is just what the mess drew. It first goes to the captain, who signs it, and the purser gives the ship's company the articles affixed to their names. On account of the prices varying so often, they are not put down on the bill, but are always hanging up in the barber's shop (by referring back to pages 21 and 22 the list of prices may be seen).

At 5 P.M. all the Kroomen were called aft to sign accounts with the purser. They are to leave us in a day or two. This seems to please the ship's company very much, as they consider it to be the first step towards home. The rumor now with all hands is that we are going to Porto Praya as soon as we get this mail, and from there to the United States. The mail is expected here (at Kabenda) on the 4th or 5th of this month. At Porto Praya we expect to meet the U.S. Sloop of War *Jamestown,* which is coming out here as our relief.

Our boys are having a great deal of sport at present. When a person has been exposed to the sun any length of time, he or they get tanned a great deal, particularly a person with a dark complexion. Aboard of this ship we have got a great many, who are all the time plagued about it by those who are a trifle whiter, calling them such names as "Moke," "Congo niggers," "Krooboy," and asking them such questions as, "Are you going to leave us at Kerbenda?" and "Why don't you go aft and sign your account?" &c &c, which they take in very good humor.

(U.S.N.) Requisition for Small Stores for Mess No. 8

No.	Names	Rank	Tobacco lbs.	Soap lbs.	Bees Wax cake	White thread lbs.	Blue thread lbs.	Ribbon pice	Tape Piece	Spools cotton	Needles paper.	Thimbles	Knives	Scissors
	Prices													
152	Frank Leston	Sea	1											
31	Gerard H. Barry	"	3	1										
37	Henry Nagle	"	2											
196	Thomas D. Elliott	O.S.		1										
201	William Leonard	O.S.	2	1										
97	Peter Daley	"	2	1										
137	Joseph Bixby	Lds.	1											
174	Robert Robinson	O.S.	2	1										
251	John Powell	Lds	3	1				1						
7	Alvah Olds	"		1										
3	Morris O Hearn	"												
101	Thomas Gaynor	S. Corp												
222	George Makins	Lds												
140	Eben B. Nichols	"	2											
	Approved													
			19	7				1						

Approved and the Purser will deliver the above articles

N.B. pepper to be served by ½ lb

for the month of March 1861 on board the U.S. Ship *Constellation*

Scrub brushes	Box blacking	D. Eye buttons	Fine combs	coarse combs	tin pots	tin pans	mustard bottle	pepper ½ lb.	Spoons	sewing silk	cotton handrf	Razor Strop	Shaving boxes	" brushes	" Soap	Shoe brushes	Clothes brushes	Mess Kettles	Mess Pans	Amount	
																				dollars	cts
			1																		
	1																				
	1																				
															2						
			1								2										
										10					2						
	2		2							10	2				4						

they being deemed by [me] necessary to the health and comfort of the men to whose names they are placed opposite

Captain John S. Nicholas

March 4th 1861   **at sea off Kerbenda/the fleet meets/ no mail yet/Hot/**

Starboard watch washed clothes. Four sails in sight belonging to the squadron. We have got but very little wind. At 9 A.M. we fired a gun in order for the gun-boats to come near us, which they did, and both their captains came on board (*Mystic*, and *Sumpter*). They are going to send the *Saratoga* prize to the United States. Kabenda is in sight two points forward of our weather beam. The Kroomen got their money today. On nearing the land four vessels were discovered laying at anchor: the *San Jacinto, Saratoga, Mystic* and the English Steam Sloop of war *Archer*. The Sloop of war *Archer* is going home. The *Portsmouth* is on our weather beam, and the Gun-boat *Sumpter* is on our port quarter. There are no signs of the *Mohican* as yet. This is the day that the fleet was to meet, and get their final orders from the flag officer, but he has deferred it until he gets the mail. At sundown we furled all the light sails, and stood off the land. It has been a very warm day, the thermometer indicating at 11 A.M. 113 degrees in the shade. At night we kept signal lights burning for the *Mohican*.

March 5th   sail ho/*Mohican* arrives with the mail/hove to/The entire
                        fleet within hailing distance/Fire 3 guns/all the captains
                        in the fleet on board the Flag Ship/rumors/no orders/
                        company during the night/at sea/drifting on to the land

At six o'clock this morning a sail was reported by the lookout on the fore topsail yard, which proved to be the U.S. Gun boat *Mohican,* which vessel we have been looking [for] for the last 2 days; she has got the mail. We are expecting to get our orders for home in it. At 9 A.M. it commenced to rain. We hove to with the fore topsail to the mast. Cleaned down the topgallant sails, and hauled up the courses, and in this position we remained all day. At 11 A.M. the *Mohican* was alongside of us, and her captain came on board with the mail. The whole squadron are around us within hailing distance: the *Mohican, Mystic* and *Sumpter* are on the port quarter and the Sloop of war *Portsmouth* on the starboard quarter. The *San Jacinto, Saratoga,* and the English Steam Sloop of war *Archer* are at an anchor in Kabenda Bay, which is about three miles astern of us.

As soon as the flag officer got the mail, he made signals for all the captains to come on board the flag ship, which they did, excepting the captains of the *San Jacinto* and *Saratoga*. They could not see the signals on account of the thick fog and rain which poured in torrents all day long. He, however, had three guns fired, which was a signal for them to get underway. The *San Jacinto* and English Sloop of war *Archer* came out to us. The captain of the *Saratoga* came out in the *Archer,* who got underway to accommodate Captain Taylor of the *Saratoga,* and partly to bid our captain good bye, they being warm friends. The captains are all on board; the ship's side is crowded with boats. They kept running all day long in the rain to and from the flagship. Various are the rumors on board, some saying we are going home direct, but these are only rumors. In the afternoon the news is that we have not got our orders, and that we are going back to St Paul de Loando again, which I believe is true. The steamers are sailing around us in great style. At four o'clock the rain ceased. At sundown, the flag officer having given most of the fleet his orders, they sailed on their course with the exception of the *San Jacinto, Mohican,* and *Saratoga,* which vessels are to stay by us until morning. In the dog watch we single reefed the topsails. The steamers

the soft answer turneth away wrath

are astern of us, with all their lights up. In the mid watch there being no wind, it was discovered we were fast drifting to the land. Shook the reefs out of the topsails, and set every stitch of canvas we had, including studding sails on both sides, and a light breeze springing up from off the land, we were soon out of all danger.

March 6th   **going back to St Paul de Loando/Secession/**
black Republicans/Politics/a hoax/at sea/food

This morning came in fine with a light breeze, the *San Jacinto* and *Mohican* in sight astern of us. At 10 A.M. the *San Jacinto* got her sailing orders, and started on her course. We are going to the southward, probably to St Paul de Loando, the *Mohican* still in company. At St Paul we expect to meet the storeship. The ship's company are all downhearted on account of the news; we expected to get our orders this mail. In the afternoon we are becalmed. At 5 P.M. the *Mohican* got her orders and sailed. We are now alone.

There is considerable excitement on board at present about the secession of South Carolina. We have got the Union dissolved here, a dozen times a day. How absurd it sounds to hear a Shellback talking politics! The Black Republican party have a great many advocates here; stump orators can be heard in all directions about the decks. The principal arguments are about the Missouri Compromise bill, Bleeding Kansas, and the Nebraska Bill which they know as much about as I do, and I am quite confident that my knowledge of either of them, is very small.[2] Our Kroomen are not going to leave us yet; the story about the U.S. Sloop of war *Jamestown* coming out to relieve us turns out to be a hoax, she is not fitted out yet. At night we got a light wind from the northward, which freshened in the mid watch. All the port studding sails set.

South Carolina seceded on December 20, 1860. Yesterday's mail brought the men of the squadron up to date only as far as late December, so they were unaware that six additional states seceded in quick succession between early January and February 1. While the sailors of the Constellation *dissolved the Union "a dozen times a day," it had already been dissolved in fact, with Jefferson Davis inaugurated as president of the Confederacy on February 14.*

One important subject I had almost forgotten to mention, that of food we get to eat, it is never too late to mend. I will give a description of it here.

American Man of War Men's Food

Monday
We are allowed Pork, and Beans. In the evening Butter and cheese, and pickles are served out, Coffee, Tea, Sugar and Molasses being served out twice a month. Navy bread being served out twice a week.

Tuesday
Is Rice day and Beef

Wednesday
Is Pork and Beans

Thursday
Is Duff day or properly, plum pudding and dried apples/also Butter, Beef, Cheese, and pickles.

Friday
Is Beef and Vegetable soup which has been lately introduced into the navy

Saturday
Pork and Beans again

Sunday
Beef, Duff, and Apples

Our Allowances
Beef, per day 1 pound or 4 pounds a week
Pork per day 1 pound or 3P a week

Flour. 1 pound a week.   Butter 4 ounces a week
Pickles 8 ounces a week.   Vinegar 1 pint a week
Molasses a week 1 pint   Cheese 4 oz a week
Apples a week 8 ounces.   Sugar 2 ounces a day.
Coffee, half an ounce a day.   Tea one eighth of an ounce daily
Bread 14 ounces a day.   Whiskey a gill per day
Beans per week 1½ pints   Rice the same (for further
                                          information see page 82 on
                                          Rations and messes.)

March 7th 1861   at sea/sail ho/suspicions/excitement/
                           fire a shot at her/she proves to be the *Portsmouth*/
                                               laughable/a rebuke/at sea

This day came in very fine, with a light wind. For this last two weeks, we have been on an allowance of water which this forenoon was taken off; we are now allowed to use what we want of it. Towards night it began to thicken up. At two bells in the midwatch [1:00 A.M.] a sail was reported on our lee bow, about a mile off. It was reported to the captain, who came on deck, and we stood down to her and set all our port studding sails. There was considerable excitement felt about the chase. The 1st lieutenant and captain being on deck during the chase, the captain gave orders to fire a shot across her forefoot, which was done promptly. She hove to and burned signal lights which proved her to be the U.S. Sloop of [War] *Portsmouth,* this being the fourth time we have chased her this cruise. The most laughable part of the affair is that we were sure we had a slaver. She looked so large that we were as sure she was the *Nightingale.* The Quarter Master of the watch (Tom Little) was sure she was, he could almost make her name out. One of the middies, being officer of the deck, was so excited that he did not know whether he was on his head or feet. Between him and the quartermaster they got the captain and 1st lieutenant as much excited as themselves—that is the reason they hove the shot. At one time the sails were all shaking in the wind and of course the ship lost her headway considerably. The quarter master runs aft, reports to the middy, "She is gaining on [us] fast, sir." He reports to the captain, "That ship is gaining on us fast, sir." He, not in a very good humor, replies, "Mr. Butts," at the same time looking at the sails, "Trim your yards, sir, and damn her gains." Which made all hands laugh. On trimming the yards properly we overhauled her fast. We did not stop but kept right on our course; we had a good breeze.

As the Portsmouth *was a thousand-ton sailing sloop with relatively trim lines, it had almost exactly the same size and silhouette as the* Nightingale, *so the confusion of the two was understandable.*

On March 7, Inman sent Lieutenant Commanding Le Roy with the Mystic *to attend a palaver (gathering of native chiefs and others) chaired by Captain Crawford, RN, of HMS* Archer *at Shark's Point at the mouth of the Congo River. Three American traders at Punta da Lenha, thirty miles up the Congo, had asked Inman for protection. Le Roy was to meet them at the Shark's Point palaver and tell them that squadron sanitary regulations forbade sending men upriver and to suggest that they move their factories to Shark's Point, where the navy could protect them. Inman added that their present location's being a notorious center of the slave trade further disinclined him to assist them. (The reader may recall that the* Virginian, *the* Cora, *and the* Nightingale *were all associated with Punta da Lenha.)*[3]

March 8th   sail ho/*John Gilpin*/race with her/beat her

This morning we were in sight of the mouth of Congo River. A sail was reported coming out. We stood off and gave her chase and at eight o'clock we made her out to be the barque *John Gilpin* of Boston, a regular coast trader. She showed her colors, and we let her pass on. She was now on our lee beam;

our captain thought he would try her sailing qualities, as she had boasted that she had run two or three of our cruisers hull down. We therefore tried her, and beat her very fast.

This day at 9 A.M. I was elected berth deck cook of No 8 mess. This is not my proper mess, this is the mizzen top mess and I belong to the main top mess. When I shifted tops I did not shift messes. The reason was I liked the mizzen the best, having one or two townsmen in it, and because the mess was composed of very sociable young fellows, whereas the main are always growling. We have had a steady cook all along till last week when he left, and nobody in the mess wishing to go cook, we had to take it in weekly turns. My term commences this morning. It being Friday and a cleaning day, I came in in a very bad time. All our tin ware had to be polished bright, mess chests scrubbed and white washed and bag lockers holystoned, and the beams white washed, and also get food ready for my mess mates. This day is called the general field day by the berth deck's cooks. I was very glad when night came, being in the Bhoys' slang played out.

At night the cooks stand their regular watches (see pages 82 and 83 about cooks and messes).

At dusk another sail was reported from the masthead. We are in chase of her and at 9 P.M. we fired a gun for her to heave to, which she did and showed a light. Our 2nd lieutenant Mr. R. [Rhind] hailed her, asking, "What vessel is that?" The answer was, "The barque *Mary* of New Bedford." "Where are you bound?" was the next question. "Cruising," was the answer. This being reported to the captain, he was not satisfied. He ordered her to keep her main topsail aback and he would send a boat on board of her. It looked very squally. We hove to and lowered the 4th cutter, and she went alongside of her. Our 2nd lieutenant gave her a thorough overhauling, but she was a whaler four months out with 100 barrels of oil. Considerable excitement was felt in this chase by the ship's company. A person living ashore cannot imagine, neither can I describe, what an excitement there is on board of a man of war during a chase. (The best I could do in this line was in the barque *Cora*'s capture—see page 147.) At 10 P.M. the boat returned, and we once more went on our course. At half past 10 P.M. we had a very heavy rain squall and it rained all night.

March 9th   **another field day/at sea/Cleanliness**

This day came in very fine with a good breeze. The starboard watch holystoned the gun deck; the cooks had to holystone the berth deck. We also had to white wash and paint all the iron work. This is another field day for the cooks. The deck is inspected by the 1st lieutenant every Sunday morning at sea, and in justice to the Master at Arms, I will say that he keeps the deck in a splendid condition. Everything is as clean as they can be. It has been remarked by visitors and old man of wars men, that she has the cleanest berth deck of any vessel they ever saw. No wonder—we are always cleaning her. We had an eight knot breeze all night.

March 10th   **a cook on a Sunday morning/high temperature/**
                            who wouldn't sell a farm and go to sea/at sea/work

Sunday, fine weather and a good breeze. The cooks had a great deal of work this morning to get the deck ready for inspection. All the clothes bags had to be taken out of the lockers, so as the men could get their mustering clothes. We had breakfast at 8 A.M. The cook at half past eight commences to clean up his mess things, stow his clothes bags, and fix his chest and lockers for inspection and wipe up all the spots in front of his mess. If grease, scrape it up, and a score of other little chores have to be done. By this time the cook feels in a temperature of 125 degrees in the shade, he now has got to look to himself and get ready for inspection. [He] washes, puts on his mustering clothes, [has] shoes to polish and his gun bright work to clean, all to be done in the short space of one hour.

At half past nine the divisions were called to quarters for inspection, after which all hands were called to muster on the quarter deck, the Articles of War were read by the 1st lieutenant, after which were piped down by the boatswain and divine service was held on the gun deck. The cook's work again commences—gets dinner ready, after which he has quite an easy time until supper time, when he again has to heave himself out of shape, his clothes bags to come out again, in order to let the men change themselves, and get their dirty clothes out ready to wash in the morning. He then goes through the same operations as in the forenoon. After supper he again has a little time to himself. When the watch goes on deck at eight bells, he has to stand his regular watch. Sometimes he has to be sweeper or has to pump water for the scuttlebutt and coppers. This, added to his other duties, gives a berth deck cook a pretty hard day's work. At night we had a good breeze. We expect to make the land tomorrow.

March 11th   **Land ho/came to an anchor in St Paul de Loando/**
                            Prize Money St Paul de Loando/
                            probable loss of the American Ship *Flora*

This morning came in wet, and very foggy, no land in sight. It is raining very hard. At one o'clock it cleared off, and land was reported all along our lee beam, which proved to be in the vicinity of St Paul de Loando. At 2 P.M. we got a fair wind going nine knots with all the port studding sails set. At 5 P.M. we came to an anchor in St Paul de Loando. It now commenced to rain very heavy. This is the rainy season here now. The American ship *Mazeppa* is still here, so is the Barque *Hazard* of Boston. We expected to meet the U.S. Store ship *Relief* in here, but she has not yet arrived. She has got a large mail for us. At 6 P.M. we sent down royal yards. This day the captain got up a petition, so as to send it home. He wants to get our prize money when we are paid off; a very good idea, all the officers and crew signed it. There is a Portuguese man of war brig at anchor here, also a large English coal ship. There is considerable talk about the American ship *Flora*. She sailed from Philadelphia, the same day the U.S. sloop of war *Saratoga* did, and eight days before the ship *Mazeppa*. Both these vessels have been out here over a month. She is loaded with coal and has a large mail for us. She is supposed to have foundered, as the *Mazeppa* reports she had some very heavy gales of wind to the north of the Line.

March 12th

This morning all hands were very busy cleaning paint work inside and out. It is a very fine day. At 9 A.M. all hands loosed sail and got out all boats. At 2 P.M. a sail was reported coming in: made her out to be the U.S. Steam Frigate *San Jacinto*. At 4 P.M. she came to an anchor, and sent down her topgallant masts. She is making repairs to her engine. At sundown we slung clean hammocks. As I belong to the gig, I had to go to the 1st lieutenant and ask him to let me finish my week cooking, which he is going to, my week being up Friday.

That is, now that they were anchored, the gig would be in use, and Leonard would normally be one of the oarsmen and exempt from other duties, but he also owed his messmates a full week as a mess cook and could not do both jobs at once.

March 13th   Gig/Fresh Beef/cleaning and painting ship/
at St. Paul de Loando/Calling away the boats/
arrival of the *Flora*/he gets ashore

Twenty-one months in commission. This morning all hands washed clothes. There is a large sail signalized from the fort coming in. This day we have got fresh beef and vegetables for dinner; we are going to have it every day while we lie here. The government allows its vessels fresh provisions in port, at the discretion of the doctors provided the price per pound does not exceed fifty cents. We are going to give the ship a thorough cleaning and painting while we lie here, inside and out. We have already begun to scrape the guns and iron work. This is done so as to have the ship look well when we get home, which we expect will be in the latter end of June or the first of July.

Another important subject I had almost forgotten, that of calling away the boats. Every boat has its regular crew and when she is called away they must go in her. In most ships the boats are called away by the boatswain's mates, with their pipes, but on board of this ship they are called away by the bugler. Each boat has its own tune. This system was originated on board here by Mr. McDonough. Below will be seen the different tunes for each boat:

Launch	Belle of the Mohawk Vale
1st Cutter	Nelly Bly
2nd do	Old Folks at Home
3d do	Dolly Day
4th do	Jordan is a hard road to travel
Barge	Wait for the Wagons
Gig	Old Dog Tray
Dinghy	Pop Goes the Weasel

"Yankee Doodle" calls away all the boats when they go on an expedition. "Fanny E[l]ssler" calls away the 1st and 2nd Divisions of small arm men. At 6 P.M. the American ship *Mazeppa* sailed. It is very warm weather here now. The sail reported proves to be the *Flora*, which vessel we thought was lost. At one o'clock at night a boat came alongside of us from her with her 1st mate, who reported her to be ashore about 15 miles below point Augustus. They mistook the harbor. It is raining very hard here tonight. We have to keep an anchor watch of one from each part of the ship.

All of the tunes chosen by Lieutenant McDonough for the Constellation's *unusual boat calls were, with the exception of "Yankee Doodle" and perhaps "Fanny Elssler," popular tunes from the 1850s. "Wait for the Wagons" (1851) is by George P. Knauff, "Bonnie Eloise: The Bells of Mohawk Valley" (1858) is by John Rogers Thomas, and "Jordan Is a Hard Road to Travel" (1853) is credited to Dan Emmett; "Pop Goes the Weasel" emerged in England in the 1840s and became very popular in America in the 1850s. Fanny Elssler, an Austrian ballerina, became a celebrity in the United States when she toured there in the 1840s; of the several songs connected with her, "Fanny Elssler in the Character of La Cracovienne" (1840) may be the only one with her name in the formal title. All the rest of the boat calls are tunes by Stephen Foster.[4] Leonard, a member of the gig's crew, would have responded to "Old Dog Tray."*

March 14th 1861. **at St Paul de Loando/coast fever on board the *Mystic* and *Archer*/*Flora* afloat**

At five o'clock this morning the launch and 1st Cutter were called away to go down to the *Flora* to get her off. The sailing master and boatswain went in the launch. At 9 A.M. the barque *John Gilpin* came in here. At 10 A.M. the U.S.

Gun-boat *Mystic* arrived; she has got the coast fever on board. She reports the English sloop of war *Archer,* at anchor in Kabenda Bay, with most of her men sick with the fever. At 1 P.M. the American barque *Swallow* came in here. She has been trading along the coast.

At 2 P.M. the launch and first cutter returned. They have got the *Flora* off. She has been out four months and four days, a very long passage. Her crew has been on short allowance of provisions for two months. We are caulking ship and side. At sundown the *Flora* is no nearer in than she was this morning. Our master is on board of her. She brought out a November mail for the squadron. My cooking week will be up tomorrow morning and I am very glad of it. I am sick and tired of the berth deck.

March 15th	out of commission/at St Paul de Loando/
	a General court Martial

This day came in very fine. At seven o'clock the *Flora* came in and anchored. At 9 A.M. my time as cook expired, and I again went back to my old duties. At 3 P.M. we went ashore in the gig, and had a two hours' run. At 4 P.M. a Portuguese Man of war steamer arrived here with the governor. He has been on a visit to the Portuguese possessions all along the coast. They are manning yards, and saluting him all over the harbor. At 9 A.M. a gun was fired and the American Jack hoisted on board the U.S. Steam Frigate *San Jacinto,* a sure sign for a General Court Martial. They are trying one of our Marines for striking an orderly sergeant. He has been very unfortunate, this being his third court martial since he has been in the ship. All hands are to work scraping, painting, and caulking ship.

March 16th	*Flora*'s crew refuse to work/Double Irons/
	American consul on board the *Flora*/
	stealing an American Flag/at St Paul de Loando/
	bad prospects ahead

Today I am boatkeeper. At 9 A.M. we went ashore and had a run, returned at twelve noon. At 2 P.M. about forty of our men went on board the ship *Flora,* to get an iron launch out of her, her own crew having knocked off work. They say they have been used very badly on the passage from Philadelphia. They are on board the Gun boat *Mystic.* At 3 P.M. we went on shore to get the American consul, who is going to dine with our captain. At 4 P.M. our men returned from the *Flora,* most of them pretty well drunk. Three of the noisiest were put in double irons, under the sentry's charge. At half past 4 P.M. the captain gave the consul, Mr. Willis, the use of the boat and crew. We brought him on board the *Flora.* Her crew was then brought on board from the *Mystic,* and were asked by the consul to turn to, which they refused to do. Her captain then accused some of them of stealing one American ensign, and forthwith had all of their chests brought on deck and searched, but it is needless to say no flag was found. The crew say that he is a perfect scoundrel, and if half of their complaints be true, he ought to be horsewhipped. Who ever heard of such a thing as stealing an American flag? It, however, is a good excuse to bluff off the consul with. The crew were again brought on board the *Mystic* and we took the consul ashore, when he gave us a dollar to drink. At 9 P.M. we returned on board the ship. The general court martial is still going on on board the *San Jacinto*. The case of our men, that got drunk on board the *Flora*, is more serious than I at first imagined; they stole the liquor by breaking open the lazarette hatch and holding the ship's cook while they got it. I think they will be court martialed.

The "iron launch" Leonard mentions was one of two iron lighters meant to be kept at Loando for use in carrying coal to and from the shore. The Flora's coal would have been added to that already piled ashore to be drawn upon by the squadron's steamers.

Lieutenant Rhind sent a letter to Fannie Hume saying he hoped to be home by June.[5]

March 17th — Bathing

Sunday, and a beautiful day, all hands dressed in white clothes. At half past nine o'clock had divisions inspection. At 10 A.M. had divine service. In the afternoon some of our men went visiting the other vessels and some of their men came on board of us. At 6 P.M. the English sloop of war *Archer* came in. Some of her men have died with the coast fever, since we saw her last. At sundown all hands went in bathing. It has been very warm all day. The *San Jacinto*'s crew are also in bathing. In the evening we got a cool sea breeze.

March 18th — new charges/at St. Paul de Loando

This morning all hands washed clothes. In the forenoon all hands were to work painting ship. At 9 A.M. the court martial on board the *San Jacinto* was resumed and at 10 A.M. the indictment was quashed on account of a flaw in it. They had one of the initials of the man's name S instead of H. He, however, has a set of new charges against him and will be tried on them in a few days. In the afternoon we went ashore in the gig and had a two hours' run. We returned at sundown. All hands then went in bathing. There are two small schooners coming in.

March 19th — visited by the Governor/21 guns

This day came in very fine, all hands dressed in white frocks, hats, and blue trousers. At 9 A.M. they began the new court martial on board the U.S. Steam Frigate *San Jacinto*. At twelve o'clock our ship was visited by the governor of the place with his suite. On his leaving we fired a salute of twenty-one guns, which salute I do not understand. They say that he is Governor General; I thought nothing but nationality or royalty were entitled to twenty-one guns. Our salute was returned by the fort. The Portuguese man of war brig also saluted him. It is a very warm day. In the afternoon we brought the captain ashore, and in coming off we had a race with one of the *San Jacinto*'s, and one of our own boats, and beat both of them. Our captain felt highly pleased. The English Gun Boat *Sharpshooter* came in here at 7 P.M.

March 20th   a sad accident

This morning, we took the boat on the beach and gave her a good scrubbing out; we rolled her over and over several times. All hands are painting and caulking ship. The court martial is still going on on board the *San Jacinto*. In the afternoon we went ashore with the captain and returned on board at sundown. A sad accident befell one of the *San Jacinto*'s men yesterday; he fell from the main top to the deck and broke his leg and several of his ribs, and fracturing his skull, he is not expected to live, he being very low.

Serious thoughts, during idle hours, in a Man of War.

In certain periods of a person's lifetime, serious thoughts will intrude themselves upon his mind, especially if such thoughts have any tendency to his future welfare. Such thoughts suggested themselves to my mind many a time while on board this ship, particularly at night in a midwatch on deck, a lookout, a masthead, or a boat keeping day, on which this article is written. I am sitting in the stern sheets of the gig, she being made fast to the starboard stern ladder. The U.S. Steam Frigate *San Jacinto* is at an anchor, about a cable's length astern of us. There is a general court martial going on, on board of her. There are also several English and Portuguese men of war at anchor here, and a great many merchant vessels. The harbor is full of fishing boats returning from the bay, together with a distant view of the City of St. Paul de Loando making what I should say (if I were a novel writer) quite a picturesque scene.

To return to my subject, the thoughts that entered my head today, are in my way of thinking, worth notice to everybody that has any interest in a seafaring life, particularly to a young man who has got any thoughts of going to sea. We all know that there is a charm or something about the sea, and the life of a sailor, to those who live in a seaport city or town, that is perfectly fascinating. Why it is so I cannot fully explain. The only reasons that I can see are 1st romance reading; 2nd a desire for adventure; 3d by hearing the sailors themselves spinning yarns of their own adventures, and what they saw, which in nine cases out of ten are false; 4th those who are compelled to go from actual necessity, of which I will say something bye and bye.

Young men, to you the first part of this article is written. In the first place I would say to you, if you can get any employment ashore do so. No matter how small the remunerations may be, it will be far superior to the highest wages that can be paid to a sailor. Just imagine what comforts a man deprives himself of by going to sea.

In the first place, he is deprived of all society, except a few who are with him. If he is taken sick nobody cares for him. Working when the people ashore are asleep or enjoying themselves, his life in danger all the time, just to gratify his foolish love for an adventurous life. He thinks by seeing a ship at anchor in harbor she looks so nice, that there must be good times, going from port, to port. Which I admit there are, but not to a sailor. As soon as his vessel arrives in a foreign port he has to work, if not discharging cargo, at the rigging or spars. If he does get ashore, which in most cases is doubtful, he goes among the lowest classes. And why? What does the generality of people think of a sailor? I will tell you partly from my own experience, and partly from what I have seen, and heard. He is associated with everything that is low, or vulgar, ashore, and at sea, he is sworn at and abused by his officers in most cases, and in some vessels if he is not a knock down character, and able to fight his own battles he is kicked and cuffed about like a dog. (If anybody doubts this statement, just look at the records of the U.S. courts in a seaport city, and judge for yourselves.) It is no wonder when he gets ashore, and has a little money, that he spends it all in dissipation. He knows he has got to go to sea again, and he is therefore bound to have a good time while his money lasts, which in most cases is not very long. After it is gone his boarding master ships him in the first vessel that is going out, no matter whether it is agreeable to Jack or not. The first thing Jack knows he finds himself on board a vessel outward bound, going through the same routine of hardship and dangers, that he went through two or three months before, and probably his advance all taken by his boarding master for some imaginary debt. And what is most remarkable about it is he is laying down plans, and ways about how he will act the next time he gets ashore. These plans are always made at sea (a sailor is a very cute, cunning, and wise man when he is at sea, at least he gives you to understand as much.) When he is ashore these plans are forgotten, at such times when Jack is carousing, and forgetting his troubles in a glass of grog. The young men to whom this article is written, see him and naturally enough think they have always such times. It is not so. He has been perhaps years accumulating the money he now spends so freely, which will last him about a week, or two at the farthest. He then has no resource left but the sea, go he must and is whining all the voyage what a fool he was to spend his money for nothing. The very next time he goes through the same operation.

During all this time he is gradually growing old. Who then is to look after him? Nobody (very few sailors ever think of laying on any thing for old age). He again goes to sea, and is not capable of doing his work; he here is abused by both officers and men. If he tries to excuse himself, he is asked such questions as, "Why in Hell did you come in a good man's place?" or "Damn your eyes, why don't you croak?" &c. &c.

This is the dark side of the picture. Now let us look at the bright side of the case, and discuss its merits, if there are any. In the first place, we will suppose that we are going to sea for the first time. We of course have got a very romantic idea in our heads. What great things we are going to see, and what great doings we are going to do. We get out to sea, and feel greatly surprised as well as disappointed on seeing nothing but sky and water, for weeks, and perhaps months. (Novel writers, and sentimental poets tell you it is a sublime scene, and so it is provided you are in the right time and place to make it so. It is very well for them to sit in a cozy parlor, or study, of a cold winter's night, and write an account of a terrible gale of wind, a lee shore, a pirate in sight, how they weathered the gale, sank the pirate, and what a sublime sight it was.) We are also surprised to be called out of our bunks in a watch below, on a cold winter's night as above, to shorten sail, or work the pumps, to keep the ship from sinking; or perhaps you are close to a lee shore, or reefs of rocks, expecting every moment to be dashed to pieces on them by the merciless waves. Add to this a thousand other little inconveniences, you will see that there is but very little sublimity in it. There might be to the aforesaid novelist or poet sitting in his parlor describing such a scene from imagination. But to you, who may be in such a scene in reality, it is quite a different thing.

We will now suppose we have had a good voyage, and arrive at our place of destination with a great expectation of seeing something wonderful. What do we see? In most cases we see about the same kind of places and things we see at home, and in nine cases out of ten not as good. On the other hand we go to a country that is strange, the people, their customs, and manners, are strange, to us, they of course interest us for the time or moment. Does this repay us for our weary voyage of months? Does this come up to our expectations? No! at least it did not come up to mine. I went when only thirteen years of age, from Boston to San Francisco. From there to Manila and from there to New York, the time occupied being a little short of eleven months. This was in 1851. I then got heartily sick of the sea, and under no consideration would I go again, although I was strongly advised to do so by my friends, and had good inducement. All to no purpose, go I would not. I remained at home until the summer of 1859, when I got the man of war fever, in consequence of which I shipped in the service, and was drafted on board the U.S. Sloop of war *Constellation,* bound to the West Coast of Africa on a two years cruise, after slavers, of which cruise I am writing a journal, this article being a part of it.

Those persons who have any prospects of becoming a master of a vessel, of course it is a good idea for them to go to sea, and get a practical knowledge of navigation. To such persons I have nothing to say. But to those who have got to go before the mast for a living, it is a life of misery and hardships. To those I would say go in an American man of war for several reasons. Which are as follows: 1st you get good pay; 2nd you get good food; 3d you get good usage; 4th you have no hard work, and you can by behaving yourself get along first rate. There is no knocking down or flogging, but there is court martialing, and they can stop your pay. But in all the court martials, that have been on board this ship (of which there have been about thirty-three), I do not know of one case, but what was brought on by the culprit's own folly or carelessness, and in most of the cases, a sort of bravado, they having a natural desire of being called hard cases, their ambition being at its height when they can say, "I have been court martialed." Anybody can get along in the Navy by good conduct. For these and several other reasons, I would advise a foremast hand to go in the navy. If he is in the service twenty years the U.S. government provides him with a home for the rest of his life, where every care and attention is paid to his comfort. [*Here Leonard seems to have had in mind the Naval Asylum in Philadelphia, which did offer such care to navy men with twenty years' service, but only if they were so old or infirm as to be "incapable of further service."*[6]]

But those young persons who have got a good common school education go in the merchant service; you there have a chance of promotion, which in the navy you have not. You might get as high as a warrant officer, such as a boatswain or gunner and there you are—where in the merchant service, you can get to be mate, or master. And who is more independent than a captain of a vessel when he treads his own deck? Is he not superior to any of your naval officers? This I believe is all I have to say upon this part of the subject. If you must go to sea, you will find my words true; out of the 400 men or thereabouts that are on board of this ship, there is not one, but what regrets that he ever went to sea.

Some people will argue that they are compelled to go to sea. Who are these compulsory ones? Why the most of them are fugitives from justice, others who are too lazy to work ashore. The only ones that are compelled to go that I can see are those who are brought up to it from childhood, and those who at an early age make it a profession.

Another part of my subject is this: fathers and guardians of boys, who think (if they are a little wild) that by sending them to sea in a man of war it will cure them of their evil ways. In such thoughts they make a grand and glaring mistake, for in almost every case they are ten times worse by it. They learn all sorts of vices, such as profanity, vulgarity, drunkenness, and several others which are too monstrous to be seen in print, but which the reader can learn of any person that has been a cruise in a man of war. To you I say do not send your boys in a man of war if you want to send them to sea, send them in the merchant service, but in no cases send them without you can help it. I say

and can argue that it does them more harm than good with any person who feels so disposed. I myself am at present but twenty-three years of age, and have not had much experience in this world, but I have seen enough during the twenty-one months that I have been in this ship to make me feel disgusted with the Navy and some of its officers. One in particular has insulted our ship's company more than once by his slurs and slanders, telling us we would starve, or be in the alms house if it were not for the Navy, and at other times, "You are a set of highbinders, rough-shod rowdies, blacklegs &c. &c." Now a sailor does not care how much he is sworn at, but to be called such names as the above, it cuts him to the quick. This man is also a prominent member of the church on board this ship. He calls himself an American (a humbug). This same church society, I should like to say something about it if I dared to. But as soon as I get out of this ship I will open on them.
to be Continued.

March 21st 1861   St Paul de Loando/arrival of the English Admiral's Ship/
She has taken a slaver the *Sunny South,* of Boston/
a prize of 900 negroes

This day came in very fine. There is a large steamer signalized coming in by the telegraph on the fort.[7] At eight o'clock she came to an anchor, she is the English Admiral's ship. Her name is the *Forte;* she has just come from the Cape of Good Hope. She saluted the Portuguese flag with twenty-one guns; she saluted our flag officer with thirteen guns, and we gave her fifteen. She also saluted the Portuguese brig, and Sloop of war *Archer.* She is painted a very odd color for a man of war, it being a cream color with a white streak in a line with her ports. The Court Martial is still going on, on board the *San Jacinto.* In the afternoon the English admiral and captain paid our ship a visit. They gave us the news of the capture of a slaver, the *Sunny South,* a Boston clipper ship with nearly 900 negroes on board. It was a gunboat called the *Speedy* that took her, but the admiral and part of the *Forte's* crew manned her when she took her; she therefore became a prize to the *Forte.* At sundown the captain went on board the *San Jacinto* and staid until 9 P.M.

March 22   no signs of the Store Ship

All hands washed clothes, it is a beautiful day. All hands dressed in white frocks, hats, and blue trousers. We are painting the white streak outside. The court martial is still going on, on board the U.S. Steam Frigate *San Jacinto.* At 5 P.M. we went ashore with the captain, and returned at sundown. The captain of the *Forte* came on board on a visit to our captain; he is a fine looking man.[8] All hands are anxiously waiting for the store ship *Relief* to come in, but as yet there are no signs of her.

March 23d 1861. St Paul de Loando/Court Martial is over/
Flora's crew turn to

This morning we holystoned all decks. At 10 A.M. we took our captain on board the English frigate and returned on board at 11 A.M. The court martial is over on board the *San Jacinto*. All bags were piped up today to air clothing. In the afternoon the captain went ashore to dine with the consul. The crew of the American ship *Flora* have gone to work again. About fifteen midshipmen from the English frigate *Forte* came on board of us, by invitation of our middies to dine. They are having a great jollification in the steerage. In coming off from shore [in the gig] we ran so close under a schooner's bow that one of her martingale guys caught our tiller head, which snapped our rudder in two. The captain was steering at the time.

March 24th Sentence of a General Court Martial/
at St Paul de Loando/Breaking of a corporal

At one o'clock this morning the Sloop of war *Archer* got underway and went to sea. In passing the admiral's ship, she gave three cheers. At 2 A.M. the admiral's ship also went to sea. Sunday and a very fine day, all hands dressed in white clothes. At half past 9 A.M. the divisions were called to quarters for inspection, and at ten o'clock all hands were called to muster to hear the sentence of a court martial. There were three charges against the prisoner, which are as follows: 1st disobedience of orders; 2nd striking his superior officer in the execution of his duty (the said superior officer being an orderly sergeant); 3d using threatening language. The 1st charge was not proved. His sentence was loss of 37 days' pay, four hours extra duty for fourteen days, after which twenty-two days solitary confinement in the brig on bread and water—every alternate day. Also in double irons. The reason he got so easy a sentence, was on account of the provocation he had in striking the sergeant, said official using very provoking language. This is the general court martial that has been going on for the last week, on board the frigate *San Jacinto*. A corporal, who was a witness in this case, at the suggestion of the president of the court was recommended to be broken [because] he refused to give any testimony in the case. He was broken there and then. At half past 10 A.M. we had divine service on the gun deck. In the afternoon some of the men went visiting. At sundown we brought the captain on board the *San Jacinto* and returned on board at 10 P.M.

March 25th coast fever on board the *Mystic*/Arrest of the U.S. Naval
Storekeeper/Refuse to bail him/war, and rumors of war

All hands washed clothes. My boatkeeping day. In the afternoon we brought the captain on board the Gun boat *Mystic*, where he is going to dine. The

Mystic has fifteen men sick with the coast fever. At sundown the captain returned on board. No signs of the Store Ship *Relief* as yet.

The U.S. Naval Storekeeper is in trouble here; the authorities have arrested him and he is now in custody. The cause of his arrest as near as I can learn, is he assaulted some Portuguese citizen, the dispute arising out of some money that he was to pay for wood. Our flag officer sent a lieutenant ashore to see what could be done for him. The governor refuses bail for him, although offered by very responsible parties, (American and English consuls), which caused great indignation among our officers. The excitement among our crew is intense; they are already laying plans for taking the forts and town. War is the only subject that can be heard. They have already begun to smell blood.

March 26th	St Paul de Loando/Our Flag officer gives notice he will fire into the town if the Storekeeper is not released at the expiration of 12 hours

This morning all hands scrubbed hammocks. Two sails reported from the fort coming in at 9 A.M. They came to an anchor; one is a Portuguese brig, and the other is an English coal barque. In the afternoon we went ashore in the gig. The excitement about the storekeeper is on the increase. At 3 P.M. we returned on board. At sundown we slung clean hammocks. At 10 P.M. our flag officer sent Captain Le Roy, of the Gun boat *Mystic,* and our 3d Lieutenant ashore, to expostulate with the governor about the storekeeper's being released on bail. If he then refuses we will fire into the town within twelve hours. There is great excitement on board.

Out of fifty in the Mystic's *crew, eighteen were reported sick, nearly all with "coast fever" (a term generally meaning malaria).*[9]

March 27th	bathing

This day came in very fine. No signs of the storeship. At 8 A.M. loosed sail. What the result of Captain LeRoy's interview was, is not yet known by anybody but the flag officer. We are having very easy times at present, nothing to do but spread awnings, and wash decks. The *San Jacinto*'s crew are painting their ship. At sundown all hands went in bathing, after which we [the gig] went on board the *San Jacinto* for the captain and returned at 9 P.M.

March 28th	at St. Paul de Loando/Death by coast fever

The excitement about the storekeeper is about all over. They have not released him as yet; they contend that he has violated the civil law, and they are going to try him by the civil law, therefore we have no business to meddle in it.

The American barque *Hazard* sailed for Boston last night. It is a very warm day. A Portuguese merchant brig arrived here today. At 11 A.M. a Portuguese hermaphrodite brig sailed from here. Today we are taking in sand, for holy-stoning purposes. One of the Gun boat *Mystic*'s Marines died today with the coast fever. Our carpenter's mate is making a coffin for him. Two of our men were taken with it this afternoon. At sundown we had a violent rain storm.

March 29th   Good Friday/Burial

This morning all hands washed clothes. Today being Good Friday, all the Portuguese vessels in the harbor have got their yards cockbilled, which gives the appearance of a cross, when you look at them from the bow or stern, the forward yards being to port and the after ones to starboard. The Portuguese observe this day with great solemnity. [*Cockbilled yards were a symbol of sorrow. With the yards on one mast tilted downward to port and on the other mast tilted downward to starboard, they appeared as an* X *when viewed directly on.*] At 8 A.M. we loosed sail, at 4 P.M. the Gun boat *Mystic*'s flag was at half mast; they are burying the man that died. He came out here in this ship, and was transferred to the *Mystic*. His name is Chambers, he belonged to Philadelphia, where he has a mother living. He is or was her only support.[10] At 5 P.M. we had a heavy thunder and rain squall. A Portuguese mail steamer arrived here. There is an American ship signalized coming in by the telegraph on the fort. At half past five we took the captain on board the *San Jacinto*. The naval storekeeper is still under arrest. Our carpenter has charge of the storehouse. No signs of the store ship *Relief* as yet.

March 30th   at St. Paul de Loando

My boatkeeping day. This forenoon all hands signed accounts and drew grog and ration money. The ship outside proves to be the U.S. Sloop of war *Portsmouth*. In the afternoon we brought the captain ashore, and returned at sundown. The *Portsmouth* has come to an anchor below the point. Her captain came on board of us.

March 31st   Easter Sunday

Easter Sunday, it is a great day ashore here. At sunrise they fired salutes, and rang all the church bells. I with a couple of towneys [*men from his hometown*] had a very good breakfast. The *Portsmouth* came up the harbor this morning. At half past nine o'clock we had division inspection, all hands dressed in white. At 10 A.M. had divine service on the gun deck. In the afternoon some of our men went visiting the other ships. We had a very good supper today, the principal feature being eggs, which we did justice to. No signs of the storeship yet. The naval storekeeper is still under arrest. At night we had a very heavy rain squall which continued all night.

April 1861

April 1st

This morning came in rainy. All hands washed clothes. The English Gun boat *Buffalo* arrived here, also a Portuguese mail boat. In the afternoon we brought the captain on board the *Portsmouth*. At 4 P.M. five of us had a stunning supper; we then went on board the *Portsmouth*. The U.S. Gun boat *Sumpter* came in at 8 P.M. At 9 P.M. we returned on board of our own ship.

April 2nd   Maggots and Weevils/at St Paul de Loando

All hands scrubbed hammocks. At 8 A.M. loosed sail. This morning I started my grog on board the ship. The only reason I do it is to try and eat the food we get, which is actually alive with maggots and weevils. The last named I do not care about, but when one of the former gets in one's mouth, it produces, a sensation which entirely destroys an appetite, no matter how voracious a person may be. Hence the benefit of taking your whisky, which improves it wonderfully. The *San Jacinto* is coaling up. At 3 P.M. we brought the captain's steward ashore, and returned at sundown. The U.S. Gun boat *Sumpter* has got some of her men sick with the coast fever. Her B.M. Steam Gun boat *Buffalo* is going to St Helena in a few days.

Up to this point, Leonard had apparently stopped his grog, meaning he got the equivalent in cash with his pay. But the bread quality drove him to change that.

April 3d   arrival of a French corvette/Coast Fever on board/19 Deaths

This morning came in wet and cloudy but cleared off at 6 A.M. A French steam corvette arrived here today. No signs yet of the store ship. There is considerable excitement on board about the secession. We have got two parties here, one the Southern and the other the Northern. We have got a rumor that fifteen states have seceded. At four o'clock the U.S. Steamer *San Jacinto* went to sea; she is to look for the Gun boat *Mohican,* which is gone for our mail, and order her to come here. We expect our orders for home in this mail. At 5 P.M. the captain of the French corvette came on board of us; her name is the *Zelee,* and is just from the Congo River. Most all of her crew are sick with the coast fever. Nineteen of her men died with it since she left the Congo. The U.S. Gun boat *Sumpter* has also got it on board.

Aboard the Constellation *Mdn. George A. Borchert, a Georgia native, penned a letter to the secretary of the navy requesting permission to return to the United States "at the earliest opportunity possible, for the purpose of resigning." Flag Officer Inman thought it presumptuous of a midshipman even to offer a resignation, exclaiming, "The assurance of the fellow. Confound him, he is only an apprentice on trial."[1] The secretary's reply to Borchert's letter, which arrived too late to matter, was for the* Constellation *to "retain [him] until the ship comes home."[2]*

The French two-hundred-ton, two-gun steam corvette Zélée *is an historical curiosity. Built as a sailing corvette in 1812, it sailed with the similar* Astrolabe *under Capt. Jules Dumont d'Urville on his south polar expedition in 1839–40, during which men first set foot on the Antarctic continent proper. In 1853 it was fitted with a steam engine and screw; that plus its small size made it suitable for duty on the African coast. The French maintained a squadron of about a dozen ships on the West African coast.*

| April 4th | indulging in a Luxury/at St Paul de Loando/ serving out money/a good sell |

At two o'clock this morning it commenced raining, in consequence of which all hands slept in until half past 6 A.M. A luxury we are but very seldom indulged in. We were then turned out, but as it still continued to rain, the hammocks were stowed between the guns, on the half deck. [*The half deck was the area of the gun deck between the mainmast and the cabin.*] At 9 A.M.
William A. Leonard.

it cleared off, all hammocks were piped up and all hands called to loose sail. At 10 A.M. the purser served out five dollars apiece to all hands. Today is my boatkeeping day.

At 4 P.M. all hands were called to haul sail out to a bowline, which order created quite a sensation on board of us, and particularly on board the *Portsmouth.* The captains of both ships' tops were aloft all day stealing, and the sails were all but furled, therefore the order took them by surprise. The captains of our tops being ordered aloft to get ready, the *Portsmouth* (which is laying a little ways astern of us) supposed we were going to furl sail [and] ordered her top men aloft. Her sails being almost furled, our flag officer signalized to them to drop their sail and follow suit with the flagship. We immediately hauled our sails out with the bowlines, which completely took them by surprise, as their bowlines were unbent. At 5 P.M. the flag officer visited the French corvette. At half past five P.M. all hands furled sail, beating the *Portsmouth* handsomely. At sundown a Portuguese hermaphrodite brig arrived here.

April 5th   **Court Martial/at St Paul de Loando/**
                                   our Master at Arms/Preparation for sea

This morning all hands washed clothes. It is very cloudy. The English gun-boat *Buffalo* sailed this forenoon for St. Helena. Our boat has been running all this forenoon to and from the other ships. There is a summary court martial going on, on board the ship today. Some of the 1st cutter's crew, including the coxswain, got drunk, and got into a fight when they came on board. The result of which is that the Coxswain, and 3 others are to be Court-Martialed.

Another of our Noticeable Characters, is our Master at Arms, or Jimmy Legs, as he is generally called by the ship's company. [He] is an Englishman by birth, and his height is about five feet eleven inches. From the fact of his having charge of all prisoners and black listers, a person would suppose he would be very unpopular with the ship's company, but he is not. On the contrary he is liked by every man, or boy, on board. He treats everybody with kindness and respect; the only ones that he has any trouble with are the berth deck cooks, who at times get him almost crazy arguing the point with him. If he was to report them they would half of the time be court-martialed. He is known to be very lenient to prisoners in the brig under sentence of a court-martial. There are a great many things done in the ship if reported by him would keep us in trouble all the time. He is always ready to crack a joke with anybody that comes along. There is not a move, or game, amongst the ship's company but what he knows. In fact, he is always On the Alert, and although we have got some smart boys, both from Boston and New York, they can't get a peg to windward of Jimmy Legs. We are going to sea tomorrow, only for a couple of days, to air the ship. At 5 P.M. we went ashore in the gig. Last evening a large centipede was killed on board, the bite of which is said to be a deadly poison unless the affected part be immediately cut out.

April 6th 1861.   **at St Paul de Loando/getting underway/a Melancholy**
                              accident and Gallant conduct of a Boston Boy/
                                   orders not to get underway until morning

This morning we are making preparations for sea. Bent all our light sail, and sent royal yards aloft at 8 A.M. At 10 A.M. got the messenger up. Very cloudy weather. Early this morning the Portuguese mail steamer sailed. At 5 P.M. all hands were called to get up anchor. In making sail the starboard main topsail sheet got foul, the clearing of which caused a very melancholy accident and also showed us an exhibition of heroism which called forth the entire thanks of officers and crew. Some of the reef points getting in the topsail sheet block, the captain of the main top, Clement A. Miller, went out to clear it; on doing which he sang out, "All clear, sir." They immediately let go the clewline, which caused him to fall. On seeing he was falling, he made a spring for the main rigging, but the clewline tripped him, causing him to fall head foremost, striking the main rigging in his fall and from the[re] onto the spars that are lashed in the chains, and overboard. The accident caused a complete panic all through the ship—the captain gave orders to clear the lifeboats, but they according to somebody's mismanagement were secured for sea, and could not be lowered under ten minutes' notice. Hardly had the man touched the water, before Eben B. Nichols, a Boston boy, was in the water, supporting the drowning man, on seeing which, a half a dozen others were overboard and between them, they supported him until the boat was lowered. On bringing him on deck his head looked as if it was literally smashed to pieces.

He was immediately carried below, where every attention was paid to him by the ship's surgeons. The extent of his injuries I have not learnt as yet. The topsails were then mast headed, but the flag officer sent up orders not to get underway until morning. We then furled sail, veered out chain, piped down and all hands called to stand by hammocks. There is no mistake but we have got a very poor system about life boats on board this ship. It was fifteen minutes from the time the man fell overboard until the boat was lowered, and then the falls had to be cut. If we had been to sea, we would have lost him sure. At 8 o'clock the man began to show signs of life. His head is cut very badly, but I believe there is no bones broken; how he escaped being killed seems to be about a miracle. At 9 A.M. all hands were piped down.

April 7th   getting underway/at sea

Sunday and a beautiful day. Had breakfast at 7 A.M. The injured man suffered very much during the night. He cannot speak, but points at his left breast; it is feared he is hurt inwardly. The doctor does not want him moved, as he fears it will kill him. They are of the opinion that he will recover. At 8 A.M. all hands were called to loose sail, and at 11 A.M. we got underway. We are only going outside of the harbor for a couple of days; the reason is the flag officer said he would not lay thirty days in any one port while he was in the ship; the longest we have laid is twenty-nine days, which was at St. Helena. At 1 P.M. we got a six knot breeze. At half past 2 P.M. the royals and flying jib were furled, at 4 P.M. tacked ship. We are now going 8 knots.

At 5 P.M. we again tacked ship, and took in top gallant sails. The ship's company are talking about getting up a subscription for two of the men that jumped overboard for the man last evening, which I think is a very good object. They deserve a reward for such an heroic act. At sundown we hauled up the courses, and stood all night under easy sail.

April 8th   **Coxswain of the 1st Cutter and 3 men**
                                      Sentenced by a Court Martial/at sea

This morning came in wet. Port watch washed clothes, at 7 A.M. made sail, had a very light wind all the forenoon. At 2 P.M. all hands were called to muster, to hear the sentence of a court-martial in the cases of the coxswain and three men belonging to the 1st cutter. The 1st case was the coxswain's, which was allowing his men privilege to go and get liquor, which they got drunk on. His sentence was reduction to the next inferior rank (which is seaman); his sentence was approved of by the captain. The next case was Frank Carr's, an Ordinary Seaman.[3] His charges were drunkenness and fighting, his sentence was loss of two months' pay, two weeks in the brig in double irons on bread and water, and two months' black list. His sentence was approved of by the captain, with the exception of 1 month's loss of pay instead of two. The next case was that of Mark Whitehouse, an Ordinary Seaman. His charges were drunkenness, fighting, and disobedience of orders, such orders being given by the 1st lieutenant. His sentence was loss of three months' pay, three weeks in the brig on bread and water in double irons and three months' black list, to consist of cleaning bright work. His sentence was approved of by the captain, with the exception of losing two months' pay instead of three. The next case was that of James Wood, Seaman, charges drunkenness and fighting. His sentence was loss of two months' pay, two weeks in the brig on bread and water, in double irons, and two months' black list. His sentence was approved of by the captain, with the exception of losing one month's pay instead of two. All hands were then piped down by the boatswain. At 3 P.M. the topmen slushed down their spars, at half past three set all the port studding sails; we are going five knots an hour. The injured man is very low today, no noise is allowed to be made around the decks. At 4 P.M. the 3d division exercised small arms. At sundown we took in all the light sails and hove to.

April 9th   **came to anchor at St Paul de Loando**

This morning the starboard watch washed clothes. The land is in sight; we are going into port today. At 9 A.M. a sail was reported which proved to be English Steam Sloop of War *Archer.* At 10 o'clock we hove to and the *Archer*'s gig came alongside with her captain. She reports the U.S. Steam Gun boat *Mohican* off Point Pedros waiting for us. She has got our mail. The *Archer* has got all the other mails. At 11 A.M. we made sail and stood in for the harbor, with a splendid breeze. We beat up the harbor, beautifully, our ship working like a yacht. All the man of wars in the harbor were watching us. At 5 P.M. we came to an anchor. There are no changes since we left. At sundown we got out the boats and sent down royal yards. The gunboats *Mystic* and *Sumpter* have got news that their orders are coming out to them.

By "Point Pedros," Leonard must have been referring to Cape Padrão, on which Shark Point (twenty-first-century Point Padrao) marked the south side of the mouth of the Congo.

List of the Officers and Crew, of the
U.S. Sloop of War Constellation
during her Cruise as Flag Ship on the African Station
in the years of 1859. 1860. and 1861.

Flag officer	Captain
Wm H. Inman	John S. Nicholas

Lieutenants

1st Charles McDonough	2nd A.C. Rhind
3d Robert M. McArran	4th E.T. Abbott

J.J. Foster acting Flag Lieutenant

Fleet Surgeon	Assistant Surgeon
Dr. Smith	John M. Browne

Sailing Master
Thomas Eastman

Purser J. Hambleton	Flag officer's Sect Vanden Heuvel
Captain Marines Doughty	Acting Lieutenant Tyler

Midshipmen
Hall, Butt, Borchert, and Kane

Purser's Clerk Worth	Captain's Clerk Wilson

Gunner	Carpenter	Sailmaker	Boatswain
Hutchison	Lowrie	J. Blackford	A. Hingerty

These are the ones that came out with us. On account of taking prizes we had to send some home and took others in their places. Our 1st lieutenant McDonough resigning, we took Lieutenant D.M. Fairfax of the *Mystic*. Lieutenant Abbott and Midshipman Hall went on board the *Marion;* we took Lieutenant Loyal and Midshipman Farquer from the *San Jacinto*. Mr. McArrann and Farquer going home in a prize, we took Lieutenant Johnson and Midshipman Schoonmaker from the *San Jacinto*. Both our Marine lieutenants were invalided home; we took one in their places, John F.R. Tattnall of the *San Jacinto*. Our purser's clerk going home, we took Mr. Bower of the Gun boat *Mystic* in his place.

(Leonard's errors and omissions of first names, initials, etc. have been left here, but a corrected version of the list of officers appears in the entry for June 16, 1859.)

Ship's Company

ships number	Name	Rate	Hammock No.
1.	George Foster	Ordinary Seaman	
2.	Joseph W. Fitzimmons	Ordinary Seaman	13.
3.	Morris O. Hearn	Landsman	
4.	George P. Cushman	captain Top	150.
5.	John Sullivan	Lds.	
6.	Michael Harrington	O.S.	
7.	Alvah Olds	Lds.	168.
8.	John McNamara	. . .	
9.	Henry Cozne	Seaman	66.
10.	James Robinson	Seaman	118.
11.	Thomas McCracken	Captain of Top	74.
12.	Henry Saxton	Captain of Top	149.
13.	William Ball	captain top	98.
14.	Richard Harden	Seaman	10.
15.	James Wilson	Captain Forecastle	2.
16.	John W. Thomson	Coxswain	
17.	Peter Anderson	Seaman	48.
18.	Henry Bryant	captain Afterguard	191.
19.	Oliver B. Rice	Coxswain	
20.	Isaac Turner	Sea	47.
21.	Charles Haines	Ships Cook	
22.	John Robie	Gunners Mate	
23.	Michael Haly	Seaman	
24.	William Lawrence	Sea	122.
25.	Henry Lawson	Seaman	
26.	William Calendar	Boatswains Mate	
27.	John Ratland	captain top	50.
28.	Daniel Malone	Quarter Master	

ships number	Name	Rate	Hammock No.
29.	William Elsworth	A.B.	
30.	James Birdwhistle	Quarter Master	
31.	Gerard H. Barry	Sea	
32.	John Penders	..	34.
33.	James Barnhum	Boatswains Mate	
34.	George Wilson	Sea	
35.	James Campbell	A.B.	
36.	Henry Cripps	A.B.	
37.	Henry Nagle	Sea	190.
38.	Henry Parsons	Sailmakers Mate	
39.	James Burns	Coxswain	26.
40.	James Duffy	A.B.	7.
41.	David H. Daniels	Boatswains Mate	
42.	Thomas Heart	Quarter Gunner	
43.	Hugh de Lancy	Lds.	
44.	Thomas Little	Quarter Master	
45.	Dixon E. Graves	Quarter Gunner	
46.	Andrew Peterson	A.B.	121.
47.	John McCarty	Seaman	26.
48.	Samuel Carson	Captain Main hold	
49.	Thomas Hoadlee	Seaman	
50.	Walter Williams	Lds.	246.
51	James Mulhearn	O.S.	120.
52.	John Lowry	A.B.	
53.	William Gurner	Seaman	
54.	Nathaniel Talbot	Quarter Gunner	
55.	William Young	A.B.	
56.	James Woods	Seaman	
57.	Charles W. Montrose	Sea	8
58.	Nicholas Myers	Sea	4.
59.	James Thomson	Quarter Master	
60.	Charles Lawson	Quarter Master	
61.	William Smith 1st	Seaman	
62.	Charles McCann	Lds	

Ship's Company (*continued*)

ships number	Name	Rate	Hammock No.
63.	William P. Upham	Coxswain	27.
64.	Sidney Conklin	Quarter Gunner	
65.	John Hogan	O.S.	112.
66.	Louis Costa	A.B.	
67.	Albert Comstock	Coxswain	124.
68.	James E. Elliott	Coxswain	
69.	John Johnson	A.B.	5.
70.	William E. Steffin	Seaman	
71.	Edward Goodson	Captain Afterguard	192.
72.	Charles Stevens	Lds.	
73.	John McGuire	O.S.	
74.	Lement A. Miller	Captain Top	
75.	John McCann	O.S.	
76.	Louis Asher	Quarter Master	
77.	James McAravy	Seaman	
78.	Charles Jones	O.S.	
79.	William Dixon	Coxswain	
80.	William Phillips	Quarter Gunner	
81.	Charles Wilder	O.S.	
82.	Samuel Arnold	Quarter Gunner	
83.	Henry Frary	A.B.	
84.	Matthew Whelan	Captain Top	49.
85.	Alexander Wilson	Captain Top	149.
86.	James Watson	A.B.	
87.	Hugh de Vany	A.B.	
88.	John McDermott	A.B.	
89.	John Bixby	Lds.	
90.	John Lewis	O.S.	31.
91.	George Brooks	O.S.	41.
92.	Michael McQuade	O.S.	
93.	William Jones	A.B.	
94.	Thomasy Brady	O.S.	
95.	John Elward	Seaman	32.

ships number	Name	Rate	Hammock No.
96.	Niel Martin	Quarter Gunner	
97.	Peter Daly	O.S.	154.
98.	James Travis	Signal Quarter Master	
99.	John Williams	O.S.	
98.	James Travis	Signal Quarter Master	
99.	John Williams	O.S.	
100.	Benjamin Gifford	Quarter Master	
101.	Thomas Gaynor	Ships Corporal	
102.	Charles Williams	Ward Room Boy	
103.	Henry Sprague	Captain of Main Hold	
104.	William Trask	2nd Class Boy	
105.	John Humphries	Ships Corporal	
106.	Thomas Woods	O.S.	
107.	Charles F. Gordon	O.S.	
108.	William Ellison	Captain Top	150.
109.	William H. Dunham	O.S.	
110.	Charles Draper	Flag officers servant	
111.	John Elsie	Flag officers servant	
112.	David Lakey	Lds.	
113.	Daniel Hooley	Lds.	
114.	Charles Hemmings	Lds.	
115.	Charles D. Murphy	O.S.	
116.	James George	Ward Room Boy	
117.	William A. Pulsiver	Lds.	
118.	Henry Adams	O.S.	
119.	Monroe Nelson	O.S.	
120.	Stephen H. Berry	O.S.	
121.	James Johnson	1st Class Boy	
122.	Warren Harrington	O.S.	93.
123.	James A. Cochran	O.S.	
124.	Samuel Higginbottom	Lds.	
125.	James T. Walsh	Lds. Jack of the Dust	
126.	John Long	O.S.	

Ship's Company (*continued*)

ships number	*Name*	*Rate*	*Hammock No.*
127.	James Johnson	Ward Room Boy	
128.	George Francis	Ward Room Boy	
129.	John Banker	O.S.	
130.	Peter B. Doran	Lds.	200
131.	Thomas Collins	Lds.	236.
132.	William H. Strowe	Landsman	
133.	Ephriam R. Foster	O.S.	
134.	Thomas Phillips	Lds.	100.
135.	John Hancock	Lds.	
136.	Thomas Mann	Lds.	
137.	Thomas J. Dwyer	O.S.	114.
138.	Daniel Benjeman	O.S. and Ships Barber	
139.	Charles Parker	O.S.	
140.	James Wisner	Lds.	
141.	Rufus Nichols	O.S.	
142.	Maurice O. Brien	A.B.	
143.	Jefferson Simonds	Lds.	
144.	John W. Elliott	O.S.	
145.	James Blake	O.S.	204. [?]
146.	Adolphus Lundergreen	O.S.	
147.	Charles Brown	O.S.	104.
148.	Edward Grayson	O.S.	
149.	Richard Spencer	Captain of Fore Hold	40.
150.	William Jones	Quarter Master	
151.	Jesse M. Furman	O.S.	75.
152.	Frank Liston	A.B.	
153.	Henry W. Higgins	Lds.	
154.	Robert Anderson	O.S.	
155.	Frederic W. Saunders	Doctors Steward	
156.	John Stenson	O.S.	
157.	Edward Lower	O.S.	
158.	Henry Smith	Lds.	
159.	Gustavas A. Bowman		

ships number	Name	Rate	Hammock No.
160.	Eben B. Nichols	Landsman	160.
161.	John Chapman	O.S.	
162.	John Jocelyn	A.B.	
163.	Thomas Glover	O.S.	
164.	Thomas W. Igo	O.S.	152.
165.	George Drew	A.B.	
166.	Daniel Laydon	Lds.	
167.	George French	A.B.	
168.	William Bainbridge	O.S.	
169.	William Thomas	O.S.	128.
170.	William Smith 3d	Lds.	
171.	James Lavin	A.B.	87.
172.	Agustus Manning	O.S.	
173.	William Shattuck	Lds.	
174.	Robert Robinson	O.S.	
175.	James D'arcy	Master at Arms	
176.	Joseph H. Mansfield	Lds.	
177.	William B. Jones	O.S.	
178.	George W. Stewart	A.B.	
179.	Zachariah Caldwell	Forward Officers Cook	22.
180.			
181.	John Fernandez	Forward Officers Steward	
182.			
183.	James Simpson	O.S.	61.
184.	Harman Rudolph	O.S.	
185.	Henry Roberts	Armorer	
186.	John C. Smith	Cooper	
187.	Mark Whitehouse	O.S.	102.
188.			
189.	John L. Nicholson	Carpenters Mate	
190.			
191.	Jarvis G. Farrar	Flag officers Body Servant	
192.			

Ship's Company (*continued*)

ships number	Name	Rate	Hammock No.
193.	John Dwyer	O.S.	
194.	William Bond	O.S.	
195.	Charles W. Batchelder	O.S.	
196.	Thomas D. Elliott	O.S.	162.
197.			
198.	John Hunter	Boatswains Mate	
199.	Joseph Vasquez	Flag officers Steward	
200.	William H. French	Lds.	
201.	William A. Leonard	Ordinary Seaman	114.
202.	James Burchstead	Lds.	
203.	Louis de Silva	Ward Room Steward	
204.	Joseph Bixby	Lds.	
205.	Henry Jones	O.S.	
206.	Bimsley P. Guilford	Lds.	238.
207.			
208.	Gavin Moffat	O.S.	
209.	Adna Legg	O.S.	18.
210.	Issac L. Nodine	O.S.	
211.	David Goggins	O.S.	
212.	Augustine Henry	Steerage Steward	
213.	William Lambert	Captains Cook	
214.	Michael J. Marshall	A.B.	89.
215.	Patrick Dolan	Captains Steward	
216.			
217.	Frank Demar	Coxswain	
218.	Clem Johnson	Ward Room Boy	
219.			
220.	William Smith 2nd	O.S.	
222.	George Makins	Lds.	
223.	Josiah Anderson	Steerage Boy	
224.	John Woods	O.S.	
225.			
226.	Issac Young	A.B.	63.

ships number	Name	Rate	Hammock No.
227.	John Lines	O.S.	
228.			
229.	William Hulin	A.B.	108.
230.	Daniel Hearn	O.S.	
231.			
232.			
233.	Antonia Wilson	Forward Officers Boy	
234.	John Glen	Captains Steward	
235.	Peter Bailey	Ordinary Seaman	104.
236.	Peter Paulson	O.S.	14.
237.	Thomas Jameson	O.S.	65.
238.	John Gavins	O.S.	
239.	Frank Keating	Pursers Steward	
240.	Joseph Ridgley	A.B.	
239.	Frank Keating	Pursers Steward	
240.	Joseph Ridgley	A.B.	
241.	Nicholas Clifford	Lds.	
242.	John Cameron	O.S.	
243.	George Fitzgerald	Yeoman	
244.	James H. Kelly	O.S.	
245.	James K. Bain	O.S.	110.
246.	John McCarthy	O.S.	
247.	Frank Carr	Lds.	
248.	Frederic Fader	O.S.	
249.	Patrick Downey	O.S.	
250.	Charles Van Amburgh	Lds.	
251.	John F. Powell	Lds.	166.
252.	James G. Beck	Painter	
253.	Andrew Ele	Captain of Band	
254.	John Boman	Captain of Band	
255.	Felix Bruner	Bandsman	
256.	Alexander Wergin	Lds. Bandsman	
257.	Theodore Dale	A.B.	

Ship's Company (*continued*)

ships number	*Name*	*Rate*	*Hammock No.*
258.	Felitia Felicia	Bandsman	
259.	George David	A.B.	
260.	Joseph Gomez	Flag officers Cook	
261.	Francisco de la Souya Bey	Captain of Band	
262.	Aresenio Marquez	Bandsman	
263.	Francisco Fernandez	Bandsman	
264.	John Fernandez	Bandsman	
265.	Joseph de Silva	Bandsman	
266.	Joachim A. Ferara	Bandsman	
267.			
268.	Fernando Andrada	Ward Room Cook	
269.	James Timblick	Ward Room Boy	
270.	Edward Lyons	Yeoman	
271.	Ferdinand Anselmo	W. Room Servant	
272.	Peter Rosello	O.S.	
273.	Peter Ridoves	O.S.	42.
274.	James McKenzie	A.B.	
275.	Ignazio Alvarez	Boy	
276.			
277.	Gregerio Gunzago	O.S.	
278.			
279.	Francisco Leandro	Lds.	
280.	Michael Hay	O.S.	
281.	Antonia Lopez	Lds.	
282.	John Brown 1st	A.B.	
283.			
284.	Charles S. Seaton	A.B.	
285.	Elsandro Ferara	Ward Room Boy	
286.	Joseph de Silva	Ward Room Boy	
287.	Antonio Fernandez	Ward Room Boy	
288.	John Wilson	Captain Top	
289.	William Young	A.B.	51.
290.	Charles Robinson	O.S.	

ships number	Name	Rate	Hammock No.
291.	Charles Stiles	O.S.	140.
292.	James Hallett	O.S.	116.
293.	Richard Drabble	Ward Room Boy	
294.	Antoine Pominique	O.S.	
295.	John Nicholas	Lds.	
296.	Richard Graham	A.B.	
297.	James Brown	A.B.	77.
298.	William Baker	A.B.	
299.	John Brown 2nd	O.S.	
300.	Leonard Beale	Lds	
301.	Joseph Ocanbraun	O.S.	
302.	Peter Lawson	O.S.	
303.	Charles Howard	O.S.	100.
304.	Benjeman F. Beck [?]	O.S.	130.

Marine Corps

Name	Rate	H. No.
J. Henrique	Orderly Sergeant	
Walsh	. . . . . .	
Rothschild	. . . . . .	288.
White	Duty Sergeant	310.
J. Edwards	. . . . . .	
Doyle	. . . . . .	
Slachoffer	Corporal	
Coyle	. . .	281.
Cleary	. . .	307.
Hefferman	Corporal	280.
Bacon	Private	296.
Becker		295.
Brandt		297.
Brumfield		287.
Carroll		313.

Marine Corps (*continued*)

Name	Rate	H. No.
Carfield		299.
Connelly		301.
Cronin		305.
Drugan		322.
Fisher	Privates	307.
Garside		294.
Gilligan		319.
Hahn		325.
Havilind		321.
Hart		303.
Hise		302.
Kean		293.
Keneen		329.
Kennedy		327.
Kimball		315.
Martin		298.
Mcleer		304.
McCarthy		192.
McKenna		300
Mell		314.
Niel		306.
Peirce		316.
Schafer		318.
Smith		326.
Smicht		309.
Stangert		323.
Ward		324.
Wammingham		328.
Griswold	Fifer	
Wood	Drummer	
Rhienline	Privates	
Chambers		
Ralph		

Ships Company Continued

ships number	Name	Rate	Hammock No.
305.	John C. Thompson	O.S.	
306.	George Callahan	O.S.	
307.	Nicholas Dan	O.S.	
308.	William Parks	Landsman	
309.	Joseph Clancy	O.S.	
310.	Thomas Peterson	O.S.	
311.	Joseph Gomez	Captains Steward	

St. Paul de Loando

April 10th 1861   **Caught in Rain Squall**

This morning all hands are busy cleaning ship inside and out. We loosed sail at 8 o'clock. We are looking for the *San Jacinto;* she has got our mail. No signs of the storeship as yet. They are going to give up the storehouse here; the provisions will not keep, the climate is too warm and damp. We are taking all the dry goods out of it. At 2 P.M. furled sail. At 3 P.M. the gig went ashore with the steward. and in coming off we got caught in a violent rain squall which soaked us through. The rain came down so hard that we did not get our hammocks until 8 o'clock P.M.

April 11th   **the Mail arrives/No Orders**

This morning the gun deck was holystoned. Two sails were reported coming in by the telegraph on the fort; one is a schooner and the other is the U.S. Steamer *San Jacinto.* My boat keeping day. At 11 A.M. the *San Jacinto* came to an anchor, and her captain came on board with the mail. I got one letter from home (J.M.). At 1 P.M. the captain went on board the *Portsmouth* to dine, and returned at half past 6 P.M. Our boys are discussing the late news from home, which are January dates. We are sadly disappointed on not getting our orders. We have got the startling news about the loss of the U.S. Sloop of War *Levant* with all hands on board. At sundown went on board the *Portsmouth* and returned at 7 P.M. At 10 P.M. had a watch over the sick man; he is getting along finely. Two Portuguese schooners arrived here during the night.

The USS Levant, *a twenty-gun sloop, left Hawaii for Panama on September 18, 1860, but never arrived. The likelihood of its having been lost at sea was published in early January.*[4]

Inman today received formal complaint about Cdr. Colhoun of the USS Portsmouth by the ship's paymaster, John Bates. Bates, a Bostonian, accused Colhoun (a Pennsylvanian) of having said that the people of Massachusetts and Boston in particular were "damned abolitionists and ought to be hung" and that he wished the South would secede and prohibit all trade with the North so that "the streets of Boston would be grown up in grass and the damned Yankees starved into submission." Bates noted that he held rank equivalent to commander and was senior to Colhoun. Colhoun denied having said such things and suggested that Bates's real motive was to share the captain's cabin, as he had been permitted to on previous ships, and remarked that "the size, habits and character of Mr. Bates would have rendered his occupancy of my apartment, most distasteful to me." Inman supported Colhoun, saying he had known him for years.[5]

April 12th   giving up the Store house at St. Paul de Loando

Today all hands washed clothes. There is an American schooner coming in. No signs of the store ship yet. She is sixty odd days out. At 9 A.M. the American schooner came to an anchor. The Naval storekeeper is still in custody; what conclusion the authorities have come to is a deep mystery to the ship's company. At 3 P.M. the Gun boat *Mystic* sailed for Elephant Bay. There is an English man of war steamer coming in, a brig is also signalized from the Fort. We were very busy all day taking stores from the store house. It is pretty near empty. At sundown went on board the *Portsmouth* and returned at 7 P.M.

April 13th

Twenty-two months in commission. At half past five this morning the gig's crew went fishing and returned at 8 A.M. At 9 A.M. all bags were piped up to air clothing. At 10 A.M. clothing was served out to the ship's company by the purser. A Portuguese full rigged brig arrived here this noon. At 2 P.M. the U.S. Sloop of war *Portsmouth* got under way and went to sea. At 3 P.M. went ashore in the gig with the captain's steward, and returned at 5 P.M. At 6. P.M. we went on board the *Sumpter* for the captain, and returned at 9 P.M. We then had to sling clean hammocks. It was a very warm night.

April 14th   arrivals/at St. Paul de Loando/a night watch over a sick man
                      and what happened/Read this/a Secessionist/Frightened

Sunday and a beautiful day, all hands dressed in white frocks, hats and blue trousers. At half past nine o'clock the divisions were called to quarters for inspection, after which divine service was held on the gun deck as usual. At 11 A.M. the English Steam Gun Boats *Sharpshooter* and *Wrangler* arrived here from the Congo River. This morning the U.S. Steam Frigate *San Jacinto* sailed for the Congo River. In the afternoon some of our men went visiting on board the gun boat *Sumpter* and the French Sloop of war *Zelee*. A Portuguese schooner arrived at half past 5 P.M. At sundown the clothes lines were got up by the fore and main top men. The man that fell from our main yard is very low today. There is but very little hopes of his recovery. His topmates stand a watch over him, it being my watch over him the night before last, from ten until twelve.

The events which happened during the two hours, being so comical, and startling, that I came to the conclusion to write it down; besides it will give a faint idea, what a man of war's decks are when all hammocks are down and all hands turned in, except those who are composed in the night watch. The sick man having gone off into a sort of uneasy sleep, I was thinking of home and friends, when the stillness of the night was broken by an unearthly yell from a hammock within ten feet of me, which brought the Corporal of the Guard, the anchor watch and myself to his hammock in a moment. We found him in a very heavy nightmare; on waking him he told us that he thought somebody was cutting his throat. I had hardly been seated ten minutes and the fan, which I held in my hand, was going mechanically, when some individual on the forward part of the berth deck sang out, "Let's have a dance!" Whether he had it or not, I do not know, for at the moment the sick man made signs for a drink, which I had to attend to. While giving it to him, another individual shouted out, "I'm not the man. I'm not the man." Whether he meant he was not the man that struck Billy Paterson, or the man that put out the big fire, I could not learn, for just then one of the hammocks on the port side of the berth deck came down by the run, letting its occupant, a marine, on his head, the force of the fall stunning him. On coming to he began abusing another marine that slept alongside of him, blaming him for the mishap, the real cause of the accident being a rotten lanyard.

In crossing over to my post again, I was very much amused to hear somebody dreaming about politics. He went in for Secession strong, and no wonder, for on my taking the pains to find out who it was, I discovered him to be a darkie we had shipped in St. Helena. Leaving the dark politician to his dreams, I once more resumed my seat besides the sick man, who at times was very uneasy. Imagining himself falling from aloft he would utter a deep groan, which sounded very dismal, it being almost midnight and everybody asleep. While uttering one of these groans I felt a light tap on the shoulder, and on turning to see who it was I beheld a figure of a man, in a light colored dressing gown. I must say that I now felt a chilling sensation creeping over me, which feeling increased as the figure stepped a pace or two backwards. It was not until he spoke that my usual feeling came back to me: he proved to be the assistant surgeon, who hearing the sick man groaning, had ventured out of the ward room to see how he was. After giving me a few instructions, he left me. Nothing more occurred during the watch of any interest. I will add to the

USS *San Jacinto* from *Gleason's Pictorial Drawing-Room Companion*, October 25, 1851. Collection of the New-York Historical Society.

above transactions the combined snoring of nearly 400 men. It now struck eight bells (twelve o'clock). I called my relief and turned in and was soon asleep.

The reader will find no Billy Patterson aboard the Constellation. *From the early 19th century until at least the 1930s, a commonplace expression indicating unknown information was "who struck Billy Patterson?" The origin is obscure and disputed, though the phrase is celebrated in a popular minstrel song.*

April 15th   the *Nightingale* still in Congo River

All hands washed clothes. No signs of the store ship. At 10 A.M. the English Sloop of war *Archer* sailed for the Congo River; the Boston clipper ship *Nightingale* is still up the river. At 4 P.M. the French corvette *Zelee* sailed for the Congo. The injured man is very low today; there is no hope of his recovery. The ship is kept very quiet. The officers take a great interest in him. It was my watch over him from eight till ten P.M., when he changed for the better.

April 16th   Rumors

Port watch holystoned the gun deck. My boat keeping day. At 9 A.M. a steamer was signalized by the telegraph on the fort, which proved to be the U.S. Gun boat *Mohican.* At 11 A.M. she came to an anchor. This morning the sail was loosed to dry, at 3 P.M. furled sail. There is a rumor ashore that the ship *Nightingale* has cleared with a cargo of twelve hundred negroes. At sundown all hands scraped hammock rails.

In Virginia, Fannie Hume's blood boiled at the news of Lincoln's call for troops, and she cheered Virginia's secession. She worked on a flannel jacket for her brother Frank to wear that night when his volunteer company left to reinforce Harper's Ferry against Federal forces.[6]

April 17th   Stealing

This day came in very fine, the sick man is getting finely. At 2 P.M. a Portuguese barque sailed from here. At 3 P.M. the English Gun Boat *Sharpshooter* sailed for Congo River. Last night one of our men had a Mok Bag (money bag) cut off of his neck while asleep with almost thirteen dollars in it. At sundown we went on board the Gun boat *Sumpter* with the captain, and returned at half past 10 P.M. It was a splendid moonlight night.

April 18th

The port watch holystoned the gun deck. All hands dressed in white frocks, hats and blue trousers. At 10 A.M. the captain went on board the U.S. Gun boat *Mohican,* and returned at 11 A.M. At sundown we got the clothes lines on a stretch. The American schooner *St. Helena* is at an anchor in this harbor.

April 19th

This morning all hands washed clothes. At 10 A.M. we went after fish for the captain. At 3 P.M. the English Gun Boat *Wrangler* sailed for the cruising ground; an English brig also sailed. No signs yet of the store ship *Relief.* The injured man is in a fair way of recovery at present. At 10 P.M. a large vessel came to an anchor off the point.

April 20th   condemning Bread

Holystoned all decks. The vessel that came in last night proved to be an English Man of war Steamer, the *Prometheus;* it is rumored that she came out here to relieve the *Archer.* At 10 A.M. all bags were piped up to air clothing. At half past 10 A.M. the gig went after fish for the captain. This forenoon all the bread was taken out of the bread rooms and was inspected by the officers, and was condemned and thrown overboard. We got bread from ashore in its place. The squadron are very short of provisions, there being none in the store house. We are looking for the store ship anxiously. At 2 P.M. a Portuguese steamer arrived, at 5 o'clock the American barque *John Gilpin* sailed on a short trading cruise all along the coast.

The HMS Prometheus *was an eight-hundred-ton, four-gun, wooden, side-paddlewheel sloop.*

April 21st   Doesticks/Prometheus

Sunday, a beautiful day, all hands dressed in blue frocks, caps, and white trousers. At half past nine had division inspection, after which divine service was held on the gun deck as usual. In the afternoon some of the ship's company went visiting on board the *Mohican* and *Sumpter.* At 4 P.M. the captain of the English man of war steamer visited our ship. My boat keeping day, which passed off very pleasantly. I borrowed a copy of the famous doings of the Elephant Club, by Doesticks, which kept me in a continued roar all day. At sundown the *Prometheus* sailed on a cruise.

"Doesticks" was the pseudonym of one of the authors of The History and Records of the Elephant Club, *a farcical narration by two popular humorists of the day.*[7]

April 22nd   an Original Character/Zeal for the Service/an Old Growl

It rained very heavy during the night. At 8 A.M. loosed sail, at half past 9 A.M. the gig went after fish for the captain, and returned at 11 A.M. after an unsuccessful search. We had fresh meat and vegetables today for dinner. At 3 P.M. furled sail, at sundown got up the clothes lines. An English brig sailed for the island of St. Helena.

Another of our Characters is William Ball, captain of the main top port watch. He is a Welshman by birth, but has been in this service since he was a boy. Consequently he is now pretty thoroughly Americanized—that is as far as matters and doings in the Navy is concerned. He is of small stature, not over five feet high, of a very dark complexion and very thin in the face. His shipmates address him with the titles of Ole Ball, Black Ball, and Old Rat. The latter appellation being given to him by the boatswain on account of his natural propensity of appropriating all spunyarn, marline, rattling, and seizing stuff to himself that comes within his reach, which he uses for his own part of the ship. He is a thoroughbred sailor, and knows his duty to perfection; in fact he is (as Marryat[8] says) all Zeal for the service. When we are in port and the sails are loosed for drying, old Ball can be seen aloft with shoes and cap off stealing sail, or in other words gathering his sails up on the yards and stopping them with ropeyarns. When all hands are called to furl sail his part of the ship are first done—they have only to pass the gaskets. This is contrary to the rules of the ship, but he being so small he can't be seen when he gets between the mast and sail. On one of these occasions he was caught, however, and put in irons in the brig, but was released at the expiration of a couple of hours, and now he is at it again. The only fault he has got is his growling propensity and O, Moses, he can growl. But that is a privilege (the Lord keep such privileges away from me) which all old sailors are allowed—it is the only comfort they have I believe. Old Ball has a double allowance of this privilege, for he turns out of his hammock growling, growls at his meals, growls at his work, turns in growling, and has growling dreams. The principal part of his time when not at work, is divided between sewing (he being a very good sewer) and growling at myself and another young fellow because he can't get us to do anything in port. We belong to the captain's boat (gig) and have to dress in our best clothes, [so] we are excused from all work in port. When he can't find anything else to growl at we come in for a large share of his attention. I have got so used to him now that I pay no attention to him, or his growling, but as this is a growling subject I will drop it with a growl and bid goodbye to Old Ball.

April 23d   Good Bread

All hands washed clothes this morning. At 9 A.M. the gig's crew went fishing, and returned at noon. It is very fine weather here now, all hands dressed in blue frocks, caps, and white trousers. At 5 P.M. a Portuguese man of war brig sailed from here on a cruise to Congo River. We got some bread from ashore today, and it is very good, being the best we have had since we went into commission. No signs yet of the store ship *Relief*; she is now 78 days out. All the divisions drilled in small arms this afternoon.

April 24th   another Original/Blue/a laughing Fit/no Partiality/
                              Favorites/Buzzards/Still another/character/an/
                              American Man of wars man/an out and outer/
                              Canoes/Boosters/grog shop sailors

Holystoned the gun deck. At 9 A.M. the gig went after fish for the captain and returned at half past 11 A.M. Very fine weather. There is a letter bag open for the U.S. going by the way of Porto Grande by the U.S. Steamer *Mohican*, which vessel is going to the northward in a few days.

Another of our original characters is a Matthew Whelan, captain of our starboard watch, foretop. He is a small man, not over five feet three inches in height. Of a sandy complexion, he is known throughout the ship by the singular cognomen of "Blue," and why on earth they call him so is a mystery to me, neither can I by any means find out why he is so called. The only conclusion I can come to in the matter is, that the name being so much a contrast to his looks, that they gave it to him, merely as a jest, but the ship's company getting hold of it (they get hold of such things very quick), they gave it to him as a nickname. It is his first cruise in the navy. He is a very good sailor, and I believe is an Irishman by birth. He is a very good humored man always laughing or poking fun at somebody. In telling a yarn, he generally gets about half through when he gets a laughing fit which breaks up the yarn, and almost busts his own windpipe (that is to judge from his appearance while he is laughing) first. As sure as he commences to laugh it turns into a violent laugh, which interesting ceremony occupies almost 15 minutes of his time. By the time he gets through his listeners are off. He is (so his topmates say) the very best petty officer in the ship, and they are right in believing so, he does not show the smallest particle of partiality. Every man in his part of the ship is treated alike. Not so with the other captains of tops, they have their favorites, who get clear of doing a great many things that they ought to do. And what's more he don't consider himself any more than a common man because he has got a Buzzard [*the petty officer insignia of an eagle on an anchor*] on his arm. Some of our petty officers would die from grief if their Eagle was taken from them. These same gentlemen are no more fit for the station they occupy than the greenest landsman that ever walked. As for Blue, he is a man every inch of him, and is liked by both officers and men.

Still another character; a man of war, I believe, is one of the best places in the world to study human nature, and if I could only express on paper what I feel, the reader of this Journal would think as I do. There is between 3 and 400 men on board this ship, and I know the character of almost every man as well as I do my own, but I lack the power to describe their peculiar traits as I would wish to. However, I do the best I can. I don't suppose there are any two characters alike, which fact makes the study of them the more interesting. The subject of this sketch is an American man of war's man, which is a very scarce article. Why it is so I cannot account for; probably they can do a great deal better by staying at home. Once in a great while you will come across one, [but] the principal part of the service is comprised of English, Irish and Dutch, who the most part of the time are talking about how well they could do when they were in such and such a service, and in such a country, when everybody knows that the American Service is the best in the world. They get the best pay, food and treatment, but as it is my intention to give this species of croaker an article to themselves, I will drop them for the present, and resume my character, whose name is James Thompson, or Old Jimmy, as he is known throughout the ship.

He on our first coming out held the rate of Captain of the Starboard watch Afterguard, and done his duty so well that he was promoted to a Quarter Master to fill up a vacancy. In height he is almost six feet two inches and very stoutly built. He is sixty odd years of age but on account of using himself in his younger days in a style that did not break down his constitution he is as sprightly as most men are at forty. Old Jimmy is never at home unless he is on board of a ship, taking his solitary walk, hat and shoes off (the aforesaid walk being about twelve feet long and two wide.)

He is also great on an argument, especially if the said argument has anything to do with the rights of man. He is also, as he styles himself, a genuine Navy man, out and out. To prove his assertion, he never alters anything he gets from the purser in the shape of clothing. His shoes he cuts down, to use his expression, from a line of battle ship to a sloop of war. Everybody in the ship knows old Jimmy's shoes by their size, their numbering somewhere in the vicinity of 13. They are styled by the waggish portion of the ship's company as "canoes." Old Jimmy is not afraid to express his opinion upon any question fearlessly, either to an officer or man before the mast. He is a warm upholder of the Northern States upon the disunion question; although he is not an abolitionist, he is strongly opposed to the slave trade. Old Jimmy has been all through the War of 1812 and relates some of his adventures, which if they are true (and I have no reason to doubt them) are very thrilling and wonderful. They also show that there is a great difference in the navy then, than what it is now; whether it is for the better or not I am not able to judge. Old Jimmy is a great favorite with the green hands; he shows them what to do and learns them if it is in his power, not like some score or two of our would-be sailor pumpkins [*slang for an important or self-important person*], who when they see a person on his first cruise trying to do a little job of sailor work, laugh, and make fun of them for not knowing how, when in reality they can't do much better themselves. It is justice to add, however, that these are the man of war sailors, who know everything about a ship, and what ought to be done and how they would do it, when they are in a grog shop, over a glass of grog, but when they are at sea, they are either loblolly boys [*ship's surgeon's assistants, i.e., not real sailors*] or the best part of their time is spent on the doctor's list. Old Jimmy likes his whiskey and what son of Neptune does not? He is also prone to growl once in a while, but not unless he has occasion to. In winding up old Jimmy's character all I got to say is, may he live to serve his country a hundred years more.

April 25th   Fishing/Bathing

At four o'clock this morning the gig's crew went fishing, the captain's clerk of the *Sumpter,* and our own going with us. We had a long pull outside of the sandbar to get onto the fishing grounds. After fishing about two hours with very poor luck, we started for the ship, meeting the Gunboat *Mohican* coming out. We arrived on board at half past eight o'clock. The *Mohican* is going up the coast to Porto Praya and Porto Grande to see if there is any mail up there for the squadron. She will be back again in a month's time. All the divisions exercised at small arms drill in the afternoon. At 5 P.M. the gig's crew took their boat on the beach and scrubbed her out; we also had a delightful bathing match. No signs yet of the store ship *Relief.*

April 26th   the American ship *Flora* again/
3 of her crew die in prison with the coast fever/
volunteers/a queer idea/a bad Regulation/Drum fish

All hands washed clothes. At 9 A.M. went after fish for the captain. My boat-keeping day. At 10 A.M. a Portuguese hermaphrodite brig sailed from here. The captain of the American ship *Flora* came on board our ship this forenoon. He wants to get some men from our ship. His crew have been in prison this last three weeks; they refuse to work. The second mate demanded his discharge, which he got; he then shipped on board the Gun boat *Mohican* as coal heaver. Three of the crew died in prison with the coast fever. Her 1st mate was taken with it yesterday, and now lies in a critical condition. Our flag officer says he will let him have some men, provided they will volunteer to go. As soon as this was known half of the ship's company went aft and volunteered, greatly astonishing our 1st lieutenant, who has got an idea into his head that a sailor man cannot live unless it be in the U.S. Navy or the alms houses (these are actually his own words). As three men were all that was wanted, they were picked out by the 1st luff. She is going to the Chincha Islands for a cargo of guano, and from there to the U.S. Her captain has got a very bad reputation. His name is Page. There were two men killed in her last voyage by her officers, but these are not the same ones.

At 4 P.M. the washed clothes were piped down. There is a curious kind of fish in these waters called by sailors drum fish. They are about the size of an American mullet and present pretty much the same appearance. The reason they are called drum fish, is from the peculiar noise they make, which at a distance sounds like the beating of a drum. They get close to the ship's bottom at night and commence operations, and there is no sleep for anybody that is inclined to be nervous. They keep up an incessant drumming all night long. While I am writing this present article an unusually large one has commenced, which sounds like the beating of a bass drum. There is no sleep for the wicked tonight.

April 27th   **singular phenomena/Startling Rumors/**
                                        Scraping Spars

This morning all decks were holystoned. At 9 A.M. all bags were piped up to air clothing. While we were washing the decks this morning, a singular phenomena presented itself to our optics. It being very cloudy, the outlines of a large ship could be seen in the clouds, in a reversed position, and at 8 A.M. she was signalized by the fort as coming in fast two hours after we had seen the reflection of her. At half past 9 A.M. she came to an anchor. She proved to be the Portuguese mail steamer that has been due here since yesterday. Our flag officer got some papers by her. There is some very startling rumors, to the effect that all the Southern states have seceded, also that the Mediterranean and Pacific Squadrons have been ordered home. There is great excitement on board of us through it. Although there is no foundation to these rumors, it is generally believed by all on board. At 11 [or 10] A.M. we went after fish for the captain and returned at noon. At half past 3 P.M. all bags were piped down. At 5 P.M. all hands were called to scrape spars. The gig went ashore, and we had a two hours run among the negroes. Our mail is looked for very anxiously by all hands. It is due in Fernando Po tomorrow; we will get it about next Friday. It is very warm here at present.

April 28th   **the store ship reported/Betting/**
                                        going to sea tomorrow

Sunday, very cloudy. Three sails in sight, one is the American barque *Swallow,* of Salem. The other is a Portuguese revenue cutter. At half past 9 A.M. had division inspection, all hands dressed in clean blue mustering clothes. At 10 A.M. divine service was held on the gun deck. Our 1st lieutenant has got information from the American consul ashore, that the American store ship has been seen off Ambriz, sixty miles to leeward of this port, which news causes quite an excitement on board. Considerable betting has been made by some of the men, that she won't be in here by one o'clock Tuesday. In the afternoon some of the men went visiting on board the Gun boat *Sumpter.* At sundown hammocks were served out so as to scrub them in the morning, but at 7 P.M. the order was countermanded by the flag officer, as he wants to go to sea tomorrow. He is getting impatient about the store ship. He expects to meet her outside. We are coming back here in a day or two.

April 29th 1861   **getting ready for sea/get underway/we speak the U.S.**
                         Store Ship *Relief*/a large mail/heavy gales of wind/
                         News/bedlam/no orders/dead calm

As soon as the hands were called, we commenced getting in all boats, bent all the light sails, got the swinging booms alongside, crossed royal yards, and by eight o'clock the ship was reported ready for sea. Four of our men went on board the coal ship *Flora*. At half past 2 P.M. we got underway with a good breeze, and sailed out of the harbor under topsails. We are only going out for eighteen or twenty hours. At half past 5 P.M. a sail was reported one point on our lee bow, and at 6 P.M. we spoke her. She proved to be the U.S. Store Ship *Relief,* which news created quite an excitement on board this ship. We lowered our 4th cutter and boarded her, she has got two of our old officers and some of our men that went home in the barque *Cora*. She brings a tremendous large mail for the squadron. I got six letters and three large bundles of papers from home. She experienced several very heavy gales of wind; she lost her flying jib boom, fore topgallant mast, and several other spars during one of them. We will now have something to eat. She has been looked for very anxiously by all the squadron. She does not bring us any important news, the mail brought us later dates. At half past 7 P.M. we hoisted our 4th cutter and stood under easy sail all night. The store ship is astern of us. The ship is full of news at present, everybody has got letters and papers. The gun deck is a perfect bedlam—one cannot hear his own words. We now do not expect our orders for home for some time, at least until the secession question is settled, which (by the present aspect of affairs) wont be for some time. We had a light breeze till twelve o'clock midnight, at which time it died off to a dead calm.

The Constellation *got mail from the states about once a month, though the contents were not necessarily so regular or timely as that might suggest. The* Relief *took eighty-five days to sail from New York to Loanda, so the letters and papers it brought were from mid-February or earlier. Flag Officer Inman had been waiting for it with as much anticipation as the crew, having told Captain Nicholas to stay within a day's sail of Loanda in order to meet it as soon as possible.*

The men from the Cora's *prize crew could tell of their voyage to Liberia and then to the United States. After leaving Liberia they had nothing but bad weather all the way across. While the anchors were being moved from the bow, a fitting gave way and Ordinary Seaman Charles Brown fell into the sea and was lost. By the time they encountered the Gulf Stream, Sailing Master East-man decided it would be impossible to make it to Norfolk as ordered and took the ship to New York.* [9]

| April 30th 1861 | Good News From home/came to an anchor in St. Paul de Loando after cruise of 24 hours |

This morning the port watch washed clothes. The land in sight all along our lee beam, the store ship *Relief* is to leeward of us. We are both standing in for the harbor—at 6 A.M. made all sail; there is hardly a breath of wind. I did not read my letters till this morning. There is roaring news in the letters, particularly from a sister (J.A.L.) and M.L.M.

At 2 P.M., a good breeze springing up, we commenced beating up the harbor. The store ship *Relief* is two miles to windward of us. We soon came up with her, and beat her, coming to an anchor twenty minutes ahead of the *Relief,* 5 P.M. At sundown sent down royal yards and got out the 2nd and 3d cutters; we then went on board the store ship with the captain and returned on board at 11 P.M. There are two of my townmen on board of her.

May 1861

This morning holystoned all decks, scrubbed paint work. Got out all boats, unbent all the light sails, spread the awnings, flemished down all the rigging, and at 8 A.M. piped to breakfast; it is a delightful day. All hands are dressed in white frocks, hats, and blue trousers. The ship is full of pictorial papers, principally Frank Leslie's, and they are a rich treat. They illustrate all that is going on at home, about secession, the Prince of Wales and several other important topics. At sundown hammocks were served out so as to scrub them in the morning.

The young Prince of Wales (later Edward VII) visited Canada and the United States from July to October 1860, being feted and admired wherever he went—including a ball in New York, three days at the Buchanan White House, and a visit to Washington's tomb. All of the prince's doings were covered in the newspapers and in heavily illustrated detail in Leslie's *and* Harper's.

May 2nd

All hands scrubbed hammocks. It is a very fine day. My boatkeeping day. At 10 A.M. the gig went after fish for the captain. At 5 P.M. the U.S. Sloop of war *Portsmouth* came in here and dropped anchor. At sundown all hands swung clean hammocks.

May 3d, 1861   **expecting the mail**

This morning all hands washed clothes. We then got a supply of bread from the store ship; it is very good bread. At 3 P.M. the gig went ashore with the captain's steward and had a run until sundown. We expect to get the English mail tomorrow from Fernando Po; The U.S. Gun Boat *Mystic* is to bring it. Our Flag officer expects some important news by it. I wrote a letter to M.L.M.

May 4th   **our men to work on board the Store Ship *Relief*/**
                                                    Sailing of the *Flora*

This morning all decks were holystoned. At 9 A.M. the gig went after fish for the captain and returned at 10 A.M. Forty of our men are sent every day to work on board the store ship *Relief.* At 2 P.M. the U.S. Steam Frigate *San Jacinto* was signalized as coming by the telegraph on the fort. I have been very busy this last two days in answering letters that I got from home. At 4 P.M. the *San Jacinto* came to an anchor. She has been to Fish Bay. At 6 P.M. the famous American ship *Flora* sailed from here for the Chincha Islands. At sundown we went on board the *San Jacinto* and returned at half past 6 P.M.

May 5th   **General Muster and reading the Articles of War/**
                           an Absconder Visiting/*Nightingale* caught at last/
                          the Captain and Supercargo escaped/a boasting captain

Sunday and it is a beautiful day, the hands very busy getting ready for the usual inspection. At half past 9 A.M. the divisions were called to quarters for inspection. At 10 A.M. all hands were called to muster. The Articles of War were read by the 1st lieutenant, we then mustered round the capstan according to our rates. We then had divine service on the gun deck. There is quite an excitement both ashore and aboard the ship, on account of one of the firm Silva & Leandro having absconded with a large amount of money. Mr. Silva being in the interior, on business for the firm. It was their intention to give up the business as soon as they could settle their affairs. The absconder went last night in the American ship *Flora,* which vessel touches in at Callao on her voyage. He did considerable business with our squadron in furnishing us with stores. It is one of the largest firms in St. Paul de Loando. In the afternoon the men went visiting the other ships, and their men are on board of us. At 2 P.M. the U.S. Sloop of war *Saratoga* was signalized coming in; at 4 P.M. she came to an anchor.

* *
Arrival of the U.S. Sloop of War
Saratoga, having captured the Famous
Clipper Ship *Nightingale*, of Boston
with almost a thousand niggers in her.
* *

The accounts of the capture as near as I could learn are these: on the 20th of April the *Saratoga* went into Kabenda Bay to water ship, the *Nightingale* being there at the time also watering ship. At 4 P.M. the *Saratoga* got underway and went to sea. When about fifteen miles from the land, one of her lieutenants told the captain that he thought the *Nightingale* would take in her niggers that night. The captain laughed at him, "But," said he, "I will let you have two boats, and you can go and see. Take some rockets with you and signalize if she is taking them in. I will stand inshore on the next tack." The lieutenant and the two boats were then sent on their way and arrived near the *Nightingale* about midnight. On approaching close to her, they were struck with the unusual jabbering of what they supposed were the negroes, which on closer observation proved to be correct. So busy were the slavers, that they did not discover the *Saratoga*'s men until they were on her decks and were ordered to surrender, which they did forthwith. During the confusion that followed, the captain and supercargo escaped in a boat. She was in the very act of taking them in when the *Saratoga*'s boats took her. Her intentions were to take in fifteen hundred, she having in over nine hundred when taken. This is the vessel that for the last three months has created such an excitement amongst our squadron, and particularly the English fleet. They could not spare time enough to coal up, so eager were they for her capture, but they got sold for once. The captain of the *Nightingale* said (when boarded by some of our vessels a month ago) that he was going to take a cargo of niggers off this coast, in spite of all the damn men of war afloat. Probably he will, but not this time. He has taken six cargoes clear; this was to be his last. There is great excitement in our vessels about it. The *Saratoga* saw the ship *Flora* down the coast, and the rumor round the decks now is that she is going to take a cargo of slaves. At sundown no signs yet of the mail.

When it arrived, the mail contained reports of Lincoln's inaugural address of March 4. Offering the slave states (of whom seven had passed bills of secession) his willingness to leave slavery as it was, Lincoln also made clear his belief that there was no right to secession and his insistence on preserving the Union. Expressing a hope that war could be avoided, he ended with an appeal to "the better angels of our nature."

Frank Leslie's Illustrated Newspaper, giving a summary of the address, commented that "we cannot shut our eyes to the fact that the Inaugural Address gives but little clue as to the means of unraveling the tangled network of our present dissensions. Its words of peace and good-will seem to be traced by the bayonet point, by a mailed hand, and overtopping the figure of Mercy frowns the shadow of Force. The issue is to come. Which will prevail?"[1] Men of the African Squadron, knowing events at home were a month or more further along than they had knowledge of, could only wonder, too, and speculate.

May 6th   **arrival of the Gunboat *Mystic* with the mail/no orders**

All hands washed clothes. All the captains in the squadron were on board the ship this morning. The topic of conversation is the capture of the *Nightingale*.

At 11 A.M. a Portuguese brig arrived here. At 1 P.M. the Steam Gun boat *Mystic* was

Be Firm to your Trust

signalized as coming in, and at 3 P.M. she came to an anchor. Her captain came on board with the mail. I got one letter (M.E. L.). About half an hour after it came on board, a crowd of about sixty could be seen in the maintopmen's gangway listening to the inaugural address of old Abe Lincoln, which was read by one of the men. The secession of Texas makes the boys feel rather gloomy; we give up the idea of getting our orders until the question is settled. At 4 P.M. the washed clothes were piped down. Dirty hammocks were served out at sundown, so as to be scrubbed in the morning. We got three new hands this day from the U.S. Gun boat *Sumpter* in place of those we sent in the *Flora*.

Texas seceded on February 1. Meanwhile, though the news has yet to reach the African Squadron, Fort Sumter had been fired upon and had surrendered. Virginia seceded on April 17, and Arkansas's legislature was on May 6 reaching the same conclusion. North Carolina and Tennessee soon followed.

May 7th   The Flag officer goes to St. Helena in the
                    U.S. Sloop of war *Portsmouth*/towed out to sea

All hands scrubbed hammocks, the U.S. Gun boat *Sumpter* sailed during the night. Early this morning the *Portsmouth* began making preparations for sea. They bent an entire new suit of sails, and got in provisions; it is not known where she is going to. At noon our flag officer made preparations to leave; he is going to St. Helena in the *Portsmouth*. At 3 P.M. the gig went ashore and had a two hours' run. At 4 P.M. the flag officer and suite left our ship and went on board the U.S. Sloop of war *Portsmouth*. On his arrival they fired a salute of thirteen guns and hoisted his pennant at the mizzen, we hauled ours down and hoisted coachwhip at the main (captain's pennant). The flag officer gave our captain the choice of going to St. Helena, or to go cruising; he preferred the latter. That is his reason for going in the *Portsmouth*. There is another large clipper ship in Congo River called the *Arab*, or *Arabian Steed*. At 5 P.M. the captain went on board the store ship *Relief*. The *Portsmouth* got underway at a quarter past 5 P.M. and went to sea. At 6 P.M. we brought the captain on board the American barque *Swallow*. She then got underway—she is going to Boston—she towed us [*that is, towed the gig while Captain Nicholas visited aboard the barque*] about three miles outside the harbor. On our way back we stopped at the *Saratoga*, and the *San Jacinto*, where we remained until 10 P.M. We then returned on board our own ship. The American schooner *St. Helena* sailed at 8 P.M. The captain of the *San Jacinto* is in charge of the squadron during the flag officer's absence.

Flag Officer Inman had voiced concern about his own health, and scurvy had broken out aboard the Portsmouth. *For some time very anxious to get home, Inman had proposed giving Captain Dornin the squadron command while he took the* Constellation *back to the States but for now left him in temporary command while he took the* Portsmouth *to St. Helena.*[2]

May 8th   **murderous assault with a knife, the injured man not expected to live/Badly Stabbed/Lynch Law talked of**

This morning we took the gig upon the beach, and scrubbed her inside and out. We also had a very nice bathing. At 8 A.M. during breakfast time a very serious and dangerous affair happened; two of the port watch of afterguard getting into a dispute at their mess about a pot of coffee, they used some very provoking words to each other. From words they came to blows and one of the parties, by the name of Thomas Collins, seized a sheath knife that lay upon the mess cloth, and inflicted a dangerous (and it is feared a fatal) wound, upon the other party, whose name is George Wilson. The knife is a common sheath knife. The whole length of the blade went into the body of Wilson, it being about three and a half inches long. He dropped instantly, and was brought into the sick bay, where the surgeons are attending him. Collins was brought to the mast, and the captain ordered him to be put in irons in the brig. The surgeons have examined the sufferer, and report him to be worse than they thought at first. There are two stabs upon him: one across his stomach which just penetrated his flesh; and the other, right under his left breast, it passed through one of his lungs, and just touched his heart. The wound is three and a half inches deep. He is in great agony. He is bleeding inwardly; they have but very faint hopes of his recovery. It causes an intense excitement among all hands. In some groups Lynch Law is talked of and is approved of by two thirds of the ship's company. We are getting in provisions and small stores. We are going to sea in a few days, for a three weeks' cruise around the mouth of Congo River and its vicinity. At 3 P.M. we went ashore with the captain's steward and returned at sundown.

Prior to departing Inman ordered that all stores be taken out of the storehouse ashore and either distributed to ships requiring them or taken aboard the Relief. *He had terminated the lease on the storehouse, establishing the* Relief *in its place as the supply depot for the squadron. Leonard mentioned earlier that the stores were not keeping as well ashore, and the naval storekeeper in charge of the storehouse was still being held by the local authorities.*[3] *Nevertheless closing down the storehouse was a major step; Inman may have been anticipating the squadron's withdrawal for operations against the Confederacy.*

May 9th   out of Danger/all hands up anchor/
the ship runs ashore/we are hard and fast in the sand/
try to get her off but cannot/11 feet in the sand/give up

This morning we commenced making preparations for sea, bent all our light sails and crossed Royal Yards. During the forenoon we were getting in provisions. The injured man was very low all last night, [but] he is considered out of danger by the doctors this morning, as he has taken a favorable turn, and at twelve o'clock noon he is considered in a fair way of recovery. At 3 P.M. we got in all boats, and by four o'clock we had everything ready for heaving up the anchor. At half past 4 P.M. the hands were piped to supper, and at 5 P.M. all hands were called to get up the anchor. There was a strong breeze blowing at the time. We were about half a mile from the beach.

On the anchor being tripped, she commenced going astern very fast—we were swinging at the same time—we now hoisted the jib, and flying jib, which made her go astern still faster, and before we had the topsails hoisted, her stern was hard and fast in the sand. We made all sail so as to drive her off, but it was no use, she didn't stir an inch. All the boats in the harbor came to our assistance and tried to tow her off, but all to no purpose. We now furled the royals and topgallant sails, and got all our large hawsers and kedge anchors. We made the hawsers fast to the store ship *Relief* and *San Jacinto,* and took them to our main deck capstan,[4] we then set all sail, and the boats commenced towing, but she resisted our combined efforts, and well she might, for on sounding in the port chains, we learnt we had seven feet of water. We draw twenty-one feet aft, and nineteen forward, which showed we were sunk about eleven feet in the sand. At 8 P.M. we again made another attempt to get her off, but with no success. As the tide was ebbing fast, it was thought best to wait for the next tide. The sails were then furled, and the batteries run out (they being run in amidships) the gun deck cleared up a little, and at half past 9 P.M. the hammocks were piped down and all hands turned in.

May 10th   trying again/swings off herself/getting underway again/
we again get foul with the *Relief*

At two o'clock this morning, all hands were called and hammocks were piped up. To get the hammocks up quick, and also prevent a great deal of unnecessary growling among the men, the 1st lieutenant, had recourse to a stratagem which produced the desired effect. It was this: on the hands being turned out he had eight bells struck. At half past 2 A.M. the ship swung off herself. We hauled her about half a mile from the beach and dropped anchor. At 10 A.M. we again made an attempt to get underway. We got up the anchor, and by means of a hawser made fast to the store ship, we warped close to her, but on loosing sail, she commenced going ahead, and in five minutes more we came in collision with the Store Ship *Relief*. Our flying jib boom going right through her mizzen topmast rigging, she had to slack up all her mizzen topmast rigging and backstays before we got clear of her. After getting clear, we made sail, and went to sea. The opinions of the ship's company about our officers is very small. As it would be high treason to express my opinions at present, I will leave it until some future period, when I hope I will be at liberty to express them freely. At 4 P.M. a sail was reported a point on our lee bow. We have got a six knot breeze. At dark we set the port studding sails. Very fine weather. The man that was stabbed is recovering fast.

May 11th   at sea./on the **Cruising Ground**

This day came in fine with a light breeze, the watch engaged in working about the rigging all the forenoon. The man that was stabbed is getting along first rate. Today our purser's steward was broke to a landsman on account of getting drunk, and another young man was appointed in his place. At 7 P.M. we took in all the light sail, hauled up the courses, and at 11 P.M. we hove to. We are now on the cruising ground, it is a very fine night and there is a good breeze blowing.

Time is money

May 12th 1861   Sail ho./Suspected vessels/boarding the schooner
                                         St. Helena nothing in her/Sail ho.

Sunday and a very fine day. At half past 9 A.M. the divisions were called to quarters for inspection, after which divine service was held on the gun deck. At 10 A.M. two sails were reported on our lee bow. Some of the old feeling is again coming among the men; as soon as a sail is reported, all is bustle and excitement. Our captain has got a list of suspected vessels that are now on the coast. They number twenty-two, among which are the barque *Kate*, and the *Cora* is said to be out here again, the *Arabian Steed* and a clipper barque name unknown, the brigs *Bonita* and *Storm King*, also the celebrated Yacht *Wanderer*. One of the sails proved to be the *John Gilpin's Bride*, and the other is the schooner *St. Helena*, which is one of the suspected vessels. We are standing for her, and gaining on her fast. At 2 P.M. we hove her to and boarded her. She had nothing in her but water casks. We then hoisted our boat and made sail. At 4 P.M. another sail was reported, which proved to be a barque rigged steamer standing to the southward. We are now in the black water of the Congo River. At night we took in all the light sail.

Leonard was not being metaphorical about the Congo. The Congo discolors the Atlantic for as much as three hundred miles offshore, the water being described as yellowish red or brownish until forty miles out, where it becomes blackish.[5]

May 13th Land ho.

Twenty-three months in commission. The starboard watch washed clothes, the port watch holystoned the gun deck in the forenoon. Land in sight all along our lee bow, supposed to be Kabenda. We tacked ship several times during the day. All the divisions were exercised at small arms. In the afternoon we have got a six knot breeze.

May 14th Shark's Point

Port watch washed clothes. It is a very warm morning, and we have got a good breeze. We are still on the cruising ground and a bright lookout is kept at the mast head. At 3 P.M. all the divisions were exercised at single sticks. At sundown we were in sight of Shark's Point. We furled royals and topgallant sails, hauled up the courses, and remained so during the night.

Shark Point was the western point of the entrance to the Congo River.

May 15th Sail ho/a Budget of Fun and a very Phunny Phellow [*sic*]
Possom Wattomie Brown./humorous/Politics/a good theory
a glutton/2nd Cruise/Ready Wit/Boarding the Barque/
after niggers a boat returns.

Early this morning we made sail. At 8 A.M. a sail was reported on our weather bow, made her out to be a barque, with French colors flying. We are now standing towards her. Land in sight all along our weather bow, we are to the southward of Congo River. At 10 A.M. the divisions are putting down for clothing.

Another of our characters is James Brown, a seaman in the fore top. Although he is but four months in the ship, he is a universal favorite. We shipped him in St. Helena from a barque, the captain of the barque refusing to comply with the articles. [*Each merchant ship carried a document, the "ship's articles" or "articles of agreement," specifying the conditions of the voyage and the employment conditions of the crew. It was a contract between the owners (represented at sea by the captain) and the individual seamen. A new one was signed at the beginning of each voyage.*] Brown, and another by the name of William Baker, knocked off, or in other words they refused to work, and they applied to our flag officer for protection. He took them on board of our ship and two others were sent in their places. Brown has, on account of his eccentricities, earned himself three nick names. The first is "the Budget of Fun," which title was given to him on account of his inexhaustible quantity of fun and good humor; the 2nd is "the Phunny Phellow," which was also given to him for the same reason as was the 1st, and also because his wit and comicalities very much resemble the fun a person derives from reading the papers with the above headings [*Frank Leslie published the monthly "Budget of Fun," with cartoons and humor; Street & Smith began publishing a humor newspaper of the title* Phunny Phellow *in September 1859—just as the* Constellation *was beginning its cruise—featuring cartoons by Thomas Nast. The "famous Osawatomie Brown," mentioned next, refers to a name given John Brown after he led the defense of abolitionists at the settlement of that name in Kansas in 1856.* Frank Leslie's Illustrated *of October 29, 1859 published a portrait of Brown after his capture, captioned "Ossawatomie Brown." The name "Possum Watomie" derives from Brown's murderous attack on settlers at Pottawatomi Creek a few months earlier. Brown's raid on Harper's Ferry took place on October 16, 1859, at which time the* Constellation *was nearing Liberia, and he was hanged December 2. Brown's name of course remained on everyone's mind for years afterward, so prominently as to make the connection with the sailor named Brown obvious, though uninspired.*]; the 3d title is the curious and singular one of "Possom Watomie Brown." Why on earth this was given to him is a mystery; it cannot be on account of his resembling the famous Osawatomie Brown, the leader of the Harper's Ferry insurrection, or because his politics are the same. The 1st assertion must be wrong, for we have had Frank Leslie's papers out here, and as he says our artist has given us a life like portrait of this distinguished abolitionist, we must give up the idea of trying to trace a resemblance between the two characters, as our Brown is an Englishman by birth, about 5 foot 5 inches in height, and very stoutly built, whereas Frank Leslie's Brown is a very tall sickly looking man, and not at all like ours.

The 1st point being settled, let us look at the second. Our Brown's politics are as different as chalk is from cheese, from Frank Leslie's Brown's politics, so that can't be the reason why he is so named. Our Brown has but very little to say about the different political questions of the days; he considers them all a humbug. His policy (as he says himself) lies in having a full stomach, which I think myself is a very good theory. Two thirds of the present politicians have this object in view when they squander the municipal and government funds in dinners, and lionizing the lord knows who. On the subject of our present sketch, [he] has a great leniency towards Gluttony. According to his messmates' stories, he in all cases scoffs [at] the government's allowance, and everybody knows, that has any dealings with our Uncle Samuel, that he allows his subjects enough food, and of a very good quality, to satisfy any man with the ordinary powers of digestion. Not so with our Brown; as soon as he is done at his mess he starts up complaining of being starved, but I believe he does this from his love for fun. He of course has got a great appetite, and when he complains of being starved, it creates a general laugh. He has been [on] a cruise in the U.S. Navy before, and to use a man of war expression, he knows every move on the board. His principal delight consists in poking fun at the captain of the mizzen top, Alexander Wilson, of which I have given a description (see pages 211 and 212). Brown in fact is the only man in the ship that can ruffle the usual good humor of Wilson. When they both get on an argument together, which is very often, Brown always comes off first best. To make the affair more interesting, both parties have their partisans, and some-times the debaters get warmed up, on perceiving which, Brown lets out some of his ready wit, which entirely destroys all ill feeling and also puts an end to the argument.

At 3 P.M., the wind dying almost to a calm, and the sail being about two miles to windward of us, we lowered our 4th cutter and went alongside of her. Our 4th lieutenant hailed her in French. He was answered by a French offi-cer dressed in Naval uniform; he told us he was from Guadalupe, bound for Congo, after a load of niggers. They take them the same as the English do the coolies. Her name is the *Marie,* of Guadalupe; she is painted white. The boat returned and we hoisted her. Shark's Point is in sight. At 5 P.M. the 2nd and 3d divisions were drilled at the small arms exercise. The air is very damp here at present, which makes it very disagreeable, our clothes being wet all the time.

William A. Leonard

Cruising at sea

May 16th   sail ho/a Calculating Yankee/a Victim of the Panic of 1857 a
Temperance advocate/a great shock to the Temperance cause/
Marvellous Yarns./Sail ho./land in sight/Sail ho/
Slave Factories in sight.

Port watch washed clothes. At 6 A.M. a sail was reported, made her out to be a steamer. There is not wind enough to give the ship steerage way. At half past 9 A.M. the division commenced drawing clothing.

Another of our characters, is Wm P. Upham, coxswain of the launch, and 2nd captain of the forecastle. He is an American by birth; he is one of those shrewd, calculating Yankees, such a one that can't be found anywhere else but in the New England States. He has been (as report says and I have no reason to doubt it) Chief Mate, of one of the fast clipper ships that sailed out of New York. But during the commercial Panic of 1857 he among the rest lost his all, and then taking to drinking, he shipped in the U.S. Navy, where we now find him. In height he is about five feet six inches. Of a light brown complexion, with a large bushy beard, he is a very intelligent man and a very good scholar. He is considered a good authority to settle all difficult questions that are brought up amongst the men, no matter what topic it is except it is religion, which topic he strictly declines to have anything to do with. I will here state that the subject of religion is rarely brought up in this ship. Every-body drops it with common consent, and it is right it should be, it creates hard feeling in any society, let alone a man of war. Country is the principal topic of conversation in a ship of war. When our ship first went into commission, a temperance society was formed by the gunner and members of the religious society, which in the course of three months had two thirds of the ship's company as members. Among the number was the hero of the present sketch, who was, and is still one of its warmest supporters. They held their meetings on the starboard side of the berth deck, two evenings in the week. His speeches exhibited a good sound mind. He would (to make his speeches interesting) relate anecdotes of the follies of intemperance. But I am sorry to say during our forty-eight hours liberty in the Island of St Helena, the Temperance Cause suffered a great shock, which caused it to break up, and now all hands can be seen twice a day at the grog tub after their little gallon, which is so called by the waggish portion of the men, except a certain few, our hero being one of the number. Upham is a great yarn spinner, he takes the lead in that line, but of all the marvelous, or fabulous, stories that could be thought of, Wm P. Upham's are the most singular that ever I heard or read of. He is also a very good sewer. Having something more to say about him on some future page, I will drop him for the present.

At 11 A.M. another sail was reported. A light breeze is springing up, which promises to be a strong breeze in a couple of hours. At 2 P.M. a good breeze sprung up, and we are now standing in for the land, also after the sail. At 3 P.M. another sail was reported by the lookout at the masthead. We made the first sail out to be the white barque, and the other is English Steam Gun boat *Sharpshooter*. We are about eight miles from Shark's Point. The slave factories can be seen distinctly on both sides of the Congo River. At sundown reduced sail, and stood out from the land. We had but very little wind during the night; the atmosphere was very damp.

May 17th	Under easy sail/Tide Ripples/Tailoring/
	Barracks/Prayer meeting

Starboard watch washed clothes; the watch on deck were busy all this forenoon, painting the weather hammock clothes. In the afternoon the divisions were exercised at small arm drill. One of the men was put in the brig, for shoving one of the kroomen out of his way while drilling. We have got a nigger loving set of officers and no mistake; they all hail from the southern states. At 2 P.M. we furled the royals and top gallant sails. This is done so as not to be seen any great ways off. As soon as a sail is reported, all sail is made, and chase given to her. Anybody accustomed to a seafaring life knows that a vessel's royals and top gallant sails can be seen before any other part of the vessel. At sundown, the wind died away and we are lying like a log upon the water. At times there is a very heavy tide ripple running which almost slows the ship. It makes a noise like a water fall while passing, which is about ten minutes.

Was busy all this day, tailoring. If there is anything I hate in this world it is in washing, and tailoring. It can't be helped, it must be done, and by myself. The cleanest set of men in the world, I believe, is an American man of war's men. They wash their clothes twice a week and their person is cleaned every day; water don't cost nothing. I have washed myself so often with salt water, that I expect to be all over barnacles before the ship goes out of commission. As the religious society are about commencing their usual evening prayer meeting, I will have to suspend writing.

May 18th   **sail ho/board her/Proves to be the English Steam Gunboat *Philomel***

This morning came in fine, with a light breeze. At half past 9 A.M. the starboard watch holystoned the gun deck. At 10 A.M. a sail was reported on our lee bow. We squared away and set studding sails; she is coming towards us. Made her out to be an English gunboat. At 11 A.M. we took in studding sails and royals, and hauled up the courses. She now being very close to us we hove to, and lowered the 4th cutter, and went alongside of her. They also lowered their gig and her captain came on board of us. He is a very young looking man for a captain. Her name is the *Philomel*. She is just out from England. She told us that the English Steam Sloop of War *Archer* had got her orders and sailed for home. He returned on board of his own vessel, and our boat also returned. We hoisted her, made sail, and stood on our course. She is a very pretty gun boat. At sundown, we shortened sail.

The Philomel, *a four-hundred-ton, five-gun screw steamer under Cdr. Leveson Wildman, RN, had just been completed and commissioned a few months earlier.*

May 19th   **Land ho./Sail ho./came to an anchor off Sharks point the mouth of Congo River/American Barque *Rattlesnake*/ Rolling a strong current**

Sunday. It is very cloudy this morning. At half past 9 A.M. the divisions were called to quarters for inspection, after which divine service was held on the gun deck. At 11 A.M. land was reported, on nearing which we discovered two sails at anchor. At half past 1 P.M. we made preparations to come to an anchor. At 4 P.M. all hands were called to bring ship to an anchor. All sail was then clewed up, the port anchor let go, and all hands were piped to supper. We are within five miles of Shark's Point, close to the mouth of Congo River. The English Gun boat *Wrangler* is at anchor close to us. The other sail we saw was the English

Speak a kind word when you can

Gun boat *Sharpshooter*. She has gone up the river. At 5 P.M. all hands were called to furl sail, the fish gear [for securing the anchor on the bow] was rove, and the messenger got up ready to get up the anchor. The captain of the *Wrangler* came on board. The barque *Rattlesnake* is up the river waiting for a cargo, also three brigs; there are rumors of other vessels being up there. There is a very heavy swell here; we are rolling so much that our guns almost touch the water. We are not going to stay here long. The land, atmosphere, water, and in fact everything here has a sickly appearance. There is a six knot current running here all the time; it requires a very strong wind for sailing vessels to get up this river.

May 20th	*Prometheus*/Our 4th Cutter with 12 men and 3 officers armed and Provisioned towed up Congo River by the *Prometheus*/*Sharpshooter* sails for home

Port watch washed clothes. During the night, the English Gun Boats *Prometheus*, and *Sharpshooter*, came to an anchor close to us. The *Sharpshooter* run ashore last night up the river, and turned back; she is going home today. We lowered the gig in the afternoon and went on board the *Wrangler*. At 4 P.M. the *Prometheus* got underway, to go up the river. Our captain had our 4th cutter manned and provisioned for twelve men and three officers. They are to be towed up by the steamer. They are to be gone two days. There are several vessels up the river that refuse to let the English cruisers board them. Each man is armed with a Colt's revolver and cutlass.

At 5 P.M. furled sail, they being loosed this morning to dry. At 6 P.M. the *Sharpshooter* got underway. And as they passed the *Wrangler*, they cheered ship, which was returned by the *Wranglers*. She has been three years and eight months in commission, has taken eight prizes, and has not had any liberty during her cruise, which is a downright shame to her officers. What would some of our countrymen do if they were penned up in a little gunboat three years and eight months? They wouldn't stand it. It is very cloudy weather here at present.

The "several vessels up the river" were refusing to let the British board them by virtue of being American. Learning this from the British, Captain Nicholas suggested they assist. Towed by the British steamer, the Constellation's *party made a seven-hour jaunt upriver. The same concern about exposing men to African fever that made it U.S. policy to forbid anyone to spend a night ashore in Africa also discouraged sending expeditions upriver unless—as was the case here—special circumstances justified it. Lt. Philip C. Johnson led the expedition.*

May 21st   Breaking of a petty Officer./Sail ho/Suspicious./
                            the Gig sent to see what she is/she proves a prize

Starboard watch washed clothes. The gig's crew were busy all the forenoon,
fixing up the boat's gear. The captain of the main top (Ball) was this day broken by the 1st Lieutenant, and another put in his place (Young). Everybody in
the ship is glad of it. He was nothing but an old growl. At 3 P.M. the washed
clothes were piped down.

At 4 P.M. a sail hove in sight; she came out from the Congo River and is
beating up towards us. She is a brigantine. There is a boat towing astern, supposed to be our 4th cutter. There is but very little wind, and a very strong current against her. We think she is a slaver that our boat has taken up the river
and sent down. At 7 P.M. the gig was called away, and manned with Kroomen,
and two officers also going in her, to board the brigantine. There is quite an
excitement on board about her. At 10 A.M. the gig returned; our suspicions
proved correct: she is a prize, and a slaver. We could not get much information
about her until morning.

May 22nd   Capture of the Hermaphrodite Slave Brig *Triton* of Indianolia.
             No Slaves Another Prize/taking of the prize/on what authority
             do you board my vessel/by the Stars and Stripes/we take/
             another prize called the *Falmouth*/give her up not worth taking/
             getting underway sailing in company with the Prize/
             we are bound to Kerbenda/came to an anchor off Black Point/
Coast fever/Supercargo not taken/everything/ready to take her Niggers

This morning all hands were up bright and early to have a look at the sla-
ver, but they were disappointed. Having but very little wind during the night,
she drifted out of sight with the strong current from the Congo River. The
Prometheus brought our party up the river fifty-six miles to a place called
Point Galina [*what Leonard heard as "Point Galina" was actually "Punta da
Lenha," the main locus of the Congo slave trade*], where the *Triton* was at
anchor. The steamer came to an anchor and our boat proceeded to board her.
The captain of the *Triton*, thinking they were English, hoisted the American
ensign at the peak, and when our officer boarded her, he wanted to know his
authority for boarding him. He showed him his buttons; that would not satisfy
him. Our officer then went to the boat and took out the boat's flag and showed
it to him. When he gave up the vessel four blue jackets and four Marines were
left in charge of her, with an officer. The rest of the party (eight blue jackets
and two officers) took the boat and pulled up five miles further and took possession of a brig called the *Falmouth*. They searched her and found nothing in

her, her sails, provisions and everything being ashore. The mate refused to tell where they were; the captain of her was murdered by the natives. Our officers, thinking she was not worth taking, prepared to leave, telling the mate, "We will keep a sharp lookout for you." "Very well," was the answer, "if I once get clear of the mouth of this river with my niggers on board I defy you."

Our party then came down to the *Triton* and got her underway and came down the river. At 8 A.M. we caught sight of the prize off our starboard quarter. At 10 A.M. we got underway and stood down to her. At twelve o'clock, we were close to her, both vessels hove to and we sent a boat alongside of her. Our men then came on board, and were immediately sent

Old Abe is Honorable

to the dispensary, where a dose of quinine was given them by the doctor. A fresh crew went on board the prize. At 1 P.M. both vessels made sail, and stood towards Kabenda, where we are going to anchor. This is the same vessel that the Gun boat *Mystic* sent home last year. [*The* Mystic *had captured the* Triton *off Loanda in July 1860. Taken to Norfolk, it was legally condemned and sold—right back into the slave trade.*] The *Falmouth* was also taken and sent home by the *Portsmouth*. [*That is, the* Falmouth *had been taken by the* Portsmouth *off Porto Praya in May 1860. It had been condemned in New York, sold at auction, and bought right back into the slave trade. The* Constellation's *boarding party decided that this time the brig was not far enough in preparing to take slaves aboard to justify seizing it, though as Captain Nicholas remarked, "She doubtless is going to take in a slave cargo."*[6]] We expect to be in Kabenda tonight; it is forty miles to leeward of Congo River. At 7 P.M. we came to an anchor about ten miles to leeward of Black Point and fifty miles from Kabenda. [*The southern tip of Loango Bay is Black Point, which is the northern end of Black Point Bay.*] The prize also came to an anchor. Her crew was then brought on board this ship, and a regular crew, consisting of eleven men and two officers, were sent on board of her. They were picked out by the 1st lieutenant. Two of her crew are very bad with the coast fever; one of her men died with it up the river. Her crew are all Americans and a very fine looking set of men. The supercargo was not taken, he being ashore when we took her, and of course he had all the money. The crew say he was captain. There are nine in all, one supposed to be the captain. She was just on the eve of taking in her niggers when our party took her: she had the slave deck laid, coppers ready, and her hold full of rice and water. Our sailing master and captain's clerk are going to take her home.[7]

May 23d the Prize going to Norfolk, Va./the Prize sails for home/
a canoe capsized/a krooman eaten by a crocodile/
4 others escaped to the Banks of the river/a quick passage

This morning the port watch washed and holystoned the gun deck. At 8 A.M. we got out two boats from the booms: 3d cutter and dinghy. We are going to give the dinghy to the prize, as she has no boats. We are giving her wood and a few provisions. One of her men is an old man of war's man. Having been twenty-two years in the service, he made a cruise in this ship when she was a frigate (1844).[8] He has about nine old shipmates among our boys. When we laugh at him, he takes it very easy and says he will try again. At 2 P.M. we hoisted in our 3d cutter. She is going to Norfolk, Va. We are going back to the Congo River, and I believe we are going to take the brig *Falmouth*, at least so the officers say. At 5 P.M. the prize got underway and sailed for the United States. Two of her men shipped with us, the rest have gone home in the prize.

While the boat's crew were up the river, the *Prometheus* lowered a canoe, and sent it ashore with five kroomen. On nearing the bank of the river, the canoe got capsized by some sudden turn in the current, which is very strong in the river (6 ½ to 7 knots an hour). While they were in the water, one of them was snapped in two by a monstrous crocodile. He made just two bites of him. The other four reached the banks of the river almost frightened out of their lives. The scent of blood attracted numerous other crocodiles to the spot. This happened in sight of the *Prometheus*. They lowered a boat but were just in time to be too late. They then went ashore for the other four kroomen, but they were so much frightened that they refused to go on board, but by dragging, coaxing and threatening they induced them to go on board.

The weather is very pleasant here at present. At sundown we lost sight of the prize; she is a very fast sailer, having made the quickest passage from the Congo River to the United States on record, 37 days.

A prize crew under Midshipman Borchert took the Triton *back to the States. Borchert, it may be remembered, is the Georgian who two months earlier had asked to return to the United States so he could resign. He was now entrusted to take the prize to New York. With him in the prize crew was the captain's clerk, Stephen B. Wilson Jr., son of the Captain Wilson whose fall on the ice kept him from taking the* Constellation *to Africa.*

at anchor off Black Point

May 24th 1861   getting underway/at sea/sail ho/came to an anchor
                          in Loango Bay send a boat ashore/
                          the Schooner *St. Helena* again/Barracoons

As soon as the hands were turned out this morning, we got up anchor, and made sail. We are going to Kabenda. At 6 A.M. the port watch washed clothes. At 8 A.M. we set all the starboard studding sails. There is but very little wind. We are running close in to the land. At 4 P.M. two sails were reported at anchor, in Loango Bay. We are standing in for them. Port watch maintop men were busy all this afternoon rattling down their topmast rigging. [*That is, they were renewing the ratlines on the topmast.*]

At 7 P.M. we came to an anchor in Loango Bay about three miles from the beach. After furling sail and putting everything to rights, the 4th cutter was called away and manned, two officers going in her to find out what the two sails are that are lying at anchor inshore. At 9 A.M. they boarded them and returned at half past 10 P.M. One of them proved to be the schooner *St. Helena,* and the other is a Spanish brig. It looks very suspicious for them to be here, as there are several slave factories, or barracoons, on the beach. They are waiting for a favorable chance to get her niggers and clear. They have not got their slave deck laid as yet, but they could rig them in an hour or two. It is a beautiful moonlight night, with a light breeze blowing.

May 25th   at anchor in Loango Bay/getting underway in Loango Bay/
                      Court Martial/No favorite/Sail ho./*Prometheus*/board her/
                      Sentence of a Court Martial/his charges/the sentence/
                      watching the Schooner *St. Helena*

This morning all decks were holystoned. The land here is very high and presents quite a beautiful appearance. It is all covered with verdure. There are six slave barracoons along the beach, and can be seen quite plain from our deck. Our 4th cutter went ashore to get some provisions for the officers. They returned at 11 A.M. After hoisting her, all hands were called to make sail, after which we hove up the anchor, and stood out from the land. At 3 P.M. preparations were made on the gun deck for a summary court martial: one of our Marines, the same one who was tried by a general court martial not long ago in St Paul de Loando; this is the fourth time he has been tried in this ship. The fact of it is, the man is no favorite with the officers; any offense committed by him lays him open to a court martial; if done by another man it would be overlooked. The man does not cringe and fawn around the officers, he is the only true man in the Marine Corps.

At 4 P.M. a sail was reported on our weather beam; she is coming towards us. At half past 4 P.M. we made her out to be the English gun boat *Prometheus;* at 6 P.M. we hove to and sent our 4th cutter on board of her. Our boatswain then called all hands to muster, to hear the sentence of the court martial. The prisoner was brought on the quarter deck by the Master at Arms. The 1st lieutenant then read his charges, which were treating with contempt the orders of his superior officer (said officer being a Dutch orderly sergeant); also telling him that he did not know how to detail the guard for duty. On account of the contradictory evidence of one of the witnesses, only a part of the charges were sustained. His sentence was twenty-one days in solitary confinement on bread and water in double irons. The hands were then piped down.

At half past 6 P.M. the captain and doctor of the *Prometheus* came on board our ship and left at 7 P.M. We then hoisted our boat, squared yards and stood in for the land. We furled royals and topgallant sails, and hauled up the courses. We are going to watch the schooner *St. Helena*. The *Prometheus* gave us the information that there is a large American ship in Congo River. At 8 P.M. we parted company with the *Prometheus*. At 10 P.M. we hove to. We are very close to the land.

May 26th

Sunday, and very cloudy. At daybreak we made all sail and stood out from the land. At half past 9 A.M. all hands were called to quarters for inspection, after which we had divine service on the gun deck. We are now going to the southward, with a six knot breeze. We tacked ship several times during the afternoon and night.

May 27th   Homesick.

This day came in very fine. At 9 A.M. all bags were piped up to air clothing. We have got an eight knot breeze. At 3 P.M. the 2nd division were exercised at single sticks; at seven bells [3:30] the starboard watch's washed clothes were piped down. At half past 5 P.M. the 1st division were exercised an hour and a half at the large guns.

I am very downhearted all this day thinking of home and friends. It seems an age since we have been out here instead of almost two years, and no wonder, there are hardly any signs of civilization in any port we go into. I long for the day that I will set my foot on shore, and can call myself a freeman again. I don't think our venerated Uncle Samuel will get my services again in this line if I can help it. Which I know I can if I feel so disposed.

W. A. Leonard

May 28th 1861.   airing bedding/calm.

Port watch washed clothes. It is a fine day, going about five knots. At 9 A.M. the hammocks were piped out of the nettings so as to air the bedding. The shot and wad men are cleaning the shot and shot lockers. At 3 P.M. the 1st division exercised small arms; at 5 P.M. the 2nd division exercised big guns. It is a dead calm, and very warm. The monthly mess bills for small stores came out today.

May 29th   exercise

Came in very fine, with but very little wind. Topmast, and topgallant, studding set on the port side. In the afternoon, the 1st, 2nd and 3d divisions exercised single sticks, small arms, and big guns. It was very calm all night. We are going to the Sd. and Ed.

May 30th   getting up and cleaning the Chain Cables

This day is fine, but no wind. At 9 A.M. both watches were set to work getting up the chain cables in order to overhaul, and clean them. At 11 A.M. the cables being cleaned, and the lockers white washed, they were put down again. At 2 P.M. the port watch holystoned the gun deck. At 6 P.M. a light breeze sprung up. Our course is to the Sd and Ed. Small stores were served out during the day. The port watch washed clothes.

May 31st   a Benefit/General Quarters/exercising the main Top men

Friday, starboard watch washed clothes. At 9 A.M. set the top gallant studding sails, it being my part's top aloft (Port watch main Top 1st part). Our sail went foul. Our 2nd luff (J.C. Rhind), being officer of the deck, gave us a hearty damning as a benefit. He then made us set the sail half a dozen times. At half past nine the drum beat to General Quarters; we exercised the starboard battery. After going through several maneuvers, the drum beat the retreat. It has been some time since we had general quarters before. Immediately after quarters, we were again sent aloft, and exercised at taking in and setting the top gallant studding sail for upwards of an hour and a half. At 2 P.M. the wind got stronger, and at 3 P.M. we were going seven knots. At 5 P.M., the wind hauling ahead, we took in the studding sails and braced the yards up sharp. We are heading to the Sd and Ed; at noon we were 83 miles to the Nd and Wd of the mouth of Congo River. At 7 P.M. we are going four knots; at 1 P.M. [*Leonard may mean* A.M. *here*] we took in all the studding sails.

June 1861

June 1st 1861   land ho/Shark's Point/sail ho/
U.S.S. *Sumpter*/the Brig *Falmouth*

At four o'clock this morning we squared the yards, and set studding sails on
both sides, and at daylight we were within eight miles of Shark's Point, the
mouth of Congo River. We then took in the studding sails, hauled up the
courses, furled the royals and hove to. We expect to see one of our steamers at
half past 9 A.M. The starboard watch holystoned the gun deck. At half past 10
A.M. a sail was reported by the lookout at the masthead, on our weather beam;
she is coming down to us, made her out to be the U.S. Gun boat *Sumpter*. She
lowered a boat and her captain came on board. She has been up the river, and
reports the brig *Falmouth* ready to take in her niggers, her slave deck being
laid. At 1 P.M. the captain of the *Sumpter* returned on board of his own vessel. We then made sail, and stood to the Sd. and Ed. We are going to St. Paul
de Loando. At sundown we were going seven knots, tacked ship several times
during the night.

June 2nd   all hands to muster, reading the Articles of War/the Gig/
a description of her crew/Parties or Cliques/
Nationality monopolizing/dead calm/drifting

Sunday and a splendid day. At half past 9 A.M. all hands were called to quarters for division inspection; we were dressed in blue mustering clothes. A 10
A.M. all hands were called to muster. The Articles of War were read by the 1st
lieutenant, after which divine service was held on the gun deck. On board this
ship there is no compulsion about attending church; those who feel inclined
to go, may, but the rest are obliged to keep perfect silence until the service is
ended. In the afternoon we have got but very little wind.

Flag Officer William Inman. Naval History and Heritage Center, Washington, D.C.

I will here give a kind of a description of our boat's crew (rather late, I know, but it is never too late is an old saying, so I will commence). Our captain's boat, or "gig" as she is called, is and has proved herself the best, and smartest pulling, boat on the Coast. We have pulled several races, and always came off victorious. She is a clinker built boat, and somewhat the shape of a yawl, and while in the water presents a very beautiful appearance. Her crew are all young fellows, not one (except the coxswain) being in the Navy before, the oldest man in the boat being 28 and the youngest 21 years. The Coxswain John W. Thomson (28 years old) is a native of Troy, N.Y.; he is 5 feet 7 inches high and weighs 147 pounds. The stroke oarsman, Charles F. Gordon, is a native of Norwich, Vt.; he is 21 years of age, height 5 feet 7 inches, and weighs 147 lbs. The next is Peter Ridovis, a native of the Island of Mahon in the Mediterranean Sea (he shipped with us from the slave brig *Delicia*); he is 5 feet 6 inches high and weighs 142 pounds, and is 25 years old. The next is Wm H. French, a native of Philadelphia, Penn.; he is 25 years of age, height 5 feet 6 inches, and weighs 137 lbs. The next in order is John F. Powell, who is a native of Charlestown, Mass.; in height he is 5 feet 7 inches, weighs 145 lbs, and is 21 years of age. The next is myself, Wm A. Leonard, a native of Boston, Mass., in height 5 feet 3 inches, weight 134 lbs., 23 years of age. I am the bowman. The boat is a 12 oared boat but we only pull 6 oars, we pull single bank, a long side stroke, the oars being 17 feet long. The captain likes his boat's crew very well; he gets us out of many a scrape. [*In the margin Leonard drew two hands, both pointing at the following sentence.*] In my own case in particular he got me out of two or three scrapes; one where I laid myself liable to a Court Martial he interceded for me, and by going security for my future behavior he got me off, and I don't think I will betray the confidence he reposes in me, although I should like very much to be out of the boat. However, the cruise is coming to an end shortly and I guess I can stand it.

We have got but very little wind at present. It is curious to notice how many different classes or cliques, there are on board a man of war, and they all have a different part of the ship where they congregate, and of course scandalize their neighbors. When I say cliques I do not wish the reader to infer that I mean political, religious, or party cliques—there is no such work as that going on in this ship, although I have heard from good authority it is a common thing on board ships of war and sometimes it is carried so far that very stringent measures have been adopted to suppress it. The cliques I have reference to are of nationality; they are I consider ten times worse than either of the aforementioned ones. For instance, ten or twelve Portuguese, Spaniards, or Dutchmen (the former in particular) will take up their position on the gratings, at the forward part of the booms where they can command a good view of the spar deck, and everybody that is on it. They then commence talking their gibberish, criticizing, and ridiculing everything and everybody that can't understand them. This is not right and there should be a law, or a clause in the Articles of War, to prevent them using any other language in this Navy but the English. Suppose these gentlemen took it into their heads to get up a mutiny, who could find it out? They could discuss their plans openly and nobody be the wiser for it.

The Kroomen monopolize the maintopmen's gangway. They in fact are the best treated individuals in this ship. They are allowed to smoke on the spar deck, as well as the gun deck. If a white man was to show his head above the gun deck with a lighted pipe in his mouth he would be instantly seized and brought to the mast, by some of these ever ready aspirants for naval fame vulgarly denominated Graybacks (marines). And there if he is fortunate enough to escape a summary court martial, he is very severely punished. These officers are not Abolitionists, o! no, not they, they are Scions of Southern Planters (a fact). If a northerner was to do this, his name would be blazoned out, and in everybody's mouth. A northern man does not put a negro above a white man, neither does he consider him his equal. If a negro goes to this ship's mast with a complaint it is immediately investigated, and if the case is not worth punishing, all hands gets abused by a certain Southern officer, who tells the ship's company, that they are imposing on the poor benighted Africans. They, knowing themselves to be in favor, will scause [*sic*] you, and actually shove you out of their way. Anyhow they have not got much longer to stay, and it will be a happy day when they are gone.

The next clique is the Marines, who take up their position in the foretopmen's gangway. They, with a few exceptions, are tolerated. The feeling a sailor has for a soldier, is about on the same principle as a cat has for a dog. Their particular star being ascendant, it is a blue jacket's policy to keep on good terms with a soldier, but as soon as they get on an equal footing a blue jacket would as soon hang himself, as be seen in company with one. Add to the above named cliques a dozen others, and you will have a faint idea, what it is to be in a man of war. It was a dead calm all night. At 8 P.M. we hauled up the courses and hove to. The current is drifting us to the Nd. and Wd. at the rate of two knots an hour.

Leonard's comments about southern officers being markedly more liberal in their treatment of blacks are noteworthy. The Constellation's *officers were, like the navy as a whole, a mixture of northerners and southerners. Captain Nicholas was himself a Virginian, as was the first lieutenant at this time, Lt. Donald M. Fairfax, and Boatswain Alfred Hingerty. They all remained loyal to the Union. Marine Lieutenant Tattnall, who "went South," was the son of Commodore. Josiah Tattnall of Georgia, who became a Confederate admiral. Of the* Constellation *midshipmen, Hall, Butt, and Borchert all joined the Confederate Navy; Butt was aboard the CSS* Virginia *during its battle with the USS* Monitor *at Hampton Roads. As was noticed earlier, Lieutenant Rhind, though born in New York, had spent formative years in the Deep South and had strong southern connections. Indeed at this very time, his fiancée was hanging a new Confederate flag outside her house near Orange, Virginia, and wondering if, when the* Constellation *returned, he would do the right thing and resign from the U.S. Navy.*[1]

William French, Leonard's boat
mate and friend. Seen here just
after his cruise on the *Constel-*
lation and decades later still in
uniform in his seventies, when
he entertained visitors aboard
the *Constellation* with stories
of the African cruise. Courtesy
of Paul and Linda Ries.

June 3d   **serving out money/off Ambrizet/Speculating**

This morning a light breeze sprang up, we set sail, [and] the port watch washed clothes. At 9 A.M. the purser served out five dollars apiece to all hands. At 10 A.M. we were going five knots. It is a very cloudy day. During the afternoon all the divisions exercised at small arms, single sticks and big guns. At sundown we had an eight knot breeze. Tacked ship several times during the night. We are now very close to Ambrizet, which is about forty miles to windward of St. Paul de Loando. There is no clothing to be served out this month, which causes the boys to speculate on the chances of getting our orders in the next mail, which we expect to get at St. Paul's. The *San Jacinto* is to bring it. I had a midnight lookout at night.

June 4th 1861.   **Intentions/Sail ho/she proves to be the**
                                          U.S.S. *San Jacinto*/we get the mail/no Orders

Starboard watch washed clothes. There is a fine breeze blowing this morning. Going about seven knots, we tacked ship several times during the morning watch. I am very busy all day, in cutting and making a suit of white sailor clothes, which are intended for a younger brother at home. During the afternoon the divisions were exercised at the usual drilling. At half past 5 P.M. a sail was reported on our port quarter coming towards us very fast. We, having studding sails set, took them in and tacked ship. We made her out to be the U.S. Steam Frigate *San Jacinto,* which was on her way with the mail for the squadron from Fernando Po to St. Paul de Loando. At 6 P.M., being close to, we clewed up the royals, hauled up the courses, braced aback the forward yards, and lowered the 4th cutter and went ahead of her. At 7 P.M. the boat returned with the mail for our ship; the flag officer's mail is kept for him by Captain Dornin of the *San Jacinto.* I got one letter (M.L.M.). At half past 7 P.M. both vessels were again on their courses. We do not get much news by this mail, the troubles to home being about the same. We expect there are some important dispatches in the flag officer's mail.

June 5th

This day came in fine with a light wind. There is no excitement at all about the news this mail brought, we have given up all hopes of getting our orders this summer. In the afternoon the divisions exercised. At 5 P.M. we set the starboard topmast and topgallant studding sails. At 7 P.M. land was reported by the cathead lookout, but it proved to be no land after getting closer to it, nothing but a fog bank. Tacked ship several times during the night.

June 6th 1861.   **swinging clean hammocks**

This day came in with a fine breeze, and very pleasant weather. Going about five knots an hour, at noon we were within twenty miles of St. Paul de Loando, but as the land is very low, and the horizon very hazy we cannot see it. We have also got a head wind. We swung clean hammocks, and [are] getting ready for port. At 5 P.M. the wind died away to a dead calm, and remained so all night. A very heavy dew fell during the midwatch.

June 7th   **Land ho/beating up the Harbor/came to an anchor in St. Paul de Loando/bad news Fort Sumter taken**

At four o'clock a light breeze sprung up, which kept increasing until 10 A.M., when we were going six knots. The starboard watch holystoned the gun deck. At half past 10 A.M. land was reported, supposed to be in the vicinity of St. Paul de Loando. We are standing in towards it. It is a beautiful day, we expect to get into port today. At 2 P.M. we hooked the clew jiggers and made preparations to come to an anchor. It is a head wind and we are beating up the harbor. When we were up about half way, the U.S.S. *Saratoga* passed us, on her way out; both vessels dipped their Ensigns. At 5 P.M. we came to an anchor abreast of the U.S. Store Ship *Relief,* and then piped to supper. The U.S. Ships *San Jacinto, Relief, Mystic,* and *Sumpter* are here; the American barques *John Gilpin* and *Lucy Johnson,* the English steamer *Prometheus,* a Portuguese mail steamer and man of war brig, besides about forty other vessels of different nations are here. At 6 P.M. sent down royal yards, and got out two boats. We then brought the captain on board the *Sumpter* and returned at 9 P.M.

The Portuguese mail steamer brought later news than our own mail. The news is very important if true; it is to the effect that Fort Sumter, has been taken by the Secessionists. It creates an intense excitement among the fleet, the ship is like a madhouse through it. We expect to be called Home. We are also expecting to see the flag officer, as there are important dispatches for him. He is at St. Helena, in the *Portsmouth.*

Fort Sumter surrendered on April 13. Virginia seceded on April 17. On April 20 Robert E. Lee, having refused command of the Union army, resigned. That same day the United States evacuated the navy yard in Norfolk, Virginia, burning ships and buildings.

June 8th   **a run ashore**

This morning, all hands were very busy cleaning ship, inside and out. Holystoned all decks, and run in the guns. At 9 A.M. got out all boats, and squared yards. We are also getting in a supply of water. My boatkeeping day. At 11 A.M. a Portuguese brig came to an anchor. At 3 P.M. the English Man of War Steamer *Prometheus* sailed for Congo River. At 2 P.M. the gig went ashore and we had a short run, returned at half past 4 P.M. It is rather chilly here now mornings, and evening.

June 9th   arrival of the *Mohican*/arrival of the U.S. Sloop
of war *Portsmouth* with the Flag officer/
arrival of the *Saratoga*/a dangerous fight between
the *Portsmouth* and *Archer's* crews at St. Helena

Sunday and a very pleasant day, a large sail is coming in. She proved to be the
U.S. Gun boat *Mohican;* she came direct from Porto Praya. At 8 A.M. she came
to an anchor. She brings no news at all. At half past 9 A.M. we had division
inspection after which divine service was held on board. At half past eleven the
captain went on board the *San Jacinto* to dine.

While waiting for the captain on board the *San Jacinto* two large square
rigged were reported coming in. At 4 P.M. made them out to be the U.S. Sloop
of War *Portsmouth* with the broad pennant of Flag Officer Wm H. Inman flying at the mizzen; the other vessel proved to be the U.S. Sloop of war *Saratoga.*
The American barque *Wm Shaler,* of Salem, came to an anchor during the
afternoon. At 6 P.M. the *Portsmouth* and *Saratoga* came to an anchor astern of
the *San Jacinto.* All the captains in the fleet went on board the flag ship. The
Portsmouth laid eight days in St. Helena. She has been up to the Congo River,
and then met the *Saratoga* and ordered her here.

The *Portsmouth* gave her men 24 hours liberty. The English Sloop of war
Archer also gave her men liberty at the same time. Both ship's companies had a
civil war while ashore, which resulted in ten of the *Archer's* men being danger-
ously stabbed, and are now in the Hospital in St. Helena. About fifteen of the
Portsmouth's crew were fined five pounds apiece. They came out 1st best. The
cause of the row, was the *Archer's* crew wanted to monopolize everything on
the island, which the *Portsmouth*s could not stand, and they didn't. At 7 P.M.
we left the *Portsmouth* and went on board the Store Ship *Relief* and remained
on board till 9 P.M., when we went on board our own ship. There was a very
heavy dew falling all night.

June 10th   the flag officer returns on board the *Constellation*/
saluting/Changing our 1st Lieutenant

Had breakfast this morning at seven o'clock. The commodore has not got
any news of importance. The *San Jacinto's* boys are sadly disappointed; they
thought their orders were in this mail. They are going on a thirty days cruise
next Thursday. Our whole squadron are now at anchor in this port, compris-
ing eight vessels consisting of eighty-seven guns. The flag officer is coming on
board today; we are making preparations to receive him. At half past 9 A.M.
the *Portsmouth* fired a salute of thirteen guns, on the leaving of the flag officer.
On his arrival on board of us, we fired a salute of thirteen guns, and hoisted
his pennant at the usual place. We are again the flag ship. I am busy writing
a letter today (M.L.M). At 3 P.M. the captain went on board the *Mohican* to

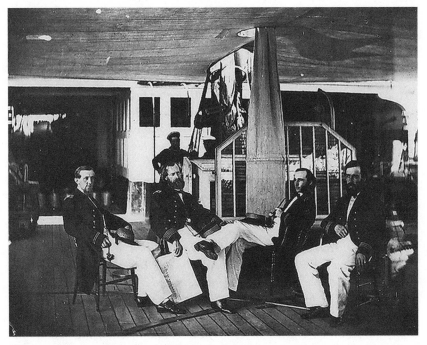

Alexander Colden Rhind (second from left). Photograph taken in 1864 aboard USS *Agawam*, which Rhind then commanded. Naval Historical Heritage Center, Washington, D.C.

dine. At 5 P.M. the U.S.S. *Saratoga* got underway and went to sea. At 7 P.M. the *Sumpter* went to sea. After supper we went to the *Mohican* for the captain, and returned at 9 P.M. Our 1st Lieutenant, D.M. Fairfax, is going to leave us, and go on board the *San Jacinto*. Our 2nd Lieutenant, J.C. Rhind, is to take his place. All hands seems very glad that Mr. Fairfax is gone; he was not liked by the ship's company. Mr. Rhind is one of the strictest lieutenants in the navy, a man that does his duty; he is a good man too, but to a man that he catches foul, he is very bitter to. I think he will be a good 1st lieutenant.

June 11th   **Rumors**

All hands, scrubbed and washed clothes. Our new 1st lieutenant Mr. Rhind took charge this morning. At 9 A.M. we went after fish for the captain. At 10 A.M. a Portuguese Brig came to an anchor. There is a rumor on board at present to the effect that our orders are on their way out here, in charge of a Lieutenant Russell, who comes out as bearer of dispatches to the flag officer. The news creates quite an excitement on board—anything so it will give us hopes

of getting home this fall. At 2 P.M. the captain went on board the *Mohican* to
dine, and returned at 4 P.M. We then went ashore with the steward and had a
run till sundown.

*Freshly returned from his recreation on St. Helena, the flag officer was not
pleased with what he found. Having sent Lieutenant Fairfax (whom he disliked but who had much earlier requested transfer) off to the* San Jacinto,
Inman got into an imbroglio with the officers of the Constellation. *He gave
Captain Nicholas a note saying, "You have permitted the discipline, military
observance, and rules of the service to be set aside on board the flagship 'Constellation,' especially among the officers, to such an extent as to have produced
disorganization, disobedience and insubordination." Inman listed various previously published orders to be adhered to and added several further require-
ments: no smoking in officers' quarters or on the gun deck; officers to be in
full uniform on duty or leaving the ship; watch always to be under an officer,
who may not converse except in line of duty. Nicholas, who could hardly
avoid taking the note as a slap in the face, posted it in the ship's order book
as a general order, publishing it to all aboard, and asked to resign his command. Inman was astounded that Nicholas had treated as a general order
what he intended as a personal direction to Nicholas. Clarifying that he was
talking about Fairfax's transgressions as Nicholas's first lieutenant, he declined
to accept Nicholas's resignation. Nicholas then asked for a medical survey on
himself, citing debilitating rheumatism. A medical board immediately found
him unfit for duty, and he was relieved of command. The* Constellation *was
the sixth and last ship he commanded. Its lieutenants and the marine officer
immediately come to Nicholas's defense. Saying the order clearly reflected on
them, they formally requested a board of inquiry into their own conduct—in
essence a way of supporting Nicholas while reporting the whole situation to
the secretary of the navy. Perhaps because Nicholas was unwilling to sit out the
months of delay the distance from home would cause, nothing further came of
that, and Nicholas was out, his career essentially over.*

June 12th   * * *

All hands scrubbed hammocks. At 9 A.M. we went after fish for the captain. At
half past ten we went ashore with the steward, and returned at 1 P.M. At 3 P.M.
we again went ashore and had a short run (G. I. AR. and G. A.B.E.). We were
very busy all day getting in wood and water. The hammocks were not piped
down on account of their being very damp. It was chilly all night.

June 13th   **Flag officer inspects the *San Jacinto***

Two years in commission, a beautiful day. We did not think two years ago that
we would be on this coast today. Our prospect for going home at present, is

very small. I am heartily sick and tired of a man of war life. At half past 10 A.M. we went ashore, and returned at noon. My boatkeeping day. At 2 P.M. we again went ashore with the captain's steward and had a run till sundown. There is considerable excitement on board the ship all day, on account of our captain, John S. Nicholas, leaving us, and also the Fleet Surgeon Dr. Smith. They are to be invalided home. It is rumored that the flag officer has done this; it is a kind of polite way of getting rid of them by invaliding them home. At 9 o'clock this morning the flag officer went on board the U.S. Steam Frigate *San Jacinto,* and gave them a general inspection. They saluted him on his arrival with thirteen guns and hoisted his pennant at the mizzen.

June 14th   our captain J. S. Nicholas leaves the ship/
                              parting with the officers/Emotion/Changing him/
                              responding/in the boat/talking to the Boat's Crew/

At five o'clock this morning the gig went ashore, to get stores for the captain, and returned at 8 A.M. At 10 A.M. the gig was called away to bring our captain to the *San Jacinto.* He is going to Fernando Po in her and from there home, by the way of England. His steward goes with him. At half past 10 A.M. all hands were called to cheer ship. The captain came on deck in company with the flag officer. The ship's company then manned the starboard rigging, the Marine Corps were drawn up on the quarterdeck with presented arms. The parting with the officers was very feeling. The captain was too full to say much; he in fact hurried over the gangway to prevent himself giving way altogether. As soon as he entered the boat, we hoisted his pennant and shoved off. As soon as we shoved off, the ship's company gave three deafening cheers, which came from their hearts. He then asked us to respond to them in his behalf, which we did, and I believe we gave three as hearty cheers, that ever proceeded from six united voices. We then gave one more cheer as a farewell, which they responded to; we then gave way with a will, and it seemed as if the boat actually had wings the way she glided over the water. She had always been his pride. The tears were glistening in the old man's eyes, as he looked at the boat, and ourselves. I almost fancied that he was taking leave for the last time, of every little familiar object in, and about, the boat. He was talking to us all the way, particularly to our coxswain, whom he thought a great deal of.

**his feelings in the boat/arrival alongside the *San Jacinto*/
parting with his Boat's Crew/the Boat returns/Thoughts**

He told us to be good boys, and when we got home, for each and every one of us to come and see him, which we promised to do. His emotion was too great to say much. He said he never felt so bad in his life as he did at the present moment on leaving our ship. On our coxswain's making a remark that he was sorry he was leaving, he turned around and looked at the ship; he gave two very deep sighs (which as long as my memory exists I never can forget) *and so am I Thompson, but I could not help it* (Nicholas speaking), while a tear was seen trickling down each cheek. He never looked better since the ship has been in commission. He always had a fatherly and venerable appearance, and he did not belie his looks, he was liked by everybody on board the ship, from the highest officer, to the smallest boys. They all felt bad at his leaving us.

On our way to the *San Jacinto* we met several boats, who tossed oars, and saluted him, caps in hand, which he returned. On arriving alongside of the *San Jacinto* I unshipped his pennant for the last time. He stood up in the stern sheets of the boat, looked at her and then at the crew, and said, "Good Bye, boys. Take care of Yourselves." What else he would have said remained in his throat. He looked behind, perceiving me standing in the bow. He took off his hat and waved it at me, which I returned with feelings of respect and gratitude. I never since leaving home felt so bad. I felt as if I was parting from one of my dearest friends. We then pulled away to our ship.

Opinions of the Captain/the Boat goes out of commission as Captain's Gig—Flag officer takes possession of her/Fleet Surgeon leaves us

It seemed as if there was a void somewhere. Although he used the boat but very little, we missed him. It was the most silent pull we ever had; hardly a word was spoken by either of us. For my part, on such occasions I like to commune with my own thoughts. It makes a person feel reconciled to the loss of a friend to think over his own mind, the many little incidents and traits in a person's character, that bind us to our friends, and he was a friend to his boat's crew, granting us privileges which no others in the ship had but ourselves. And in fact he was a good friend to the ship's company, but he very seldom exercised his authority. He was a very easy going man, and our No. 1 took the advantage of it and prejudiced his mind against us. Which made it very bad for us.

Our No. 1 has gone and they have got rid of the captain, now we will see what kind of a time we are going to have. On arriving on board the ship the boys besieged us with all sorts of questions about how he parted with us, which questions we evaded by off-hand answers. It is very strange how quick a person's good qualities, are found out, after he is gone. Just so in this case, as soon as the Old Man was gone, every body was saying what a good man he was, and how sorry they felt that he did not go home in the ship. Their opinions two days ago were altogether different; they said he was a mean old devil, he never looked after the ship, and that he gave No. 1 the whole sway, which in fact was partly true, but instead of giving him the sway, he took it on his own responsibility. More than twenty instances, while we were coming to an anchor, has the captain given orders, which the 1st lieutenant disobeyed. This has been done in presence of the whole ship's company; what he has done in private, nobody knows. This and several other instances combined caused the captain to leave this ship, and if I was to say, or write half of what I know I suppose they would put me down as a mutineer, so I will say no more at present.

We were very busy all the afternoon cleaning out the captain's apartments. Our new 1st luff, Mr. Rhind, called our coxswain and told him our boat has gone out of commission as the captain's gig, but, said he, the flag officer is going to use her altogether, and he will give you your orders. At 3 P.M. the flag officer sent for the coxswain, and told him that he wished him to continue on as before. He said that he was going to use the boat altogether for his aide de camp and steward. He also said that he knew that we had good times in the boat and that we still would have them, and he also told us not to be downhearted. We went into commission at half past 3 P.M. and went ashore with the aide de camp. At four o'clock the *San Jacinto* got underway and steamed out of the harbor. Our Fleet Surgeon Smith also goes home in her. During the day three men from the store ship came on board of us, having changed with three of our boys. At sundown the boat was hoisted in her old place.

June 15th   naval storekeeper again/dispatch Boat/Captain De Camp

This morning all decks were holystoned. At 9 A.M. we went ashore with the flag officer's aide de camp, and returned at 11 A.M. We returned on board with the celebrated Mr. Burney [Birnie], the U.S. Naval Storekeeper at this port, the one that made such a sensation among the fleet two months ago. His trial is a mystery. He is got a certain time to leave here for the U.S. Our boat is now called by the ship's company the Flag Officer's Dispatch Boat. The barge men do not like it, as it deprives them of a good many runs ashore. At half past 3 P.M. we went ashore with the flag officer's steward, and his body servant (vulgarly denominated "bone polisher" [*slang for "footman"*]). There is considerable talk on board, as to who is to be our next captain. It is whispered that the captain of the Store Ship *Relief* is coming. His name is De Camp, and they say he is a very good man. He is a very tall man, being six feet four inches. It was very chilly during the night.

Storekeeper Birnie had been tried for assaulting a local man who had come to do business at the naval storehouse (Birnie's version of the event was different) and breaking his arm. He was convicted and sentenced to ten days' imprisonment and being banished from the Province of Angola. Having been imprisoned since March 25, he boarded the Constellation *to go home.*[2]

June 16th   **inspection by the Flag officer**

Sunday and a very fine day. At half past 9 A.M. the drum beat to quarters for inspection (something that has not been done on a Sunday since the ship has been into commission). The flag officer inspected the ship's company. At 10 A.M. divine service was held on the gun deck. All hands are dressed in white frocks, hats, and blue trowsers. In the afternoon those of the ship's company that wanted to go visiting the other ships were allowed to go. Our ship was crowded by the visitors from other ships. At four o'clock we went ashore with the flag officer's steward. After washed clothes, and returned at sundown.

June 17th 1861.   **Boat Sailing/a Regatta**

Anniversary of the Battle of Bunker Hill. The day came in beautiful. All hands dressed in white frocks, hats, and blue trowsers. At 9 A.M. we went ashore with the flag officer's steward, and had a good run of two hours, had a good dinner of fresh provisions. At 3 P.M. we went ashore with the flag officer's aide de camp, and returned at half past four o'clock. In the evening we had a very pleasant boat sail, beating several boats belonging to the other ships. Was occupied the best part of this day in writing a letter home (M.L.M). At sundown the clothes lines were got on a stretch. The officers are getting up a regatta, to come off on the 4th of July. There are three prizes; what they are to be I have not learnt. It is to come off in this harbor. There is considerable talk about it throughout the squadron.

June 18th   **a General Court Martial**

All hands washed clothes. My boat keeping day. At half past nine A.M. we went ashore with the flag officer's aide de camp, and had a two hours run. Returned at noon. At nine o'clock this morning a gun was fired, and a jack hoisted on board the U.S. Sloop of war *Portsmouth,* as a signal for a general court martial. They are going to try the man that stabbed another, on board our ship. The man has recovered his usual good health. At 3 P.M. we went ashore with the flag officer's steward, and had a run until sundown. We were blacking the ship outside today. She now looks very neat.

June 19th   **landing a sailors Brigade/Military movements**

This day came in very fine. The general court martial commenced again at nine o'clock on board the *Portsmouth.* The coxswains of the different boats are picking out crews, practicing all day pulling. Our 4th cutter beat our 1st and 2nd cutters. During the day we painted the boom cover and hammock clothes. [*Hammock clothes or cloths were canvas covers put over the hammocks when they were put above the bulwarks in the hammock rails or nettings.*] In the afternoon at 5 P.M. all the boats in the ship were practicing pulling.

At nine o'clock this morning, the 1st and 2nd battalions of small arms men, and the launch's crew, landed on the beach with their arms and accoutrements. The launch's crew landed a howitzer. All the Marines also landed in charge of Lieutenant Tattnall. We all went through several military maneuvers, which as the officers say, reflected great credit to the name of the ship. We

Be kind to thy Mother

landed as a Sailor's Brigade. The movements were marked as being very orderly; in disembarking and embarking they showed very good discipline. At twelve o'clock we returned on board the ship.

June 20th   cock of the walk/will sweep the field/
                                 we'll whip the crowd/

Early this morning, our boats were out pulling and practicing for the race. It is their intention to pull every morning and evening until the race comes off. The *Portsmouth*'s 1st cutter pulled across our ship's bow at 9 A.M. with a live cock lashed on her stem, which signified that they thought themselves cock of the walk. At 10 A.M. the *Relief*'s launch pulled across our bow with a broom sticking up, which meant "we'll sweep the field." Our boys wanted to take our launch and pull her round both the other ships with a whip sticking up, which means, "we'll whip the crowd," but our officers would not allow it. There was nothing of any interest transpired today, but the excitement about the regatta is so great that we forget all about home. I have got a copy of the challenge that our officers sent to the other ships, and I give it here word for word. The clothes lines were got up at sundown.

[new page unpaginated in journal]

Challenge to the Squadron

The undersigned, on the part of the officers of the Flag Ship Constellation beg leave to assure the officers of the Squadron, that without the least desire to brag, it is their opinion that the "Gig" — "4th Cutter" — and "Launch" of the Constellation are the fastest Boats, of their respective rates, to be found under the American Flag, on the African Station, and moreover that the aforesaid "Gig" will sweep the field, on any occasion upon which the Officers of the Squadron shall decide to test the question? Should they Dare!

The undersigned respectfully, suggest that the 4th of July next be the day selected for a race between such boats as the vessels of the Squadron may desire to enter
(signed)
Officers of the Constellation

Conditions.

To prevent wind on the stomach, that's in the discussions sure to
proceed and follow the Regatta, projected for the 4th of July next.
Benton Mint Drops to the amount of $2.50 should be contributed by
each individual who may desire to participate in the proposed sport.

The amount so subscribed to be made up into 3 purses to be distributed as follows. One to the boat that sweeps the field—one to the
Launch, that may prove victorious over all other Launches, and one
to the Cutter that proves herself the fastest among the others entered.

For the above objects we the undersigned do subscribe the sums,
set opposite our respective names

(signed) By the Officers of the Constellation

the above challenge was written on the 17th of June, and sent on board the
U.S. Sloop of war *Portsmouth,* and the Gun boats *Mohican,* and *Mystic,* also
the store ship *Relief,* and they have accepted the Challenge, and they are now
practicing their respective boats. Each Coxswain is allowed the privilege of
picking their men, and do whatever they please to make their boat better
for pulling in the race. Our boats are very well practiced, particularly our
"Launch," which is a splendid pulling boat for her size; she pulls 16 oars.

*"Benton mint drop" was a slang term for gold or silver coin, from Sen. Thomas
Hart Benton's efforts in the 1830s on behalf of such money rather than paper.*

**a character/fatigue and privation/all through the Mexican War/
in the Navy/Taking French/almost left behind/coal bunkers/
shipped again/Barrier Forts/wounded/he gets a pension on conditions/
again in the navy/his pension stopped/U.S.S. *Niagara*/a queer dodge**

Another of our noticeable characters is a Thomas Gaynor. Born in Ireland in
1826, consequently he is 35 years old, but coming to the United States at a
very early age, he is now pretty thoroughly Americanized. Few men of his age
have been through the fatigue and privations that he has. In 1846 he commenced his public life by entering the Navy in the store ship *Senator,* but very
soon after left her. At the breaking out of the Mexican War, he joined the New
York Volunteer Regiment, and under General Scott he fought in almost every
battle, throughout the campaign. After returning to New York at the close of
the war, he again entered the Navy, and made a three year cruise in the U.S.
Sloop of war *Preble.* After spending his money he again shipped in the navy
and was drafted to the *Preble* again, and this time he made over three years
in her. After staying ashore a short time, we again find him in the U.S. Steam
Frigate *Powhatan,* bound for a cruise of two years on the China Station.

The *Powhatan* on her way out stopped at St. Helena, and our hero, belonging to the captain's gig, took it into his head one day to take French (which

means in a man of war, borrowing a few days liberty on your own responsibility). He and another left the boat. After staying ashore three days, and seeing their vessel making preparations to get underway, they came to the conclusion to go on board, which they did just as she tripped her anchor. This adventure cost Tom and his companion a five months' sojourn in the *Powhatan*'s coal bunkers heaving coal.

After running through all the money that he made in the *Powhatan* cruise, he again joined the navy, and was drafted to the U.S. Sloop of war *Portsmouth* on her last cruise on the China Station, and was at the taking of the Barrier Forts, where he received a wound from a musket ball, for which on arriving home he received a pension from government. The conditions he got the pension, was if he entered the navy again it was to be discontinued. He then went to work in the Navy Yard at Brooklyn, but here he remained but a short time. His love of adventure again caused him to join the Navy, but he tried to keep this to himself so as to save his pension, and Jew our venerated Uncle Samuel out of some of his money, but he was not smart enough. In a drunken spree he let the cat out of the bag, or in other words he told on himself, and his pension was stopped.

He was then drafted to the U.S. Steam Frigate *Niagara,* and was in her at the laying of the Famous Telegraph Cable. In this ship our hero got so severely punished that he suffers from the effects of it until this day. While the *Niagara* was lying at Plymouth, England, he and another used to go ashore every night, and return early in the morning, unawares to the officers. This dodge they kept up for two weeks. They used to get into the fire room, and by crowding along the main shaft to the propeller, and from there onto the wharf. They had the watchmen bribed.

severe punishment/paid off/shipped again/a drunken spree/
Delirium Tremors/his life despaired of/he recovers/
mind your own business

They were caught one morning; the watchman being changed during the night, he nabbed them both and brought them on board their ship. For this sport they were triced up to the beams by the wrists for over a week, and so strictly did the master at arms do his duty that our hero feels the effects of it now. After coming home from the *Niagara* he again joined the navy in New York.

When this ship went into commission, he was drafted to her from the receiving ship *North Carolina* and was made ship's corporal, which duty he performed to the entire satisfaction of both officers and crew, when on liberty at St. Helena, in Jan 1861 our Tom unfortunately got on a drunken spree, and stayed over his liberty two days. The last day he got the delirium tremens. I was with him most all day, but I did not notice anything strange about him, but he then was in the worst stages of the most terrible disease; the liquor is what sustained him. He was brought aboard the ship, and immediately put under the doctor's charge, who despaired of his life for over a week. It was necessary to bind him to his cot, to keep him from killing himself. It was heartrending to see what poor Tom suffered from the phantoms he created in his own mind.

After three weeks' severe illness he recovered so as to walk about and is now in his usual good health, but his billet of ship's corporal is no more. He has now the rate of an Ordinary Seaman, and is stationed in the Afterguard. But he is in the same mess as myself. He has a brother in the Gun boat *Mohican*. Tom and I are on very intimate terms, and if he was to know that I was giving a description of him, he would be very apt to give me a grand talking to (the subject being, mind your own business). In height he is about five feet four inches, of a dark complexion, which by hard usage is inclining to an iron grey. His front teeth are all gone, which defect he consoles himself with the idea of getting a false set put in when he gets home. He wears a goatee, and an enormous moustache, which on bean soup days it looks like a white wash brush.

a great blower/ridiculing/gets floored/Boston versus New York/ a 6 cent dinner/a funny statement/Remarks

He is a great politician, but his arguments are on the western stump orator's style. He is a great blower on the New York system, he runs away with an idea that nothing can be done unless it is done there, by a New Yorker. His particular aversion being against Boston, and everything that is Bostonian. Knowing that there are two or three Boston boys in the mess, he takes advantage of every opportunity of poking fun at them about their peculiarities, but in every instance he is floored by the ever ready wit, and cutting remarks of the aforesaid Bostonians. This statement calls forth another remark from me which I think is in keeping with the above article. The ship's company are mostly composed of Boston and New Yorkers who are always at each other, talking about the merits of their respective cities. The only way they get ahead of the Boston Boys, lies in the size of their city, which difference is soon made up by the Bostonians in quality. Tom in particular calls us the Baked Bean fraternity, which he says is the most favorite dish with us. We retaliate with a remark, which in one of his unguarded moments he let fall, which was to the effect that in New York, they could get a dinner in any restaurant for the sum of six cents, which remark we take advantage of by calling him the six cent dinner man. He knows he was wrong, but he will not back out of the assertion. To make the matter more ridiculous they had to eat the above meal with a fork, knives he says being out of fashion with New York Society. This to the reader might seem a very silly subject to write upon, but I can assure you, it is a very important matter with us.

Tom has been married, but his wife died some years ago. But it is his intention of marrying again, the 1st favorable opportunity. He is of a very cheerful disposition, and very good hearted. He has an aged mother and a sister in New York City who depend on him and his brother for support. If he should by chance ever read this article I hope he won't be offended at the liberty I am taking in devoting a few pages in describing him. In closing I will say there is not man, or boy, on board but wishes him well.

W.A.L.

June 21st   **Sentence of a general court martial/an easy sentence**

This morning, all hands washed clothes. At 9 A.M. had division inspection. We have inspection now twice a day since Mr. Rhind has been 1st lieutenant. [*Inspections twice a day would be considered normal, but that had apparently not been done.*] At 10 A.M. the boatswain called all hands to muster, to hear the sentence of a naval general court martial, which finished on board the *Portsmouth* yesterday. The prisoner was brought on the quarterdeck by the master at arms. His name is Thomas Collins, this is the man that stabbed another on board this ship (an account of which see page 280). His charges were fighting and using provoking language; 2nd^ly fighting and stabbing. On the 1st two counts he was found guilty, and on the 2nd counts not guilty. His sentence was thirty days in solitary confinement, and the loss of three months' pay, the court having recommended him to mercy. The flag officer remitted that part of the sentence which alluded to the loss of pay. This sentence was the easiest one that has been in this ship, considering the offence—he was within a hair's breadth of killing the man—but they took it in the light of self defense. At 12 o clock the Gun boat *Mystic* went to sea, for a short cruise. At 4 P.M. the gig went ashore with the flag officer's steward, and returned at sundown.

June 22nd   **our Launch beats the *Portsmouth*'s/ wishes to destroy himself**

All decks were holystoned. Our launch has been fitted with a new sail, and had a race with the *Portsmouth*'s launch, and beat her in every point. There is considerable rivalry between both ships, and I believe if both ships were to give liberty together there would be a civil war. At 3 P.M. the gig went ashore with the flag officer's steward and returned at sundown. A Portuguese barque came to an anchor at 7 P.M. One of the men that we took in the Slave Brig *Triton* has been confined for making a remark last [night], which was to the effect that he would destroy himself if he was not allowed to go home. He won't ship with us, and the authorities won't allow us to let him land here. Our officers are waiting for a chance to send him home in some ship. I believe the man is insane. He is a down east yankee, and is very tall, being about six feet four inches. He weighs about 230 pounds.

June 23d   **Divine Service**

Sunday, a very Cloudy morning. At seven bells [7:30] went to breakfast. All hands dressed in white frocks, hats, and blue trousers. By the way, the officers are very injudicious about dress [in] this chilly weather; everybody is complaining about having cold, and I should [think] they had, for everybody is barking all day, and night. At half past nine the drum beat to quarters for inspection, and [we] were reviewed by the flag officer, who is acting the double duty of captain and commodore. At 10 A.M. had divine service. My boatkeeping day. During the afternoon the men went visiting. At sundown, the clothes lines were got on a stretch. All hands were kept awake by a young fellow that is sick with the coast fever; he is out of his head. His lungs must be in good condition, for he hollored like a bull.

The typical temperature in Loanda in this season would be in the mid to high sixties Fahrenheit.

June 24th   **another Death on board by Coast Fever/**
                                      disrating a Coxswain

All hands washed clothes. At 8 A.M. the gig went ashore with the flag officer's aide de camp and returned at 9 A.M. Just as we got alongside the young man that was sick with the coast fever expired. This makes the fifth death on board our ship. He was a wardroom boy, and the officers thought a great deal about him. His name was James George. He was a native of the island of St. Helena, where his parents are now living. He was about twenty-four years of age. He is going to be buried this afternoon ashore; the carpenters are making him a coffin.[3] The gig made two more trips ashore during the forenoon. Sail was loosed at 9 A.M. At 2 P.M. we again went ashore and returned at 3 P.M., when all sail was furled. We then went ashore with the flag officer's steward and returned at sundown. While we were ashore the 2nd and 4th cutter went ashore and buried the man that died. The coxswain of the 4th cutter was disrated this afternoon for disobeying orders.

The *Portsmouth* has been making preparations all day for sea. At sundown, her orders being countermanded, she got out all boats and sent down her royal yards. We were also making preparations for sea this morning to go to sea tomorrow, but just as we had the royals bent the order was countermanded.

June 25th 1861. arrival of an English Coal ship

This day came in fine. At 9 A.M. a sail was signalized by the telegraph on the fort. At 2 P.M. we took the gig and went out to see what she was; at half past 3 P.M. we came alongside of her. She proved to be an English coal ship, the *Thornhill*, 95 days out from Cardiff, England. At 4 P.M. we returned. A Portuguese revenue cutter came to an anchor. During the day the divisions exercised at big guns, small arms, and single sticks. At 6 P.M. the American barque *Wm H. Shaler* sailed on a trading cruise along the coast. At 7 P.M. the *Thornhill*, an English coal barque, came to an anchor. There is a very strong sea breeze in this harbor every afternoon, commencing about 1 P.M. and lasts till about 7 P.M.

Though he did not mention it in his journal, Leonard had learned earlier of the death of Miss Isabella Blood, "Bella," who urged him when parting to "be of good heart." Today he wrote a long letter in her memory, addressed to their mutual friend Miss Mary L. Moloney of Charlestown. At the closing he remarked that "the above lines were written at a time, when death had taken one of our ship's company, whose dying hours are much too sad to contemplate." Mary became Mrs. William Leonard on September 18, 1862.[4]

June 26th exercising

Cloudy, and chilly. The gig did considerable running this morning before breakfast. At half past 9 A.M. had inspection, after which the 3d division exercised big guns. A gang has been to work all day breaking out storm sails. At 3 P.M. the gig went ashore and returned at 4 P.M. The launch's fighting boat's crew exercised the boat and howitzer; at sundown the regatta boats' crews exercised the boats they are to pull in on the 4th of July.

July [June] 27th General court martial

This day came in very fine. At 10 A.M. a gun was fired, and a jack hoisted on board the *Portsmouth*. They are general court martialing a corporal of marines, for conspiracy. At 2 P.M. the gig went ashore and returned at 3 P.M. The boats were exercising all the afternoon with their regatta crews. At sundown the clothes lines were got up, so as to wash clothes tomorrow morning.

July [June] 28th Pulling boats

All hands washed clothes; my boatkeeping day. The regatta boats have been pulling all day and they have been timed. The gig had made the best time yet, being nine seconds ahead. I don't know what the distance was, but I should judge it was a mile and a quarter. The washed clothes were not piped down today on account of their being damp. The general court martial is still going on, on board the U.S. Sloop of war *Portsmouth*.

June 29th   [Flag Drawing in Margin] *Hankow*/a New York Steamer/
                                Bad News from Home/excitement/
                          expecting our orders in the next mail/Patriotic/

❊ ❊

Arrival of a Steamboat from New York, Called the *Hankow* with very important News

❊ ❊

This morning a steamboat was signalized coming in. As she had an American flag flying, we did not know what to make of her; some had it she had
been sent out by the U.S. with important dispatches for the flag officer. She
very soon came up the harbor, and [as] she passed us, she dipped her ensign,
which salute was returned. She is painted white, and is a side wheel boat; she
is just like one of the sound boats. The gig was manned and the flag officer's
aide de camp was sent on board of her to get the news. On seeing us coming
she stopped and we boarded her. She is a bran[d] new steamer, built in New
York, expressly for the China Station. She is a river boat, and is intended to
run between Hong Kong and Shanghai. She is six weeks out from New York.
She stopped seven days at Porto Grande for coal. She put in here for coal. She
brings news up to the 13th of May. We got the news of the destruction of the
shipping at Norfolk, and all the political news. We got several papers. At 8
A.M. we returned on board our own ship and told the news, which created the
greatest excitement I ever heard in so small a space. It seemed as if the ship's
company were going mad. On reading the papers, the excitement was worse
than ever—nothing talked of now, but the North, and the South, War to the
death, Abolitionism, and Secession. We have forgot all about the regatta, we
see by the papers that our squadron are supposed to be on the way home, but
we have got no orders as yet, although we expect them in the next mail, which
is due here the 5th of July. All hands are anxious to get home, so as to join the
Naval Brigade. I believe there is not a man on board this ship, but what would
tender his services to the Federal government, immediately after we got home;
their sentiments are very patriotic. The news has given us an excitement which
promises to last some time.

                        a Boat Race between the *Portsmouth*,
                          and *Mohican*/read.read.read/
                        a challenge not accepted/Big Talk

The gig has been kept going all this day by the flag officer. We were ashore four
times during the day. At 9 A.M. clothes bags were piped up, to air clothing. At
noon, while we were at dinner, we got a new excitement in the shape of a boat
race. The boats were the *Portsmouth*'s 1st cutter, and the *Mohican*'s 1st cutter,
and our ship's company take a very lively interest in the race. When we first

came out here the *Portsmouth*'s crew had been out here some time, and had their boat fixed up, and a good crew picked out and practiced for her. When we came in here, they challenged our 1st cutter to pull them a race for eighty dollars, our boys accepted it, and the next day was set upon as the time. They hoisted their boat and black leaded her bottom, while our boat was allowed to lay at the boom and the next morning she was sent to market. Besides she had no regular crew; when she came back, anybody that wanted to jumped into her, and they pulled the race, and lost it. But beating our boat did not satisfy the *Portsmouths*. When their cutter passed under our bow, somebody in her sung out, "That is the way we intend to beat your ship, bye, and bye." In two weeks' time we both got underway together and went to sea. Our ship outsailed them on every point (see page 68–69). They then allowed their ship was not in trim, but we have beaten them several times since, beating their ship in about everything they did.

When the present regatta was proposed for the 4th of July, these feelings were again brought up by them. They went on board the *Mohican,* and challenged their 1st cutter to pull them a race, for 300 dollars, but the *Mohicans* could not get the money and at that time they refused the challenge. The *Portsmouths* then went on board the *Mohican,* and told them how they beat us, and, said they, if they saw they were going to beat us, they were going to pitch into them and lick them (which would have been the toughest job they ever undertook to do). They also tried to get the *Mohican*'s boys against us, but that they couldn't do. We had been on liberty with the *Mohicans,* and made ourselves good friends. When they saw that this ruse was no good they turned on both of us, and tried to make all the ridicule they could. How far they succeeded in this, this Journal will show.

Ridicule/another Challenger/going to the Race/ *Mohican*'s Boats beat them a ¼ of a mile/ Red shirts and White Caps/our boys cheer the *Mohican*/Hurrah

They took their 1st cutter every morning and pulled under both ships' bows, with a live cock on their bow, making themselves cock of the walk. This lasted until the day before yesterday, when the *Mohicans* sent them a challenge of sixty dollars to pull them, which they accepted, but they wanted it to be $100, which was agreed to by the *Mohicans,* and today at 4 P.M. was the time selected. The distance was three miles, from Point Agustus [Lagostas] to a buoy astern of our ship, one of our lieutenants being the stake holder. At 3 P.M. both boats started down to the bluff, the *Mohican*'s boat sailing and the *Portsmouth*'s pulling. Both ships' launches also went down. Considerable money has been bet among the officers and men. The *Portsmouth*'s boat was the favorite, at two to one, the distance being so great we could not see them start. The *Portsmouths* dressed in red shirts and white caps, and the *Mohicans* in their blue clothes. At half past four the boats got near enough to tell them, the *Mohican*'s boat ahead and gaining very fast, five to one on the *Mohican* boat and no takers. They came in half a mile ahead of the *Portsmouth*'s boat and tossed oars, thus winning the race. They then cheered our ship. We jumped into the rigging and gave them three hearty cheers, they then put up a coach whip and pulled around the *Portsmouth*'s boat, and from there to the store ship, where they were cheered. This so tickled our boys, that they are almost jumping out of their shoes.

The *Portsmouths* were so sure of winning that they had red shirts and white caps made on purpose. They also had a live cock in the boat ready to put on their bow if they beat. They were so mortified that they did not come near our ship, but slunk away to their own as fast as they could. The ill feeling will be doubly increased between our ship and theirs now. The three cheers we gave didn't allay the feelings very much.

The general court martial ended on board the *Portsmouth*, at 3 P.M. in the evening. The excitement was on the increase, the principal theme being the boat race.

my hammock comes down by the run/stunned

I was dreaming all night about Secession, North and South, Abolitionism, Niggers, boat racing, fighting, and a host of others, in the midst of which my hammock lanyard parted, which brought me down on my head with such force, that I was stunned for over ten minutes. After getting to rights again, I turned in and slept sound until we were piped up by the boatswain.

June 30th					**all hands to muster/reading the Sentence of
							a General court martial/Rather a hard Sentence/
							visiting/Fuddled/Naval Brigade**

Sunday, very cloudy. All hands dressed in white frocks, hats, and blue trousers. At half past 9 A.M. the drum beat to quarters, and the flag officer inspected the ship's company. At 10 A.M. had divine service. At 11 A.M. the flag officer paid a visit to the steamer *Hankow*, and returned at half past eleven. A quarter before twelve o'clock all hands were called to muster to hear the sentence of a general court martial which finished on board the *Portsmouth* yesterday. The prisoner was a corporal of marines on board the *Portsmouth*, and his crime was sedition against the peace and honor of his sergeant. He was found guilty of the charges and specifications, and was sentenced as follows: 1st to be reduced to the ranks, two months' solitary confinement, and to forfeit half the pay and sustenance now due him; also to be dishonorably discharged from the U.S. Navy. His name is Shuttleworth. He has about 350 dollars due him.

During the afternoon the ship's company went visiting. Some of the Portsmouths were on board of us, and if they didn't get a drubbing from our fellows. It was a caution, remarks such as, "What are you going to [do] with the red shirts?" "Where's the rooster?" &c, &c. The Mohicans were pretty well represented here today, they are very much pleased at our cheering them last night. Some of our boys were on board the storeship, and come back fuddled. Accounts were signed with the purser during the day. At sundown the hammocks were piped down, and the boats hoisted and the regular evening's amusements commenced, talking politics. All hands are sure of getting our orders in the next mail. They are talking about the Naval Brigade.

Col. William A. Bartlett was organizing a naval brigade in New York, intended originally as a coastal patrol unit. It was soon reorganized as the Ninety-Ninth Infantry Battalion.

July 1861

July 1st

sending down top Gallant yards and Masts/
Tarring down/overhauling Rigging/
Massachusetts Boys/some pumkins [*sic*]

As soon as the hands were turned to, the topmen were sent aloft, to send down the topgallant yards, and masts, also all the rigging, which was going to give the rigging a thorough overhauling fore and aft, rattle and tar down. We (the gig's crew) are excused from all work after breakfast. At half past 8 A.M. we went ashore with the flag officer's steward, and returned at noon. All hands to work tarring, rattling, and setting up rigging. At 3 P.M. a Portuguese mail steamer called the *Don Pedro* arrived here from Fish Bay. At 4 P.M. all the rigging work was finished, and the topgallant masts are ready for going aloft; they will not be sent until tomorrow. The decks are in an awful mess from tar and slush; they are to be scraped tomorrow morning.

The officers are certain of our orders in the next mail. The secession business is still in everybody's mind. We understand from the papers that the southerners are bitter against the Massachusetts boys, and will whip them if they can. I wish they would come across some of our ship's company, and see if they could whip them. I think they would have to work harder than they did since they were born. We can whip as many southerners, as would take to garrison Fort Sumpter, and we only muster 300 fighting men.

Leonard had apparently been reading about the Baltimore Riot. Maryland was a slave state with strong Southern sympathies. On April 19 the Sixth Massachusetts Regiment moved through Baltimore on its way to Washington. To switch trains the troops had to march or ride in horse-drawn cars through town from one station to the other. In the process they were confronted by an angry mob of Southern sympathizers throwing rocks and bricks. Shots were fired, and a number of troops and citizens died before the soldiers left on their train to Washington, where they were the first to arrive of the troops called up by President Lincoln. (When Lincoln had had to pass through Baltimore en route to his inauguration, he had done it as covertly as possible.)

July 2nd **Scrubbing the boat/serving out money**

This morning the starboard watch scraped the spar deck. At 8 A.M. a Portuguese brig came to an anchor. At 9 A.M. the gig's crews went on the beach to scrub their boat and returned at noon. All hands to work about the rigging. The flag officer has given the boat up to the crew, in order to practice for the regatta. The purser served out five dollars apiece to those that wanted. The topgallant masts were scraped, and the heels of them painted white. Considerable betting is going on in the ship, about getting our orders in the next mail. The regatta excitement swallows up every other topic now. We expect the mail next Saturday.

July 3d 1861. **all hands up/top Gallant Masts/another challenge to the**
***Portsmouth*/Catamaran Race/getting ready to decorate/**
Waiting for an answer

This morning, the decks were holystoned, and all hands washed clothes, piped to breakfast at 8 A.M. All the forenoon was spent in setting up the topgallant and royal backstays, also the fore and aft stays. By noon everything was a-taunt-oh. At 1 p.m. the U.S. Gun boat *Mystic* arrived here. Our regatta boats were practicing all the afternoon. Our boys have raised a purse of 270 dollars, and sent it on board the *Portsmouth*. We bet that our launch will beat theirs, and if they want to we will make the bet 500 dollars on our launch.

Our carpenter has fixed up our catamaran, and bets she will beat the *Portsmouth*'s. They are to pull with two shovels and is to be steered by an oar; ours is to be steered by the captain of the fore hold, Peter Daly (a very comical fellow). The quarter masters are rigging signal halliards from the flying jib boom, over the mast heads, to the spanker boom, so as to decorate the ship tomorrow in honor of the day. Our boats were practicing all the evening. Our gig and the *Mohican*'s launch had a race; our gig came up victorious. Our boys are very anxiously waiting to see what action the *Portsmouth*'s crew are going to make to our challenge; we are very anxious that they should accept it. Our mail is expected tomorrow; it is coming in the Steam Frigate *San Jacinto*.

July 4th **Sunrise/dressing ship**

✻ ✻

4th of July 1861
Grand Gala day

At sunrise this morning the topgallant yards were crossed and the ship dressed from the flying jib boom over the mast heads to the end of the spanker boom. At each mast head an enormous American flag was flying, also one at the spanker gaff. The Sloop of war *Portsmouth*, gun boats *Mohican* and *Mystic*, the Store Ship *Relief*, the *Hankow*, and two English coal ships also dressed ship at the same time with flags

* *Union* *

* *

[page heavily adorned and bordered with stars]

Hurrah for the 4th/preparation for the Regatta/ The Regatta/*Portsmouth* ahead/our boats takes [*sic*] to Prizes/ excitement/Great saluting/a good Dinner

and streamers of all nations. The harbor presents quite a holiday appearance. The messes have made arrangements to have a dinner cooked ashore, in honor of the day. The weather is delightful. All hands dressed in white pants, hats, and blue frocks. After breakfast the regatta boats commenced making preparations for the race. Each boat has got their own uniforms. They have anchored buoys, in a parallel line with our ship, each boat having a separate buoy with a flag flying on it. Our buoy has a blue pennant. At 10 A.M. the boats started down to the point. There are eight boats entered: our ship enters the launch, 4th cutter and gig; the *Portsmouth* entered her launch and 1st cutter; the *Mystic* entered her 2nd cutter and the *Mohican* entered her launch and 1st cutter. At 11 o'clock the boats started, but they were too far off for us to tell which was which. At half past eleven we could tell them—they were now within a quarter of a mile of the buoys, the *Mohican*'s 1st cutter being the favorite from the beginning. The excitement on board of us was immense, [much] betting going on. Our launch looked to be the 1st boat. At twenty minutes of 11 A.M. the race was decided, the *Portsmouth*'s 1st cutter coming in first, our launch next, being only two seconds behind, our 4th cutter next, and the gig next, the *Mohican*'s boats being next; the 1st prize (forty dollars) being given the 1st Cutter of the *Portsmouth*, the 2nd (thirty-five dollars) to our launch, the 3d (thirty dollars) to our 4th cutter. The boats as they came in were cheered by their own ships.

The *Mohican*'s boats did not pull: they did not have any encouragement from their officers, and they determined not to pull. There is great disputes among all hands about the race. The excitement is intense. Our catamaran is going to pull at 1 P.M. At twelve o'clock, we fired a National Salute of twenty-one guns. The *Portsmouth, Mohican,* and a Portuguese man of war brig also fired a salute of twenty-one guns each in honor of the Day. At a quarter past twelve piped to dinner. Our mess had a roast pig and fixings from ashore, as had the other messes. We made a splendid dinner of it.

over

* *

4th of July at St. Paul de Loando

[*page heavily adorned and bordered with stars and flags*]

**catamaran/Sport/Fun/Cheering/our catamaran gets beat/
Laughing/invitation to dinner/they did not try to pull/
Sailing/our launch Beats**

At half past twelve our catamaran was manned by two Kroomen and the captain of the fore hold as coxswain; he had an oar and the Kroomen had shovels. The Kroomen wore strait jackets and the coxswain wore a suit of clothes that Jerry Clip wore at our theatrical performance. They had a live cock lashed to a pole on the forward part of their catamaran. (A catamaran is 4 casks lashed together and is used to scrub the copper with; it as broad as it is long.) The coxswain had a large sheet of paper about three feet square with a challenge to the Store Ship *Relief*. On his arrival they gave him three cheers and accepted his challenge. They rigged their launch, put one oar in her, and two kroomen with two large swabs to pull her. They started from the *Relief* and pulled round the *Portsmouth* to our ship. In consequence of starting with the wind, the launch gained on our catamaran and beat her, about thirty yards. I never in my life laughed so much, all hands were perfectly crazy with laughter. They were cheered again and again by every ship in the squadron; it was the most comical sight I ever witnessed. The officers, particularly the flag, took great interest in it. Both coxswains came on our quarter deck, and were handed three dollars apiece. The coxswain of our catamaran claimed the race, in consequence of the other boat fouling him. My throat is hoarse from laughing at the race. There were about four officers on our quarter deck witnessing the sport.

Several of our men have been invited on board the *Relief*; her crew have got up a grand dinner. The ship's company were allowed to visit the other ships during the afternoon. Several of the *Mohican*'s crew that pulled today have been put in double irons, for not trying to pull. There is no doubt but what her boats would have won the race if they tried to, but they had no encouragement and they said they would not pull. They sent word to us last night not to bet on them because they did not intend to pull. Several hundred dollars was bet on her by her own officers, but they made a draw of it. Our launch and the *Portsmouth*'s have been sailing all the afternoon. Our launch beats her on every point.

*328.

Incidents and Items in the Cruise of the U.S.S. Constellation.

St. Paul de Loando / July 3d 1861.

all hands } This morning, the decks were holystoned, and washed clothes, piped to breakfast at 8 A.M. at sig top Gallant } 9 A.M. all hands were called to send up top Gallant Masts. Masts. } the forenoon was spent in setting up the topgallant and Royal Backstays, also the fore and aft stays. by Noon everything was A Taunts, at 1 P.M. the U.S. Gun boat Mystic arrived here.

another } our Regatta boats were practicing all the afternoon. our boys challenge to } have raised a purse of 250 dollars, and sent it on board the Portsmouth } the Portsmouth, we bet that our Launch will beat theirs, and if they want to we will make the bet 500 dollars on our Launch our Carpenter has fixed up our Catamaran, and bets she Catamaran } will beat the Portsmouth's they are to pull with two Shovels Race } and is to be steered by an oar. ours is to be steered by the captain of the fore Hold, Peter Daly (a very comical

getting ready } fellow) the Quarter Master, are rigging Signal Halliards to decorate } from the Flying Jib boom, over the Mast heads, to the Spanker Boom, so as to decorate the ship tomorrow in honor of the day.

Waiting } our boats were practicing all the evening, our Gig and the Mohican for an } Launch had a race, our Gig came off Victorious. our boys are Answer. } very anxiously waiting to see what action the Portsmouth's crew are going to make to our Challenge we are very anxious that they should accept it. our Mail is expected to Morrow it is coming in the Steam Frigate San Jacinto.

July 4th } 4th of July 1861.
Grand Gala day.

Sunrise } At Sunrise this morning the Top Gallant yards were crossed and the ship dressed from the Flying Jib boom over the Mast heads to the end of the Spanker boom, at each mast head an enormous dressing } American flag was flying also one at the spanker Gaff. the ship } Sloop of war Portsmouth, Gun boats Mohican and Mystic the Store Ship Relief, the Hankow, and two English Coal ships also dressed ship at the same time with Flags Union.

Leonard's journal for the Fourth of July 1861.

While "Flag Ship of the African Squadron." — by W.A.L.

Hurrah for the 4th and streamers of all nations, the harbor presents quite a holiday appearance, the messes have made arrangements to have a dinner cooked ashore, in honor of the day, the weather is delightful all hands dressed in White pants, Hats, and Blue Frocks

preparations for the Reggatta after breakfast the Reggatta boats commenced making preperations for the race, each boat has got their own uniforms they have anchored buoys, in a parralel line with our ship each boat having a separate buoy with a flag flying on it our barge flies a blue pennant, at 10 A.M. the boats started down to the point, there are 8 boats entered, our ship enters the Launch 4th Cutter and Gig, the Portsmouth entered her

The Reggatta Launch and 1st Cutter, the Mohican entered her Launch and 1st Cutter, the Majestic entered her 2nd Cutter, at 11 Oclock the boats started, but they were too far off for us to tell which was which at ½ past 11 we could tell them they were now within ¼ of a mile of the buoys the Mohicans 1st Cutter being the favorite from the begining, the excitement on board of us, was immense, betting going on our Launch looked to be the 1st boat at

Portsmouth ahead 20 minutes off 11 Oclk. the race was decided, the Portsmouth 1st Cutter coming in first, our Launch next being only 2 seconds behind, our 4th Cutter next, and the Gig next, the Mohicans boats

our boats takes two Prizes. being next the 1st prize 40 dollars being given the 1st Cutter of the Portsmouth, the 2nd 35 dollars to our Launch, the 3rd 30 dollars to our 4th Cutter, the boats as they came in were cheered by their own ships, the Mohicans boats did not pull they did not have any encouragement from their officers, and they determined not to

excitement pull, there is great disputes among all hands about the race, the excitement is intense, our Catamaran is going to pull at 1 P.M.

great saluting at 12 oclock, we fired a National Salute of 21 Guns, the Portsmouth Mohican, and a Portuguese Man of war Brig also

a good Dinner fired a salute of 21 guns each in honor of the Day, at ½ past 12 piped to dinner, our Mess, had a roast pig and fixings from ashore, as had the other messes, we made a splendid dinner of it

over

At half past 4 P.M. all hands were called to

* *

July 4th 1776

* *

4th of July 1861.   **splicing the Main Brace/National Songs**

Splice the Main Brace, after which the boatswain piped to supper. At sundown, the signals and colors were lowered. Our officers are having a grand 4th of July dinner, and by the way some of them are acting, I believe something besides patriotic feelings are in them. At five bells (half past 6 P.M.) hammocks were piped down. All hands are now in the gun deck singing national songs. There is but very little secession feeling among us. Altogether the day has been a very pleasant one to everybody. Thus ended our Independence Day.

* *

July 5th   **The *Hankow* sails/Summary Court Martial**

All hands washed clothes. We are now looking anxiously for the mail. Our boat again is under the flag officer's orders. At half past 10 A.M. we went ashore with the flag officer's body servant and returned at noon. At 3 P.M. we went ashore, and returned with two ladies, a girl, and a gentleman (Portuguese); they asked permission of our flag officer to visit our ship. At 5 P.M. we brought them ashore again, and on the way we had a race with one of the *Portsmouth*'s cutters and beat her. The American steamer *Hankow* sailed for China at half past 5 P.M. We had a very social time with the flag officer's steward ashore. We returned on board at 7 P.M.

There was a summary court martial on board of us today. It finished at half past 3 P.M. He was a marine. His charges were talking to a blue jacket while on post. The orderly sergeant reported him to the Marine lieutenant and he preferred charges against him (our Marine lieutenant is a son of Commodore Tattnall.)

Commodore Josiah Tattnall, a distinguished U.S. naval officer, had famously explained his assistance to British forces under fire at the Taku Forts in China by saying, "Blood is thicker than water." Upon his home state of Georgia leaving the Union, he went to Washington to tender his resignation personally to President Buchanan on February 21, 1861. He became a Confederate admiral.

Meantime this month two squadron officers, Lt. H. K. Stevens of the Portsmouth *(from Florida) and Master H. H. Dalton of the* Saratoga *(from Mississippi) resigned.*[1]

July 6th   *San Jacinto* arrives with the Mail/No Orders/
                                Disappointment/Discouraged/The Brig *Falmouth*
                                taken by the *Sumpter*/a Comet

This morning the decks were holystoned. At half past 6 A.M. a steamer was
signalized coming in; she proved to be the Portuguese mail steamer. She came
to an anchor at 11 A.M. At half past 11 A.M. we went ashore in the gig and
returned at noon. The U.S. Steam Frigate *San Jacinto* is coming in. She has
got the mail. At half past twelve she came to an anchor ahead of us. Her
captain came on board with the mail. There was but very few letters for the
ship's company. She brings us no news, but what we have had by the steamer
Hankow. All hands are expecting our orders in this mail; every vessel in the
squadron expects to go home, this mail. Considerable money had been bet on
getting the orders. The U.S. Sloop of war *Saratoga* has taken another prize, a
Spanish brig. She had no slaves. At 3 P.M. the U.S. Gun boat *Sumpter* came to
an anchor.

The excitement is all over, we have got no orders, everybody feels bad
about it. No vessel is going home, it is a sad disappointment to everybody.
Walking along the decks, you meet everybody with faces a yard long. At half
past 3 P.M. the gig went ashore and returned at 5 P.M. The English Steam Sloop
of war *Electro* came in here this afternoon.

We are going to sea the 1st part of next week. We begin to feel discouraged. It is enough to make one feel so, two years on this miserable station. It
is rumored around the ship that we are going to the island of St. Helena again
for liberty. The coxswain of our boat got bad news from home, it being the
death of his mother. The Gun boat *Sumpter* has taken the brig *Falmouth*. She
had no niggers in; she run right in the way of the *Sumpter* and they had to
take [her]. There is a very beautiful sight here every evening in the shape of a
Comet. It made its appearance two weeks ago, and gets brighter every night.
It is a very brilliant one.

The ship whose name Leonard heard as "Electro" is actually the HMS Alecto,
an eight-hundred-ton, four-gun wooden sidewheel sloop.

The Sumpter *captured the* Falmouth *on June 14, off Red Point, about 150
miles south of Loando.*[2] *Readers will remember that the* Falmouth's *mate, confronted by* Constellation's *officer at Punta da Lenha, had said, "I defy you."*

*The Great Comet of 1861 was not only very dramatic in appearance, but
its track was such that for a while the Earth was actually within the comet's
tail. Captain Dornin aboard the* San Jacinto *describes it as "a long comet in
the NW at a low altitude, tail to the SdEd."*[3]

July 7th   all hands to muster/reading the articles of war/
                                Sentence of a Court Martial/a run ashore

Sunday, at three bells this morning we took the gig on the beach, and scrubbed her inside and out. We returned at seven bells. All hands are dressed in white frocks, hats, and blue trousers. At nine o'clock we went ashore with the flag officer's steward, to get stores for the flag officer. It is a beautiful day, and as we rambled over the city, we were very much amused by the costumes of the natives, as they were in holiday attire. We returned at noon. At half past 9 A.M. the ship's company were inspected by the flag officer, after which all hands were called to muster. The Articles of War were read by the 1st lieutenant (A. C. Rhind). It being his 1st time, we got them read thoroughly. He laid great emphasis on the word "Rebel" in particular; whether he was thinking of the secession troubles or not I could not say (he is a northern man, and is for the Union). All hands then passed round the capstan, according to their rates.

Lieutenant Rhind's fiancée, Fannie Hume, spent July 4 reading old letters and wishing, "Oh! If I could have a glimmering of how things will be! 'Tis all in the hands of a wiser than I."[4]

At half past ten A.M. all hands were again called to muster to hear the sentence of a court martial. His charges were disobedience of orders, and talking to a blue jacket on post (the prisoner is a marine and this is his 3d court martial in this ship). His sentence was the loss of one month's pay, and two weeks extra police duty.

At half past ten A.M. divine service was held on the gun deck. During the afternoon the ship was full of visitors from the other ships in the squadron. Some of our men also went visiting. At 4 P.M. the gig went ashore and returned at sundown. There are three vessels signalized from the fort as coming in. One of them is supposed to be the U.S. Sloop of War *Saratoga*. At eight P.M. a Portuguese brig came to an anchor astern of us. The topgallant yards were sent down while we were ashore * [*large star*] this morning. The decks were cleared, all the light sails were bent, and the fish gear rigged. At 8 A.M. the top gallant and royal yards were crossed. We are going to sea this afternoon. At 9 A.M. all hands got in boats and got everything ready for sea. At noon the gig went ashore and returned. At 2 P.M. all hands were called to get up the anchor and make sail. The anchor had a very good hold; we had to get deck tackles onto the messenger to start it. At half past 3 P.M. we were on our way out of the harbor. We do not know where we are going to—it is rumored we are going to St. Helena. At 6 P.M. we were going five knots. It is quite chilly. One of the *San Jacinto's* doctors is on board of us. He is only a passenger with us.

July 9th **bound to St. Helena**

Port watch washed clothes. During the divisions [we] put down for clothing. We are steering a S.W. course and we are bound for St. Helena. The divisions exercised during the afternoon at big guns, small arms, and single sticks. We are expecting to get another liberty when we get to St. Helena.

Today, as the Constellation *headed for St. Helena, Midshipman Borchert brought the prize brig* Triton *into New York, rather than Norfolk, due to bad weather. He anchored one hundred yards out from the receiving ship* North Carolina *at Brooklyn Navy Yard. Young Stephen Wilson was not aboard; he died at sea and was buried on Ascension Island. While Borchert went ashore to report in, the* Triton's *captain and two other prisoners made their escape. The other two were recaptured, but the captain was not. After completing the legal and administrative work on the* Triton, *Midshipman Borchert left the navy and headed south to join the Confederate navy. The* Triton *was, for the second time, condemned.*

July 10th 1861. **all hands to muster/two men sentenced by a Court Martial/on the Muscle**

This morning came in fine, going about 9 knot. At half past 9 A.M. had division inspection. At 10 A.M. clothing was served out by the purser. At twelve o'clock two men got fighting and were put in double irons. At 12 P.M. the paraphernalia for a summary court martial was rigged on the port side of the half deck. The two men that were fighting this morning are the unfortunate individuals. At 3 P.M. the 3d division exercised at small arms, the 1st at single sticks. At 4 P.M. all hands were called to muster to hear the sentence of a court martial. The charges were disorderly conduct; they both pled guilty. They were sentenced to deprivation of all liberty on foreign stations, one month's black list, consisting of whatever the executive officer shall decide, and ten days solitary confinement in double irons. Considering that we are going to have liberty in a few days, it comes rather hard. (Their names are John Gavin and John Dwyer.) Rather a bad thing to be on your muscle, in a man of war.

July 11th

Port watch washed clothes. At half past 9 A.M. the drum beat to general fire quarters. Our 1st lieutenant is drilling the marines at big guns. They don't like it at all. It was almost a dead calm all the afternoon; the breeze freshened towards evening.

July 12th **Elected Sweeps/General Quarters**

This morning the starboard watch washed clothes. At 7 bells I was elected Main Top Sweeper for a week. If there is anything I hate it is sweeping. O

Lord, only think knight of the broom, a dustpan, 3 swabs, and 8 spit boxes to look after.

At half past 9 A.M. the drum beat to general quarters. After drilling at big guns, repelling boarders and sail trimming for over an hour, the drum beat the retreat at noon. We were 870 miles from St. Helena. We now have got but very little wind. We expect to get the S.E. trade winds every minute. If we don't get them soon we will make a long passage. At 7 P.M. we were going four knots. The principal part of this Journal is written by candle light on the berth deck in the dog watches.

Ellen M. Leonard

In addition to keeping the maintopmen's assigned area of the deck spotless by use of his broom, dustpan and swabs, Leonard must also deal with the spit boxes, the wooden version of spittoons. As having so many as eight in this one area of the ship suggests, chewing tobacco was immensely popular in America at this time, especially aboard a ship where smoking was curtailed.

July 13th   **S.E. Trade wind**

Twenty-five months in commission, a very fine morning. At one o'clock this morning we got the S.E. trade winds, and at 6 A.M. we are going 8 knots an hour. At 9 A.M. the gun deck was holystoned, and the paint work scrubbed by all hands. At noon we were going seven knots, the port F.T. mast and top gallant studding sails set. Towards evening the wind began to die away, but in the mid watch it freshened again. Port watch had eight hours in.

July 14th   **Sunday.**

Sunday. Fine weather, and an eight knot breeze. All the Port Studding sails set. At half past nine A.M. the flag officer inspected the ship's company at quarters. At 10 A.M. had divine service on the gun deck. Am writing a letter to a friend (M.C.). At 5 P.M. the wind commenced to slacken, and at 6 P.M. we were only going 4 knots. At noon we were 600 miles from the island of St. Helena.

July 15th   **Provoking**

Port watch washed clothes. The wind is very light this morning; going about three and a half knots, at noon we were over 500 miles from port. At 2 P.M. the 3d division exercised at small arms. We are now going four and a half knots. At 5 P.M. the 1st division exercised big guns. The wind acts curiously for the S.E. trade; in the day time the wind is strong but at night it dies away almost to a dead calm. It is provoking to us, who are expecting liberty. The *Portsmouth* made the passage in six days and six hours; here we are eight days out, and 500 miles to go and by the way the wind acts, we have a good prospect of being eight days more. Heigh ho—we will get there sometime.

July 16th   Musket Drill under difficulties

Starboard watch washed clothes. The wind is very light this morning. Going three knots at 8 A.M. During the afternoon the division exercised at big guns, small arms, and single sticks. The 1st Division are very unfortunate in respect to drilling. We have had no less than six different officers drilling us during the cruise, and each one has an entirely different way of drilling, which makes it very bad for us. If we don't know their peculiar way, they blame us and give us an extra hour or two at the muskets for not doing their way. This afternoon, we were exercised an hour and a half at small arms by Mr. Johnson, our 2nd luff. It being his first time, he gave us his ideas, which are very good in their way, but our present 1st luff used to drill a great deal better. At noon we were 440 miles from St. Helena; at 6 P.M. we were going 1 knot an hour, with a good prospect of going less before midnight.

July 17th

This day came in fine, with but very little wind; at noon we were 372 miles from St. Helena. During the afternoon the divisions exercised at their usual drill. We had a very light wind all night. I was busy writing all this day (M.L.M.).

July 18th   Politics again

Starboard watch washed clothes. We have got a five knot breeze. At half past nine A.M. we had General Fire Quarters. At twelve o'clock we were Latitude 12°.38 South Longitude 5°.55 West, distance from St. Helena 274 miles. At 1 P.M. we were going six miles an hour. We averaged six and a half knots an hour all this afternoon. Politics is the only question that is argued now by the ship's company, and by the way that some of them talk, a person would think that the federal government had made a great mistake in not having them in some other capacity besides a sailor. Fort Sumter could be retaken in no time, according to their plans. Fort Pickens could be held by them against the world.

July 19th   a good breeze

Port watch washed clothes. We have got a seven and a half knot breeze. We are heading half a point off of our course. At noon we were 160 miles from St. Helena. At 1 P.M. we were going eight knots. At half past 9 A.M. we had General Quarters. After exercising for a half an hour, the drum beat the retreat. We expect to get into port tomorrow afternoon, if the wind holds, which as at this writing has every prospect to. At sundown all hands swung clean hammocks. We had a roaring breeze all night.

July 20th   Land ho.

At 5 A.M. the watch on deck was set to work scrubbing paint work inside and out. At daylight land was reported by the cat head lookout, which proved to be the island of St. Helena.

Came to an Anchor off the Island of St. Helena/ Death on board the Brig *Triton*/we are going to have 24 hours Liberty/Spotted Dog

We are about forty miles off. We expect to be in by noon. The watch was busy all the forenoon taking off chafing gear, hooking clew jiggers and getting ready for port. Two other sails are making towards the island from the southward. As I have described the island before, it is useless to say any more about it. At eleven o'clock we came to an anchor, a little farther out than we did before. We came to an anchor in very good shape, opposite Rupert's Valley. There are at anchor here about sixteen merchantmen from China and the East Indies; English, French, Dutch, and Swedish. We sent down royal yards, got out the 2nd and 3d cutters, and dinghy. We also got the swinging booms out and piped to dinner at half past twelve o'clock.

By a letter that our doctor got from the island of Ascension, we learnt that the brig *Triton* (the last slaver we took) put in there and buried our late captain's clerk. [*Stephen B. Wilson Jr., the son of the Captain Wilson mentioned at the beginning of this journal.*] He died two days after we parted company with them at Kabenda, of the coast fever. At 2 P.M. the barque *Sarah Scott*, of Sunderland, England, came to an anchor. An American ship passed in sight of the island at 3 P.M. and showed her private signal. It is winter time at the island, but the weather is delightful. At half past 3 P.M. we went ashore in the gig, but returned immediately. At sundown a Swedish barque sailed, bound to the northward.

We are going to have twenty-four [hours] liberty commencing Monday. All those that wanted money put down for it today at the purser's clerk's desk. At 7 P.M. all the boats were hoisted and the hands called to stand by hammocks. Visions of the Spotted Dog, the Jolly Sailor, and the Heart of Oak, celebrated drinking houses, are running in the minds of ship's company. Politics yesterday, and Liberty today.

July 21st   Sunday

During the night two Dutch ships arrived here. The decks were thoroughly holystoned. At half past 9 A.M. the flag officer inspected the ship's company at quarters. All hands dressed in blue clothes and white hats. At 10 A.M. had divine service on the gun deck. At 2 P.M. a Bremen ship arrived here, two English ships and a barque sailed to the northward, several visitors came on board in the afternoon. An English barque came to an anchor at 5 P.M. A draft of blue jackets are going ashore tomorrow for twenty-four hours. It was rather chilly here today. There is a French barque to leeward of the island trying to beat up. There is a very strong current running here all the time.

Today, at home near Orange, Virginia, Fannie Page Hume heard that a battle had begun at Manassas at five o'clock in the morning. The next day she helped send food into town for forty or fifty wounded Confederates brought there after the battle.[5]

July 22nd **a Draft goes ashore/the Gig's crew wait all night ashore for the Flag Officer**

The clipper ship *Game Cock* of Boston arrived here this morning, also three English East Indiamen. At 9 A.M. the 1st part of the starboard watch were ordered to get ready to go ashore on liberty. The barge's crew are also going ashore; we are to be under his orders until they come off. [*That is, because the crew of the flag officer's barge was being given liberty, the gig was substituted until they return.*] At 10 A.M. the draft went ashore. Petty officers get ten dollars, seamen seven and a half, and the rest five apiece.

At ten we brought the flag officer ashore and had orders to wait for him, go on board and get our meals, and come back. At half past 1 P.M. the boat was called away. On coming to the gangway our rudder was missing, also a brass yoke, and some yoke ropes. The yoke was valued at 30 dollars. Nobody knew where it was. The 1st lieutenant called the boatkeeper and gave him fits. He took him out of the boat, and stopped his liberty. We used the 2nd cutter's rudder the rest of the day. It must have been a great piece of carelessness on his part; it must have unshipped while the boat was going astern and sunk. We then went ashore and waited until supper time. We came on board and had supper, and went ashore again. We had a good run till the nine o'clock gun fired, when we had to return to the boat, as nobody is allowed to go outside of the town after that hour without a pass. We waited in the boat until 6 A.M. We were chilled through. We returned on board at half past six and staid there. During the night six English ships went to sea.

July 23d **We go on Liberty/ashore/ Singing the Jolly Tar/P. R./Rum Mills**

This morning I feel as if I had been drawn through a knot hole; I am all of tremble, cold and sick. It rained during the night, and we were almost wet through. At 8 A.M. we were told to get ready to go on liberty. We got our money and dressed ourselves in clean blue mustering clothes. The 2nd part of the starboard watch and part of the Marine Corps are going today. The ship *Game Cock* sailed at 9 A.M. for New York (I sent 4 letters in her). [*The*

Game Cock was also taking Clement Miller, the captain of the top whose fall from the main yard Leonard mentioned on April 6 and who required hospitalization.][6] At 10 A.M. the draft that went ashore on liberty came on board in very good order, with one or two exceptions. We were then sent ashore with instructions to behave ourselves and be off the next day at 10 A.M. We struck the beach at half past ten and walked up to the town. As I have said something about the appearances of the place, on our previous liberty, I think it is sufficient, as there has been but very little changes since we were here before.

As I had made no arrangements as to what I should do, I took a ramble among the grog shops and there met some of our boys. Although we were but little over an hour ashore, some of them were in the 1st, 2nd, and I may say the 3d stage of drunkenness. One fellow in particular got a notion into his head that I liked to hear him sing (and so I do in the proper time and place, if it is a good singer) but this fellow, being about half tight, commenced the greatest howling I ever heard. His lungs, I must say, were in good order, and his voice was pitched in a key that defies all the rules that ever were made by professors of music. It was a mixture of G sharps and B flats and at times it would go high, resembling the yelp of a lean dog when somebody tramps on his tail, and at the conclusion he would break out in a yell. The song or ballad, I made out to be after a while, was called "Oft in the Stilly Night."[7] I had to drink with him, and I in a moment after left the place. By the way, the name of it was the Jolly Tar. They know how to get the affection of a blue jacket, by calling a place after him.

As soon as old Barnacle Back gets shot (a sailor phrase for being drunk), he is right on his shape, or in other words he likes to tell everybody what he can do, and what he might have done. Of course the landlords of these places coincides with him, and makes him think he is somebody and the first thing Jack knows is nothing at all. He probably wakes up next morning after sleeping in the gutter all night, minus his money [and] the best part of his clothing, and he is very lucky if his nose is on or both ears in their places. It is a frequent occurrence to see a man with his nose hanging, an ear off or an eye out, coming on board a man of war after a general liberty. There are a great many grievances and old scores to be settled by a man of war's crew. When they get on liberty and drinking it breaks out, and a fight is the consequence, and if an outsider is unlucky enough to interfere, he gets a hiding. It is common to see about twenty or thirty couples at it at once. The rules of the P.R. [*London Prize Ring Rules of 1838*] are not observed much in these contests. If by accident one man get his nose or ear close to his antagonist's mouth, ten chances to one but he will snap at it.

I had just run clear of the Jolly Tar, when I run right into one of these crowds, and then I had my handful for over an hour with a young fellow that was an old schoolmate. Finally by coaxing and force I got him away and staid by him until 7 P.M., visiting all the noted rum mills on the island.

Shorty/Light Fantastic Toe/Ship Tavern/a mixed assembly/ description of an Orchestra/a gay party/a free fight

We had a dinner, and supper, at a man's house that is known by the name of Shorty. He came here about two years ago in an East Indiaman; she was condemned and he took up with one of the women of the island. He is a great favorite with all our squadron. He furnishes meals for us. Being a sailor himself, he knows what they want. He is also very accommodating. If any of our boys gets robbed of their clothes, Shorty is on hand to supply them with a suit.

After eating supper we started on a tour through the town. I had almost forgotten to mention that one of our boatmates bought an accordion, and we hired a room, and had a good time, tripping it to the light fantastic (as the newspapers say). My companion commenced to get pretty well corned by this time, and it was as much as I could do to keep him from getting a sound drubbing several times, and at one time I came within an ace of being licked myself, through him. After leaving here, the Jolly Tar had to be visited by him again and here he got into a dispute with me, and abused me in a good style. Here I left him and went on my own [illegible].

Falling in with another young fellow, we visited the Ship tavern, where we heard music. We went upstairs, and entered the ballroom, and here the assembly almost baffles description. In the first place the music was composed of a fiddle played [by] a soldier of the S.H.R. [St. Helena Regiment] with one string, which made a noise like the squeaking of a cart wheel that wanted oiling. The next was a tambourine played by a darkie of the Uncle Tom style; next came a fife played by a Yam Stock [*a native of St. Helena*],[8] who judging by his appearance had but a very poor share of wind, for at times he would break down and all at once he would strike up again, with a piercing shriek that would make the assembly turn pale with fright. I have heard it said that the fife was a soul stirring instrument but I never knew it until then. The last piece in the orchestra was a drum, and by the looks of it, it might have been mistaken it for a wash tub, and the noise it made would help to confirm your opinion. At intervals he would stop to talk to an old courtezan at his side, and he then would strike in, but always in the wrong place, which would cause the company to stop and commence again. The music was seated on a plank set on the head of two empty barrels, the crowd was composed of all sorts— soldiers, sailors, niggers, Yam Stocks, prostitutes—about forty in all.

I got perched on the window sill where I could command a good view of the party, when the music struck up a waltz and if there wasn't fun to see it, I wouldn't say so. The liquor began to work, and they commenced brawling when we left, not before one of our fellows tripped one of the soldiers, who fell, and the rest followed suit. He got up and accused another soldier for doing it, and they went at it, and in five minutes it became general. We left in the middle of it, and the prospect then was at that time it would be kept up all night. On passing the window, the drum came out, and after it came benches, chairs, and tables. Here the police interfered, marching about a dozen of them to the lockup. As it was getting late we began to look around for some place to sleep, which we obtained at Shorty's. He had a spare room, which he gave us, giving us some of his own bedding.

July 24th   second day ashore/Return on board/
                                       a poor time/a poor place for Liberty

Being tired, we slept soundly until half past eight A.M. Fixing up and eating breakfast, we had another dance. Our accordionist furnished the music. We at half past 10 A.M. marched to the beach, and returned on board. Coming alongside, we sung a little more [word uncertain]. Reporting ourselves to the officer of the deck, we returned to our duty. The decks are covered with men lying dead drunk. Two of our men went home in the *Game Cock*. As for saying that I enjoyed my liberty, I cannot. It is the meanest, miserablest dirty hole I ever got into, and I think that the West Coast of African Squadron ought to send a petition to the U.S. Government, for a place to give liberty in. It is supposed to recruit the men, in giving them liberty. But here we cannot get anything to eat, it is so enormously high. The poorest kind of fresh beef is 36 cents a pound, eggs 75 cents a dozen, and everything else in proportion. When men are six and eight months penned up in a ship, on such a station as this, fresh provisions is a godsend. Here we don't get anything. To be sure, rum is cheap, and a sailor will drink it. Coming on board of his ship after his liberty and going right on to his salt provisions again is not very pleasant. At Madeira, we had everything we wanted, but we are not allowed to go there, as it is too far off of the station. Two English East Indiamen came to an anchor at 2 P.M. A Swedish and a French barque sailed at 4 P.M. Two of the 1st draft were brought off by the St. Helena police, they having broken their liberty. The reward is five dollars. [*It was standard navy practice when a man overstayed his liberty to pay the local authorities five dollars to bring him in.*] The 2nd part of the port watch went on liberty at 10 A.M. At night we had a grand breakdown on the gun deck.

July 25th   Death/a Dance/Home sweet home/two men
                                       brought off by the Police/abusing an Officer/
                                       as much as they can do/taking in bread

As soon as hammocks were piped up, we went ashore with the steward. We do it every morning; we have to wait for him, thus giving us a two hours run every morning. On going up Napoleon St. we met several of our boys who had been sleeping in the street all night. It rained during the night, and they were covered with mud from head to foot. They had been robbed, of course. We gave them something to drink, and they went aboard.

At 8 A.M. we returned on board. At 10 A.M. the draft came on board, four of theirs being left ashore in jail. They had a fight with the police. At half past 10 A.M. a Dutch barque arrived here with her colors at half mast, her captain having died coming in. He is to be buried on the island. At 11 A.M. the 1st part of the starboard watch went ashore. This is the last draft. At ten o'clock an English troop ship arrived here from Melbourne. This is a very disagreeable day, very chilly with rain squalls. We have been ashore five times during the day. Two English ships and a French barque sailed during the afternoon.

In the evening it cleared up. Several ladies came on board and the officers had a dance until 10 P.M. On leaving, our band played "Home, Sweet Home," and it sounded beautiful. The night was so still it made me wish that I was home. God grant that we soon may be.

This afternoon two of our men were brought off by the police, one a boatswain's mate, and the other a seaman (W.C. and Jim B.). The boatswain's mate has belonged to the Religious Society all the cruise, and was also a prominent member of the temperance cause. On coming on board he made an awful noise. He abused the 1st lieutenant Rhind in a shocking manner, calling him all the sons of B-hs he could lay his tongue to. He was put in double irons and gagged. He will be court martialed, I suppose. There is also about twenty in the brig for being drunk and noisy. The officers have as much as they can tend to, to look after the ship's company. Everybody is more or less drunk; as soon as they get one fellow fixed, two or three others break out and it is over an hour before they are safe in irons. The men are not slow in expressing their opinions of the officers when they are drunk. The ship to me seems to be upside down. Several of our religious characters broke out this time. They—to alter or reverse the text—cast off the Lamb, and assumed the Sheep. At 7 P.M. the American whaling barque *Greyhound,* of New Bedford, came to an anchor. During the night four vessels arrived and one sailed. We got in several thousand pounds of bread during the day.

July 26th   **Trophies of Victory/a drunken Boatmate spouting Shakespeare/**
in the Brig/getting ready for sea/arrival of the Flag Officer/
attacking the St. Helena police/a dangerous wound/
a speech by the 1st luff/Excited/no more Liberty

It rained very heavy during the night, and was raining when we turned out. We went ashore at 6 A.M. with the steward. We met about six of our fellows, sitting on the steps of a drinking house called the Victoria, waiting for it to open so as they could get their morning bitters. They were in an awful condition, all covered with mud; they slept in the gutter all night. Some of this draft had a grand row with some of the St. Helena Artillery men. As trophies of the victory our boys have got a soldier's cap apiece, which they are going to keep. At 8 A.M. we returned on board. We are taking in water. At 9 A.M. we went ashore with the flag officer's valet, and had orders to wait for him until supper time, which we did. One of our boat's crew (J.C.) got drunk, and was very noisy during the afternoon. He is the same one that I had so much trouble with when I was on liberty. The police mistook [him] for a man that broke his liberty, and were taking him aboard when our coxswain interfered and got him off. At 5 P.M., the valet not being in sight, we went on board and had supper. Our drunken boat mate, being a little Tragedy inclined, began to spout Shakespeare. His audience (the 1st luff) not liking [his] style put him in double irons in the brig. What he will do with [him] I do not know. The coxswain of the 1st cutter came on board drunk and abused the 1st luff horribly. He is in irons in the brig. There has been two or three changed in our boat since we left Loando. During the afternoon, all hands have been getting the ship ready for sea. I believe we are going tonight. All liberty men are off but two. The police are after them. At 6 P.M. we again went ashore, but returned immediately and hoisted, and secured the boat for sea. The flag officer came on board at 7 P.M. The capstan bars were shipped, and the messenger brought to [*these are preparations for weighing anchor*]. We are now waiting for the two men. At half past 7 P.M. the two men were brought on board by the police. They were dressed in shore clothes. They were very drunk. In coming over the gangway one of the police was struck in the head with a heavy wooden spitbox and the other was almost knocked overboard by a blow from somebody's fist. The 4th cutter was then hoisted. One of the policemen was coming up the main hatch ladder, when some one fired a hand holystone and struck him on the forehead, inflicting a very dangerous cut. He fainted, and on coming to he was brought down into the dispensary where it was dressed by the doctor. The cut is about three inches long and an inch deep. The 1st luff, while they were dressing him, came into the port gangway, and gave us a piece of his mind. He said that the man that done such a cowardly act was a cold blooded assassin, he would shrink from his gun in action, and Dare Not face his enemy, and, said he, "By the Eternal God I would give 100 to 1000 dollars out of my own pocket to find him out, and I would do my best to have the Damn Traitor hung at the Yard Arm of this ship. He is not an American. No American would not disgrace his flag by doing such a dastardly action." He also gave the P.O. [police officer] a touch and after a few more words he went below. The flag officer was on deck at the time, and said that there would be no more liberty given in the ship if she staid out three years longer, and said he there is not a man in this ship will get a big discharge unless the man that done it is found out. I believe there is not five men in the ship knows who done it. The affair happened just as we were going to hoist the 4th cutter. After the 1st luff got through, we hoisted her. The affair caused quite an excitement all through the ship. The police, while our men were ashore, struck two or three of the men with clubs while they were drunk, and this is the cause of the trouble.

Mysterious/the Drum beats to quarters and all the Marine Corps with muskets escort the police over the ship's side/all hands up Anchor/Drunkenness/Underway/leaving the island of St. Helena

They now being ready to go ashore, they would not under any consideration go over the side; they were afraid of being murdered. The flag officer had the drummer beat to quarters. The Marines with their muskets then escorted them over the side. When they were about half a mile away from the ship, the drum beat the retreat, and the boatswain called all hands to get up anchor. We had about sixty fathoms of chain to heave in. I never in my life see an anchor come up so slow. We were about an hour getting it up. The reason could be seen plain enough. One draft of our men [had] just come off; they were about all drunk, and of course were used up. Besides, the rest of the ship's company were two thirds drunk with smuggled liquor, of which there was oceans of. At 9 P.M. we tripped our anchor, and the topsails and courses were loosed, the anchor was then catheaded and fished, and sail made. At half past nine the starboard watch's hammocks were piped down, and they were piped below. My first gangway [watch]. The ship seems to be turned upside down, so different, everything goes from what it used to. At 10 A.M. the topgallant sails were set. We are going direct to St. Paul de Loando for our mail. At 12 P.M. we had an eight knot breeze, the island very plain in sight.

July 27th   **at Sea/Prisoners**

This morning came in fine with a light wind from the Sd. and the Ed. The island is out of sight. At 9 A.M. the starboard watch payed the messenger below; all bags were piped up to air clothing. The starboard watch holystoned the gun deck. All hands seems to be perfectly used up. Everybody you see has got a black eye or a broken nose. At 2 P.M. we were going eight knot. At 3 P.M. we rigged preventer backstays. The brig and gun deck forward are full of prisoners, the victims of liberty. We shipped three men in St. Helena as Ordinary Seaman.

Preventer backstays were extra lines running from the masts to the rails abaft the masts, to strengthen the mast when carrying a press of sail on a steady course for a prolonged period.[9]

July 28th 1861.

Sunday. Came in fine with the S.E. trades very strong, going eight knots on a taut bowline. At half past 9 A.M. the ship's company were inspected at quarters by the flag officer. At 10 A.M. had divine service. A person cannot hear anything but adventures and exploits that happened during our liberty. Two of our petty officers lost their billets by getting drunk and abusing the officers. We had several light rain squalls during the day. At sundown we were going eight knots.

The "taut bowline" indicated that the ship was sailing close to the wind.[10] _The Constellation was having a swift, easy cruise back toward Loanda._

July 29th   **3 Blue Jackets and a marine tried by a Summary Court Martial/
                  Sentences of a Court Martial/rather a dear liberty/
                  very unfortunate/Refusing Duty/Piped Down**

Port watch washed clothes. We had a very large wash morning; the liberty clothes got a nice coat of mud while they were ashore. At 8 A.M. we were going eight knots. Some of the men were let out of the brig this morning. Some of the men in the brig have charges preferred against them. At 2 P.M. the signal quarter master rigged up the port side of the gun deck with flags, a sure sign for a summary court martial. They are going to try three blue jackets and a Marine. Two of the blue jackets are the ones that were brought on board by the police the night we left. The other is our boatmate, the one I had so much trouble with while on liberty. The Marine is one that had been tried before for refusing duty. He is tried now for the same cause. During the afternoon the divisions exercised at the usual weekly drill. At 5 P.M. all hands were called to muster by the boatswain to hear the sentences of a summary court martial. It finished at half past 4 P.M. The prisoners were brought up on the quarter deck by the Master at Arms, and the 1st Lieutenant A.C. Rhind read the sentences, which were as follows: the 1st was Isaac Young, a seaman. His charges were disorderly conduct and breaking his liberty. He pleaded guilty and was sentenced to twenty days in solitary confinement in double irons on bread and water, [and] the loss of three months' pay. He also had to pay ten dollars reward besides his liberty money (seven and a half dollars), which made it rather a dear liberty, fifty-four going with the court martial, ten reward and seven and a half liberty money, making in all seventy-one and a half dollars. [_That is, he spent $7.50 on liberty, lost three months' pay at $18 per month, and had to reimburse the $10 paid out to the local police for bringing him in._] The next was Henry Jones, an Ordinary Seaman. His charges were the same as Young's. He pleaded guilty and was sentenced to twenty days in solitary confinement in double irons on bread and water and the loss of three months' pay. His sport altogether cost him fifty-seven dollars. He was in company with Young all the time. The next was our boatmate, James Cloney. He was very unfortunate. He had been in the boat only three days. The boat's crew tried to persuade him to be quiet, but no, he would see us damned first. In coming off, the officer of the deck saw how he was, and reported him. His charges were as follows: that the said J.C. on or about the 26th of July 1861 did while on duty get drunk, which rendered him incapable of performing his duty. He pleaded guilty and was sentenced to be reduced to the next inferior rank, a Landsman (he being an Ordinary Seaman); the loss of two months' pay (28 dollars) and one month's Black list.

The next was the Marine, John Wamingham. He spilt some oil on the berth deck, and when the master at arms asked him to clean it, he refused. He was reported and charges preferred against him, which were disobedience of orders. He pleaded Not Guilty; after mature deliberation the court found him guilty and sentenced him to seven days in solitary confinement, every alternate day on bread and water, 1 month's extra duty to be given at the discretion of the flag officer.

All hands were then piped down. All hands say these are the hardest sentences for so slight an offense that they ever heard of. Such words as, "Keep your weather eye lifting," and, "[Keep] them skinned for the 1st luff" can be heard all over the deck. At 6 P.M. we were going eight knots. We are heading our course.

July 30th   **a Photographic View of the ship taken**

This morning came in fine with a good breeze. The starboard watch washed clothes. The 1st lieutenant is giving some of the boys fits, tricing them up, and giving them the lee wheel for not behaving properly while on liberty. While we lay in St. Helena, a photographic view of our ship was taken by an officer of the St. Helena Regiment. They pronounce us to be the handsomest man of war, that ever was there. During the afternoon the divisions drilled at big guns, small arms, and single sticks. At 6 P.M. we were going six knots. We expect to be in St. Paul de Loando the latter end of this week.

Nellie & Charlie Leonard

July 31st

This day came in fine with a good breeze, going about seven knots. The division bills are out so as the men can put down for clothing. So are the mess bills. During the afternoon the divisions were drilled at big guns, small arms, and single sticks. At 6 P.M. we were going five knots.

August 1861

August 1st   another Court Martial/Sentence of a Court Martial/
a speech by the 1st luff

The starboard watch washed clothes. This morning a man struck another on the quarter deck. He will be court martialed. Small stores were served out this morning. This forenoon the hammocks were piped into the rigging so as to air clothing. At 2 P.M. the quartermasters rigged up the paraphernalia for a summary court martial. It has been very cloudy all day. We have got a good breeze, going about six knots. At 5 P.M. all hands were called to muster to hear the sentence of a court martial. The 1st lieutenant read the charges, which were as follows: that James McKenzie, seaman, did feloniously attack and assault John Chapman, an ordinary seaman, on the quarter deck. He pleaded guilty to the charges, and was sentenced to twenty days in solitary confinement in double irons in the brig, on bread and water, and the loss of three months' pay (54 dollars), which was approved of by the flag, and executive officers.

The 1st luff then made a short speech, which was to the effect that ever since he had been in the ship it was a frequent occurrence to hear one man call each other by very insulting epithets. He said if he heard of it any more, or anybody reported another for it, and could prove it, he would punish them to the fullest extent of the law, and if anybody should take the law into his own hands, he would treat them in the same way. We were then piped down by the boatswain. At 6 P.M. we were going five knots. It is very cloudy.

August 2nd

This morning came in fine, with an eight knot breeze. The port watch washed clothes. At half past 9 A.M. the drum beat to General Quarters. We exercised the starboard battery for half an hour, when the drum beat the retreat.

Be Just, and Fear Not

Clothing was served out during the forenoon. At sundown we had a very strong breeze, which lasted all night. At midnight we were going ten knot[s].

August 3d   a Collation/Bad Bread

This morning came in fine, with a strong breeze; going eight knots. Being Saturday, the bags were piped up to air clothing, and the gun deck was holystoned by the port watch. At noon we were 270 miles from St. Paul de Loando. We expect to be in there Monday. We also expect the mail.

In the dog watch, I had quite a nice collation, given by the cook of our mess (Eben B.N.) to a few of his friends. It came in very acceptable, as I had but a very poor supper. Our bread is in a state that would turn a person's stomach; it is black, dirty, and full of maggots. We got it in St. Helena and it probably came out of some very condemned vessel there, or most likely from some captured slaver, the bread being used for the niggers. On handling it a cloud of mouldy dust comes from it, that makes a person sneeze; it smells horridly. Old sailors say that it is the worst bread they ever saw, rather a bad state for one of the U.S. men of war to be in.

August 4th   General Muster/reading the Articles of War

Sunday. At half past 9 A.M. the drum beat to quarters and we were inspected by the officer of the divisions. At 10 A.M. all hands were called to muster. It being the 1st Sunday in the month, the Articles of War were read by the 1st luff and all hands mustered around the capstan, according to their name and rate. At half past 10 A.M. the bell rang for divine service. Towards evening the wind began to die away; at midnight it was almost a calm.

August 5th

This morning came in cloudy, not a breath of wind. At 9 A.M. we braced the head yards aback and remained so all the forenoon. The starboard watch washed clothes. It rained during the forenoon. It was a dead calm all this day. At sundown the courses were hauled up close, the royals and flying jib furled, they being useless, as there is no wind whatever.

Meanwhile, at Loanda, Commander Godon of the Mohican, *senior U.S. officer present while both Inman and Captain Dornin were elsewhere, had received a generous offer from the governor general of Angola. The squadron had for some time had occasional money problems. News of the increasingly serious problems in the United States made it difficult for the American navy to obtain money locally at all, even at very steep rates of exchange. Hearing of this, the governor general had offered to provide whatever money was needed. Godon was grateful but said he could not accept. (Adding to Godon's money problems was the ship's lack of a paymaster, with the captain himself and then a clerk temporarily having acted as one—a desperate expedient caused by the chronic squadron personnel shortages.)*[1]

In Virginia a bed had been moved into "Selma's" parlor to convert it into a sickroom for two ill Confederate soldiers returned from the Battle of First Manassas/Bull Run. Fannie Hume was looking after them.[2]

August 6th   Land ho/came to an anchor in Bengo Bay

It remained calm all night. At 4 A.M., a light air springing up, the royals and courses were set. It is very cloudy and chilly this morning. At 10 A.M. land was reported on our weather beam, supposed to be in the vicinity of St. Paul de Loando. At twelve o'clock, the fog clearing, we could see the city very plain. We are about fifteen miles off; we are going about one mile an hour. At dark we were about seven miles from Point Augustus, and at 10 P.M. we came to an anchor in Bengo Bay, about three miles from Point Augustus. We then got our hammocks. The anchor watch was set, I having 1st watch.

August 7th   underway/we get the mail/
good News at last/Home Sweet Home

At daylight the hands were turned out, but as it was a dead calm, we did not get underway. At 6 P.M. the 4th cutter was manned and went up the harbor. At seven bells we had breakfast, and at half past 8 A.M., a light air springing up, we got up the anchor and made sail. A Portuguese mail steamer is coming in. We are drifting into the harbor. At 9 A.M. the 4th cutter came alongside with the mail. By the looks of it, there is not much prospects for our orders.

At ten o'clock the flag officer came on deck, and told one of our middies that our orders had come, which being overheard by a messenger boy, [he] posted into the gangway and told the news

* * *

* *We get Our Orders for home* *
* * *

We thought he was jestering, but his story being confirmed by the officers, we had to believe. In less than ten minutes all hands knew it, and if there wasn't excitement I wouldn't say so. Everybody has a smile upon his countenance. The 1st lieutenant had to come forward several times in order to obtain silence in the ship, but as soon as he went aft, the noise broke out again with redoubled vigor. The news is very important—we have got the news of the engagement at Harpers Ferry, VA. and the death of Colonel Ellsworth, of the Zouaves—but as important as it

HOME

is, it is nothing compared with our orders.[3] All the squadron are going home, with the exception of the *Saratoga*, which is to remain out here. The flag will be represented by a Capt Wilkes, who is on his way out here in a coal ship. She has also got our original orders.

We are going to Portsmouth N.H./came to an anchor in St. Paul de Loando/ Babel/all hands down Top Gallant and Royal Yards/all hands having a good time/Rejoicing

We having received duplicate copies by the mail, our ship and the *Portsmouth* are ordered to Portsmouth, N.H., the *Mohican* to Boston, the *San Jacinto* and *Sumpter* to New York, and the *Mystic* to Philadelphia, Penn.

At twelve o'clock we came to an anchor in the harbor of St. Paul de Loando. All the vessels in the squadron are here but the *Saratoga*. There are also three American barques, the *John Gilpin*, of Boston, *Wm. H. Shaler* and *Lucy Johnson* of Salem, Mass.; two Portuguese mail steamers, and about thirty brigs and schooners of all nations. At 2 P.M. we went ashore in the gig and returned at 3 P.M. The other vessels are overjoyed at getting their orders. It is not every day that we get orders to leave such a miserable station as this. It sounds like a modern Babel in the ship. We are making preparations for home. Our boat has been running all day to and from the different ships in the squadron.

At 6 P.M. hammocks were served out, so as to scrub them in the morning. At sundown all hands were called to send down the top gallant and royal yards. They are to be thoroughly overhauled and in fact all the running and standing rigging. The yards came down better than ever they did before—all hands work with a will. The clothes lines were then rigged, and the boatswain called all hands to stand by hammocks. As soon as the hammocks were down, fiddles, fifes, accordions, and banjos came into requisition, and such a dancing, singing, and raising the Devil I believe was never known before.

The *Mohican* is to take all the Kroomen in the squadron to Monrovia, and leave them. She then goes home direct. The Store Ship *Relief* is going home. Although the news from home is very important, our orders takes all the interest from it. At eight o'clock I turned into my hammock to dream of home. W.A.L.

Upon arrival Inman at last received Secretary of the Navy Gideon Welles's order, sent three months earlier (May 9, with a postscript of May 14), ordering the squadron home. The Saratoga *alone remained on station.*

After transferring San Jacinto's *Captain Dornin to command the* Constellation, *Inman ordered the* San Jacinto, *under the temporary command of the disliked Lieutenant Fairfax, to proceed to Fernando Po, where Capt. Charles Wilkes will come aboard and assume command. Wilkes was to take the ship to Monrovia to drop off kroomen and then go to Philadelphia. The* Saratoga *met its new captain, William M. Glendy, at Fernando Po, and Glendy became senior officer in command of his squadron of one ship. The* Portsmouth *will head for Portsmouth, NH. The* Sumpter *and* Mystic *will steam to Monrovia to drop off kroomen and then to New York and Philadelphia, respectively. The* Mohican *is ordered to Boston, the* Relief *to New York, and the* Constellation *to Portsmouth.*[4] *It is really the end of the U.S. African Squadron.*

August 8th   getting ready for Home/Captain Dornin

All hands scrubbed hammocks. During the forenoon, we were getting in wood, water, and provisions. We went ashore with the flag officer's steward, to get provisions, and returned at 1 P.M. The Kroomen are cleaning the ship's bottom, the guns being run in for that purpose. [*That is, the guns were run in on one side and out on the other, giving the ship a list that exposed the bottom further on the side where the guns were run in.*] All the carpenter's gang are busy making hen coops for the officers. The boatswain is got all hands to work about the rigging. There is a rumor on board that Captain Dornin, of the *San Jacinto*, is coming to be captain of our ship, the flag officer having instructions to take him. He is a Southerner, and he thinks he might run her into a Southern port and give her up. He has a son, and a son in law, in the Southern service. I believe we are going to sail Sunday, the 11th. The *Portsmouth* is to sail tomorrow. In the evening the usual sports commenced and were kept up until 9 A.M., [P.M.] when the hands were piped down.

The rumor about Captain Dornin coming on board of us is true.

August 9th   The U.S. Sloop of War *Portsmouth* sails for Home/
Saluting/Cheering/Garibaldi/Boating

This morning all hands scrubbed, and washed clothes. At 9 A.M. we went ashore with the steward, to get stores for the flag officer and Captain Dornin. The *Portsmouth* is preparing to go home. We gave her a month's bread; she had none, they were going to St. Helena for some, but her crew went to the mast and told her captain that they were willing to go on allowance, provided he would go straight home. He approved of it, and is going to start today. We also gave the *Mohican* a month's allowance of bread. The store ship *Relief* bent all her sail this forenoon. She is to sail next week for New York. At twelve o'clock we returned on board. At twenty minutes past twelve the *Portsmouth* made sail and hove up her anchor for home, and by the way it came up there was many a light heart on board of her. She fired a parting salute of thirteen guns to our flag officer; we returned them nine guns, she then cheered every vessel in the squadron. Every vessel returned it with a will. There is but very little wind. It makes us all feel good because we know that we are soon to follow.

All is bustle and excitement on board. The ship sounds like a poultry yard. The gun deck is covered with chicken coops.

As the plan was to make as direct and swift a run home as possible, there was little reason to worry about going to general quarters, so the ship was stocking up on poultry to provide fresh food instead of salt pork or beef during the transit. At times this might be done only for the officers, but from Leonard's description it seems that this time the entire crew benefited.

At 2 P.M. we again went ashore and returned at half past 3 P.M. The *San Jacinto* is going to Fernando Po to wait for the ship *Garibaldi*, where she gets a Captain Wilkes who is going to bring her home. She goes to Fernando Po in charge of Lieutenant Fairfax. At 4 P.M. the telegraph on the fort signalized the U.S. Sloop of war *Saratoga* as coming in. At 5 P.M. the Portuguese mail steamer sailed for the island of Madeira. She takes two of our musicians who were discharged at their own request. At sundown we bent new topgallant sails. I am (to use a vulgar phrase), about played out today. We [*the crew of The gig*] have been pulling all day long ashore and to the other ships. My [arms] are fairly aching. At eight bells I turned in.

August 10th   Captain Dornin comes onboard/Kroomen leave the ship

This morning the launch was sent ashore for wood. At 8 A.M. the topgallant yards were crossed. At 9 A.M. we went ashore with the steward and returned at 11 A.M. We are taking in wood and water. The *Saratoga* is at anchor abreast of us. At 1 P.M. the Kroomen were paid off and left us. They cheered us on leaving. At half past one Captain Dornin left the *San Jacinto*. They gave him three hearty cheers. He was received by the flag officer and all our Lieutenants. He took charge immediately on his arrival. He has a splendid name by the *San Jacinto* crew.

Our Lieutenant of Marines, J.R.F. Tattnall, is going home in the *San Jacinto* as a prisoner. He is a son of Commodore Tattnall, who is in the Southern service. It is rumored that some of his correspondence has been intercepted, and in it there are documents that warrant his arrest. His room is better than his company on board this ship. He looks on a blue jacket, in the same light as an executioner does a condemned felon.

Actually Lieutenant Tattnall was not sent as a prisoner but at his own request was put in charge of the marines aboard the San Jacinto, *and he had himself informed Inman of letters received from his home state of Georgia encouraging U.S. officers to switch allegiance to their state. On the other hand, Captain Dornin's son had "gone South," and so his allegiance was suspect too; Secretary of the Navy Gideon Welles had ordered Inman to relieve him. Instead, bringing Dornin (who strongly protested his loyalty) to the* Constellation *avoided humiliating him while putting him where Inman could keep an eye on him, and sending Tattnall to the* San Jacinto *prevents having both the flagship and its marines commanded by men of questioned allegiance. Dornin's case marks a rare moment in the annals of the navy when a man was outraged while being given command of a ship, and a flagship at that.*[5]

In Virginia this day, Fannie Hume was in the parlor tending to one of the Confederate soldiers in the last moments of his life.

> the Gun boat *Mystic* sails for Home/Cheering/we go into Commission as Captains Gig again/the *San Jacinto* sails for Home/Saluting/the Gun boat *Sumpter* sails for Home.

The English Steam Sloop of war *Electro* [*Alecto*] came in here during the night. At 4 P.M. the U.S. Gun boat *Mystic* fired a salute of thirteen guns to the flag officer. We returned her five guns; she then weighed anchor and steamed close under our stern. We then manned the rigging and gave her three cheers, which they returned. The *Relief, Saratoga, Sumpter, San Jacinto, Mohican,* and *Electro* then cheered her. They returned their cheers and made out of the [harbor]. On her way home, she touches at Fernando Po; Monrovia, where she leaves her, and part of our, Kroomen; then at Porto Grande, and the island of Barbados, for coal. From there she proceeds direct to Philadelphia. At half past four the flag officer gave up the gig to Captain Dornin. That brings it into commission again.

At 5 P.M. all hands was called to get in boats, and just as we got on deck the *San Jacinto* tripped her anchor, and fired a parting salute of thirteen guns to our flag officer. We endeavored to return her five guns, but owing to a mistake of a quarter gunner they fired six, this giving him one more than he was entitled to. They then cheered us. We returned it. They then cheered all the other vessels and they returned it. They then hoisted in the boats, and they came in quicker than they ever did this cruise before. At 6 P.M. hammocks were piped down and all hands commenced singing homeward bound songs. At half past 9 P.M. the Gun boat *Sumpter* got underway and came close under our stern, but as all hands were turned in, she made no parting salutes. She takes part of the Kroomen. She touches at Fernando Po, Monrovia, Porto Grande, island of Barbados, and from there she goes direct to New York. The *Mohican* sails direct to Boston Mass. She will probably sail about the 12th or 13th· We are going to sail tomorrow afternoon. We are almost full of water. We expect to make the passage in forty-five days.

August 11th 1861. Preparations for Sea/hoisting the Boats/Huzza for home/ heaving short/making sail/*Mohicans* Cheers and salutes us/ all hands pitch their white Hats Overboard/the *Saratoga* salutes and Cheers us/*Relief* and *Electro* cheers us/at Sea

Sunday. This day came in fine. Both decks were holystoned. At half past 9 A.M. the drum beat to quarters for inspection, all hands dressed in blue frocks, trowsers, and white hats. We were inspected by our new captain and the flag officer. At a quarter of ten the drum beat the retreat. Royal yards were then crossed, and the 3d cutter and dinghy hoisted in, swinging booms were got alongside, the accommodation ladders unshipped, and at 11 A.M. we got up the messenger, and at half past eleven we were ready to heave up the anchor. Our captain then took the boat, and went on board the *Mohican* and *Relief*. We returned at twelve o'clock. We are now waiting for the sea breeze to set in. We were then piped to dinner. At 1 P.M. we hoisted the barge, gig, and 4th cutter and secured them for sea. At half past 1 P.M. the sea breeze set in, but very light. At two o'clock the boatswain called all hands to get

*Up Anchor for Home

And in an instant all was bustle and rejoicing. The men worked with a will—we hove short in about five minutes—when we were again called to make sail, which was done in very short notice. The way the topsails were sheeted home and hoisted was a caution; the topgallant sails and royals seemed as if they were set by magic. We were then sent down to the bars [of the capstan], and such a scrambling down the hatchways I never saw before. The anchor was hove up in about ten minutes, and we were then pointed for home. The U.S. Steam Gun boat *Mohican* then fired a parting salute of thirteen guns and we returned her seven guns. She then manned the rigging and gave us three cheers, we manned our rigging and returned her three cheers with a will, and during the third cheer all hands threw our white hats overboard. Our 1st luff told us we were a set of Damn fools, (but as his opinion was expressed voluntarily we did not care about it). The *Mohican* then gave us one parting cheer, and we answered it—we then cat headed, and fished—parting salute of 13 guns, we returned her 7 guns. She then cheered us, we returned hers, the store ship *Relief* then cheered, and answered it. H.B.M. Steam Sloop of war *Electro*, then cheered us, we answered it, and she gave one parting cheer which we also returned. We now laid out of the rigging and set the port studding sails and cleared up the decks. We are crawling out of the harbor very slow, but the breeze is freshening. At 6 P.M., the wind having freshened, we are now going seven knots. The men are already laying plans of what they are going to do. The different routes between Portsmouth and Boston, New York, and Philadelphia and their fares are about the principal points of discussion to those who belong to the respective cities, and the rest are talking of boarding houses and landlords.

August 12th   Distance

This day came in fine with a good breeze, port watch washed clothes. We were going seven and eight knots all night, the port fore topmast and topgallant studding sails set. At half past 9 A.M. we were called to quarters for inspection.

During the afternoon, the divisions exercised big guns, small arms, and single sticks. At 6 P.M. we were going seven knots. We unbent the cables during the afternoon and sent them below. The distance in a direct line from St. Paul de Loando to Portsmouth, N.H. is 5661 miles, but I suppose we will sail double that distance. We have got a very fair start of it, we have averaged seven knots on our course since we have been out.

August 13th	Sail ho/she proves to be HBM Frigate *Arrogant*/ she salutes us with 13 Guns

Two years, and two months in commission. This morning came in fine, going eight knots, the topmast and topgallant studding sails set. Starboard watch washed clothes. At half past 9 A.M. a sail was reported by the lookout on the fore topmast crosstrees two points on our lee bow. At 10 A.M. made her out to be H.B.M. Steam Frigate *Arrogant*. She hoisted the American ensign at her fore and fired a salute of thirteen guns. She being about five miles to leeward, we could not hear the report of her guns, owing to the strong wind that is blowing. We then hoisted the English ensign at our fore, hauled up our courses, lowered the fore royal, and returned her a salute of thirteen guns. She then being under steam, squared away, loosed, and made all sail. She is heading towards St. Paul de Loando. We then set all sail and stood on our course. During the afternoon the division exercised at big guns, small arms, and single sticks. At 5 P.M. the hammocks were taken out of the sail room and stopped on the clothes lines to dry. At 6 P.M. we were going seven and a half knots.

The Arrogant *was the flagship of Commodore William Edmonstone, senior British officer on the West Coast of Africa. An exchange of salutes between the two commodores is proper procedure, though this time the Royal Navy squadron was in effect bidding farewell to the U.S. squadron.*

August 14th	Exercising

This day came in fine with an eight knot breeze, port topmast and topgallant studding sails set. During the afternoon the divisions exercised at big guns, small arms and single sticks. The launch's fighting crew were exercised at howitzer drill, and the master's division with the carbines. At sundown the wind died away to a dead calm. In the middle watch a light air sprung up.

August 15th

This day came in fine with a very light breeze; going three knots. Starboard watch washed clothes. The watch on deck was to work all the forenoon scraping pin rails. The latitude at noon was 6 [?] 19 S [cut off]. We also had general fire quarters. This forenoon the wind freshened in the afternoon, and at 6

P.M. we were going seven knots. Today the bandsmen were stationed in the afterguard. There is only three left of them. The fore and main topmen have to keep masthead lookouts again, the fore one day and the main the next. The weather is getting warmer as we approach the Equator.

August 16th   General Quarters/Sailing

Port watch washed clothes. We have got pleasant weather and an eight knot breeze this morning. The port lower, topmast, and topgallant studding sails set. At half past 9 A.M. the drum beat to general quarters; cast loose both batteries, and exercised the port guns. We had the longest drilling at the guns this time, than ever we had before. I suppose it is on account of our going home. This ship will be inspected by the Commodore of the Portsmouth Navy Yard and it is a common occurrence if a ship is not properly drilled, to send them on a six months' cruise in the Gulf to learn a little more. During the afternoon the wind freshened, and at 6 P.M. we were going ten knots. In the midwatch it got a little stronger, and the topgallant studding sails and royals were taken in, when in all conscience they ought to be on her. A Middy had the deck (we have only got four deck officers now, two lieutenants and two midshipmen; the last named knowing but very little makes it bad). We are all very anxious to beat the time of the U.S. Sloop of War *Portsmouth*, which vessel sailed 48 hours before us. Considerable money has been bet on both ships, but when we get a little puff of wind the sails that does the most good are taken off of her. It is enough to make a person swear rather hard, particularly when we are on our way to a civilized country. As soon as the watch was changed the sails were set, and we went from eleven to twelve knots.

August 17th

This day came in with a roaring breeze, all the port studding sails set at 9 A.M. A new fore, and main sail, spanker, fore topmast staysail, jib, and flying jib were bent by the starboard watch. The port watch was to work all the forenoon, holystoning the gun deck. At twelve o'clock we were making almost a due west course, in order to cross the Line in Longitude 32 or 33 West, in order to take advantage of the trade winds. We have now got the S.E. trades and they may take us right into the N.E. trades, and if they do the probability is that we will make a very quick passage.

The region near the equator, with calms and light variable winds, is the doldrums, where a ship can move slowly, or not at all, for days on end. In a band to the south of that, where the Constellation *was at this point, blow the southeast trade winds, and in a band to the north of the doldrums the northeast trades blow, in both cases in a westerly direction. Leonard was hoping for a quick transit of the doldrums into the northeast trades.*

August 18th   **Sunday inspection/a beautiful night**

Sunday. The wind is very strong this morning. We are going ten and eleven knots. At half past nine A.M. the drum beat to quarters for inspection, which was done by Captain Dornin. The ship's company were dressed in blue mustering clothes. Their appearance, with their cutlasses, pistols, and bright work, together with the decks, almost milk white, pleased our captain very much. At 10 A.M. divine service was held on the gun deck. At twelve o'clock we were going nine knots. We are now 980 miles from St. Paul de Loando. We were in 3 W. Longitude. We were going seven and eight knot[s] all the afternoon, all the port studding sails set. The evening is surpassingly beautiful, a full moon, and not a speck to be seen on the horizon, together with a wind which is driving us at a rate of eight knots an hour, which in this latitude is very refreshing (5 S and 3 W). It reminds one of reading some poetical romance. I had a midwatch lookout in the gangway, which time was very pleasantly spent in building air castles.

August 19th   **Projects/Exercise**

Good wind, and a fine morning. Starboard watch washed clothes. All the men are making grand preparations for washing and making clothes, money belts, &c. &c. It is amusing to hear what plans, and maneuvers some of the men are going to do when we get home. There is not one but has got a project so that he will make his living ashore. They are never coming to sea, o' no, not they. This time they only came for pleasure, and I fancy they have seen a great deal. As for myself, I hardly know what I will do; it depends a great deal on circumstances which, for good reasons, I do not wish to make known, whether I come again or not. Certain it is, that I will if I can stay at home.

Homeward Bound at sea

Anything is preferable to this dog's life of a sailor. A person of any spirit might as well be in the infernal regions as in a man of war.

During the forenoon the mizzen topmen bent a new mizzen topsail. The afternoon was occupied in exercising the divisions, at big guns, small arms, and single sticks. The wind towards evening began to die away and at six P.M. we were going five and a half knots. In the midwatch the wind again increased to an eight knot breeze.

August 20th   **mess bills**

This day came in beautiful, with a seven knot breeze. The mess bills for September came out this forenoon, and the purser's steward notified the ship's company that it is for the last time. During the afternoon the gun deck divisions exercised big guns, small arms, and single sticks. At 6 P.M. we were going seven and a half knots. In the morning watch the port watch washed clothes; they were piped down at seven bells in the afternoon watch.

August 21st

Since six o'clock last night we have averaged nine knots an hour. Today the weather is delightful. We have got a good wind, going eight and nine knots, the wind being a little on our port quarter. All the port studding sails are set. At twelve o'clock noon the Latitude was 5.9 S and Longitude 11.53 W. During the afternoon the divisions exercised at big guns, small arms, and single sticks. The launch's fighting boat's crew were drilled with the howitzers. Six P.M. we were going eight knots.

August 22nd   Beating to General Quarters at midnight/ taken by surprise/Black List

Port watch washed clothes. We have got an eight knot breeze. This morning at half past 9 A.M. the drum beat to general fire quarters and the men were inspected at their stations by the 1st lieutenant. At 10 A.M. the drummer beat the retreat. At noon the latitude was 4.38. S Longitude 14.41 west, we having run 201 miles during the last twenty-four hours. At 5 P.M. the 4th division were exercised with carbines. At 6 P.M. we were going nine knots. Port watch eight hours in.

At a quarter before twelve midnight the watch below was startled by hearing the drum beating to general fighting quarters. Instantly all was excitement —dressing themselves hastily, lashing their hammocks, and bringing them on deck, was done in a very short space of time; then to our guns, casting loose, and getting ready for action was done in silence and with dispatch. The ship was reported ready for action to the captain in seven minutes and a half from the time the drum commenced beating. He inspected the ship to assure himself of this fact. This is not near as quick as we have done it. We have done it in 4 minutes, but then we knew it, and were prepared for it; this time it was a complete surprise to everybody; not a soul knew it. The captain came on deck and ordered the drummer to beat to quarters, in a time when everybody in the ship was asleep, with the exception of the lieutenant of the watch and the lookouts. It stupefied some, they hardly knew what to make of it.

A person would think there would be a great deal of confusion in such a scene, but it is not so. Everybody has a certain duty to perform, which he does quick, and in silence. The only time there is anybody in confusion is when they are dressing, lashing up their hammocks, and carrying them up the hatchways to the nettings. Those that have their hammocks stowed are trying to get down, and the others are trying to get up, some with their pants on, and some with them off. If a fellow is very hard to wake, he has to hurry up his cakes or stand the consequences. Some get so absent minded that they forget to take up their hammocks. Their numbers are taken, and the next day they are honored with a prominent position in the Black List. The scene on the gun deck of a man of war when they beat to quarters for action, at night is beyond description: all the paraphernalia for battle before your eyes, battle lanterns lighted, the men with their faces at the guns, ready at a moment's notice from their commanding officer to spread death and destruction to their fellow beings. Such a scene as this at midnight made its impression on my mind. At half past twelve the drum beat the retreat, hammocks were piped down, and the regular watch was again set.

August 23d   heavy Rolling

Starboard watch washed clothes. We are going eight knots this morning. The wind during the night shifted dead aft, and we have now got all studding sails set alow and aloft. We are rolling frightfully, the swinging booms dipping every other time. At half past nine we went to quarters, but on account of the ship's rolling we dispensed with the usual general quarters, but we secured the guns afresh. This suited the boys first rate and some of them prayed that she might roll so until we got home.

At noon we were going nine knots. Longitude 18.15 West. As we are making a due west course, the latitude is about the same as it was yesterday. We averaged eight knots during the afternoon. At night the ship rolled so heavily that it was almost an impossibility to get asleep; the guns, boats, ladders, and bulkhead kept up an incessant squeaking all night.

August 24th   a good breeze/Longitude 21.23 W.

This morning came in splendid with a roaring breeze, wind dead aft, going ten knots. At 6 A.M. the mizzen topgallant sail and royal was furled, and the topsail lowered on the cap, and the reef tackles hauled out. This was done in order to let the sails on the main to be full, and it proved to be a good move, for we went a knot and a half faster when the log was hove. Our studding sail gear, being rather old, kept parting all day long. First a tack would go; that would hardly be fixed before a halyard or sheet would snap, and down the sail would come, then "Hurrah there, my lads, and get that sail on her, as quick as you can," would be the cry of the boatswain, or lieutenant of the watch. At 6 P.M. we were going eight knots. The gun deck was holystoned in forenoon, and the masts slushed down in the afternoon. Port watch eight hours in.

August 25th

Sunday, and a beautiful morning going eight knots, studding sails both sides alow and aloft. At half past 9 A.M. the ship's company was inspected at quarters by the captain, all hands dressed in blue mustering clothes. At 10 A.M. had divine service on the gun deck. At noon we were in 24.15 West Longitude. We

USS *Constellation* with studding sails set alow and aloft. As seen here, studding sails were set on spars that could be extended out on both sides from the regular spars. More often they were used on one side or the other, but here, with the ship running "wing and wing" ahead of the wind, they have been set, as Leonard mentions on August 25, 1861, "alow and aloft on both sides." Painting by C. R. Patterson, courtesy of Washington County Museum of Fine Arts.

averaged seven knots all this afternoon. We made about twelve hundred miles this week.

August 26th   Sail ho.

Came in fine with a good breeze, going eight knots. At noon the Latitude 2. 59 South Longitude 27.2 West. During the afternoon the 1st division were exercised at dismounting guns, the 2nd division at small arms, the 3d division at single sticks and the 4th division at carbines. At 2 P.M. a sail was reported by the lookout at the masthead heading to the Nd and Ed. We hoisted our ensign, and she showed English colors. She is a large ship, probably bound to Europe. At 6 P.M. we were going seven knots and a half. The port watch washed clothes this morning.

August 27th   **Sail ho.**

Starboard watch washed clothes, a fine morning. Good wind, going seven and a half knots. At half past 10 A.M. two sails were reported by the masthead lookout. They were close-hauled on a wind standing to the southward. They being so far off we could not make out what they were. At noon we were in 1^deg and 31^miles to the southward of the Equator, 29^d 39^m west Longitude. As we approach the Line, the weather gets warmer. We expect to cross it tomorrow. During the afternoon the divisions exercised at dismounting guns, small arms, and single sticks. At 6 P.M. we were going nine knots, which is considered something remarkable so close to the Line, where it is generally calm. At 10 A.M. the wind hauled a point ahead, the yards were braced and we were going eight and a half knots.

August 28th   **crossing the Line**

This morning came in fine with a nine knot breeze. We expect to cross the line this afternoon. At six minutes of twelve o'clock, we crossed the Line in

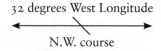

32 degrees West Longitude

N.W. course

with a ten knot breeze, all the port studding sails set. At noon we were one mile North Latitude. During the afternoon the divisions exercised big guns, small arms, and single sticks. At 6 P.M. we were going eight knots, we have still got the S.E. trade winds.

August 29th   **all hands cleaning the Cables**

Starboard watch washed clothes. This is a beautiful morning, a seven and a half knot breeze blowing all the port studding sails set. At 9 A.M. all hands were set to work on the gun deck, getting up the sheet cables so as to overhaul and clean them. Port and starboard watch on their respective sides, one watch trying to beat the other, the starboard was ahead, but in stowing their chain they made a grand mistake: their locker was chock full, and thirty fathom of their chain still on deck. They had to get it up again, and stow it over, which occupied all the afternoon. The port watch got through theirs at half past two P.M. They are having a great laugh at the starbowlines [*slang for the men of the starboard watch*].

The sheet cables are chains used with the sheet (secondary) anchors.

Lines, On the Ocean.

on the ocean, in the ocean—
on the brave old ocean sea.

we are sailing—proudly sailing
o'er the waters blue and free.
Day is dying sun is sinking,   [Star Graphic]
And the night clouds gather gray
Ocean winds of night are sighing
Dirges o'er the passing day.

Rising, like the queenly Venus
Rising from her beauty bath,
O'er the azure world of waters
[American Flag Graphic]   Rises Luna o'er our path;
O'er our path a million star gems
Twinkle, twinkle in the sky;
Sky, and waters—Sky and waters,
Naught but these do fill our eye.
On the ocean, on the ocean—
on the dear old ocean wave
Proudly speeds our gallant vessel,
Freighted with the fair and brave,
Now, at lightning speed we're flying—   [Star Graphic]
Speeding, on our voyage far,
And we're steering—homeward steering—
Steering, by the evening star.

the wind is beginning to die away. At 6 P.M. we were going five knots. The Latitude at noon was 1.38 North. We had a good breeze all night.

August 30   Division Bills

My birthday came in very fine with an eight knot breeze. All the port studding sails set. At half past 9 A.M. the drum beat to General Quarters. Both batteries were cast loose, exercised the starboard battery for over [an hour?] and then beat the retreat. At noon we were in 3 degrees 9 miles North Latitude. We had an eight knot breeze all the afternoon. Port watch scrubbed and washed clothes in the morning watch. The division bills for clothing came out today for the last time. The wind freshened in the first night watch to a ten knot breeze.

August 31st   Starting all Rations/Anxiety

This day came in fine with an eight knot breeze, all the port studding sails set. At half past 9 A.M. the port watch were sent to holystone the gun deck. All bags were piped up to air clothing. At twelve o'clock we were in four degrees thirty-three miles North latitude, Longitude 38.17 west. At five o'clock a squall came up on our port bow. Studding sails, royals and flying jib were taken in and the yards braced sharp up. We are now steering a N.E. course, we are now looking for the N.E. trade winds. At noon today we were over 3000 miles from St. Paul de Loando, it being over half the distance to Portsmouth N.H. Today all the rations were started; each mess now draws its full allowance. I am getting awful anxious to get home, every day seems a month to me. Although we have averaged eight knots an hour since we started, it hardly seems if we went, so impatient does it make me feel that I [am] almost crazy.

It appears that the chickens were good for three weeks, and now the crew was back to the usual salted meat diet. With the last chicken coop probably tossed overboard, the gun deck was unencumbered for firing the guns, as would be done on the next clear day.

Homeward Bound Passage,
at Sea

Homeward Bound

1st
For the fair land of freedom, we hope soon to sail,
For the land of the true, brave, and free.
Our hearts, shall be light as we sing to the gail [sic]
That flits past us as we bound o'er the sea

Chorus
Then a cheer brave boys, as we gaze around,
On the happy smiles of the homeward bound
Huzza, huzza, we're homeward bound,
Huzza, huzza, huzza, we're homeward bound

2nd
Years have passed since we sailed from our own native soil,
Our commerce and rights to mantain [sic]
But now we'll return with the fruits of our toil,
To our much loved Columbia again.

3d
The thoughts of reunion is dear to the heart,
of the wanderer, poor though he be.
He dreams of his home, and wakes with a start,
He is still far away on the sea

4th
Then a hail to the Star Spangled Banner, all hail,
Long, long, may it wave to the breeze.
Let this be our song, as we crowd on each sail,
Our Frigate's the pride of the sea.

These verses were Composed by John C. Thompson expressly for this Ship on the Homward bound passage from St. Paul de Loando to Portsmouth N.H.   U.S.A.

September 1861

September 1st Doldrums/Rain Squalls/uncomfortable/Torrid Zone

Sunday came in wet and squally. It rained very heavy in the morning watch. The men improved the time by giving themselves a thorough washing, which makes them look two shades whiter. The usual Sunday's inspection was dispensed with on account of the weather. At 10 A.M. it commenced clearing off. At half past 10 A.M. Divine Service was held on the gun deck. At 11 A.M. the sun came out, and the rest of the day was very pleasant. At noon we were in 6 degrees 21 miles north latitude and 39 degrees 12 miles west longitude.

We are now in the latitude of the Doldrums, or variable wind. A squall rises here very suddenly, and hardly are you aware of it, before it bursts upon you, and then, "Hurrah, there, and take in sail!" One of the squalls was brewing on our starboard quarter all the afternoon, and at 6 P.M. it came upon is, but it being almost aft we hardly felt it. It sent us along for two hours, at the rate of twelve knots. At 11 P.M. another squall with very heavy rain came upon our lee bow and caught us aback. Royals, topgallant sails and flying jib were furled; courses and spanker were hauled up.

The whole of the midwatch it rained a 2nd deluge. The watch was kept to work at the braces, and at eight bells there was not a man but what was wet through. During the intervals between bracing, the watch would stow themselves on the booms, under the boom cover, and it would make a horse laugh, to hear some poor fellow come in soaking wet, edging in, and swearing, he'd be D_d if he would ever come to sea again, he'd sooner go to the poor house first. And I can safely say it is not very comfortable, the wind whistling through the rigging, and the rain coming down Tremendously. Add to this a night so dark that you can hardly distinguish an object until you are upon it. You may get dozing under the lee of something on deck, when you are called to lay aft to the braces, you are probably wet through to the skin, and shivering, and then perhaps you have to go aloft to furl some sail, the same as we had. Then you will not wonder, if a person forms a resolution, not to come to sea again. But just as soon as the weather gets pleasant again, it is all forgotten. (The reader must bear in mind that we are now in the warmest part of the world; what it must be in the cold latitudes he can form his own opinion).

September 2nd   **Washing/all hands Reef Topsails**

Came in wet and squally. At 7 A.M. it cleared off a little, but just as soon as the port watch came on deck, it thickened up, and commenced to rain, and it came down good. All hands are washing themselves, blankets, clothing, and in fact everything that belongs to them. It is a rich treat to a sailor to get a little fresh water once in a while, that is if there is not much wind with it. At 11 A.M. it cleared off again, and the clothes lines, and rigging was covered with washed clothes and pea jackets. At noon, the master could not get an observation on account of the weather, but according to dead reckoning we were in 8.37 North latitude, and 39.29 West Longitude. During the afternoon, it commenced to thicken on our lee bow, and at 5 P.M. we had a passing squall. Royals and flying jib were furled, but were loosed and set again at half past five. It looks very threatening on our lee bow, and promises to be a nasty night. At four bells the boatswain called all hands to reef topsails. One reef was taken, and the topgallant sails and royals were set over them. This was done so as to be prepared, in case it should come on to blow during the night. We expect to get the N.E. trade wind out of all these squalls. We had several very heavy rain squalls during the night. The wind came from all points of the compass.

September 3d   **6 round of shot and 1 of shell fired at a Target/Rain**

In the morning watch the reefs were shaken out of the topsails, and all sail made. Port watch washed clothes. It is a fine morning but no wind, and half past 9 A.M. the drum beat to general quarters. The carpenters rigged a target (a barrel with a white flag and staff), it was dropped overboard, both batteries were cast loose, manned the starboard guns. The object was at the distance of 1200 yards. Each gun had orders to fire as soon as they could bring the object to bear. Six round of shot and one round of shell was fired from each gun. The firing gave satisfaction to the officers, although the target was still standing when we ceased firing. At half past twelve the drum beat the retreat, and all hands were piped to dinner. The latitude at noon: 9.44 North. We are now in a dead calm; at half past three P.M. we had another rain squall, but no wind. At 6 P.M. it was still calm. In the midwatch it rained very heavy for over an hour.

September 4th   **Serving out Clothing**

Came in wet, and no wind. At 6 A.M. it cleared off and old Sol came out screeching hot. Clothing was served out by the purser, for the last time. At noon the Latitude was 10 North, the ship having run 16 miles the last 24 hours. Very encouraging for homeward bounders. At 3 P.M. we had a light rain squall, with a light wind from the N.E. Some of the men say they are the Trades. At [illegible] P.M. the 3d division was exercised at dismounting guns and the 2nd division at small arms. At 6 P.M. we were going three knots, and it is awful warm. The
Warren Darlington
wind is from the Nd and Ed. The wind was very light all night.

September 5th   **Rain squalls/Reefing**

Port watch washed clothes, fine morning but no wind. At half past 9 A.M. had general fire quarters. At noon we were in 11 degrees North Latitude. At 5 P.M. we had a very heavy rain squall, and two more in the first watch. We had nothing but cat's paws, all day long from every point in the compass. In the midwatch we had a very severe squall, the topgallant sails and royals were furled, and one reef taken in the topsails; the fore, and main sails were then hauled close up and she remained so all the watch.

September 6th   **2419 miles from Home/Reefing/the North Star.**

This morning came in wet and squally. The reefs were shaken out of the top-sails, and the royals and topgallant sails set. The winds we get in these squalls are always in our favor. It rained heavy all this forenoon watch. We averaged four knots this forenoon. At noon the Latitude was 12.10 North, and Longitude 40.56 West, course N.W. and by N. Distance from Portsmouth, N.H. was 2419 miles. During the afternoon we had very little wind. At 6 P.M. we were going three knots. It looked very squally all round the horizon. One reef was taken in the topsails by the starboard watch, so as to be prepared on account of the bad weather. The usual general quarters for this week was dispensed with.

We are now in the latitude of the West India Islands, and it is very warm, but as we have been used to hot weather, we don't mind it much. We have given up the idea of getting the N.E. trade winds; we have now been about a week in the Doldrums and no signs of them yet. Last night the North Star was plainly visible during the last dog watch. We had several rain squalls during the night.

September 7th Holystoning

This morning came in wet and squally, with cat's paws from all points of the compass. At noon we were in 13.7 North Latitude. We did not clean the gun deck this forenoon on account of the weather, but at 2 P.M. the wind coming from the Eastward and beg[inning] to clear off, the port watch were sent down to holystone it. We scraped all the iron work and gave the deck a thorough holystoning. We had several passing rain showers during the afternoon, with a very heavy swell from the Nd. and Ed., a good sign of the N.E. trade winds. In the dog watch we set all the starboard studding sails. We were going seven knots. The wind was very steady all night.

September 8th North East Trade winds at last/reading the articles of war/Fighting/Sport/Traveling

Sunday came in fine with an eight knot breeze from the N.E. which we have no doubt are the Trade winds. At half past 9 A.M. had division inspection, and at 10 A.M. all hands were called to muster by the boatswain. The Articles of War were read by the 1st lieutenant. At half past ten we were piped down, and divine service on the gun deck. The wind is freshening; at 11 A.M. we were going eleven knots and a half. Everything is creaking and groaning. At noon we were in 15 degrees 27 miles North Latitude. It is a beautiful day and a glorious breeze. During the dinner hour two men got fighting on the gun deck. They were put in double irons in the brig and were told by the 1st luff that they would be court martialed tomorrow. It is a common occurrence to see one or two fights a day, but they don't get caught. If they have a dispute during the day, it is postponed till the hammocks are down and then they can have it without being disturbed. The next morning if a man has both his eyes shut up, or his nose broken, it is attributed to his last night's sport. The officers look and wonder, for they are never the wiser of it. It is only a hot-headed fellow that has a set to in the day time. At 2 P.M. we were going ten and a half knots. We averaged ten knots all this afternoon. At 6 P.M. we were going twelve knots. The wind still increasing, the topgallant studding sails were taken in.

September 9th 2 men tried by a Summary Court Martial/ Sentence of a Court Martial

This morning came in rainy, with the N.E. trade winds. Port watch washed clothes. It rained all the watch, starboard studding sails set alow and aloft. It cleared off; at 10 A.M. the main royal yard was sent down to fix the sail. At noon we were in Latitude 17.12 North and Longitude 467.26 West. At half past twelve sent up the main royal yard at 2 P.M. the two men that were fighting yesterday were tried by a summary court martial; the screen was up about fifteen minutes and then taken down. It does not take them long to put a fellow over the coals. During the afternoon the 2nd and 3d Divisions exercised small arms and single sticks, and the 1st division launch's fighting boat's crew were drilled at their howitzer.

At half past 5 P.M. all hands were called to muster to hear the sentences of a court-martial, which was as follows: James Hallett, Ordinary Seamen, charged with fighting and disorderly conduct (he pleaded guilty); his sentence was loss of one month's pay (fourteen dollars), two weeks in double irons in the brig in his watch below, and two weeks' Black List. The other was an O.S. named Peter Lawson; his sentence was loss of 1 month's pay (fourteen dollars), two weeks' Black List, and two weeks in double irons in the brig in his watch below. All hands were then piped down. At 6 P.M. we were going ten knots.

September 10th 1861.   sail ho/Spring our main top gallant yard

This morning came in fine with the North East trade winds. Going ten knots. The starboard watch washed clothes. Last evening we sighted a brig, going to the southward with all her studding sails set; at dark we lost sight of her. In the morning watch we sprung our main topgallant yard, and sent it on deck. At 11 P.M. we sent a new one aloft. At noon we were in 19.18 North Latitude and 51.30 West Longitude. We have been going nine knots all this forenoon. During the afternoon the 1st, 2nd, and 3d and 4th divisions exercised at big guns, small arms, single sticks and carbines. At 6 P.M. we were going eight knots.

September 11th   Sail ho

This morning came in very fine, N.E. trades going eight knots. Port watch scrubbed all the paint work on the spar deck in the morning watch. At noon we were in 21.26 North Latitude and 53.42 West Longitude. This afternoon the 2nd and 3d divisions exercised at big guns and small arms. The spar deck was painted by the port watch. At 6 P.M. we were going seven knots. At 7 P.M. a sail was reported by the cathead lookout on our starboard bow, it being so dark we could not make her out. She was standing to the southward.

September 12th 1861.   Gulf weed/Dolphins and Flying Fish

This morning came in fine with an eight knot breeze. At 9 A.M. all hands were sent on the gun deck to scrub paint work, finished at 11 A.M. At noon we were in 22 degrees and 21 miles North Latitude and 55.37 west Longitude. At half past twelve o'clock we took in all the studding sails and hauled close on a wind. We are now heading N.W. We were 1385 miles from Portsmouth at noon. There is plenty of Gulf weed passing by. The sea, as far as one can see, is full of dolphins and flying fish; some of them are very large. At 6 P.M. we were going eight knots. We painted the hammock clothes this afternoon.

September 13th sail ho

Two years, and 3 months in commission. This day came in fine with an eight knot breeze. Port watch washed clothes. This morning we commenced paint- ing the gun deck, on account of which we dispensed with the usual weekly general quarters. At half past ten A.M. a sail was reported on our weather beam, standing to the southward. We soon lost sight of her. At noon we were in 24.45 North Latitude and 59.41 West Longitude; the distance from Ports- mouth N.H. was 1195 miles. We averaged eight knots all this afternoon. At 6 P.M. we were nine and a half knots an hour.

September 14th sail ho/Painting

This morning came in fine, with but very little wind. Starboard watch washed clothes. At 9 A.M. two sails were reported by the lookout on the fore topmast crosstrees. Standing the same as we are, at noon we were in 25 degrees 41 miles North Latitude and 62.41 West Longitude. At 2 P.M. the wind died away to a dead calm. At 6 P.M. it is still calm; the two sails are still in sight. The ship's painter and his gang have been to work all day painting the gun deck. It remained calm all night.

September 15th catch a Shark

Sunday, and a dead calm. Courses are hauled up close, the ship has not got any steerage way. The sun pours down with a vengeance. At half past 9 A.M. all hands were called to quarters for inspection; we were dressed in white frocks, pants, and white hats. At 10 A.M. divine service was held on the gun deck. The Latitude at noon was 26.19 North Longitude 63.24 West. During the after- noon the forecastle men caught a large shark; after cutting off his tail they let him go again. It continued calm all this day and it is very warm. A sail is in sight on our lee bow, supposed to be the same one we saw yesterday.

September 16th 1861 Summary Court Martial/
Sentence of a Court Martial/Sail ho

This day came in calm. Starboard watch washed clothes. During the night a marine and a blue jacket got into a fight, and were put in the brig. They are to be tried by a summary court martial. The painter and his gang are to work, touching up the paint work. At noon we were in 26^d.30^m North latitude having made 11 miles since 12 o clock yesterday. Longitude 63.57 West. At 2 P.M. the summary court martial commenced. The 2nd and 3^d divisions exercised single sticks and small arms during the afternoon. At 3 P.M. we got a light wind from the Nd and Wd.

At half past 5 P.M. all hands were called to muster by the boatswain, to hear the sentences of a summary court martial. It was as follows: John Dwyer, Ordinary Seaman, charge disorderly conduct—specification of charge, that during his watch on deck he had a fight with John Hart, a marine private. He pleaded not guilty to the charge, but the court after mature deliberation found him guilty, and sentenced him to the loss of one month's pay (fourteen dollars); two weeks in the brig in double irons, during his watch below; and two weeks' extra police duty, to be assigned by the executive officer. The other, John Hart, marine private, had the same charges and specifications, and had the same sentence (his month's pay amounts to eleven dollars, it being his first enlistment).

There have been two brigs in sight all day. At 6 P.M. we were going four knots, heading W by N., being five points off our course. This 1st lieutenant is an awful man; if a person looks crosseyed at him, he will have him court martialed. He is a terror to both officers, and men. At eight o'clock it again became a dead calm.

September 17th   Dead Calm/Horse Latitudes

This morning came in calm with but very little wind. Port watch washed clothes. A sail is in sight on our port quarter. We are getting short, and the cooks were put on half allowance. The messes' [illegible] have been stopped; it occasions considerable murmuring among the ship's company. At noon the Latitude was 26.36 North, being six miles further north than we were yesterday. 65.07 West Longitude during the afternoon. The 1st 2nd and 3^d divisions exercised small arms, big guns, and single sticks. It had been a dead calm all this afternoon. At 6 P.M. all hands swung clean hammocks.

The surface of the sea is like glass, not a breath of wind to be seen anywhere. Vessels have been known to be becalmed here, at times, for twenty and twenty-five days. It is called in Nautical parlance the horse latitudes, the reason why I don't know, but according to all old salts' stories (and they have a story for everything) it is as follows: Between the West India islands and the United States, a number of vessels used to be employed in transporting horses from the latter to the former. When in and about this latitude they got becalmed for days and weeks, and getting short of water, they were obliged to throw their living cargo overboard, so as to save themselves from want, and also not to be spectators of the poor animals' death by that most horrible of deaths, thirst. This is the cause according to their account why they are so named Horse Latitudes.

September 18th   still calm

This morning came in very warm, and no wind whatever. The starboard watch scrubbed hammocks. The sun today is very hot; awnings spaced fore and aft the spar deck. At noon we were in 26 degrees 49 miles North Latitude, and [blank] West Longitude. It still continues calm. At 3 P.M. the 2nd division exercised small arms; at 5 P.M. the 1st and 3ᵈ divisions drilled at big guns. There is no sign of any wind as yet. We are looking for a breeze with a change of the moon, which will be full tomorrow. It is awful to be within a 1000 miles of home, and be becalmed. Everybody is under its influence. If you ask a person a question, you must not be surprised at getting a surly answer, and any attempt at joking is looked upon as an insult by those to whom it is directed.

The USS Sumpter *arrived in New York Harbor on September 15. Lieutenant Armstrong, commanding the* Sumpter, *remarked that "we do not return to our country with the glad emotions we hoped to realize after an absence on distant service, for armed rebellion and treason has desecrated our soil;—but we return with the desire to aid the Government in suppressing it, in upholding the honor of the Flag, in maintaining the Union we love, and the Constitution we are sworn to defend."* [1]

Fannie Hume, engaged to the Constellation's *First Lieutenant Rhind but now a full-hearted supporter of the Confederacy with her brother in the Confederate Army, was at home near Orange Court House, Virginia. She read in her newspaper of the* Sumpter's *return and that the rest of the African Squadron was homeward bound. Anticipating Rhind's return, she wrote in her journal, "The crisis, I suppose, is near at hand. I try not to feel anxious and impatient of the result. I hope to have strength to do my whole duty. I read over the package of old letters in lieu of later ones."* [2]

September 19th   A Breeze

A light air sprung up during the night, and this morning we are going a knot and a half with all the port studding sails set. Port watch scrubbed hammocks. We went three knots an hour all this afternoon. At noon we were in 27.22 North Latitude and Longitude 66.03 West, the distance from Portsmouth N.H. being 980 miles. During the afternoon the 4th division were exercised at carbine drill. At 6 P.M. we had the light breeze, going three knots. The brig is still in sight astern of us.

September 20th   890 miles from Home

During the morning watch we had a heavy rain squall. Starboard watch washed clothes. We had several rain squalls during the forenoon watch, which kept driving us ahead. At 11 A.M. it cleared off and left us a six knot breeze, right after which we improved by setting all the studding sails both sides. The brig is about ten miles astern of us. At noon we were in 28 degrees 36 miles North Latitude and 66 degrees 44 miles west Longitude, the distance from Portsmouth N.H. being 890 miles. We had a good breeze all the afternoon. At 6 P.M. we were going six and a half knots the brig is still in sight.

September 21st   Sail ho

During the midwatch last night we passed a vessel outward bound. She was too far off to be made out. This morning the port watch washed clothes. We had several light rain squalls during the watch. All the port studding sails set, at 9 A.M. all bags were piped up, and the starboard watch holystoned the gun deck. A rain squall coming up at 11 A.M., the bags were piped down. The brig is still in sight on our port quarter. At noon we were in Latitude 30.34 North and Longitude [blank] West. At 2 P.M., being my masthead, reported a sail, right ahead standing to the Eastward. At 3 P.M. the brig was out of sight astern. We went six knots all this afternoon. At 6 P.M. we were going six and a half knots, all the port studding sails set.

September 22nd   Struck aback in a heavy Squall/Bermudas, and
                                Cape Hatteras/Gulf Stream/Two sails in sight/
                                           latitude 32. 48 longitude 68.15

Sunday. At five o'clock this morning, we were struck aback with a heavy squall from the Nd, and Wd. We had the topmast and top gallant studding sails set, and the watch ahead just commenced scrubbing the spar deck down with sand, before the topmast studding came in, the yard snapped in halves, and the sails were tore to ribbons. The royals and top gallant sails were furled, topsails lowered on the caps, and reef tackles hauled out, and courses hauled up. The watch then double reefed the topsails. All the running gear was foul, being coiled up on rails, and all the gun deck ladders were unshipped to be scrubbed. The officer of the deck made noise enough to awaken all the watch below.

We had several squalls during the forenoon with rain. At 11 A.M. we got a roaring breeze from the Sd, and Wd, which sent us along at the rate of twelve knots an hour. The usual inspection was dispensed with today on account of the bad weather. We get no observation today, but according to dead reckoning we were 640 miles from Portsmouth N.H., where we can't expect anything else but bad weather. There is a couplet among sailors about these islands which says—"If the Bermudas let you pass, then beware of Cape Hatteras." We expect to cross the Gulf Stream tonight. At 2 P.M. a sail was reported on our starboard bow going to the Ed. At ½ 2 P.M. [2:30] we were going twelve knots. At 3 P.M. another sail was reported on our port bow, close hauled, under close reefed topsails, her topgallant sails, royals, and mainsail furled. We have got all the port studding sails set running before it. At 6 P.M. we were going eleven knots. Every fair wind we get, the hands are prophesying that we will get in such and such a time, but as soon as it dies away or comes ahead, their tune changes in another direction. By their calculations now, we are to be in Wednesday afternoon sure. At 7 P.M. a sail was reported by the cathead lookout, bearing a point on the port bow. We went eleven and twelve knots all night.

September 23d   Head Wind

This morning came in with an eleven knot breeze. All the port studding sails set. The port watch washed clothes. Had a light rain squall during the forenoon. At noon we were going twelve knots. Latitude 36.12 North Longitude [blank] West. At ten minutes past twelve the wind shifted to the N.W., which to us is dead ahead. Took in all the studding sails, and furled the royals. This makes all the boys feel blue again. Toward evening the wind began to shift to the Eastward; tacked ship. At 6 P.M. we were going five knot.

September 24th   Blowing/Reefing topsails/Gulf Stream/
Sail ho/Reefing the Foresail/a gale

This morning came in cloudy. Starboard watch washed clothes. At 6 P.M. we had a rain squall from the Nd and Ed. At 10 A.M. it began to blow very fresh; the topgallant sails were furled, topsails lowered on the caps and the reef tackles hauled out; the courses were hauled up close. At half past ten we put three reefs in the topsails, and one reef in the mainsail, and set them. At noon, we were in 37.21 North Latitude and [blank] West Longitude. We are now in the south edge of the Gulf Stream, going six and seven knots; the wind being from the N.E., it is very chilly. We are abreast of New York. Being about 220 miles from it, we are 350 miles from Portsmouth N.H. at 5 P.M. the lookout on the foretopsail yard reported a sail on our starboard bow, under close reef topsails. She is standing more to the westward than we are, probably bound to New York. At 6 P.M. we were going five and a half knots. The reefs are still in the topsails and mainsail. At intervals we have a light rain.

At half past 7 P.M., the wind increasing, the foresail was reefed. Such a hollering there is when a sail is reefed is enough to make a person deaf. The 1st luff gives an order, which is repeated by the 2nd, 3ᵈ and 4th lieutenants, four midshipmen, the boatswain and his four mates and all the captains of the tops, and the men are singing out to let go this, or haul up that, or light the sail over to windward; [everything] must be repeated by every man on the yard. The sails were reefed today in the watch. At eight o'clock, the wind still increasing, the port watch close reefed the fore and mizzen topsails, and furled the mainsail. Everything now being snug, the watch stowed themselves in the hammock nettings, and on the booms. Once in a while a heavy spray comes over. It blowed very fresh all night.

September 25th   **Shaking out the Reefs/Sail ho/Shindig/Sounding**

This morning came in cloudy. The wind is moderating; at 6 P.M. we shook two reefs out of the topsails, and fore and mainsails, and set the topgallant sails and jib, and at 10 A.M., the wind going down, we shook out all the reefs, and set the royals and flying jib. We are now going ten and eleven knots on the wind. We are three points off of our course, two sails in sight to windward heading the same as we are. At noon, by observation we were in 39 degrees North Latitude and 70 degrees 53 miles west Longitude, that being eight miles to the westward of our port, and the wind still driving us to the westward. At 2 P.M. all hands drew their grog and ration money. Everybody but the boys drinks their grog now. At 4 P.M. the masthead lookout reported two more sails. At 6 P.M. we were going five knots, the wind coming from the Nd, and Wd. It is clear and cold, stockings and underclothes are in great demand. In the last dog watch the boys got up a shindig on the gun deck, and they employed themselves finely until eight bells. We hove the deep sea lead two or three times during the night, but got no soundings. We are about 245 miles from Portsmouth, N.H.

September 26th   **scrubbing paint work/bending the Cables/**
                                     Nantucket Shoals

This morning came in fine, the wind is ahead. Starboard watch washed clothes, and the [*sic*] scrubbed the lower masts from the tops down. Seven sails in sight. At 6 A.M. we got a cast of the deep sea lead, and found bottom at forty-six fathoms, a blue mud sticking to the lead. We are about forty-five miles from Block Island and about fifty miles from Sandy Hook. At 9 A.M. the port watch scrubbed the white streak. We tacked ship several times during the forenoon. At noon we were in 40 degrees 22 miles North Latitude, but we are away to the westward of our port, the distance from Portsmouth N.H. being 280 miles, which is a great ways with a head wind. The cables were bent at 2 P.M. by the starboard watch. [*That is, the anchor chains were attached to the anchors in preparation for anchoring.*] At 6 P.M. we were going nine knots. We are now close to Nantucket Shoals, standing off so as to get a good offing. The air here is beautiful, pure, everybody on board feels invigorated by it. As for myself I feel like a new person; the coast of Africa made a person's system drowsy and heavy. Although I did not feel sick, I can't say that I felt as well as I could wish to. We get soundings several times during the night.

Hearing today indirectly from Lieutenant Rhind's sister, Fannie Hume knew the Constellation *was on its way home on August 12. She wondered anxiously what Rhind's sentiments about the conflict would prove to be: "Oh! If I could only know!!"*[3]

September 27th   Land ho/a Row with the Boatswain/cutting remarks/
Hailing the Lookout/Gay head/Sail ho/
Nantucket Shoals/Light Ship/a good Breeze

During the night a light was reported on our lee bow, supposed to be Gay Head Light; we tacked ship and stood off. At four o'clock we again tacked ship and stood in. At daylight, it being my masthead, I went aloft after washing my clothes (it being our watch's wash morning). The lookout is stationed on the main topsail yard. I, wishing to have a good look, took a tramp up to the royal yard, and on looking sharp I discovered land on our lee bow. A fog bank just rising obscured it from view in a few moments. I sang out in a lusty voice, "Land ho!"—"Where Away?"—was the response from the officer of the deck. I answered, "Broad on our lee bow." I had hardly time to get the sentence finished, when I was greatly astonished and a good deal surprised, on hearing somebody calling me a Damn Fool, and also that I had a substance in my eyes that is altogether out of place in that locality. On looking to see who it was, I perceived our boatswain perched on the foretopsail yard. He then added, "Youngster, you are very highminded (alluding to my position on the royal yard) and you had better keep your eyes open, and not report a fog bank for land." Being stung by his last remark, and also feeling confident that I saw the land, I told him that I saw houses on it. This started him up: "O you bugger, Damn you, it is lucky for you, that I ain't near you." By his gestures I know he meant business, but there being the space between the fore and main masts between us, I did not feel alarmed. He then went down, and reported to the officer of the deck, that it was nothing but a fog bank. The captain, coming on deck at this stage, hailed me, "Topsail yard, there! Sir—go up to the royal yard and see if you can see what you reported as land now." I told him that I could see it from where I was. He then sent the boatswain with a spy glass on the foretopsail yard, to see if he could make it out.

In about five minutes he made it out; the fog bank now rising, the white sandy banks of Gay Head were to be seen plainly from the deck about ten miles to leeward. The boatswain then in a very handsome manner apologized to me for his previous abuse. He also said that I had very good eyesight to see through a fog bank. (My eyesight is not good, I was for six months unable to read any kind of print, caused by the African Coast weather, but now they are in good condition.) I now reported three sails, one on our weather quarter, and two more close under the land. At eight bells I was relieved, and coming on deck I was complimented by my watchmates as being the 1st one that saw the broadside of America. At half past eight o'clock we tacked ship and stood off so as to weather the shoals of Nantucket. We are about twenty-five miles to leeward of the Nantucket light ship, South Shoals.

At 2 P.M. we sighted the light ship a quarter of a point on our weather bow. We made two tacks, and passed the light ship a quarter of a mile to windward going nine knots. She hoisted the stars and stripes at her peak, and dipped it to us; we returned the salute. It is the first one we have seen since leaving St. Paul de Loando. Every vessel we have seen hoisted English colors, which makes us think that something is wrong at home. It is almost four months since we have had any news from home.

The wind is freshening; at eight bells we squared yards, and set studding sails alow and aloft, both sides. We expect to get in tomorrow; it is 135 miles from the light ship to Portsmouth, N.H. The ship's company are now light-hearted on account of the prospect of getting in so soon. At ten o'clock we were going ten knots and a half across Massachusetts Bay.

September 28th	Reefing/Land Ho/The Pilot comes on Board/ The News/a Head Wind/Fort Constitution/ Came to an Anchor in Portsmouth N.H./Cheering/ Maine and New Hampshire/Down Royal Yards/ Scraping spars/*Mohican San Jacinto* and *Sumpter*

We averaged ten and twelve knots all night. At 5 A.M. it began to thicken up, and [we] furled the royals and topgallant sails, hauled up the courses. The wind increasing to a gale, we close reefed the topsails. It is very thick and foggy. At 9 A.M. the wind abated a little, and the fog began rising. We discovered land on our weather bow, about fifteen miles off. We set the topgallant sails, and we went eight knots. At half past ten we hove to, and took a fisherman on board to pilot us in. At eleven o'clock, we were in sight of the Isle of Shoals. We hove to, and took a regular pilot. We learnt from him that the U.S. Sloop of War *Portsmouth* arrived here last Tuesday, thus beating us two days on the passage, she being forty-six days and our ship being forty-eight days. We also learnt the particulars of the Battle of Lexington, and all the news generally. It being a head wind for us, we cannot go up the river to the Navy Yard. The river being very narrow, we will have to come to an anchor off of Fort Constitution, until we can get a fair wind. We are now going nine knots, took in the topgallant sails.

We passed Fort Constitution at a quarter before twelve o'clock, within a stone's throw. We were hailed by some individual with a trumpet that looked big enough for a steamboat's smoke stack, in the following style: "Ship Ahoy!" —"Halloa," from our 1st luff. "What ship is that?"—"The U.S. Ship *Constellation*," was the answer, when they fired one gun, and gave us three hearty cheers. We at this moment clewed up the topsails, and dropped anchor in eleven fathoms water, abreast Fort Constitution, Portsmouth, N.H. After furling sail and getting the ship to rights, we got ready to fire a salute of thirteen guns for the Commodore of the Navy Yard. We fired it, and it was returned from the battery at the Navy Yard. We were now saluted from Fort McRea, which is on the right, of the river, with nine guns; what that was for I could not learn.[3] They also gave us three cheers; we returned the salute, and manned the starboard rigging, and gave them three cheers back. We then manned the port rigging, and cheered the volunteers on Fort Constitution, in return for their cheer and salute of welcome.

This place at this position looks very bleak and dreary. The Isle of Shoals, with its lighthouse, is to be seen, with the sea breaking over it (there is a N.E. wind blowing, which accounts for that), Fort Constitution is on the left of the river's entrance, and Fort Mc Rea on the right. We are anchored, between the two, within a stone's throw of either. The states of Maine and New Hampshire are very close here; nothing but a rivulet separates them. The Navy Yard is in the town of Kittery, Maine, and Portsmouth is across the river, in New Hampshire. We will have to wait here, for a fair wind to go up the river to the Navy Yard, which is about a mile and a half from where we are at anchor. There are two lighthouses at the entrance of the river.

The *Portsmouth* crew are stripping their ship; they expect to go ashore Monday the 30th. At 2 P.M. we went to dinner, and when the hands were turned to, we sent down royal yards and scraped spars, and began to get the ship to rights. At 5 P.M. we went to supper. The ship is just like a bedlam, everybody talking and no listeners. Union, Secession, War, getting paid off, are among the principal topics of conversation. We have got today's papers from Boston, and learnt of the arrival of the *Mohican*, which vessel, according to their own accounts, was going to make the passage in thirty days. We also heard of the arrival of the *San Jacinto,* and *Sumpter.* All hands are in excellent spirits, and elated with the prospects of being paid off soon. The weather here to us is very chilly. Indeed, this is the place where, all sailors say, that the people dig up sunrise with a shovel, and also that this is [the] place, that the missionaries from the civilized countries come to, in order to teach them Christian doctrine. In fact the appearances, from where we are at anchor, are not very good. This evening was very chilly.

| September 29th | Holystoning Decks/Painting Ship/Jerry Gullison the Bum Boat Man/His appearance |

Sunday. The hands were turned out at two bells (5 o'clock). It was very chilly and some of the boys expressed their feelings by chattering their teeth and slapping their hands together. After the hammocks were stowed in the nettings, orders were passed by the 1st lieutenant, for each part of the ship to get up holystones and sand, and holystone all the decks; three hands from each part of the ship to go outside and scrub paint work. These orders did not suit the boys at all, but they couldn't be disobeyed, go they must, and at it they went. The water was very cold to us, tramping about the decks, ankle deep in water. At seven bells (half past seven o'clock) we had them dried, and they are as white as snow.

As soon as the hands were turned to after breakfast, stagings were rigged over the side to paint ship. Everybody went at it with brushes and rags, and by ten o'clock we had her painted from the hammock rails to the water's edge. She now looks splendid both inside and out. The river is full of boats, looking at us, and they say she looks beautiful. We are now waiting anxiously for a fair wind to go up to the Navy Yard.

Ever since we left the Coast of Africa the ship's company have been talking about an individual by the name of Jerry Gullison, a bum boat man and boarding house keeper. Those that have had any dealings with him, say he is a notorious rascal. He swindled some of our men when they came home last cruise. There has been more talk about him, than there has been about Old Abe himself. Every boat that came alongside, somebody would sing out, "Here is Jerry Gullison," when every body would ask to see him, so anxious were they to get a glimpse of him. After getting sold a number of times by this dodge we at last saw him on board, and I believe the whole ship's company were on the spar deck looking at him. His appearance does not justify the remarks made about him; he looks like a very respectable sort of personage. But as appearances are deceitful, we must not judge him by his looks. As I do not know him personally I can't say much about him. We are very anxious to know whether we are to be paid off or not. At 6 P.M. hammocks were piped down, and by half past eight o'clock everybody was turned in.

The 1860 U.S. Census shows a Jeri Gunnerson, trader, age forty-six, in Kittery, Maine.

September 30th	Fair wind/Boarding house keepers from Boston and New York/Heaving Short/up anchor/underway/in the Harbor/at Anchor off the Navy Yard/Down Royal Yards/Kittery Navy Yard/To be inspected/Romantic

The spar deck was holystoned. We then took the gig, and oiled the copper. At eight A.M. crossed royal yards and piped to breakfast. There is a fair wind this morning and we are going up to the Navy Yard as soon as the tide turns. At 9 A.M. the messenger, was got up, and the cable brought to, and at 10 A.M. everything was in readiness to get underway. The flag officer and his baggage left us this forenoon; the captain went ashore in his boat at 11 A.M. The boats were hoisted at half past eleven. We are now waiting for the pilot. He is expected every minute. At twelve o'clock piped to dinner. The ship is full of boarding house keepers from Boston and New York. There is great news by them, about old acquaintances &c. &c. At 2 P.M. the pilot came on board and ordered ninety fathoms of starboard cable to be taken out of the lockers, and ranged on the gun deck. We are to moor the ship close to the Navy Yard with both anchors. At half past 2 P.M. he gave the order to heave short, which we did in very quick time. When the boatswain called all hands to loose sail, everything was loosed but the royals. We then hove up the anchor, and sheeted home the topsails only. The jib and flying jib were hoisted, and at 3 P.M. we were on our way up the river. There is a five knot current running with us. We have just sail enough to give the ship steerage way. The river is very narrow— a copper could be tossed ashore on either side. The country on both sides presents quite a beautiful appearance; in fact more than could be expected, to judge from the looks of Fort Constitution. The river on both sides is full of sailing boats, following us.

At 4 P.M. we entered the harbor or bay, and within a hundred yards of the navy yard, we let go the starboard anchor, and ran out ninety fathoms of cable. The port anchor was then dropped, and the topsails clewed up. The ship brought up like a swan, in presence of 2000 spectators in the navy yard. The *Portsmouth* is at the wharf close to us. We then hove in the starboard chain to 50 fathoms, the yards were then squared, messenger payed below, royal sheets, and clew lines, topsail reef tackles unbent and sent below. We then went to supper, and at sundown we sent down royal yards. The *Portsmouth's* crew have stripped their ship down to her lower rigging, topmasts housed; they are now taking out the provisions.

This is quite a pretty place. Portsmouth is about half a mile from us. There are about 2000 men at work at this Navy Yard. They are building three new gun boats; one is about ready for launching. There are two large ship houses here. In one, is the *Franklin,* the steamer we heard so much talk about on the coast. The *Alabama,* 74 line of battle ship, is in the other. There is quite a large dry dock here, in which there is one of the gun boats. There are also several other large buildings, among which are the naval store houses and steam saw mills. The harbor is like a mill pond, but there is very deep water. It is occupied almost exclusively by government vessels, and a few coasting schooners. It is full of moorings and buoys. At half past 6 P.M. hammocks were piped down, and the men had quite a shindig on the gun deck. We are to be inspected at General Quarters tomorrow, by the Navy Yard officials. I never since I have been in this ship knew things to work so well as it has today. Everybody with a will, it is a credit to us, the way she was brought to anchor here. I am not a very romantic individual, but the way the city of Portsmouth looks with all its lights, and the ringing of the bells, is music to my ears. I suppose being away from such things so, has the effect of producing such a sensation.

October 1861

1st Captain Pearson and others inspecting the ship's
company/U.S. Sloop *Portsmouth* goes out of commission/
Exercising the batteries/Dismounting guns/Small Arms Drill/
Single Sticks/Out Boats/Man and arm boats/
Landing a Sailors Brigade/all over/comments/Boats

As soon as the hands were turned to, all three decks were holystoned. We were
all the morning cleaning the ship for inspection. At 6 A.M. we took our three
Lieutenants: B. P. Loyal, W.R. Butt midshipman, and Lieutenant Steven of the
Portsmouth, in our boat, and two other gentlemen. They are under charge of a
U.S. Marshall, they are going to Fort Levenworth [*sic*], La Fayette. At half past
9 A.M. our boat went ashore, and brought on board Captain Pearson [*commander of Portsmouth Navy Yard*], two Lieutenants, and several other gentlemen, to inspect the ship and crew. They arrived on board at a quarter of ten
A.M. The *Portsmouth*'s crew now manned their rigging, and gave three cheers,
and their flag was hauled down, thereby putting her out of commission. Her
crew then went out of her with their bags and hammocks. At ten o'clock our
drum beat to General Quarters, cast loose both batteries. After looking all
over the ship to see if everything was in its proper place for an engagement,
they worked us at both sides for half an hour, and then we manned the starboard battery and worked it for another half an hour. The 1st captain, 1st
loader, and 1st sponger of each gun, acting as captain alternately. The inspectors asked questions of the guns' crews, relating to their duties. They overhauled the most minutest things; this being done with satisfaction, they shifted
guns from one side to the other, and dismounted others. Orders were then
given to run out and secure, which was done very quickly. The sailtrimmers
were then piped away, and they with the master's division, fished some of the
masts, and spars. They shot most of our braces away. They were stoppered,
and preventers got up, in very quick time, The drum then beat the retreat, and

the 1st division of small arm men were ordered aft upon the quarter deck, with their muskets, and drilled in most all the Light Infantry movements for twenty minutes, when they were dismissed. The 2nd division were then exercised at single sticks, and gave general satisfaction.

This being all the inspectors wanted to see of this kind of drill (we had general fire quarters between this), they gave orders to out boats, and the way the booms were cleared, yard and stay tackles got up, was a caution; all the boats were out in fifteen minutes after the order was given. They then gave orders to man and arm all boats, which was done very quickly. The howitzers were in the launch, the 1st and 2nd Cutter carried the Marine Corps. We all formed in a line with the launch in the centre, under command of our 2nd Lieutenant. Orders were then given to land on the beach, which was done in very good order, the launch's howitzers firing, as soon as they got it ashore, the small arm men going through several important maneuvers. Orders were given to embark, and we returned on board. It being now 1 P.M. and the inspectors being entirely satisfied that the ship's company were well drilled, gave orders that we should cease drilling and go to dinner, which we did at one bell (half past one o clock [*oddly Leonard is mistaken here: half past one is* three *bells*], it being three and a half hours' drilling). We landed on the beach near the Navy Yard, in presence of all the workmen. It being the dinner hour, they had a good opportunity of seeing the Elephant in a new style. I don't think the inspectors could find a worse place to land in the harbor, all rocks, and grass, which prevented the boats to come within fifteen yards of the beach. There was no help for us, we had to go, up to our middle in mud and water.

The inspection generally gave good satisfaction to the inspectors, but I can safely say that it was almost the worst general quarters that I have seen in the ship since she went into commission. The reason was we had no officers. Our officers resigning as soon as they came in made it very bad for us. There was nobody to give us the orders, and cheer us on in our exercise. Only one lieutenant exercised the gun deck batteries, when there ought to be four [lieutenants] and three midshipmen. The men did better than could be expected under the circumstances. During the afternoon some of the boats were brought to the Navy Yard for good. We are going to take out the powder and shell tomorrow and haul alongside of the wharf, we are going to strip the ship and take everything out of her, the *Portsmouth*'s crew are to be paid off Thursday, so we understand. At six o'clock hammocks were piped down.

The three officers who refused to swear allegiance to the Union were taken to Fort Lafayette (not Leavenworth — Leonard's slip of the pen), an old fort located near New York City, where the eastern support of the Verrazano-Narrows Bridge now stands, which was used throughout the war to hold political prisoners and prisoners of war.

The Portsmouth, New Hampshire, Navy Yard. *Gleason's Pictorial*, July 23, 1853. Gilliland Collection.

Lt. Benjamin P. Loyall became a lieutenant and eventually commander, Confederate States Navy.[1] *Mdn. Walter R. Butt became a Confederate midshipman and was aboard CSS* Virginia *during the Battle of Hampton Roads. Lt. H. K. Stevens was by the following June executive officer of the CSS Arkansas, at Vicksburg.*

October 2nd — Taking out Powder/Warping alongside the Wharf/ Important Rumors

At seven o'clock this morning, all hands went to breakfast. The fires were then put out, and at 8 A.M. we commenced taking out powder, shot, and shell, and it came out with a will. At 9 A.M. we took Captain Dornin's baggage ashore, and had a run all over Portsmouth until dinner hour, when returned on board. The powder is all out. We are now waiting for slack tide to warp the ship alongside the wharf. The decks are lumbered up with chains, hawsers, tackles, and mooring chocks. We had to heave up both anchors, which was a very hard job. At half past 2 P.M. we were alongside the wharf. We then had dinner. All the afternoon was occupied in mooring the ship, we had to get the off moorings. We then cleared up decks and piped to supper, which was at half past 5 P.M.

At half past 6 P.M. all hands have got a story afloat, that we are to be sent out again, which causes quite an excitement. The Boston papers say that all those on board our ship that have six months to serve, have got to go. That order brings me in, as I have eight months to serve after the 13th of this present month, I then being two years and four months shipped. It is hard, but it can't be helped. I am perfectly willing to go provided they give me time to see my friends before I go, which I suppose the government will allow. Hammocks were piped down at half past 6 P.M. I got two letters from home this evening. Good news.

October 3rd — Stripping the Ship/the *Franklin*

This morning the decks, were [illegible]. Had breakfast at 7 bells. and at 1 bell we commenced to strip ship. We unbent sail, and sent down all yards and topgallant masts, and took all the gun gear out, all the rigging and spars were handed on wharf by 3 P.M. we housed the topmasts, and left the main yard standing. The men worked nobly today, we are going to leave her, as soon as everything is out of her, which will be by Saturday afternoon. I had a good run over the Navy Yard and had a look at the *Franklin*, she is a perfect beauty.

The Franklin, *a five-thousand-ton screw frigate, had been laid down in 1854 but was not launched until 1864, when it was sent to the European Squadron.*

It is a sight worth seeing to look at a person's friends coming to see them after so long an absence. Brothers, sisters, fathers, and mothers, our ship's company are with a very few exceptions all young men and it being their first trip from home, their folks are overjoyed at seeing them. We are going to break out the hold tomorrow and take out the provisions &c. &c.

At 6 P.M. the hammocks were piped down. For my part I am very tired, I being aloft all day, and I calculate to make a good night's sleep, and by the appearances of my brother tars, they are no better off than I am.

October 4th   Breaking out the Hold/Sharpers & Sailors/
                                       Taking in a sailor/piped down

The hands were called at 5 o'clock this morning, the After Guard, and port watch Mizzen top men, were set to work breaking out the after sail room; all the maintopmen, and the Starboard watch mizzen topmen are breaking out the fore and main holds, and cable tiers; the forecastlemen and foretopmen are to work at the forward sail rooms and yeoman's room, and the way that the provisions, and sails &c. &c. are coming out is a caution, one gang is on the pier stowing them as fast as they are coming out.

The ship and wharf is crowded with landsharks, and sharpers, ready to light on some shellback. These sharpers are very good judges of human nature, and have also a good insight into the study of phrenology. If in their observations, they come across any of our boys whose craniums are profuse with the bumps of benevolence or any of the other foolish bumps, they draw them into conversation, the result of which is, that a mysterious looking black bottle is passed from sharper's coat pocket into the shirt bosom of the son of Neptune, who may be seen an hour afterwards, practicing a corkscrew walk or trying to walk on his head. The next thing he does is go to one of the officers, and abuses him, for some real, or imaginary wrong, done him by the aforesaid officer sometime during the cruise. Our hero is then ironed hand and foot and put below, where in his sober moments he can repent of his folly. In the meantime sharper is not idle. When Jack gets paid off he looks out for him, and he is not slow in bringing to Jack's memory the favor (if it can be called such) he done him. Jack, not wanting to be under a compliment to anybody, asks him to go round with him. They go carousing together and the first thing our late shipmate knows, his money and sharper is missing. This is only one of a thousand ways that a sailor is robbed.

At 5 P.M. the hold was clear. We knocked off for the day and cleared up decks. The spirit room is to be broke out tomorrow, also the shot lockers. At half past 6 P.M. hammocks were piped down, some of the boys, got a fiddler, and had a dance on the starboard side of the gun deck. All hands are in excellent spirits, with the prospect of getting out of the ship tomorrow. At 9 o'clock all hands were piped into their hammocks and by a quarter past everything was still.

October 5th 1861. Breaking out the spirit room and shot lockers/all hands
to muster/a speech by the 1st luff/Leaving the ship/
Hurrah for Boston/taking the oath of Allegiance/
Arrival in Boston/At Home/going to Portsmouth/
Paying off/Prize Ticket/Observations

At 5 o'clock this morning, the hands were turned out, and hammocks, were stowed on the half deck between the guns, on account of the rain. It is a very disagreeable morning, raining heavy, and very chilly. Part of the men are to work clearing the Spirit Room. At 11 A.M. we broke out the shot lockers and rolled the shot onto the wharf. Most of the boys are selling their clothes, bedding, &c. for almost nothing. Those who are buying, will make something on them [but] these very same men who are selling their clothes now, will be shipped [will reenlist] in less than two weeks, and will have to get a new outfit. At 12 o'clock the boatswain piped to dinner. Everything is done in the ship now.

At half past 12 all hands were called to muster, on the half deck on account of the rain. A short speech was made by the 1st Lieutenant (A.C. Rhind). He said, "Men! the work being now all done in the ship I have got orders to let you go from the ship. You will get your discharges, and you will also be paid off on Monday or Tuesday. Which, I am not certain. The purser has written to Washington for your prize money, but he has not got an answer as yet; therefore I do not know whether you will get that money when you are paid off or not." (At this moment one of the boys sung out, "Three cheers for Uncle Sam!" and it was given with a will.) He then proceeded, "I do not want to hear any confusion while leaving. You can now take your bags and hammocks, and go. The marines will stay by the ship until further orders." Three more cheers were given, and all hands started for their luggage, and the way that the bags and hammocks went over the side into the boats was a terror to the boatmen.

The old ship *Constellation*'s crew leave her

About ten of us got into a little sloop and started for Portsmouth in the middle of a rain squall, and at ten minutes of 2 P.M. we arrived at the wharf, overjoyed at finding ourselves once more free. We got our luggage on an express wagon, took a look at the old ship, that we spent so many days together in both good and bad, and started for the Railroad Depot, as it was our party's intention to go to Boston. The rest of the ship's company started in different directions. At half past 2 P.M. we arrived at the depot, and had our baggage checked. The train not started until half past 5, we rambled about the town, but it being a very wet day, there was nothing to be seen.

Two circumstances happened which I had forgotten. Yesterday afternoon, Captain Pearson of the Navy Yard came on board, and all hands had to take the Oath of Allegiance, by holding up their right hand and swearing, "So, help me God." Nine cheers was given for the Union, and we were then piped down. We swung clean hammocks last evening.

U.S. ship *Constellation* goes out of commission

At 5 P.M. we arrived at the depot again, and waited for the train that was to bring us to Boston, and some of us to our homes. At half past 5 P.M. we got aboard the cars, and started. The train was full of Sharpers, Blacklegs, and Courtesans. There was about 40 blue jackets in the train. Some of our boys, feeling merry, sang all the way. About ten minutes past 8 P.M. we arrived, at the Eastern Railroad Depot for Causeway St., Boston, where some of the boys' relations and friends were ready to receive them. Two of us put our things on an express wagon, and started for Charlestown, Mass. where we arrived a little before 9 P.M., and it is needless to mention here what a reception we met with at home, it is too good to be described. My folks are all well, and in excellent spirits, and overjoyed at seeing me safe home.

The next day I remained at home, and was visited by my former friends and acquaintances, who were very glad to see me, and they gave me invitations to visit them, which if I do nothing else it will take me a month to fulfill.

During his time aboard, the Constellation *covered 42,950 miles while under way 406 days.*[2]

Paid Off, and Discharged from the
United States Navy
On Thursday the 10th day of October 1861.
after a
Two year, three months and twenty eight days
Cruise

Having learnt that we would not be paid off until Wednesday, we did not go up to Portsmouth Wednesday morning. We went to the depot, and met our 2nd lieutenant, who told us we would not be paid off until the next day. We of course did not go up. The next morning we took the half past 7 A.M. train, and started for Portsmouth, N.H. where we arrived at 10 A.M. and then started for the Navy Yard. At 11 A.M. they commenced paying off. At half past 12 o'clock I got my money and discharge from the navy, also a prize ticket, or a paper which certifies that I was on board the *Constellation* when she captured the barque *Cora,* and brig *Delitia* on the Coast of Africa. I suppose it will cost us all of it to get the money. Uncle Sam is very mean in respect to prize money. He gives it to the officers, but the men have to get it through a lawyer, who takes the whole of it in fees. At half past 2 P.M. we again arrived at Portsmouth, and it being a fine afternoon we had a walking observation of the city, the fashion, &c. &c. Four of us had our Ambrotypes taken together in sailor's clothes. I always thought I was homely, but the picture that we had taken today, makes me look as if I had lost all my friends. But I suppose the picture is a good one. But some people have a conceit about their looks. I am one of that class; if the picture don't flatter me, I am not satisfied. My comrades tell me it is a good picture, and I set myself down, as one of the ugly ones. At half past 5 P.M. we again took the cars for home, where we arrived at a quarter before 9 P.M.

All's well that ends well.

The following is an exact copy of our Prize tickets

no. 201. I certify that William Leonard Ordinary Seaman was on board the U.S. Ship Constellation when she captured the barque Cora, on the Coast of Africa 25th of Sept 1860. and is entitled to share in said prize Also in the brig Delicia captured 21st Dec 1859 by same vessel

approved   Jno. W. Hambleton
                  pay master
J.S. Nicholas   Captain

The Cora was sold at auction by the U.S. marshal in February 1861. The ship brought $8,900.00, and its cargo brought $696.62. Subtracting $824.94 of costs left $8,771.68. By statute half went to the Naval Retirement Fund, leaving $4,385.84 as prize money to be divided among the crew of the Constellation.[3]

The greater prize was the African recaptured slaves. For each of 696 landed alive in Liberia, the government gave a bounty of $25.00, or $17,400.00 also to be divided among the Constellation's crew. Leonard's share was about $23.00.

Epilogue

William Leonard, paid off from the *Constellation* on October 10, 1861, went home to Charlestown. On September 5, 1862, he enlisted in the local Hamilton Guard. Two weeks later, on September 18, 1862, he married twenty-two-year-old Mary Moloney. They had six children, of whom three survived to adulthood. The Hamilton Guard became a company of the Fifth Regiment of Massachusetts Volunteer Infantry, for nine months' service. Shipped to North Carolina, the regiment conducted various operations against the Confederates. Though the regiment served until July 1863, Leonard was mustered out early for medical reasons; while on picket duty near Washington, N.C., he was hospitalized for a severe bout of malaria. Discharged from the hospital and the army on March 4, 1863, he returned home and began employment in the rigging loft at the Charlestown Navy Yard on March 26.

In March 1864, despite all the warnings he had written into his journal aboard the *Constellation*, Leonard again enlisted in the navy, this time for service aboard the USS *Cornubia*. Built as a coastal steamer for a Welsh shipping line, the *Cornubia* was purchased by the Confederate government for service as a blockade runner. Captured by the U.S. Navy, it was commissioned as the *USS Cornubia*. With Leonard in the crew, it served on the Gulf Coast until being decommissioned in August 1865.

Leonard presumably lived and worked in the Boston area from then on, though the first available record from that period has him working as a messenger for the Osgood and Co. express company on October 26, 1869. In this job he shuttled the 63 miles between Boston and Worcester on the Fitchburg and Worcester and Nashua Railroads, traveling by his reckoning a total of 151,872 miles during the next three years. When that company suspended operations on October 1, 1872, Leonard went to work as a driver for the U.S. and Canada Express Company. On December 19, 1889, at the American

Express Co. stable in south Boston, he was killed by falling through a scuttle to the floor twelve feet below.

Flag Officer William Inman was placed on the retired list effective December 1, 1861. Promoted to commodore on the retired list in 1867, he died in Philadelphia in 1874.

Capt. John Smith Nicholas returned to his home in Bound Brook, New Jersey, where he died on July 18, 1865.

Fannie Page Hume broke off her engagement to Lieutenant Rhind. Unable to return his letters because of the war, she finally burned them on Christmas Day 1862. On February 18, 1865, she married a cousin, Confederate artillery officer Lt. Col. Carter Braxton. She died in Richmond on June 16, 1865.

Lt. Alexander Colden Rhind failed in his efforts to reconnect with Fannie Hume, but the war made his career. Given command of the USS *Crusader* two months after leaving the *Constellation,* he distinguished himself in taking and destroying Confederate works on rivers in the vicinity of Edisto Sound. On April 7, 1863, he commanded the ironclad USS *Keokuk* participating in an unsuccessful attack on Fort Sumter. Riddled with ninety hits from Confederate guns, the ship sank the next day. In December 1864 Rhind took the USS *Louisiana,* loaded with powder, to explode under the walls of Fort Fisher, near Wilmington, North Carolina. After the war he held various commands afloat and ashore, retiring in 1883 as a rear admiral. He died in New York City on November 8, 1897. He never married.

Notes

Unless specifically noted otherwise, correspondence cited here is from National Archives RG 45 (Naval Records). Within that group letters to the secretary of the navy (Isaac Toucey until March 1861 and Gideon Welles after that date, except for a brief period when the identity of Lincoln's secretary of the navy was not yet known to the African Squadron and letters were addressed simply to "Secretary of the Navy") from Flag Officer Inman as commander of the African Squadron will be found in the African Squadron file. Other official correspondence will be found in the appropriate files of "Letters received by" or "Letters from" the secretary of the navy.

June 1859

1 *Boston Daily Advertiser*, June 27, 1859.
2 *Boston Daily Advertiser,* September 14, 1859; Bartlett, *Presidential Candidates.*
3 Federal Census 1860, Massachusetts, Suffolk County, Boston, Ward Eleven, 402; Boston City Directory.
4 Inman to Toucey, June 16, 1859.
5 *Boston Daily Advertiser*, May 30, 1859.
6 The names given here are accurate, based upon the crew list, the *Boston Daily Advertiser,* and comparison with official correspondence. The editor has substituted these corrected names for those actually given in Leonard's manuscript. As so often elsewhere, Leonard must have taken pains to get the information as completely as he could at the time but, probably relying upon what he heard, gives many of the names either incompletely or misspelled.
7 Theodore F. Kane, midshipman, also served aboard USS *Mystic.*
8 Grog ration.
9 *Boston Daily Advertiser*, June 17, 1859.
10 The *Constellation's* small arms included 86 rifled muskets, 54 Jenks carbines, 111 boarding pistols, 22 Colt revolvers, 112 swords, and 70 boarding pikes. Dornin, *Journal,* unnumbered page titled "Constellation's Battery," apparently written August 10, 1861, when Dornin took command.
11 The *Boston Daily Advertiser,* September 15, 1860, raises this issue while noting that all of the U.S. Navy's squadron commanders seem to have an old-fashioned preference for sail-powered flagships.
12 A sailor who absented himself temporarily with the intention of returning to his ship was said to have taken "French leave."

13 Captain Jarvis to Secretary of Navy, June 6, 1859, shows eight sent to the hospital plus seventy-one remaining aboard on sick list.

14 A Mr. J. F. Boyd had offered the navy a patented device for reefing and reducing topsails from the deck, and Secretary Toucey chose the *Constellation* to test it. It does not seem to have been adopted. Toucey to Nicholas, July 8, 1859 (Confidential File).

July 1859

1 Leonard, letter to Mary Moloney, copied on page 594 of Leonard's journal.

2 Dornin, *Journal*. Dornin specifically says the two after guns are "in the cabin." If so it would have crowded further the space that was already divided between the captain and the flag officer.

3 Callan and Russell, *Laws of the United States*, 125–41.

August 1859

1 Toucey to Maxwell, April 18, 1859.

2 Leal, *Portugal Antigo*, 872.

3 Church identification from Tony Hughes-Lewis of Funchal, Madeira, personal e-mail.

September 1859

1 The *Boston Daily Advertiser*'s correspondent reports Phillips's death and burial ashore on September 13, with two officers and about twenty seamen attending. He notes it was "90 in the shade." *Boston Daily Advertiser,* November 26, 1859.

2 Inman to Toucey, October 1, 1859; *New York Times,* November 25, 1859; *Boston Daily Advertiser,* November 26, 1859.

3 Eason, *US Ship* Marion, 51.

4 *New York Times,* November 25, 1859.

5 *Boston Daily Advertiser*, August 25, 1859.

6 Small steamers used on coastal runs by the Cromwell Company of New York, they had been leased for $3,000 a month with a purchase option. Refitting the seven leased steamers before sending them to Paraguay had cost the navy $141,000 and purchasing them added $137,000 more, adding up to about $40,000 per ship. To those sums must be added the cost of the considerable renovation done before sending them to Africa.

October 1859

1 Grey to Conover, March 21, 1859, enclosed in Inman to Toucey, October 25, 1859.

2 Inman to Grey, October 24, enclosed in Inman to Toucey, October 25, 1859.

November 1859

1 "Extracts from Logbook of *San Jacinto*," enclosed in Inman to Toucey, October 24, 1859.

2 Ibid.

3 *New York Times* "Further Details of Interest —American Vessels on The Coast–Naval Intelligence," American Vessels," March 2, 1860, 1.

4 Cdr. Thomas Brent to Toucey, April 23, 1859, with enclosures, gives all the details. In this case as in others, the Royal Navy captain was exercising the right of visit claimed by the British but denied by the U.S. government.

5 Howard, *American Slavers,* 170–76.

6 Sarah J. Hale, "Our Thanksgiving Union," *Godey's Lady's Book,* November 1859, 466.

7 Livingstone, *Missionary Travels,* 257.

December 1859

1 *New York Times,* November 12, 1859.

2 Canney, *Africa Squadron,* 209.

3 Capt. Thomas Morgan was sentenced to a two-thousand-dollar fine and two years in jail, first mate Byron Chamberlain to two years in jail, and William Dunham, second mate, to twenty-one months in jail; each mate was also fined one dollar. The court did not find sufficient evidence to indict Morgan under the "Piracy Act," under which a death sentence was possible, and after he changed his plea from not guilty to guilty, the stiffest sentence possible under the lesser crime of aiding the slave trade was imposed. *New York Times,* October 6, 1860; *Boston Daily Advertiser,* October 3, 1860, and October 5, 1860.

4 Inman to Toucey, December 15, 1859.

5 Nicholas to Inman, December 21, 1859, enclosed in Inman to Toucey, December 21, 1859.

6 *New York Times,* February 10, 1860.

January 1860

1 Inman to Toucey, January 11, 1860.

2 Inman to Toucey, January 13, 1860; Howard, *American Slavers,* 199.

3 Inman, January 18, 1860, to Cdr. Henry Walke, enclosed in Inman to Toucey, March 28, 1860.

4 E-mail from Prof. Dale Cockrell to editor, November 15, 2010.

5 *Constellation* crew records at Historic Ships in Baltimore.

6 Inman to Toucey, January 11, 1860.

February 1860

1 Inman to Toucey, January 13, 1860; Howard, *American Slavers,* 199. Lt. George Brown commanded the prize crew and was accompanied by marine lieutenant Henry B. Tyler, who had left Boston aboard the *Constellation* but was then transferred to the *Portsmouth.*

2 Selby, *Robert Macaire.*

3 Morton, *Box and Cox.*

4 Inman to Toucey, February 11, 1860; Inman to Toucey, February 13, 1860.

5 Howard, *American Slavers,* 220.

6 *Boston Daily Advertiser,* April 3, 1860.

7 *Boston Congregationalist,* June 17, 1859; Lenhart to Toucey, April 19, 1859, and July 14, 1860; Toucey to Lenhart, April 20, 1859, and July 19, 1860.
8 Inman to Toucey, August 15, 1860, with enclosures, esp. Colhoun to Toucey, February 17, 1860.
9 Selby, *Robert Macaire,* 7.

April 1860

1 *Boston Daily Advertiser,* May 11, 1860.
2 Dornin, *Journal,* 2.
3 Nicholas to Inman, May 1, 1860, enclosed in Inman to Toucey, May 2, 1860.
4 Inman to Dornin, April 23, 1860, enclosed in Inman to Toucey, April 23, 1860. In response to Inman's report of that date, Secretary Toucey reversed a number of Inman's orders, ordering on May 19 that Armstrong regain command of the *Sumpter;* McDonough return to the *Constellation;* Fairfax to the *Mystic;* Lieutenant Downes to the United States, "as his transfer to the *Supply* was entirely contrary to the wishes of the dept."; Hughes back to the *San Jacinto.* Secretary of the Navy note on back of Inman to Toucey, April 23.
5 *Boston Daily Advertiser,* April 3, 1860; the anonymous correspondent, writing from Loando on February 10, says, "We [and the *Portsmouth*] shall both sail tomorrow for Porto Praya, where we shall provision and water ship and then cruise to the northward, touching at the Canary Islands, as far as Madeira, where we are to remain until August next. The Portsmouth will cruise upon the South coast until June, when she will join us at Madeira." The correspondent's full remarks show good knowledge of the entire squadron's activities and plans.
6 A discrepancy of chronology here: in his personal journal, Dornin says, "I therefore on the 23 April took passage in a Portuguese steamer and left for Lisbon en route to Cadiz—I was fifty hours only going to Lisbon." Dornin, *Journal,* 2.

May 1860

1 Luce, *Text-book of Seamanship,* 309.
2 Special thanks to John Pentangelo for suggesting this interpretation.
3 Inman to Toucey with enclosures, May 27, 1860.
4 The *Portsmouth* had captured the brig *Falmouth.*

June 1860

1 Inman to Toucey, August 11, 1860, with enclosures; Inman to Toucey, August 15, 1860, with enclosures; Eason, *US Ship* Marion, 77–78.
2 These letters included a complaint from Capt. D. B. Vincent of the American brig *Johossee* of Charleston, dated Whydah Roads, January 23, 1860. Captain Vincent complained of having been arrested by force by the HMS *Falcon.* Lieutenant Boggs of the *Falcon* sent a note of January 14, thanking Vincent and mate J. N. Barmeau for helping him work the *Johossee* on the passage to Whydah from Adeffie, when the greater part of the prize crew were inebriated and incapable. J. P. Clark of the bark *Edwin,* at Accra, complained of treatment by British. Captain Godon of USS *Mohican* relayed a complaint from the brig *Belle* of Camden,

having been boarded by the HMS *Lynx* without asking permission. On July 2 Inman gave the admiral correspondence regarding a complaint about the American bark *Iowa* having been boarded by the HMS *Archer* on March 31.

July 1860

1 *Boston Daily Advertiser,* October 8, 1860.

August 1860

1 Inman to Toucey, August 7, 1860.
2 Inman to Toucey, November 3, 1860, from "Bengo Bay, 8 miles from Loanda" (in Area File, microfilm Roll 18); *Africa Pilot,* 390–91.
3 He had been transferred to the *Marion* back in early September 1859 to fill a shortage of officers. On that ship he was acting master until January, when severe ophthalmia disabled him and he was sent home aboard the *Vincennes.* After recuperating at home in Macon, Georgia, for two months, he requested active duty and was sent to the *Niagara.* Then Inman truncated his voyage to Japan (with the agreement of the *Niagara*'s Capt. William McKean) by drafting him back into the African Squadron. Cdr. Thomas W. Brent to Toucey, January 28, 1860; Wilburn B. Hall to Toucey, March 31, 1860; Hall to Toucey, May 31, 1860; Hall to Toucey, June 21, 1860; Inman to Toucey, August 15, 1860, enclosed in Inman to McKean, August 14, 1860.
4 *Boston Daily Advertiser,* October 8, 1860. The correspondent states that the *Sebastian Cabot* arrived on the eleventh and not the fourteenth, as Leonard has it. He describes its grounding and the rescue by Lieutenant Johnson with forty of *Constellation*'s crew.
5 Inman to Toucey, August 14, 1860. Dornin's report to Inman, dated August 12, says he has arrived at Loanda "this day." Dornin to Inman, August 12, 1860, in the letterbook section at the back of Dornin's journal. The present editor notes the three different dates given for Dornin's arrival but ventures no explanation.
6 Howard, *American Slavers,* 128–29.
7 Eason, *US Ship* Marion, 96.
8 Inman to Toucey, August 23, 1860.
9 The deceased was apparently Lt. Sydney Metcalfe, given as "Lieutenant Sidney Midcraft"; *Boston Daily Advertiser,* November 3, 1860; *Times,* (London) January 8, 1861.
10 Inman to Toucey, August 29 1860.

September 1860

1 Inman to Toucey, September 3, 1860.
2 *Boston Daily Advertiser,* December 6, 1860; the details in this account corroborate Leonard's, except for mentioning four shots fired instead of three. Both disagree in some ways with Wilburn Hall's, which was written decades after the event and is thus less to be relied upon.

October 1860

1 Wells, *Slave Ship* Wanderer, esp. 21–22, 30–31.

2 Leonard's gig-mate, William French, writing sixty-four years later, remarked that a member of the *Cora*'s crew was found to have been an owner not only of the *Cora* but also of the *Wanderer*. Martinoli, *Paine-French Genealogy*, 81.

3 Inman to Cdr. Benjamin M. Dove (commander of the store ship *Relief*), October 6, 1860; Inman to Judge of the District Court for the Eastern District of Virginia, September 26, 1860. (Both enclosed in letters from Inman to Toucey of the same dates.)

4 *New York Times*, March 21, 1861.

5 *New York Times*, December 8, 1860.

6 *Boston Daily Advertiser*, December 6, 1860.

7 *New York Times*, January 7, 1862.

8 *New York Times*, March 18, 1861.

9 Hall, "Capture," 130.

10 Inman to Toucey, October 8, 1860.

11 *Boston Daily Advertiser*, December 15, 1860.

12 Dornin to Capt. Andrew H. Foote, October 15, 1860, Area File.

13 *Boston Daily Advertiser*, January 9, 1861.

November 1860

1 *The Vermont Wool Dealer* (1838), a popular farce by Cornelius Ambrosius Logan; *The Widow's Victim* (1848), a one-act farce by Charles Selby; *Omnibus* (1831), an "interlude" by Isaac Pocock.

2 Buchanan to Secretary of State General Lewis Cass, December 15, 1859, Buchanan Papers Roll 51, 0082.

3 This would be a large bat, likely an Angolan fruit bat, common in great numbers in this part of Africa.

4 *Boston Daily Advertiser*, February 16, 1861; *Sailing Directory*, 775–76. Though Leonard refers to the location as "Fish Bay," it is clear from his comments that he is referring to Little Fish Bay and not to Great Fish Bay (Baia dos Tigres) at 16°30'S.

December 1860

1 *Boston Daily Advertiser*, February 16, 1861.

2 Having taken command of the *San Jacinto* at Cadiz in May, Captain Dornin brought it back to join the squadron by way of Fernando Po and Prince's Island.

3 *Boots at the Swan* (1842), by Charles Selby, remained a very popular farce for professionals and amateurs for many years.

4 *Ambrose Gwinnett* (1828) is a melodrama by English playwright Douglas William Jerrold.

January 1861

1 Foster to Toucey, December 20, 21, 24, 27, 29, 1860; January 1, 5, 7, 13, 24, 1861. There is an odd discrepancy in the number of slaves aboard the *Bonito*: Foster's reported 622 aboard and 616 landed is surely correct, as it would have been verified by the agent for recaptives there, and prize money was involved. Yet Inman reported 750, and *Bonita* crewman Charles Blaus said that 765 were

loaded at the Congo. Inman to Toucey, October 15, 1860; *New York Times,* June 23, 1861.

2 *Boston Daily Advertiser*, March 8, 1861.

3 Hume, *1861 Diary*, 7.

4 Dornin, *Journal*, 15, mentioned learning the news on Jan. 5 from the *Mystic*, which had brought the mail from Fernando Po to Loanda, where Dornin was with the *San Jacinto*. The *Constellation*'s anonymous correspondent explicitly stated that Dornin brought the news to St. Helena when he arrived on the sixteenth; *Boston Daily Advertiser*, March 8, 1861.

5 No Pedro is listed among the persons taken from the *Cora* (Inman to Toucey, September 26, 1860), but this is almost certainly Peter Ridovis, who shipped aboard *Constellation* from the *Delicia* and, as a member of the gig's crew, was well known to Leonard (John Pentangelo communication with editor).

February 1861

1 Inman to Cdr. Alfred Taylor, February 6, 1861, enclosed in Inman to Secretary of the Navy, April 30, 1861.

2 Midshipman Butt rejoined the *Constellation* on the ninth; Midshipman Kane joined on the sixth from the *Mystic*. Midshipman Farquhar (who was sent with the *Constellation*'s prize, *Delicia,* to Charleston) returned on the *Saratoga* with the marines and two lieutenants and was sent to the *Mystic*. *Boston Daily Advertiser*, April 28, 1861.

3 LeRoy to Andrew Hull Foote, February 12, 1861, Area File.

4 Hume, *1861 Diary*, 14.

5 The reader may notice that in the table of ship's complement Leonard gives later, he lists thirty-six privates, four corporals, four sergeants, one drummer, and one fifer for the marines. This total of forty-six was close to the allowance of a frigate (forty-nine) rather than a sloop (twenty-six). Also his total here of forty does not match the breakdown, which adds up to thirty. Brady, *Kedge-Anchor,* 316.

March 1861

1 *Boston Daily Advertiser*, May 21, 1861.

2 The Kansas-Nebraska Act of 1854 nullified the Missouri Compromise and resulted in such violence in the Kansas Territory between those for and against slavery that it became known as "Bleeding Kansas."

3 Inman to Le Roy, March 6, 1861, enclosed in Inman to Secretary of the Navy, April 30, 1861.

4 The Phrase Finder, www.phrases.org.uk; American Memory, memory.loc.gov. "Fanny Elsller" might have been one of several tunes associated a few decades earlier with the Austrian ballerina of that name.

5 Hume, *1861 Diary*, 33.

6 "Proposed rules and regulations . . . ," no. 550, American State Papers, Naval Affairs, 4:540.

7 This telegraph was a large, mechanical semaphore device.

8 Capt. (later Adm.) Edward Winterton Turnour commanded the *Forte*. The English admiral is Rear Admiral Sir Henry Keppel, KCB.

9 *Boston Daily Advertiser*, May 21, 1861.

10 The deceased was Pvt. William G. Chambers; *Boston Daily Advertiser*, June 29, 1861.

April 1861

1 *Boston Daily Advertiser*, July 2, 1861.

2 Note by Toucey on Borchert to Secretary of the Navy, April 3, 1861.

3 Likely the Frank Carr listed below as a landsman.

4 *New York Times*, January 7, 1861.

5 Bates to Inman, April 11, 1861, and Colhoun to Inman, April 11, 1861, both enclosed in Inman to Welles, April 15, 1861.

6 Hume, *1861 Diary*, 27.

7 *The History and Records of the Elephant Club*, by Knight Russ Ockside, M.D. and Q. K. Philander Doesticks, P. B. [Edward F. Underhill and Mortimer Neal Thomson] (New York: Livermore & Rudd, 1856).

8 Capt. Frederick Marryat (1792–1848), English novelist and pioneer of "the sea story."

9 Eastman to Toucey, December 8, 1860.

May 1861

1 *Frank Leslie's Illustrated Newspaper*, March 16, 1861, 258.

2 Inman to Welles, May 7, 1861.

3 Inman to Commander DeCamp, May 7, 1861, enclosed in Inman to Welles, July 15, 1861.

4 The *Constellation* had a double capstan. The spar deck capstan could be used for raising and lowering yards, and the main deck capstan (which had room to accommodate more men at the bars) could be used for raising the anchor.

5 Findlay, *Sailing Directions*, 754.

6 Nicholas to Welles, May 22, 1861; Howard, *American Slavers*, 220.

7 Actually it was not the sailing master who took this prize home but rather Midshipman Borchert.

8 Of course the USS *Constellation* the old sailor saw in 1861 was not the frigate he sailed on in 1844. The frigate, launched in 1797, was dismantled in 1853. Leonard's *Constellation* was not the old frigate cut down to a sloop but a completely different ship constructed in 1854.

June 1861

1 Hume, *1861 Diary*, 39.

2 Dornin, *Journal*, June 14, 1861; Edward R. Birnie to Secretary of the Navy, April 24, 1861, in "Letters received . . . from navy agents and naval storekeepers," RG45.

3 Like most of the St. Helena population, he was of African descent; he came aboard as part of the original crew at Charlestown in June 1859; John Hambleton's endorsement on Surgeon Browne's report of death, enclosed in Inman to Toucey.

4 Letter and comment copied into back section of journal volume.

July 1861

1 *Boston Daily Advertiser*, August 30, 1861.
2 Lt. George W. Young to Gideon Welles, July 29, 1861.
3 Dornin, *Journal*, July 4, 1861.
4 Hume, *1861 Diary*, 46.
5 Ibid., 50.
6 Inman to Welles, July 26, 1861.
7 "Oft in the Stilly Night," lyrics by Thomas Moore, continues to be performed.
8 Partridge, *Dictionary of Slang*, 1059.
9 McEwen and Lewis, *Encyclopedia of Nautical Knowledge*, 54.
10 A bowline is "a single rope leading forward from a bridle made fast to a square sail's weather leech [edge], used when sailing close-hauled to flatten out the sail as much as possible." McEwen and Lewis, *Encyclopedia of Nautical Knowledge*, 413.

August 1861

1 Inman to Welles, August 5, 1861.
2 Hume, *1861 Diary*, 54.
3 Col. Elmer Ellsworth, twenty-four years old and a friend of Abraham Lincoln, was killed on May 24, 1861, while removing a Confederate flag from a hotel in Alexandria, Virginia. Famous for organizing the colorfully dressed regiment of "Fire Zouaves," recruited from the firemen of New York City, he was the first Union officer killed in the Civil War. His life and death were covered at great length in the illustrated papers.
4 Inman to Welles, August 11, 1861.
5 Inman to Welles, August 10, 1861.

September 1861

1 Armstrong to Welles, September 15, 1861.
2 Hume, *1861 Diary*, 66.
3 Ibid, 68.
4 Nine guns was the salute given a navy captain. As a flag officer, Inman rated thirteen. But he had turned over his squadron command upon leaving Africa, so the nine-gun salute would be correct. However, the salute given by HMS *Arrogant* suggests that Inman was still flying his broad pennant, which rated thirteen guns.

October 1861

1 After the war Loyall petitioned the government for his share of the *Cora* prize money. He was denied.
2 *Boston Daily Advertiser*, September 30, 1861.
3 Marshal's return to U.S. District Court, Southern District of New York, February 27, 1861, *Cora* File.

Bibliography

Archival Materials

(Note: The logs of USS *Constellation* for the entire period concerned are lost.)

Buchanan, James. President James Buchanan Papers (Philadelphia Historical Society).

Cora File. National Archives RG 21. U.S. District Court for the Southern District of New York, Entry 83, Admiralty Case Files 1828–1912, Box No. 195, File A16–216, at National Archives, Philadelphia.

Dornin, Thomas A. *Journal & Remarks on Board the U. States Frigate San Jacinto of 15 guns*. Manuscript journal and letterbook, 1860–1861. HM 30205 and HM 30206. Huntington Library, San Marino, California.

Eason, Henry. *US Ship* Marion *at Sea 1858*. Manuscript journal, online from Mystic Seaport G. W. Blunt White Library. http://library.mysticseaport.org/initiative/Page Image.cfm?

Marion Log. USS Marion *Log 1858–1860*. National Archives, Washington, D.C.

National Archives RG 45 (Naval Records), specifically "Letters from the Secretary of the Navy" and "Letters to the Secretary of the Navy" in various categories and the "African Squadron" and "Area File" letters.

Periodicals

Boston Daily Advertiser
Congregationalist (Boston)
Frank Leslie's Illustrated Newspaper
Godey's Lady's Book
Harper's Weekly
New York Times
Times (London)

Books and Articles

Africa Pilot, H.O. No. 105, Washington, D.C.: Gov. Printing Office, 1916.

American Colonization Society. *Annual Report for 1860*. Washington, D.C., 1860.

American State Papers, House of Representatives, 23d Congress, 1st Session.

Bartlett, D. W. *Presidential Candidates: Containing Sketches, Biographical, Personal and Political, of Prominent Candidates for the Presidency in 1860*. New York: Burdick, 1859.

Bathe, Basil W. *The Visual Encyclopedia of Nautical Terms under Sail*. New York: Crown, 1978.

Bopp, Lawrence J., and Stephen R. Bockmiller. *Showing the Flag: The Civil War Naval Diary of Moses Safford, USS* Constellation. Charleston, S.C.: History Press, 2004.

Boston City Directory for 1860.

Brady, William. *The Kedge-Anchor; or, Young Sailors' Assistant.* 4th ed. New York: William Brady, 1849.

Busk, Hans. *The Navies of the World.* New York: Routledge, Warnes & Routledge, 1859.

Callan, John F., and A. W. Russell, comps., *Laws of the United States Relating to the Navy and Marine Corps.* Baltimore: Murphy, 1859.

Canney, Donald L. *Africa Squadron: The U.S. Navy and the Slave Trade, 1842–1861.* Washington, D.C.: Potomac Books, 2006.

Chisholm, Donald. *Waiting for Dead Men's Shoes: Origins and Development of the U.S. Navy's Officer Personnel System 1793–1941.* Stanford: Stanford University Press, 2001.

Correspondence with the British Commissioners at Sierra Leone, Havana, the Cape of Good Hope, and Loanda, and Reports from British Vice-Admiralty Courts, and from British Naval Officers, relating to the Slave Trade. London: Harrison, 1862.

Findlay, Alexander George. *Sailing Directions for the Ethiopic or South Atlantic Ocean, Including a Description of the Coasts of South America and Africa.* London: Richard Holmes Laurie, 1883.

Gilliland, C. Herbert. *Voyage to a Thousand Cares: Master's Mate Lawrence with the African Squadron 1844–1846.* Annapolis, Md.: Naval Institute Press, 2004.

Hall, Wilburn. "The Capture of the Slave-Ship 'Cora." *Century,* May 1894, 115–30.

Holland, John H. and Mark Myers. *Seamanship in the Age of Sail.* Annapolis, Md.: Naval Institute Press, 2006.

Foote, Andrew H. *Africa and the American Flag.* London: Dawsons of Pall Mall, 1970.

Howard, Warren S. *American Slavers and the Federal Law 1837–1862.* Berkeley: University of California Press, 1963.

Hume, Fannie Page. *1861 Diary of Miss Fannie Page Hume, Orange Virginia.* Introduction by James W. Cortada. Orange, Vir.: Orange County Historical Society, 1983.

———. *The Fanny Hume Diary of 1862: A Year in Wartime Orange, Virginia.* Edited by J. Randolph Grymes Jr. Orange, Vir.: Orange County Historical Society, 1994.

Instructions in Relation to the Preparation of Vessels of War for Battle. Washington, D.C.: Navy Department (Bureau of Ordnance), 1852.

Laws Relating to the Navy and Marine Corps, and the Navy Department. Washington, D.C.: Navy Department, 1865.

Leal, Pinho. *Portugal Antigo e Moderno,* Vol. 11. From copy in local document provided by Funchal Diocese clerk, fax, July 25, 2011.

Lever, Darcy. *The Young Sea Officer's Sheet Anchor: or, A Key to the Leading of Rigging, and to Practical Seamanship.* Boston: Lauriat, 1930.

Levy, Uriah P. *Manual of Internal Rules and Regulations for Men-of-War.* New York: Van Nostrand, 1862.

Livingstone, David. *Missionary Travels and Researches in South Africa.* London: Murray, 1861.

Luce, S. B. *Text-book of Seamanship: The Equipping and Handling of Vessels under Sail or Steam.,* 4th ed. Revised by Lt. W. S. Benson. New York: Van Nostrand, 1898.

McEwen, W. A., and A. H. Lewis. *Encyclopedia of Nautical Knowledge.* Cambridge, Mass.: Cornell Maritime Press, 1953.

Manual for Exercise of Broadside and Pivot Guns in the United States Navy as Practiced on the United States Gunnery Ship Santee. Washington, D.C.: Govt. Printing Office, 1869.

Martinoli, Beverly Marion. *The Paine-French Genealogy.* N.p.: Trafford, 2010.

Morton, John Maddison. *Box and Cox.* New York: French, n.d.

Partridge, Eric. *Dictionary of Slang and Unconventional English.* Abridged ed. London: Routledge & Kegan Paul, 1973.

Selby, Charles. *Robert Macaire.* London: Duncombe, [1853?].

———. *The Widow's Victim.* New York: Douglas, 1848.

U.S. Navy Department. *Report of the Secretary of the Navy.* December 1859.

U.S. Navy Ordnance Bureau. *Instructions in Relation to the Preparation of Vessels of War for Battle.* Washington, D.C.: Navy Department, C. Alexander Printer, 1852.

Ward, W. E. F. *The Royal Navy and the Slavers.* New York: Pantheon, 1969.

Wells, Tom Henderson. *The Slave Ship* Wanderer. Athens: University of Georgia Press, 1967.

Williams, Glenn F. *USS* Constellation: *A Short History of the Last All-Sail Warship Built by the U.S. Navy.* Virginia Beach: Donning, 2000.

Wines, E. C. *Two Years and a Half in the Navy: or, Journal of a cruise in the Mediterranean and Levant on board of the U.S. Frigate* Constellation *in the Years 1829, 1830, and 1831.* Philadelphia: Carey & Lea, 1832.

Index

Page numbers in italics refer to illustrations or tables.

Abbot, E. T., 253
Abbott, Trevett, 11
admiral, 14
African fever, 15
African Squadron, Royal Navy: burial of
  officer of, 137–38; complaints against,
  by U.S. merchant ships, 392–93n2;
  Crimean War and, 3, 10, 86–87;
  mission of, 2; ships captured by, 184,
  244; U.S. African Squadron and, 2, 3,
  8–10, 48, 86–87, 121. See also specific
  ship
African Squadron, U.S.: British African
  Squadron and, 2, 3, 8–10, 48, 86–87,
  121; challenges for, 56–57, 124–25;
  Congo patrol area, xiv; cruising
  ground, xiii, 105, 112–13; establishment of, 2, 7; fleet, 2–3, 7, 30–31,
  37, 41, 77, 98, 119, 163–64, 390n6;
  health risks for sailors in, 15–16; ineffective commanders in, 27–28, 77–78;
  liberty conditions of, 16; mission of,
  1, 2, 7, 8–10; ordered home, 346–48,
  350; rendezvous, 3, 27; restrictions on
  actions of, 160; shortages of officers
  and crew in, 133, 135–37, 158; slave
  ships and prize money taken by, 53,
  131–32, 134, 147–50, 157–58, 225–
  26, 279–80, 291–92, 293, 329; storehouse at St. Paul de Loando, 62, 63,
  64, 68, 75, 246, 265, 266, 282; tactics
  of, 68, 157. See also specific ship
afterguard, 12, 23
Agawam, USS, 305

aguardiente, 38, 61
Alabama, HMS (line of battle ship),
  377
Alecto, HMS (steam sloop), 329, 350,
  351
Allen, William, 53
Ambriz, 80, 89, 157
Ambrose Gwinnett (play), 181, 183,
  198–201
American Colonization Society, 47
American Express Co., 386–87
anchors and anchor chains, 13, 21,
  141, 153
Anderson, Peter, 209–10
Annabon Island, 88–89
Ann & Mary (U.S. merchant barque),
  139
Arab (clipper ship), 281
Arabian Steed (clipper ship), 281, 284
Archer, HMS (steam sloop), 60, 61, 133,
  134, 137, 138, 162, 165, 169, 207,
  208, 230, 233, 238, 244, 252, 269,
  289, 304
Ariel (slave ship), 132
Arkansas, CSS, 378
armorer, 218
Armstrong, J. F., 56, 369, 392n4
Arrogant, HMS (steam frigate), 136,
  137, 139, 140, 141, 352
Articles of War, 23
Ashburton, Lord, 2
Astrolabe (French corvette), 249
Aurelia (U.S. barque), 198
Austro-Sardinian War, 6–7

Baker, William, 285
Ball, William, 271, 291
ballast, 20–21
Baltimore Riot, 322–23
Banana Point, 56
barber, ship's, 26, 30, 224
barge, 18, 216, 217
Barnum, P. T., 207
barracoon, 55
Bartholomew Diaz (Portuguese steam
  frigate), 138
Bartlett, William A., 321
Bates, John, 266
battalions, 216
Bayman, Robert, 29, 101
beeswax, 21
Bengo Bay, 129, 131, 346
Benjamin, Daniel, 123
Benjamin, M., 108
Benson, Stephen Allen, 47
Benton, Thomas Hart, 312
berth deck, 5, 11, 83, 217
Birnie, Storekeeper, 309
Bishop of Madeira, 32
Blackford, George D., 11, 133, 140, 253
blacksmith, 218
blankets, 22
Blood, Bella, 17, 317
boatkeeper, 16, 110–12
boat races, 65, 68–69, 144, 240, 311–12,
  315, 318–20, 323–25
boatswain, 11
boatswain's mates, 219
Bonita (slave ship), 157–58, 188, 284,
  394–95n1
Booth, John Wilkes, 64
Boots at the Swan (play), 180, 198–201
Borchert, George, 11, 249, 253, 293,
  300, 331
Boston Daily Advertiser, 7, 8, 124, 155,
  197, 392n5
bowline, 397n10
boxing matches, 123
Brady, Thomas, 39, 197
Braxton, Carter, 387
Brazil, 2, 3, 10

Brent, Commander, 48, 120–21
Brooks, George, 197
Broome, John L., 158
Brown, Charles, 277
Brown, James, 285–87
Brown, John, 46, 64, 286
Browne, John M., 11, 174, 253
Buchanan administration, 3, 10, 28, 170,
  278
Buffalo, HMS (gun boat), 137, 165, 169,
  248, 249–50
bumboats, 29, 120, 158–59
Bunker Hill, Battle of, 12, 310
Butt, Walter R., 11, 132, 253, 300, 378,
  381
buttons, 22

cables, 21; slipping, 141
calling of boats, 236–37
Camera de Lobos, 27
Cameron, J., 168, 200
Campbell, Pete, 154, 156
Cape Fly Away, 161
Cape Padrão, 253
Cape Verde Islands, 3, 36, 37, 44
captain, ship's, 10, 14
Captain of Marines, 11
captains: of after guard, 221; of fore-
  castle, 220; of the holds, 219; of tops,
  217, 221, 272
carpenter, ship's, 11
carpenter's mate, 218
Carr, Frank, 252
Carroll, Mary E., 147
Cass, Lewis, 77
catamaran, 73, 325
cathead, 153
caulking, 102
chafing gear, 21
Chamberlain, Byron, 391n3
chaplain, 88
Chapman, John, 344
Charlestown Navy Yard, 6, 7, 8, 9, 20,
  386
China, 15
Chincha Islands, 274

Christmas Day, 72, 183

Civil War, 1, 188, 231, 248–49, 266, 269, 275, 281, 300, 303, 318, 322–23, 328, 335, 345–46, 348, 349–50, 378, 379, 386, 387, 397n3

Clark, J. S., 124

clerks and secretaries, ship's, 11

Clip, Jerry, 325

Cloner, J., 168

Cloney, J., 200, 343

clothing, 21–22

coast fever, 15, 245–46, 247, 249, 274, 316

Cochituate, USS (store ship), 126

cockbilled yards, 247

Colhoun, Commander, 86, 90, 120, 266

Collins, Thomas, 282, 315

Colorado, USS (steam frigate), 8

combs and brushes, 22

comet, 329

commander, 10

commodore, 14

compensation for sailors: disbursements for liberty, 103, 107; grog and ration money, 82; prize money, 384–85

Comstock, Albert, 108

Congo River, 55, 56, 57, 284, 290, 293

Conover, Commodore, 27, 77

Constellation, USS, 28, 209, 357; African Squadron deployment of, 2–3, 8–10; berth deck, 5, 11; boats of, 216–17; burial of Corporal Edwards at sea, 151; calling of boats of, 236–37; Civil War loyalties of crew of, 300; command structure of, 214–15; construction history of, 1, 8, 396n4; crew list, 254–65, 389n6; design details of, 1, 8, 396n4; discharge of crew of, 383–84; duration of cruise of, 384; foreign-born crew of, 299; fully dressed, 17–18; gun deck, 4, 21, 163; historical significance of, 1; Marine corps aboard, 222, 395n5; officers of, 10–11, 253, 300; ordered home, 346–47; petty officers of, 217–21, 253; prize money earned by, 384–85;

return to U.S. of, 373–75; roles of seamen aboard, 219, 221; rules of behavior on, 25–26; sailors' diversions aboard, 99–100, 165–69; signals and orders aboard, 215–16, 236–37; slave ships captured by, 70–71, 147–48, 154; small arms aboard, 389n10; spar deck, 5; watches aboard, 217

cooks, ship's, 220, 234, 235

coolie trade, 184–85

coopers, 218

coppers, 57

Cora (slave ship), 4, 145, 147–50, 154, 155, 156, 157–58, 234, 276, 284, 384, 385, 394n2, 397n1

Cornubia, USS (coastal steamer), 386

corporals, 83, 217, 219, 222

cost of articles, shipboard, 21–22, 209–10, 227

courses, 161

court martial charges and proceedings, 35, 39, 54, 71, 72, 101, 106, 107, 120, 127, 134, 135, 138, 139, 142, 146, 151, 159–60, 169, 171, 175, 180, 181, 182, 204, 210, 211, 238, 239, 240, 243, 244, 245, 250, 252, 294–95, 310, 315, 317, 320, 328, 330, 331, 339, 342–43, 344, 365–66, 367–68

coxswain, 217, 287–88

crank, 20

Crawford, Captain, 233

Crimean War, 3, 10, 86

crocodiles, 293

crossjack braces, 38

Crusader, USS, 387

Cuba, 2, 3, 10

Cumberland, USS (sloop of war), 8, 27, 28, 77

cutters, 216–17

Cyane, USS, 2

Dahlgren boat howitzers, 24

Daley, P., 168

Dalton, H. H., 328

Daly, Peter, 323

Davis, Jefferson, 7, 231
De Camp, 309
Delicia (slave ship), 71, 132, 384
deserters, 15, 35
de Vaney, Hugh, 197
Dickens, Charles, 7
dinghy, 216–17
discipline, 19, 83, 91, 97, 100, 217. *See also* court martial charges and proceedings
displacement of USS *Constellation*, 1
division bills, 22, 25
doctor's steward, 220
Doesticks, 270
doldrums, 353, 362–65
Don Pedro (Portuguese mail steamer), 322
Doran, P., 109, 168, 200
Dornin, Thomas A., 101, 102, 103, 158, 347, 348, 349–50, 381
Doughty, Isaac T., 11, 253
Douglas, Stephen, 7
Downey, P., 168
Dramatic Club, 85, 86, 88, 89, 91, 99, 102, 106, 107–9, 157, 161, 165–69, 174, 179, 180, 181, 183, 187, 190, 198–201
drinking and carousing, 12, 18, 32, 71, 91, 97, 100–101, 105–6, 120, 175, 188, 189, 238, 239, 241, 250, 252, 288, 313–14, 336, 337–38, 339–41, 382
drum fish, 275
Dunham, William, 391n3
Dunnington, Lieutenant, 132
D'Urville, Jules Dumont, 249
duty sergeants, 222
Dwyer, John, 331, 367–68

Eastman, Thomas H., 10, 11, 124, 150, 253
Echo (slave ship), 129
Edmonstone, William, 352
Edwards, James, 151
Edwin, 124
Electro. see Alecto, HMS (steam sloop)

Elephant Bay, 169, 171
Elizabeth, 2
Ellen (slave ship), 48
Elliot, J. E., 84, 85
Ellsworth, Elmer, 397n3
Elsie, J., 85
Elssler, Fannie, 237
Emily (slave ship), 64
Emmett, Dan, 237
Erie (slave ship), 132
Eveline (British barque), 189
Express (slave ship), 226
eyes of ship, 218

Fader, F., 200
Fairfax, Donald McNeill, 79, 79, 88, 253, 300, 305, 306, 347, 349, 392n4
Falcon, HMS, 120, 137
Falmouth (slave ship), 291–92, 293, 297, 329
Fanny (U.S. whaling schooner), 203
Farce of Box and Cox (play), 86, 107
Farquhar, Norman J., 65, 71, 126, 132, 253, 395n2
Farragut, David, 15
Farrar, J. G., 84, 168
Farrar, Jarvis Y., 84
Fernando Po, 30
Ferreira, Maria, 52, 53
Fifth Regiment of Massachusetts Volunteer Infantry, 386
fire quarters, 124, 216
first class boys, 221–22
Fish Bay. *see* Little Fish Bay
Fish Town, 27, 104–5
Fitzsimmons, Joe, 211
Flag Lieutenant, 11
Flag Officer, 11, 14
flamingo, 101
Flora (U.S. coal ship), 236, 237, 238–39, 245, 274, 279
Flying Dutchman, 160
food and water, 16, 18, 29, 44, 67, 82, 91, 102, 231, 236, 248, 270, 271–72, 348–49; cooks, 220, 234, 235; dining arrangements, 82–83; rations, 82, 232

Forte, HMS (Admiral's ship), 244, 245
forward officers, 11
Foster, J. J., 253
Foster, James P., 11, 132, 158, 188–89
Foster, Stephen, 237
France, 61
Francis, G., 84
Franklin, USS (steam frigate), 377, 381–82
Franz Joseph, Emperor, 6
Frederick, Morgan, 150, 155
French, William H., 84, 85, 168, 200, 299, 301, 394n2
French leave, 14, 389n12
French Point, 56
Funchal, 27, 33, 101, 110

Game Cock (U.S. clipper ship), 335–36
games, 26
gander sets, 113
Garibaldi, 6, 153
Garibaldi, HMS, 349
Gavin, John, 331
Gay Head, 373
Gaynor, Thomas, 312–15
general quarters, 151, 216, 355–56, 368–79
George, James, 316
Georgia, 154
gig, 12, 93, 216, 217, 298–99
Glendy, William M., 347
Godey's Lady's Book, 58
Godon, Captain, 124, 135, 140, 207, 345
Gordon, C. F., 84, 85, 167, 168, 197, 299
Gordon, Nathaniel, 132
Grampion (British coal ship), 127
Great Britain: ban on slave trade in, 2, 8–10; U.S. relations with, 10, 80, 86, 121. *See also* African Squadron, Royal Navy
Grey, Rear Admiral, 48, 104
Greyhound (U.S. whale ship), 339
grog rations, 82, 248
guano, 274

Guilford, B. P., 200
Guilford (British barque), 210
guitar, 105
Gulf Stream, 23, 370, 371
Gullison, Jerry, 376
gun crew: commands and signals for, 215–16; in *Constellation* command structure, 214, 215; exercises and drills, 13, 18, 24, 25, 36, 38, 41, 45, 50, 51, 54, 66, 74, 90, 100, 114, 117, 123, 124, 142, 144, 163, 176, 177, 181, 204, 210–11, 216, 295–96, 302, 331, 332, 333, 343, 351, 352, 353, 354, 355, 357, 363, 364, 366, 368–69; general quarters, 151; members of, and their duties, 13, 18, 118, 215, 218–19; small arms companies of, 216
gun deck, 4, 21
gunner, 11
gunner's mate, 218
Gunnerson, Jeri, 376

Hale, Sarah J., 58
Hall, Wilburn B., 11, 133, 150, 156, 253, 300, 393n3
Hallett, James, 366
Hambleton, John N., 11, 253, 385
Hamilton Guard, 386
handkerchiefs, 22
Hankow (U.S. steamboat), 318, 324, 328
Harper's Weekly, 7
Harrington, Warren, 85, 168, 200
Hart, John, 368
Hartford, USS (steam sloop), 8, 15
hats and caps, 22
Hazard (U.S. barque), 236, 246
health, sailors', 15, 61, 95, 133, 140. *See also* coast fever
Heenan, John C., 123
Henry, Gus, 168, 200
Heuvel, Apthorp Vanden, 11, 253
Hewitt, Commander, 86
Higginbottom, S., 168, 169
Higgins, H. W., 108
Hingerty, Alfred, 11, 78, 126, 253, 300

History and Records of the Elephant Club, The (Doesticks), 270
Home Squadron, 15
Homeward Bound (Thompson), 361
horse latitudes, 368
howitzers, 24
Hume, Fannie Page, 11, 198, 208, 239, 269, 330, 335, 346, 350, 369, 372, 387
Humphries, Henry, 133
Hunter, John, 108, *166*, 167, 168, 200
Hutchinson, James, 11

idlers, 222
Igo, T. W., 168, 200
indenture contracts, 184–85
Independence Day, 17–18, 122, 325–28
Ingolls, Moses, 7
Inman, William, 8, 11, 14, 39, 40, 58, 66, 67–68, 76, 80, 86, 101, 103, 104, 105, 107, 115, 120, 124, 134, 135, 140, 150, 157, 207, 208, 233, 249, 253, 266, 276, 282, 298, 304, 306, 347, 349–50, 387, 392n4
insanity plea, 6
insubordination, 107, 134, 135, 151
Italy, 6–7

jackets, 21
Jack of the Dust, 219, 220
Jackson, Thomas, 64
Jamestown, St. Helena, 185, *186*
Jamestown, USS (sloop of war), 225, 231
Japanese diplomatic mission, 129–31, 133, 153
Jimmy Legs, 217, 250
John Gilpin (merchant ship), 60, 61, 205–6, 233–34, 237, 270, 303, 347
John Gilpin's Bride (merchant ship), 284
Johnson, Philip C., 79, 174, 253, 290
Jones, Henry, 342–43
Jones, W., 84

Kabenda Bay, 67, 69, 70, 158, 225, 229–30, 279–80
Kane, Theodore F., 11, 133, 253, 395n2

Kansas and Nebraska Act, 231
Kate (slave ship), 284
Keating, F., 85
Keenan, Michael, 226
Keokuk, USS (ironclad), 387
Keppel, Henry, 104, 121, 124
Kinsembo, 89
Knauff, George P., 237
kroomen, 45, 47–49, 56–57, 95, 124, 142, 160, 204, 227, 299–300, 347, 349

Ladder Hill, 187, 196, 197
Lady of Lyons, The (play), 85
La Forte, HMS (steam frigate), 104, 109
Lamar, Charles, 155
landsman, 221
Latham, John, 150, 154, 155
launch, 216, 217
launch crews, 35
Lavin, James, 197
Lawson, Peter, 366
Lee, Robert E., 64, 76
lee wheel watch, 23
Legg, Adner, 191, 197, 200
Lenhart, John, 88
Leonard, Catherine, 147
Leonard, Charles, 147
Leonard, Ellen M., 147
Leonard, James, 147
Leonard, Jane A., 147, 277
Leonard, Mary E., 146, 147
Leonard, William, 168, 169, 299; birthday of, 34, 138, 359; discharged from *Constellation,* 383–85; historical milieu of, 6–7; life after *Constellation,* 386–87; on life of sailors, 240–44; parents and siblings of, 17, 147; prize money earned by, 384–85; seafaring career of, 6; shipboard assignments of, 36, 37–38, 142, 162; shipboard journal of, 3–4, *111*, 190, 326–27; wife and children of, 20, 386
Le Roy, William E., 39, 66, 155, 208, 233, 246

Leslie's Illustrated Newspaper, 6, 278, 280, 285–86
Levant, USS (sloop of war), 265
Liberia, 2, 45, 47–49, 134
liberty, 99, 105; African Squadron rules, 16; in Madeira, 31–33, 103, 104–6, 107; money for, 103, 107; in St. Helena, 185, 189–97, 334, 335–38, 339–41
lieutenant commander, 10
lieutenants, 10, 11
life boats, 251
Lincoln, Abraham, 7, 170, 280, 323
Lind, Jenny, 207
Lines, on the Ocean, 358–59
Little, Tom, 233
Little Fish Bay, 169, 171–77, 182, 394n4
Live Yankee (U.S. clipper ship), 184
Livingstone, David, 60, 174
Loango Bay, 292, 294
loblolly boys, 274
Long, William, 56–57, 78, 126
Longwood, St. Helena, 192–93, 194–95
Louisa's Rock, 115
Louisiana, USS, 387
Lowrey, Henry M., 11, 253
Loyall, Benjamin P., 65, 88, 253, 378, 381, 397n1
Lucy Johnson (U.S. barque), 303, 347
Luis I, King of Portugal, 141
Lytton, Edward Bulwer, 85

Madeira, *Constellation* at, 26–35, 101–13
mail, 30, 40, 85, 98, 105, 115, 121, 126, 153, 156, 170, 180, 205, 206, 208, 227, 230, 231, 236, 252, 265, 272, 274, 275, 276, 280, 281, 302, 329
malaria, 15–16, 245–46, 247, 386. *See also* coast fever
Malone, Daniel, 24, 151
Marie (slave ship), 287
Marines, 216, 217, 222, 300; *Constellation* crew list, 263–65, 395n5

Marion, USS (sloop of war), 30–31, 32, 34, 35, 38, 40, 56, 65, 75, 80, 83–84, 86, 88, 120, 126, 127, 133, 134–35
Marshall, M., 197
Martin, William J., 146
Mary (U.S. whaling ship), 234
master, 11
master at arms, 83, 217
mattresses, 22
Maxwell, Charles D., 31, 112
Mayo, 44
Mazeppa (U.S. coal ship), 206, 235–36, 237
McArann, Robert M., 11, 71, 253
McCrachen(d), Thomas, 108, 168
McDonough, Charles, 11, 72, 75, 107, 120, 134, 138, 139, 237, 253, 392n4
McIntosh, Alexander, 118
McKenzie, James, 344
McNamara, J., 200
McQuade, M., 197
Medusa, HMS, 48
mess bill, 22–23, 226–27, 228–29
mess divisions, 82
messenger, 43
messes, 82, 217, 234
Mexican War, 226, 312
Mexico, 15
midshipmen, 10–11, 300
Miller, Clement A., 251, 336
Minnesota, USS (steam frigate), 8
minstrel shows, 76, 77, 83, 84–85, 99
Missouri Compromise, 231
Mobile Bay, Battle of, 15
Mohican, USS (steam gun boat), 98, 115, 119, 120, 121, 124, 132, 135, 137, 140, 142, 164, 170, 179, 181, 184, 185, 188, 189, 198, 205, 207, 211, 226, 230, 231, 249, 252, 269, 272, 274, 304, 305, 318–20, 324, 325, 345, 347, 348, 350, 351, 375
Moloney, Anna, 126, 147
Moloney, Mary L. (M. L. M.), 20, 147, 277, 278, 302, 304, 317, 386
Monitor, USS, 300
Monrovia, 45, 47–49, 150

Montague (U.S. whale ship), 157
Morgan, Thomas, 56, 57, 66, 77, 391n3
Morse, William H., 44, 97
Morton, John Maddison, 86
Mossamedes, 173
Murphy, C. D., 84, 108
music and dancing, 20, 28, 61, 66, 74, 76–77, 83, 84–85, 91, 99, 106, 108, 109, 113, 337, 338, 347, 382
muster, 19
Mystic, USS (steam gun boat), 38, 39, 40–41, 52–53, 56, 57, 61, 65, 66, 76, 77, 85–86, 87, 90, 92, 129, 131–32, 135–37, 143, 152, 154, 156, 160, 163, 164, 169, 172, 205, 208, 209, 210, 225, 230, 233, 237–38, 245–46, 281, 292, 303, 315, 323, 324, 347–48, 350

Namibe, 173
Nantasket Roads, 20
Napoleon Bonaparte, 76, 183, 191–92
Napoleon III, 6
Narragansett, USS (steam gun boat), 8
Nast, Thomas, 286
National Salute, 324
Naval Academy, U.S., 11, 33
Naval Asylum, 243
Navy, U.S.: foreign-born sailors in, 273; officers' ranks in, 10, 14; prices of required articles in, 21–22; squadron deployments of 19th century, 2. *See also* African Squadron, U.S.; *Constellation,* USS
Navy Efficiency Board, 14
neckerchief, 22
Netherby (British ship), 185
New Year's Day, 74
Niagara, USS (steam frigate), 129, 130, 133, 313
Nicholas, John S., 10, 11, 13–14, 71, 104, 115, 150, 167, 253, 276, 300, 306, 307–9, 385, 387
Nichols, E. B., 200, 251
Nightingale (slave ship), 207–8, 209, 214, 223, 224, 233, 269, 279–80
Ninety-Ninth Infantry Battalion, 321

Nodine, Isaac L., 108, 167, 200
Northwestern Boundary Dispute, 80

Officers of the Deck, 217
officers of U.S. Navy, 14; *Constellation* command, 10–11
Ohio, USS (receiving ship), 8, 17, 18
Olds, Alvah, 168, 200
Omnibus, 165
orderlies, 222
ordinary seamen, 221
Oregon, 12
Orion (slave ship), 48, 55–57, 65–66, 76, 77
Osgood and Co., 386

Pagalu, 89
Page, Captain, 274
painter, ship's, 218
Paraguay Expedition, 3, 7, 39, 41, 390n6
Patterson, Billy, 267, 269
Patterson, Lieutenant, 135
pea jackets, 21
Pearson, Commander, 378, 384
Pedro V, King of Portugal, 140, 141
Peninsula War, 118
Perry, Matthew C., 2
pets, 159
petty officers, 217–21, 272
Phillips, Thomas, 38
Phillips, W., 169
Philomel, HMS (gun boat), 289
Phunny Phellow, 285–86
Pig War, 80
pikemen, 13, 215
Pioneer, HMS (exploring steamer), 174
pipes (whistles), 219
pivot guns, 20, 21
Pluto, HMS (steam gun boat), 65, 66, 76
Plymouth, USS (sloop of war), 31, 33, 34
Pointe Francaise, 56
Point Langosta, 129, 131
Point Pedros, 252–53
Point Santo Antonio, 56
Ponta Padrão, 56
Porto Grande, 36, 37, 38, 115

Porto Praya, Cape Verde Islands, 3, 43, 44, 96, 115
Portsmouth, New Hampshire, 374–85, *380*
Portsmouth, USS (sloop of war), 31, 56, 64, 65, 67–69, 70, 75, 76, 86, *87*, 89–90, 103, 115, 134, 137, 142, 144, 156, 157, 163, 180, 207, 212, 213, 226, 230, 233, 247, 248, 249–50, 265, 266, 278, 281, 282, 304, 310, 311, 313, 315, 318–20, 323, 324, 328, 332, 347, 348, 353, 374, 378
pots and pans, 22
powder monkey, 13
Powell, John F., 73, 108, 168, 191, 197, 202, 299
Powhatan, USS (steam frigate), 312–13
Preble, USS (sloop of war), 312
preventer backstays, 341
Prince of Portugal, 139–41
Prince of the Congo, 89
Prince of Wales, 278
Prince's Island, 30, 52, 89, 90–92, 119, 124
privates, Marine, 222
Prometheus, HMS (man of war steamer), 270, 290, 293, 294, 303
pumpkins, 273
Punta da Lenha, 233, 291
purser, 11
purser's steward, 219

Quail (Liberian gun brig), 47
quarter gunners, 218–19
quarter masters, 219, 273

Rascius (U.S. whaling barque), 172, 175, 189
ratlines, 29
Rattlesnake (cargo ship), 290
rattling down, 29
rear admiral, 14
Redovis, Peter, 84
Relief, USS (supply ship), 150, 152, 153, 156, 158, 270, 272, 274, 275, 276, 277, 279, 282, 284, 303, 311, 324, 325, 347, 348, 351

religious practice, 19, 88, 287–88, 297
rendezvous, 3, 18, 27
Rhind, Alexander Colden, 11, 19, 198, 208, 239, 253, 300, 305, *305*, 309, 315, 330, 342, 369, 383, 387
Ridovis, Peter, 299, 395n5
Robert Macaire (Selby), 86, 107
Roberts, John S., *59*
Royal Navy. *see* African Squadron, Royal Navy
royal yards, 209
Rudolph, H., 200
Rufus Choate, 15
Rules for the Better Government of the Navy of the United States, 23

sail maker, 11
sail maker's mate, 218
sail trimmers, 215
salutes, 13, 14, 17, 18, 27, 28, 29, 31, 32, 35, 37, 44, 61, 78, 89, 90, 97, 119, 126, 129, 133, 134–35, 137, 138, 139–40, 163, 173, 187, 205, 240, 244, 304, 307, 318, 324, 348, 350, 351, 352, 374–75, 397n3
San Antonio, 115
San Jacinto, USS (steam frigate), 37, 38, 44, 48, 56, 60, 64–65, 67, 70, 76, 77, 78–79, 101, 102, 132, 134–35, 138, 143, 146, 157, 159, 163, 169, 179, 180, 199, 201, 203, 207, 208, 213–14, 230, 231, 236, 238, 239, 245, 249, 265, 268, 279, 281, 302, 307, 329, 347, 349, 350, 375
Santa Antão, 37
Sarah Scott (British barque), 334
Saratoga, USS (sloop of war), 163, 204, 205, 206, 206–7, 210, 212, 225, 230, 279–80, 303, 304, 305, 329, 346–47, 349
Savannah, USS (frigate), 15, 16
Sayers, Tom, 123
scurvy, 103, 282
seamen: crew list of *Constellation,* 254–65; discharged from *Constella-tion,* 383–84; foreign-born U.S.

seamen: crew list of *Constellation* (continued) sailors, 273, 299; Leonard on life and character of, 240–44, 272–73; pay for, 221; skills of, 221

Sebastian Cabot (U.S. coal ship), 133

second class boys, 221–22

Second War of Italian Independence, 6–7

Selby, Charles, 86

Sennott, William, 146

Seward, William, 7

sewing materials, 22

Shark Point, 253, 285, 288

sharks, 125, 146, 211, 367

Shark's Point, 55, 56

Sharpshooter, HMS (gun vessel), 162, 207, 208, 240, 266, 269, 289–90

shaving materials, 22

Shaws, Ira B., 146

sheet cables, 358

shirts, 21

shoes, 22

Sickles, Daniel, 6

side tackleman, 13

Silva & Leandro, 279

Sixth Massachusetts Regiment, 322–23

slave factories, 55, 120–21, 233, 294

slave trade: African facilities for, 55; British ban on, 2; challenges in prosecuting traders in, 56–57, 160; characteristics of ships in, 57–58, 64, 148, 149; flags and titles of ships in, 65–66, 131–32, 149, 160; in mid-19th century, 10; mission of African Squadron to interdict, 1, 3, 7, 121, 124–25, 160; mortality among slaves in, 77; punishment for participants in, 132, 391n3; sale of captured vessels used in, 53, 155, 184; U.S. ban on, 1–2; U.S. Civil War and, 188–89; voyage of yacht *Wanderer* in, 154–55. *See also* African Squadron, Royal Navy; African Squadron, U.S.

sleeping arrangements, 8, 123

slush fund, 30

slushing, 30

small pox, 12, 31

Smith, Dr., 253, 307, 309

Smith, Henry, 72

Smith, Thomas L., 11

soap, 21, 22

socks, 22

spar deck of *Constellation,* 5

Speedy, HMS (gun boat), 244

spit boxes, 332

Spitfire, HMS (gun boat), 60, 61, 69, 137, 140, 150, 157, 158, 173, 174

spitting, 26

St. Helena, 65, 76, 112, 138, 183–201, 331, 332, 334–41

St. Helena (U.S. schooner), 270, 281, 284, 294

St. Paul de Loando, 58, 59, 60–68, 63, 73–79, 83–84, 126–31, 135–41, 152, 153–57, 161–63, 178–80, 205–8, 235–36, 237–40, 244–50, 265–76, 303–30, 347

St. Thomas, 54, 89

St. Vincent, 36

steerage boat, 12

Stenson, J., 200

Stevens, H. K., 328, 378, 381

Steward, P., 108, 109

stewards, 220

St.Jago, 115

Storm King (slave ship), 134, 284

Storm King (U.S. barque), 185, 187

straw hats, 22

Street & Smith, 286

Strowe, W. H., 168, 200

Stuart, Jeb, 64

studding sails, 357

sugar production, 2

Sumpter, USS (steam gun boat), 39, 40–41, 55, 56, 75, 78–79, 87, 120, 121, 126, 133–34, 137, 142, 143, 156, 164, 205, 214, 248, 267, 269, 275, 281, 297, 303, 305, 329, 347–48, 350, 369, 375

Sunny South (slave ship), 244

Supply, USS (storeship), 60, 61, 73, 76, 78

surgeon, fleet, 11
Surprise (pleasure yacht), 20
Swallow (U.S. barque), 238, 275, 281
sweeping, 331–32

tarring, 29
Tattnall, John F. R., 253, 300, 349
Tattnall, Josiah, 300, 328
Taylor, Captain, 230
Temperance Society, 95, 99, 288
Termagant, HMS (steam frigate), 31, 34
Thanksgiving Day, 58
Thomas, John Rogers, 237
Thomas Achorn (slave ship), 131–32
Thompson, James, 273–74
Thompson, John C., 361
Thomson, J. W., 197, 299
Thomson, T. R. H., 53
Thornhill (British coal ship), 317
thread, 21
tobacco, 21, 332
Todd, Midshipman, 132
top men, 13
Totten, Commander, 77–78
Toucey, Isaac, 3, 28, 41, 103, 104, 134, 392n4
transatlantic cable, 129
Trident, HMS (steam gun boat), 67, 104
Triton, HMS, 48
Triton (slave ship), 131–32, 291, 292, 315, 331, 334
trousers, 21, 22
Tyler, Henry B., Jr., 11, 253

uniforms, 18
United States: ban on slave trade, 1–2; relations with Britain, 80, 86, 121. *See also* African Squadron, U.S.; Civil War
Upham, William P., 287–88

Vendique (French barque), 124
Vermont, USS (Line of Battle ship), 8
Vermont Wool Dealer, 165
Vincennes, USS (sloop of war), 77–78, 83–84, 85, 154

Viper, HMS (steam gun boat), 65, 86–87
Virginia, CSS (ironclad), 300, 381
Virginia, USS (Line of Battle ship), 8
Virginian (brigantine), 86
Walpole, 20
Wamingham, John, 343
Wanderer (slave ship), 154–55, 284, 394n2
wardroom boat, 12
War of 1812, 2, 10
War of Reform, 15
warrant officers, 11
Warren Hallett (U.S. ship), 187
Washington Monument, 76
Washington's Birthday, 90, 212
watch rules, 25, 26, 217
Webster, Daniel, 2
Webster-Ashburton treaty, 2, 7, 8–10, 27, 66
Welles, Gideon, 347, 349
Whelan, Matthew, 272
Whitehouse, M., 197, 252
Widow's Victim, The (play), 165, 179, 181, 183, 198–201
Wildman, Leveson, 289
Wilkes, Charles, 347, 349
William Shaler (U.S. barque), 304, 317, 347
Willis, John G., 61, 238
Wilson, Alexander, 211–12, 286–87
Wilson, George, 282
Wilson, S. Byard, 11, 13, 253
Wilson, Stephen B., Jr., 293, 331, 334
wind sails, 92
Wood, James, 252
Worth, James M., 11
Wrangler, HMS (steam barque), 159, 205–6, 209, 266, 270, 289, 290

Xavier de Moura, Don Patricio, 32

yellow fever, 162, 163, 170, 179
yeoman, 217–18
Young, Isaac, 342

Zélée (French corvette), 249, 267, 269

About the author

C. HERBERT GILLILAND is a professor of English at the U.S. Naval Academy in Annapolis, Maryland, and a retired captain in the naval reserve. His recent book *Voyage to a Thousand Cares: Master's Mate Lawrence with the African Squadron, 1844–1846* received the John Lyman Award from the North American Society for Oceanic History. He also co-authored *Admiral Dan Gallery: The Life and Wit of a Navy Original.*